GLOBALISATION AND THE
FUTURE OF TERRORISM

This book sets out to explain how international terrorism is shaped, how it evolves over time and what we are to expect in the future. It offers a fresh contribution by drawing upon research and methods outside the traditional terrorism research genre, and by taking both a theoretical and a practical predictive approach still unusual in the field of terrorism studies.

While predicting terrorist activities is a highly speculative business, Brynjar Lia has identified a number of long-term causes and driving forces. He combines these research findings with predictive literature on various aspects of globalisation, and underpins his analysis by numerous case studies. The result is a set of propositions about future patterns of terrorism, which are not simply best guesses, but backed up by the latest research in the field.

Lia finds that the current wave of deadly terrorist attacks is rooted in global structural factors, including the current unipolar and interventionist world order, proliferation of weak transitional states, globalisation of organised crime, privatisation of policing and warfare, migration and ethnic heterogenisation, growing information interconnectedness, and diffusion of deadly technologies. These systemic causes will shape the future terrorist landscape, and will sustain a high level of transnational terrorism in the foreseeable future.

This book will be of invaluable interest to students, researchers and practitioners in the field of terrorism studies.

Dr Brynjar Lia is a senior researcher at the Norwegian Defence Research Establishment. He is widely regarded as one of Norway's foremost experts on international terrorism. He was a Visiting Fulbright Scholar at Harvard University in 2001–2. Lia is the author of *The Society of the Muslim Brothers in Egypt 1928–42: The Rise of an Islamic Mass Movement* and *A Police Force Without a State: A History of the Palestinian Security Forces in the West Bank and Gaza* and has published more than 20 research reports and articles.

CONTEMPORARY SECURITY STUDIES

GLOBALISATION AND THE FUTURE OF TERRORISM

Patterns and Predictions

Brynjar Lia

Routledge
Taylor & Francis Group

LONDON AND NEW YORK

First published 2005
by Routledge
2 Park Square, Milton Park, Abingdon, Oxon, OX14 4RN

Simultaneously published in the USA and Canada
by Routledge
270 Madison Ave, New York, NY 10016

Routledge is an imprint of the Taylor & Francis Group

Transfered to Digital Printing 2006

© 2005 Brynjar Lia

Typeset in Times by
RefineCatch Limited, Bungay, Suffolk

British Library Cataloguing in Publication Data
A catalogue record for this book is available from the British Library

Library of Congress Cataloging in Publication Data
Lia, Brynjar.
Globalisation and the future of terrorism : patterns and predictions /
Brynjar Lia.
p. cm.
Includes bibliographical references and index.
1. Terrorism. 2. Terrorism–Forecasting. 3. Globalization. 4.
International relations. 5. World politics–1989– I. Title: Globalization
and the future of terrorism. II. Title.
HV6431.L498 2005
303.6′25–dc22
2005005339

ISBN10: 0–7146–5261–X (hbk)
ISBN10: 0-4154-0296-4 (pbk)

ISBN13: 978–0–7146–5261–0 (hbk)
ISBN13: 978-0-4154-0296-5 (pbk)

Printed and bound by CPI Antony Rowe, Eastbourne

To Hilde

CONTENTS

CONTENTS

ILLUSTRATIONS

Figures

Tables

Boxes

ACKNOWLEDGEMENTS

This study grew out of the Terrorism and Asymmetric Warfare Project, which was launched in 1999 at the Norwegian Defense Research Establishment (FFI) and which I have directed more or less continuously since then. Back then when I wrote the research reports, that later became the basis for this manuscript, I benefited greatly from the stimulating academic environment at FFI, a truly multidisciplinary and future-oriented research institute, where my first attempts at forecasting and predicting were not met with academic condescension. Instead, my ideas and thinking about long-term evolutions of terrorist movements and ideologies were shaped in an environment where bold and speculative ideas about future scenarios were encouraged and reshaped by constructive criticism. Needless to say, aspiring to capture the multifaceted effects of globalisation on contemporary terrorism is a daunting task and the current study is admittedly more akin to an essay than to a strictly scientific study.

A number of people deserve to be mentioned, some for their practical assistance and others for their academic inspiration. Annika S. Hansen worked with me at an early stage of this project and assisted me in shaping Chapter 3. Others have provided inspiration during my work on this book. Director of Research Jan Erik Torp deserves mention for providing the right mixture of academic and practical-administrative guidance for me and the Terrorism and Asymmetric Warfare Project-group. Other FFI researchers have been very helpful. I am grateful to Katja H.-W. Skjølberg for assisting me on a related study on the causes of terrorism, from which this book has benefited. Iver Johansen and Tor Bukkvoll in particular have offered constructive criticism in a number of areas. Pål Aas has given me useful feedback on my writings on biological and chemical weapons, and Steinar Høibråthen has shared with me his insight on nuclear and radiological arms and proliferation risks. Kjell Olav Nystuen and Janne Merete Hagen provided me with background material and guidance on my writings on future cyberterrorism threats and critical infrastructure. Rolf-Inge Vogt Andrésen, now Principal Lecturer at the Russian studies department at the Armed Forces' School of Intelligence and Security, was helpful in sharing his knowledge of the terrorism–organised-crime nexus in Russia. Bjørn Olav Knutsen, now foreign-policy adviser in the Norwegian Parliament for the Conservative Party, shared with me his broad insight into theories of international relations (IR) and helped shape my thinking on the future of IR. My colleagues Laila Bokhari, Thomas Hegghammer and Petter Nesser have provided constructive criticism to several draft chapters. My research assistants Truls H Tønnessen, Synnøve Marie Kvam and Cathrine Westad have been very helpful in collecting sources.

Many others deserve special consideration for having facilitated this research. Professor Cemal Kafadar, Director of Center for Middle Eastern Studies (CMES) at Harvard University provided me with an excellent working environment by appointing me as Visiting Scholar at CMES in 2001–2. Let me also thank my Frank Cass and Routledge editors and the anonymous reviewers for their insightful comments, which assisted me in improving this book. All errors and flaws are of course my responsibility alone.

I have devoted this study to my wife, Hilde, whose patience with my absent-mindedness during the past few years cannot be overstated.

ABBREVIATIONS

ADF	Allied Democratic Forces
AMU	Arab Maghreb Union
ASALA	Armenian Secret Army for the Liberation of Armenia
ASEAN	Association of South-east Asian Nations
AU	African Union
BW agent	biological warfare agent
BWC	Biological Weapons Convention
CBRN	chemical, biological, radiological and nuclear
CBW agents	chemical and biological warfare agents
CW agent	chemical warfare agent
CWC	Chemical Weapons Convention
CIA	Central Intelligence Agency
CIS	Commonwealth of Independent States
CSIS	Canadian Security Intelligence Service
CTB	Comprehensive Test-Ban Treaty
CTC	Counter-terrorism Committee
DRC	Democratic Republic of Congo
ECOWAS	Economic Community of West African States
ELN	Ejército de Liberación Nacional de Colombia, National Liberation Army of Colombia
EPR	Ejército Popular Revolucionario, Popular Revolutionary Army (Guerrero, Mexico)
ETA	Euskadi Ta Askatasuna, Basque Fatherland and Liberty or Basque Country and Liberty
EU	European Union
EZLN	Ejército Zapatista de Liberación Nacional, Zapatista National Revolutionary Army (Chiapas, Mexico)
FALN	Fuerzas Armadas de Liberación Nacional, Armed Forces of National Liberation (Puerto Rico)
FARC	Fuerzas Armadas Revolucionarias de Colombia, Revolutionary Armed Forces of Colombia
Fateh	Palestinian National Liberation Movement

FBIS	Foreign Broadcast Information Service
FFI	Norwegian Defense Research Establishment
FLQ	Front de Libération du Québec, Liberation Front of Quebec, Canada
GATT	General Agreement on Tariffs and Trade
GDP	gross domestic product
GIA	Groupe Islamique Armée or Armed Islamic Group (Algeria)
HEU	highly enriched uranium
HTI	Hizb al-Tahrir al-Islami, The Islamic Liberation Party
IAEA	International Atomic Energy Agency
ICBL	International Campaign to Ban Landmines
ICC	International Criminal Court
ICISS	International Commission on Intervention and State Sovereignty
IEA	International Energy Agency
IED	improvised explosive device
IEMF	Interim Emergency Multinational Force (deployed in Bunia, DRC, June 2003)
IIRO	International Islamic Relief Organization
INGO	International non-governmental organisations
IRGC	Iran's Revolutionary Guard Corps
ISAF	International Security Assistance Force
ISI	Inter-Service Intelligence (Pakistan)
IT	information technology
JF	Jamaat al-Fuqra, Community of the Impoverished
KADEK	Kurdistan Freedom and Democracy Congress
KFOR	NATO Kosovo Force
KLA	Kosovo Liberation Army (also known as UCK)
KRL	Khan Research Laboratories
LDCs	less developed countries, least developed countries
LNG	liquefied natural gas
LSE	London School of Economics
LTTE	Liberation Tigers of Tamil Eelan (Sri Lanka)
MILF	Moro Islamic Liberation Front (in the Southern Philippines)
MKO	Mujahidin e-Khalq, People's Mojahideen of Iran
MNLF	Moro National Liberation Front
MONUC	United Nations Organization Mission in the Democratic Republic of the Congo
NAFTA	North American Free Trade Agreement
NATO	North Atlantic Treaty Organization
NUPI	Norwegian Institute of International Affairs
NY	New York
OAS	Organization of American States
OAU	Organisation of African Unity

ABBREVIATIONS

OIC	Organisation of the Islamic Conference
OSCE	Organization for Security and Co-operation in Europe
PAM	Policy Analysis Market
PFLP-GC	Popular Front for the Liberation of Palestine – General Front
PIRA	Provisional Irish Republican Army
PKK	Partiya Karkeren Kurdistan, Kurdistan Workers' Party
PLO	Palestine Liberation Organisation
PMC	private military companies
POLISARIO	Frente Popular para la Liberacion de Saguia el Hamra y Rio de Oro
PRI	Partido Revolucionario Institucional
PRIO	Peace Research Institute Oslo
RAF	Rote Armée Fraction or Red Army Faction
SAARC	South Asian Association for Regional Co-operation
SADC	South African Development Community
SCO	Shanghai Co-operation Organisation
SFOR	NATO Stabilisation Force
SPLA	Sudanese People's Liberation Army
TCOs	transnational criminal organisations
TNCs	transnational corporations
UN	United Nations
UNAMSIL	United Nations Mission in Sierra Leone
UNCTAD	United Nations Conference on Trade and Development
UNDP	United Nations Development Programme
UNIFIL	United Nations Interim Force in Lebanon
UNITA	União Nacional para a Independência Total de Angola, National Union for the Total Independence for Angola
UNMEE	United Nations Mission in Ethiopia and Eritrea
UNMIK	United Nations Mission in Kosovo
UNMIL	United Nations Mission in Liberia
UNMISET	United Nations Mission of Support in East Timor
UNOCI	United Nations Operation in Côte d'Ivoire
UNODC	United Nations Office on Drugs and Crime
UNPO	The Unrepresented Nations and Peoples Organisation
UNSC	United Nations Security Council
US	United States
WHO	World Health Organisation
WMD	weapons of mass destruction
WTC	World Trade Center
WTO	World Trade Organisation

1

INTRODUCTION

The [9/11] attacks showed that, for all its accomplishments, globalisation makes an awful form of violence accessible to hopeless fanatics.[1]

(Stanley Hoffmann, 2002)

When two passenger planes crashed into the World Trade Center and another flew into the Pentagon building in Washington on 11 September, 2001 the word 'globalisation' quickly became a buzzword in nearly every expert commentary on the background for the attacks. While globalisation had long been touted as mostly a force for good, at least for the Western world, the horrifying onslaught of death and destruction in the world's greatest metropolis of power and capital highlighted the 'dark side of globalisation'. Analysts warned about a rapidly changing world coming apart, unhinged by sinister forces not properly understood or anticipated. In the shadow of a remarkably long period of economic growth and the spread of the market democracies in the post-Cold War world, religious fanaticism had returned with a vengeance, shattering the Western sense of tranquillity and insulation from the ills and maladies affecting distant zones of conflict. The new evil was said to be feeding itself on abject poverty, glaring inequalities, remnants of Western colonial domination and a visceral hatred of the West's wealth and success. It thrived in a growing number of Third World failed states, from where it could attack a Western metropolis, the traditional barriers of distance and geography had fallen thanks to the revolution in communication and transportation. These factors, it was argued, provided the ideological and material basis for a new professional warrior class of determined martyrdom-seeking terrorists, seeking to dethrone the world's remaining superpower, punishing it for its political arrogance, its hypocritical foreign policy and its infidel values of individual freedom and liberal democracy. To many observers, the 9/11 attacks were the culmination of previously observed trends where terrorism was becoming increasingly more irrational in its logic, fanatical in its ideological manifestation, global in its reach, and mass-casualty-causing in its modus operandi. Nearly all previously held assumptions about terrorism as a political phenomenon were dismissed as anachronistic and outdated, and all but the most alarmist and hawkish predictions about terrorism were considered naïve and irrelevant.

There has been a flood of research on terrorism after 9/11. For obvious reasons, terrorism studies have become distinctly more actor-focused. Understanding the rise of al-Qaida, the resilience of its organisation and its support networks and the variety of local affiliate groups and predicting al-Qaida's next step have been on everyone's mind. The impact of globalisation on terrorism has become an important topic in the post-9/11 writings on terrorism.[2] A common theme is that the new terrorism is a manifestation of resistance to globalisation and the global spread (or imposition) of values of Western market democracies, a kind of reactionary backlash against modernisation.[3] Others argue that since the world is globalising, so is terrorism. Hence, one is witnessing a globalisation of terrorism since patterns of terrorism reflect overall societal changes. The tendency towards loosely organised terrorist 'networks' rather than hierarchical organisations, the multinational characters of the new terrorist organisations and their global reach are characteristics which have obvious parallels to how the globalisation process has affected the business economy, national and identity politics, as well as socio-cultural trends.[4] The growing lethality of terrorism may, for example, be linked to one aspect of globalisation, namely the growing vulnerability of globalising societies to terrorist attacks. During the era of globalisation terrorist groups have gained access to new means, making them more lethal and more global in reach. A related theme is the enormous political impact of terrorism in the age of globalisation. The new-found destructive capabilities of terrorist networks have empowered them and elevated them to being significant actors in international politics and the international economy. Hence, they may also have the power to change the very course of globalisation.[5]

Beyond various public debates, academic studies of globalisation's impact on terrorism have until recently excelled in their near-absence, especially in terms of the overall future impact of globalisation.[6] Even if there is broad agreement that globalisation is perhaps the single most important process shaping our future, there have been few scholarly contributions in the terrorism literature that aim at capturing long-term shifts caused by the globalisation process.[7] After all, nothing is more risky than prophesising in the midst of rapidly unfolding 'wars', be they in Afghanistan, Iraq or the global 'war on terror'. Even though 'the future of terrorism' has been a favourite title for books on terrorism for a very longtime, the terrorism-research literature has traditionally drawn surprisingly little from the large body of futuristic studies. Also, general social-science research has also been somewhat ignored, despite the potentially important contributions of conflict theory and quantitative peace research studies to our understanding of terrorism.

Since the mid-1990s, literature on terrorism trends address the future of terrorism under labels like the 'new terrorism' 'the new face of terrorism' and 'new generation of terrorists', but without linking these predictions to processes of long-term societal changes.[8] These studies mostly foresee increasingly more lethal forms of terrorism, (which turned out to be true), but argued that the increased lethality would be caused by non-conventional terrorism or weapons of mass destruction (WMD)-terrorism, (which so far has not proven to be correct). This literature drew its conclusions primarily from a few trend-setting events in the mid-1990s such as the first WTC-bombing, the Sarin gas attacks by the Aum Shinrikyo sect and the Oklahoma bombing, as well as an apparent predominance of religiously motivated (mostly Islamist) terrorist groups in transnational terrorism. Without pondering the enormous destructive *potential* of conventional terrorism, forecasts and prognoses focused almost exclusively on WMD-terrorism.[9]

Towards a framework for predicting future patterns of terrorism

Since its inception in the 1970s, the voluminous literature on modern terrorism contains numerous attempts to predict the future of terrorism. Most of these attempts are unsystematic, however and lack a theoretical foundation.[10] The future of terrorism literature has generally suffered from the lack of systematic thinking about how changing societal conditions can produce a variety of both permissive and inhibiting environments for terrorism, resulting in constantly evolving patterns of terrorism. It is often based on observation of related events and extrapolations from single cases, while the evolving contextual or underlying factors shaping the very environments in which terrorism thrives or declines are not properly analysed or understood. Or it tends to focus merely on insufficiently substantiated 'conditions', which allegedly have an aggravating effect on the occurrence of terrorism while the countervailing forces are ignored. Consider the following example:

> Nearly all conditions thought to breed terrorism will probably aggra-
> vate in the short and medium future. Value nihilism; the search for
> new beliefs, especially by the young generation; disappointment
> with the established order; and broad public malaise will probably
> increase. Scarcities, unemployment, ethnic tensions, nuclear angst,
> acute ecological problems, and the frustration of welfare aspirations
> are sure to increase in most democracies. Value cleavages and intense
> disconsensus [. . .] may well grow. International anarchism, hosti-
> lities, and fanaticism will expand. Poor Third World countries, well
> equipped with weapons, but unable to handle their problems, will
> probably direct their hostility at democracies. The confrontation
> between communism and democracy will continue and perhaps
> escalate. Technical tools for expanding terrorism and the vulner-
> ability of democracies to terrorism will increase. [. . .] At the same
> time basic democratic freedoms will provide a convenient space for
> terrorism to operate in. Aging population, additional leisure-time

facilities, and continued urbanisation will provide 'soft' human targets. Modern energy facilities, data networks, roboted factories, and the like will add critical material targets. The ease of international communications and movements, mass-media attention to terrorism and informal networks that support terrorism constitute further trends that will permit or encourage terrorism.[11]

Needless to say, the author is obviously wrong in assuming that almost every societal process of change will lead to more terrorism. The author identifies a wide range of societal trends that may well have an impact on terrorism, but without any basis in the research literature on the causes of terrorism and without any systematic analysis of variables that 'breed terrorism', it is clear that the outcome of such exercises has limited value only. Therefore, one needs a far more stringent methodological approach if the results are to be anything other than mere speculations.

A method that it is widely used in the literature as well as among practitioners is to extrapolate from current trend patterns, assuming that the future will be more of the same and that emerging trends can be spotted by monitoring closely various indicators.[12] Although indispensable for short-term predictions, such research strategies need to be complemented by alternative methods. Extrapolation of current terrorism trends remains inevitably an uncertain method of long-term predictions. The risk is that long-term shifts are only understood after they have occurred. Or a temporary short-lived surge in certain forms of terrorism may be erroneously interpreted as a long-term change.

While being primarily a set of tactics used by a plethora of groups, terrorism in its various manifestations and permutations is also intimately linked with armed conflicts as well as socio-political and economic characteristics in those societies where it is prevalent. Even though terrorist cells sometimes live isolated lives in underground movements, they are rarely entirely unaffected by the outside world. Assuming for a moment that the causalities of terrorism remain the same, we still live in an era of rapid societal change and globalisation of economy, culture and politics, and thus, the conditions, which cause terrorism to occur and to remain resilient, are rapidly changing. This has increasingly been acknowledged in much of the recent literature on terrorism. A couple of years before 9/11 Walter Laqueur argued that much of what we have learnt about terrorism in the past may be irrelevant to understanding the 'new terrorism'.[13]

The present study aims at unearthing the forces shaping future terrorism patterns and understanding where they lead us. This will not be done by presenting one coherent picture or by outlining a number of possible scenarios. Instead, by exploring the complex picture of both permissive and countervailing forces, the book highlights most salient processes at work. In order to improve our ability to prognosticate about terrorism, this book offers a new research strategy or analytical framework for prediction. It relies on projecting trends in societal changes known to have an influence on terrorism, rather than projections based simply on previous patterns of terrorism. The framework consists of two main building blocks: first, propositions about future societal changes, and second, causes of terrorism. Put simply, those societal conditions, which appear likely to affect patterns of terrorism in one way or another are identified and studied with a view to predicting how these conditions are changing. On this basis it is possible to guess intelligently about the future of terrorism. A very simplified illustration of this research strategy is given in Figure 1.1.

The advantage of this framework is that many societal processes of change move slowly and are to a great extent determined by its previous evolution. Hence, they are predictable, and therefore useful, analytical tools for understanding the future. A pivotal part in the framework is causes of terrorism, that is various causal relationships linking societal patterns and characteristics to the occurrence and patterns of terrorism. As Martha Crenshaw has noted, prediction about terrorism can only be based on theories that explain past patterns.[14] Conceptually, the approach is not unusual in similar fields of research. In an influential paper on the future of armed conflict, the editor of the *Journal of Peace Research*, Nils Petter Gleditsch, noted that there is a limit to what trend projection can tell us. We need to 'ask ourselves what factors *cause* war, and whether these factors are improving or deteriorating [. . .].'[15] At the end of this introductory chapter, I have provided a survey of existing 'theories' on the causes of terrorism, focusing on the national-societal and the international/world-system levels. This survey provides us with the necessary tools to derive likely terrorism outcomes from a variety of future developments.

The present framework is attractive because of its simplicity and flexibility, and it may easily be adapted to encompass future theoretical findings on the causes of terrorism. Its strength lies in its ability to uncover possible future shifts, which do not seem very apparent, or even likely, by looking only at recent patterns of terrorism. Rather than aiming at presenting 'the face of terror in 2020', this study arrives, through its analyses, at a set of long-term implications for terrorism of current and future societal developments. Like

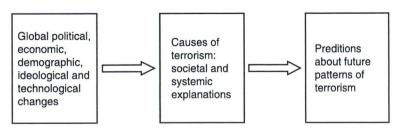

Figure 1.1 Predicting future patterns of terrorism.

other global-trend studies, there is no single trend or driver that completely dominates the future of terrorism. Nor will the trends identified here have equal impact in every region. Some trends also work at cross-purposes, instead of being mutually reinforcing.[16] Still, through a survey of key global trends in six broad areas: globalisation and armed conflicts, international relations, the global market economy, demographic factors, ideological shifts and technological innovations, I am able to analyse what these drivers mean for the future of terrorism.

The actual analytical units of this study are the 'postulates', which are basically general propositions about the future evolution of a particular phenomenon or societal process. The first of these postulates deals with the future evolution of globalisation. As will be seen, the literature offers several theories of causal linkages between globalisation and patterns of terrorism. In most cases, however, globalisation's impact on terrorism is analysed in terms of its impact via intermediary factors such as state capacities, socio-economic inequality and armed conflicts.[17] Similarly, the future of armed conflicts is also examined in relatively broad terms with a view to under-standing the implications for patterns of terrorism. As for the other categories of postulates, they are subdivided into more specific propositions, accom-panied with sets of implications for terrorism patterns. For example, in the international relations category, one analytical unit is 'democratisation' and its postulate is: 'the number of states in transition to democratic rule or which are neither autocracies nor fully fledged democracies will remain high and possibly increase.' The postulates are formulated, based on a reading of relevant research literature, in this case, the voluminous literature on democratisation.

The initial selection of postulates was done intuitively, and they were subsequently refined, following several workshops in the Terrorism and Asymmetric Warfare Project Group with participation of invited scholars and practitioners. A set of selection criteria has also been applied: the postu-lates are assumed to correspond to or at least have a certain minimum of influence on one or more of *the causal factors of terrorism*; the predicted changes must be *global* in the sense that they involve more than just one country or one region; and the set of postulates should reflect *the most likely future scenarios*.[18] Admittedly, postulates cannot be verified or validated. At best, one may reduce uncertainty by applying a set of methodological rules. *Inconsistencies* between various postulates should be clarified and avoided; results from *contemporary research literature* should, as far as possible, pro-vide a basis for or give support to the postulates. The literature used for this study varies greatly. Recent social-science and political-science literature has been used extensively to understand causalities and dynamics, as well as to review specialist opinions on expected future developments within various fields. A great number of strategic assessments, trend studies and other futur-istic works have been drawn upon in formulating the postulates. Area-studies literature is similarly used to exemplify and concretise how developments play out in real life. A final criterion for selecting postulates is that they should primarily include *broad societal and global processes* of change, which move slower, are largely determined by their past evolution and hence are more predictable than discrete events. Still, some judgements about the future will be more reliable than others. Predictions about demography will necessarily be more reliable than postulates about the future of democratisation, socio-economic inequality and political ideologies, since the former can draw upon scientific extrapolation of current demographic patterns, while the latter will be a more speculative assessment, informed by *inter alia* past patterns, an understanding of causal relationships, and a good deal of guesswork based on specialist opinions.

Our set of postulates is just one of many possible inputs in the analytical framework for predicting future shifts in the patterns of terrorism. The overall aim has been to identify the most important processes of change, influencing the occurrence of terrorism. In the case of the postulate on democratisation trends, for example, I find that the trend towards more semi-democratic states 'will cause heightened risks for state collapse, intrastate conflicts and civil violence. Higher levels of domestic terrorism in some of these states are likely. New sources of international terrorism may also emerge as a by-product of these conflicts, especially if they cause state collapse' (see p. 59).

As expected, I do not find identical implications for each and every postulate, but instead, some postulates indicate increased levels of terrorism, others a possible long-term reduction. Several trends work at cross-purposes. In some cases, I am also able to predict changes in certain types of terrorism (left wing, right wing, separatist, politico-religious, etc.) as well as their modus operandi (international, domestic, mass-casualty terrorism, etc). The final step is to assess the emerging picture of trends with a view to identifying a cluster of coinciding predictions, based on postulates and causal relationships with higher validity than opposing trends, as well as the internal consistency of postulates. This is done in the concluding chapter. An illustration of the research strategy is outlined in Figure 1.2.

Needless to say, this analytical framework is unable to capture short-term shifts or local variations. After all, any terrorist attack is the result of a decision by an individual or group who are not necessarily obedient instruments in a greater game ordained by social-science theory on the causes of terrorism. There are other weaknesses: causality is an extremely complex phenomenon in social sciences, and the present study must necessarily simplify causal relationships in order to make them useful. I have relied heavily on studies that have demonstrated non-spurious correlations between certain societal conditions and the occurrence of terrorism. Existing research in this field is admittedly somewhat weak, since many hypotheses have not yet been rigorously tested in, for example, comparative cross-country studies.[19] As is usually the case in social-science research, there are also several conflicting

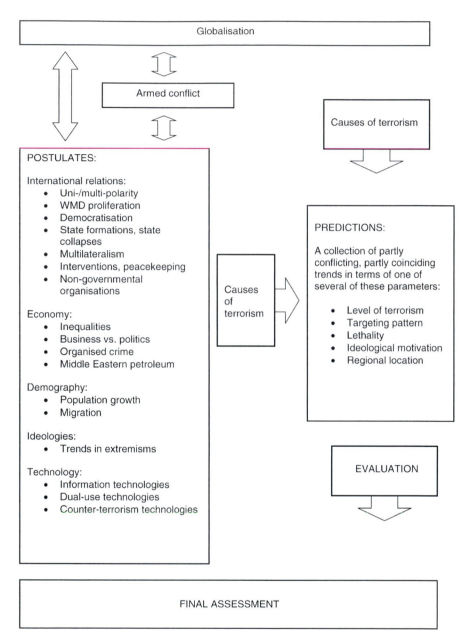

Figure 1.2 Predicting future patterns of terrorism: analytical units.

theories and competing 'schools'. No single theory on the causes of terrorism has been embraced wholeheartedly among the community of terrorism researchers. The range of possible scenarios in each of the fields examined in this book only highlight the degree to which futuristic studies are marred by constant uncertainty. Hence, the present study is an exercise in educated guesswork. Even if the research design is admittedly ambitious, the goal of this study cannot go beyond the identification of processes and trends, which are more educated and reliable than those that are offered in the research literature today.

The main finding of this study is that there are important structural factors in nearly all fields of societal conditions, creating more propitious conditions for both domestic as well as transnational terrorism. There are also several factors facilitating the growth of mass-casualty terrorism. The inhibiting factors are fewer and, in most cases, they do not seem to carry the same probability and weight – at least not in the short run – as those factors aiding and abetting the rise of terrorism. In view of the past few years of al-Qaida-related terrorism, these findings may not come as a surprise. Still, our analysis demonstrates the degree to which terrorism is rooted in *structural* factors in the international world order and the global market economy, as well as in demographic and technological trends. We also find that there are structural processes facilitating more *domestic* terrorism, especially in developing countries undergoing difficult transition processes to market democracies.

This book is structured around the two building blocks of the analytical framework as presented above. The present chapter has introduced the methodological rules for the subsequent analysis. It also discusses definitional issues and approaches to studying terrorism and its relationship with armed conflicts. Finally, it deals with the causes of terrorism, summarising the research literature on this topic. Chapter 2 discusses the impact of globalisation and armed conflicts on future patterns of terrorism. The subsequent chapters explore separate fields of societal change and their possible implications for terrorism, including the future international state system, the global economy, demographic changes, ideological shifts, and finally, technological innovations. The main findings are presented and discussed in the concluding chapter.

Defining terrorism

Terrorism is a very pejorative term. Both democracies and autocracies use the term in political discourse to delegitimise their political enemies, while terrorist groups usually avoid the terms to describe their activities, preferring other more positively-laden labels such as revolutionary cells, urban guerrillas, Islamic fighters or mujahidin, etc. According to Bruce Hoffman, *Lehi* or *Stern Gang*, one of the Jewish terrorist groups active in Palestine during the 1940s, is believed to be the last group actually to describe itself publicly as terrorist.[20] Terrorism as a positive term has not disappeared entirely in the writings of radical ideologues, however. For example, the famous Brazilian revolutionary Carlos Marighella lauded 'terrorism' as a tactic the revolutionary should never abandon in his seminal treatise *Minimanual of the Urban Guerrilla*.[21] Contemporary radical Islamist ideologues, such as the Saudi Shaykh Hamud bin 'Uqla al-Shu'aybi, cite the Koranic verse, which urges the believer to gather strength and 'strike fear in the enemies of God (*wa turhibuna bihi 'aduw Allah*)' as a theological basis for the argument that there is a kind of terrorism (*irhab*) which 'is legitimate, sanctioned and ordered by God, which is to prepare strength and be mobilised for resisting the enemies of God and his prophets.'[22]

Terrorism has long been a controversial term in academia for very good reasons. While there is much good research on individual terrorist groups, their campaigns and the conflict areas in which they operate, the study of terrorism as a generic phenomenon has suffered from serious problems. Charles Tilly, for example, has warned social scientists against reifying the terms 'terror', 'terrorism', and 'terrorist', since they 'do not identify causally coherent and distinct social phenomena.'[23] The extensive literature on the topic, most of it written after 1968, either falls into the trap of being ideologically biased, purely psychological, speculative commentary or built on data of uncertain quality. Terrorism databases do exist, but they have been criticised for not being entirely scientifically coded. Furthermore, none of them are comprehensive, at least not when it comes to domestic terrorism.[24] In the social-movement and political-violence literature, terrorist incidents are usually not coded separately, but instead they are melded in with other forms of collective political violence.[25] Thus, the literature has suffered from a relative lack of good empirically tested findings on patterns and causes of terrorism. Ted Robert Gurr argued back in the 1980s that the research questions raised about terrorism often are considerably more interesting than most of the evidence brought to bear on them.[26] Alex Schmid and Albert Jongman followed up the critique, arguing that

> There are probably few areas in the social science literature in which so much is written on the basis of so little research. Perhaps as much as 80 per cent of the literature is not research-based in any rigorous sense; instead, it is too often narrative, condemnatory, and prescriptive.[27]

There has been a considerable resurgence in terrorism studies during the 1990s, and especially after 9/11, and significant progress has been made in understanding the sources and context for terrorism. Still, basic conceptual and methodological questions remain unresolved, especially in terms of integrating terrorism studies fully into the field of social science. Senechal de la Roche noted in 2004 that the field of sociology had been 'caught badly off guard' on 11 September, 2001 and 'had little to tell the world' about the nature and causes of terrorism.[28] Being event-based, instead of utilising aggregated data similar to civil-war studies, quantitative terrorism research still faces enormous challenges. For example, even if terrorism is sometimes paradoxically understood to be 'the lowest level of violence', despite its deliberate shock and horror effects, the boundaries between civil wars and terrorist campaigns are blurred in the research literature.[29] There is a strong tendency to label anti-Western and anti-Israeli violence, including attacks on military targets, as terrorism, while less publicised terrorist campaigns against ethnic groups and government targets in developing countries are greatly under-reported in the terrorism databases used by most researchers.

While no generally accepted definition of terrorism exists, there appears to be a growing consensus in academia on the definitional issue. Moreover, in the post-9–11 world it is also acknowledged that 'terrorism' is a term that has to be taken more seriously in political and social sciences. The most widely used definition of terrorism is the one used by the US Department of State in its annual reports *Patterns of Global Terrorism*, and which it has used for statistical and analytical purposes since 1983. Terrorism is defined here as 'premeditated, politically motivated violence perpetrated against noncombatant targets by subnational groups or clandestine agents, usually intended to influence an audience.'[30] Terrorism is furthermore defined as international when it involves 'citizens or the territory of more than one country.'[31] Terrorism is often implicitly understood as international or transnational terrorism, since such acts attracts most political and media attention. (The terms 'international terrorism' and 'transnational terrorism' are often used interchangeably, but international terrorism may also be associated with state sponsorship, while transnational terrorism is not. Both terms will be used in this study.) Statistically, however, most acts of terrorism are domestic, and perhaps as few as 5–10 per cent are by definition 'international'.[32] Apart from the domestic–international categorisation, terrorism is usually subdivided into four or more types according to the perpetrators' ideological motivations: socio-revolutionary terrorism (left wing and right wing), separatist terrorism (usually by ethnic-minority groups seeking autonomy or independence), single-issue terrorism (anti-abortion activists, environmental militants, animal-rights defendants etc.), and religious terrorism. These categories often overlap. For example, single-issue anti-abortionist militants are often religious extremists. Al-Qaida's Islamist terrorism is both religious and revolutionary. In some regions, such as Kashmir and the southern Philippines, it also furthers irredentist or separatist goals. Finally, separatist terrorism, such as in the case of PKK and ETA, often contains leftist ideologies with strong socio-revolutionary tendencies.

Terrorism is obviously just one of many forms of non-governmental collective political violence, and the term is perhaps more aptly defined by delimiting it from other related terms. It must be seen as part of a broader violence continuum where some acts are more 'terroristic' (i.e. share more of its definitional characteristics) than others. For example, it is common to distinguish terrorism from guerrilla warfare and armed insurgencies by the former's deliberate targeting of non-combatants, and by the fact that terrorist groups are commonly, but not always, small conspiratorial groups with no capacity or ambition to *physically* defeat the enemy or control territory. Terrorism is often associated with political violence by non-state actors in societies at peace.[33] Large-scale indiscriminate violence against civilians in civil wars has other names, such as 'war crimes', 'atrocities', 'massacres', 'ethnic cleansing', etc., and is more rarely termed terrorism. For example, the label 'terrorism' was not commonly used in the international press about the systematic targeting of civilians during the Balkan wars in the 1990s. By contrast, Serbian and Yugoslav journalism had been replete with examples of Serbs labelling Albanians as 'terrorists' since the 1980s. Nor has it been commonly used about the brutalisation of civilians in Africa's many civil-war zones, with the possible exception of the Algerian war for liberation in the 1950s and early 1960s and the Islamic insurgency in Algeria during the 1990s.

To study terrorism in isolation from the larger body of political-violence and civil-war studies is problematic. Terrorism and armed conflicts are closely linked and the causalities explaining variations in civil wars may also help us in understanding the causes of terrorism. In some armed conflicts, violence assumes the form of terrorism; in others terrorism is only a subordinate tactic. In yet other conflicts, terrorism occurs as an extra-territorial by-product, a response, a spillover, etc., from ongoing or past armed conflicts.

Terrorist campaigns are sometimes seen as an escalation of radical political activism, and occur when political groups no longer find it sufficient to pursue their cause vis-à-vis the authorities through political dialogue, demonstrations or civil disobedience only. In weak states, disaffected groups are often able to form large militias and stage region-wide insurrections. In stronger states, militant opposition groups apply urban terrorist tactics instead since an armed uprising is unfeasible. In both cases, however, the insurgents see themselves as guerrillas, freedom fighters, mujahidin, and not 'terrorists', engaged in a 'war' against an enemy. While not being accepted as legitimate military units, terrorists nevertheless see themselves as such and conceptualise their activities within the framework of an armed struggle, usually on behalf of a constituency, such as the Aryan nation, the Islamic *umma*, the Jewish people, the colonised Third World or the oppressed proletariat. They also form contacts and sometimes alliances with groups in other countries, fighting similar 'wars' be it against the 'Zionist Occupation Government', the 'Jewish-Crusader Alliance', 'Arab terrorists', 'US imperialism' or against 'fascist regimes'. This self-perception is important, not because terrorist ideologies should be taken at face value, but simply because it suggests the need to investigate the relationship between terrorism and armed conflict, and its applicability to understanding long-term patterns of terrorism.

Alex Schmid's classic typology from 1988 illustrates how terrorism is situated in the landscape of collective political violence: political motivation separates terrorism from criminally and pathologically motivated violence, and its oppositional character (i.e. non-state vs. a state) distinguishes terrorism from vigilante violence (non-state vs. non-state), state terror (state vs. non-state) and state-sponsored terrorism (state vs. state).[34]

More recently, the two sociologists Senechal de la Roche and Donald Black have proposed new sociological conceptualisations of terrorism.[35] They argue that like many other forms of violence, terrorism is also 'social control' in the sense that it defines and responds to deviant behaviour and that it is 'violent self-help', meaning that it handles a grievance with aggression. It is also collective violence, a group project. Collective non-governmental political violence can be divided into four categories: terrorism, vigilantism, lynching and rioting, which are organised in a 2×2 matrix, based on a logic of the victims' liability (individual or collective) and the participants' degree of organization (low or high). In this matrix, terrorism occupies the lower left square as it presumes both high organisation and collective liability.[36] While victims of vigilantism and lynching usually are selected on the basis of their assumed individual wrongdoings, this is not the case with terrorist victims, nor victims of riots. Acts of terrorism are planned, organised and recurrent and lack the relative spontaneous character of lynching and riots.[37] Moreover, terrorism, despite its warlike appearance, is distinguished from warfare by its covert and unilateral character, its civilian targeting and its lack of the game-like elements of warfare, such as respect for the Geneva Convention.[38] Donald Black proposes an ideal-type definition: 'pure terrorism is self-help by organised civilians who covertly inflict mass violence on other civilians.'[39] He supplements Senechal de la Roche's typology by adding the *intercollective* and *upward* direction of pure terrorism, as it targets civilians associated with another collectivity (for example, another state or ethno-religious group), as well as social superior targets such as members of a politically dominant community.[40]

The terrorism literature also offers many other characteristics of terrorism, such as 'its anxiety-inspiring method of repeated violence', the use of victims 'as message generators', the distinction between targets and victims of violence and its use of mass media.[41] An important school in terrorism research is the conceptualisation of terrorism in the framework of symbolic communication theory, viewing 'terrorism as theatre' and as a medium of communication.[42] Hence, as a symbolic act, terrorism can be analysed much like other communication processes, consisting of four basic components: transmitter (the terrorist), intended recipient (target), message (bombing, ambush) and feedback (reaction of target). The terrorist's message necessitates a victim, but the target or intended recipient of the communication may not be the victim.[43] Deduced from this theory is the famous dictum by the Rand Corporation's terrorism emeritus Brian Jenkins that 'terrorists want a lot of people *watching*, not a lot of people dead.'[44] Quantitative studies of European terrorism over the past decades also reveal that only a small minority of terrorist attacks cause fatalities, indicating a preference for acts that symbolise rather than cause violence.[45] This is technically still the case, although the emergence of al-Qaida's mass-casualty terrorism has shattered Jenkins' oft-cited maxim and swayed many people to adopt a new dictum, that of a 1994 statement by former CIA Chief R. James Woolsey: 'Today's terrorists don't want a seat at the table, they want to destroy the table and everyone sitting at it.'[46]

Being primarily a set of tactics of politically violent struggle, terrorism can occur in a multitude of contexts and be used by a variety of actors. Terrorist groups often employ other forms of political violence as well, such as guerrilla warfare when circumstances permit and vigilantism to assert social and political control over their constituent communities. A further complicating factor is that non-political organisations also commit acts of violence that bear a strong resemblance to terrorism. Mafia organisations and crime syndicates carry out car-bombings and assassinations to intimidate rival factions, punish recalcitrant businessmen or deter governments from acting against their members and business interests. The sky-bombing operations by the Colombian drug cartels in the 1980s and the numerous political assassinations in Russia by a variety of mafia organisations in the mid- and late 1990s are two cases in point.[47]

Given the definitional and conceptual problems of studying terrorism generically, one has argued that it is better to use a political definition of terrorism, namely illegal violent activities practised by groups listed as outlawed terrorist organisations by the USA and more recently by the European Union (EU). The advantage of this approach is that this relieves the researcher from applying a scientifically problematic definition, but the drawback is that it makes it impossible to study causalities and trends based on the framework proposed in this book. Hence, I will adhere to the US State Department definition, since it is the most commonly used definition today, but without accepting the official list of Designated Foreign Terrorist Organisations as the only actors involved in perpetrating terrorism. In order to avoid inaccurate generalisations I have sometimes chosen to refer to other categories of collective political violence, (armed insurgencies, civil violence, violent conflict, etc.) of which terrorism is often an integral part. This is because our knowledge about these sociological terms and their causalities are greater than the admittedly poorly developed sociology of terrorism. For this reason it is relatively easier to make reliable predictions about the increasing or declining likelihood of internal violent conflicts than about upwards or downwards trends in terrorism. Prognostications about armed conflicts are useful to us, since terrorism frequently appears as a tactic in such conflicts. Furthermore, transnational terrorist acts are often inspired or motivated by armed conflicts occurring somewhere else. This study has therefore relied relatively more on the long academic tradition of armed conflict studies than has previously been common in terrorism research.[48]

Causes of terrorism

Terrorism is a multifaceted phenomenon, and theories and hypotheses explaining its occurrence and resilience are necessary components of any prognostications about it. Some theories are well grounded in theoretical and empirical studies, others admittedly are not and should be seen as working hypotheses. Despite their shortcomings, they are the best we have got when it comes to making long-term predictions. Below, I have summarised the most important causal relationships, focusing on factors on the societal/national and international/world-system levels:[49]

- *Relative deprivation and inequality*: widespread perceptions of deprivation and inequality, especially among culturally defined groups, serve as the basic condition for participation in collective civil violence. Terrorism may be part of this violence.
- *Terrorism by spoilers*: peace processes based on negotiated settlements are frequently accompanied by increased levels of terrorism by rejectionist groups.
- *The contagion theory*: the occurrence of terrorism in one country often leads directly or indirectly to more terrorism in neighbouring countries. Terrorists learn from one another, and new tactics are usually quickly emulated. Spillover occurs in a variety of ways.
- *Terrorism and mass media*: paradigmatic shifts in modern mass media appear to influence patterns of terrorism, by enhancing its agenda-setting function, increasing its lethality and expanding its transnational character.
- *Rapid modernisation* makes societies more exposed to ideological terrorism. Societal changes associated with modernisation create new and unprecedented conditions for terrorism such as a multitude of targets, mobility, communications, anonymity and audiences. Socially disruptive modernisation may also produce propitious conditions for terrorism, especially when it relies heavily on natural-resources export, causes widespread social inequality and environmental damage and creates mixed market–clientalist societies.
- *Poverty, weak states and insurgencies*: poor societies with weak state structures are much more exposed to civil wars than wealthy countries. Economic growth and development undercut the economics of armed insurgencies. Economic growth and prosperity also contribute to lower levels of transnational terrorism.

- *Democratisation*: states in democratic transition are more exposed to armed conflict and terrorism than democracies and autocracies. Because of pervasive state control, totalitarian regimes rarely experience terrorism. States with high scores on measures of human-rights standards and democracy are less exposed to domestic ideological terrorism. Levels of transnational terrorism also seem to be highest in semi-authoritarian states, especially when undergoing a democratisation process.
- *Political regime and legitimacy*: terrorism is closely linked to a set of core legitimacy problems. Lack of continuity of the political system and a lack of integration of political fringes tend to encourage ideological terrorism. Ethnic diversity increases the potential for ethnic terrorism. A high density of trade-union membership in a population has tended to contribute to a lower level of domestic ideological terrorism.
- *The ecology of terrorism*: technological developments offer new and more efficient means and weapons for terrorist groups, but also increase the counter-terrorist capabilities of states. Transnational organised crime and terrorism are partly inter-linked phenomena, and growth in transnational organised crime may contribute to increased levels of terrorism.
- *Hegemony in the international system*: an international state system characterised by strong hegemonic power(s) is more exposed to international terrorism than a more multipolar system. High levels of bipolar conflict in world politics invite the use of state-sponsored terrorism as a means of war by proxy. A strongly unipolar world order or a world empire system, on the other hand, will experience high levels of transnational anti-systemic 'anti-colonial' terrorism.
- *Economic and cultural globalisation*: economic globalisation has mixed impacts on transnational terrorism, depending on how globalisation is measured. Cultural globalisation, measured in the rate of international non-governmental organisations (INGOs), tends to cause higher levels of transnational terrorism, especially against US targets.
- *The proliferation of weak and collapsed states* seems to have a facilitating influence on terrorism. Failed or collapsed states, caused by civil wars, underdevelopment, corrupt elites, etc., may contribute to international terrorism in a variety of ways.
- *Ongoing and past wars*: while terrorism in some cases is an armed conflict in its own right, terrorist motivations are often rooted in ongoing or past wars in one way or another. Armed conflicts also have various facilitating influences on transnational terrorism.

This list of causal relationships is by no means exhaustive, but represents the most useful theories for the purpose of this study. I have made no attempt at discussing these theories at length in this book, and readers should consult my 'Causes of Terrorism: An Updated and Expanded Review of the Literature', for an in-depth survey and an assessment of this literature.[50]

2

GLOBALISATION AND ARMED CONFLICTS

> One illusion has been shattered on 9/11: that we can have the
> good life of the West irrespective of the state of the rest of the
> world [. . .] The dragon's teeth are planted in the fertile soil of
> wrongs unrighted, of disputes left to fester for years, of failed
> states, of poverty and deprivation.[1]
>
> (Prime Minister Tony Blair, November 2001)

Globalisation, in its various aspects, and armed conflicts are arguably among
the most important determinants for the future of terrorism. Their multiple
impacts are not necessarily direct, however, even if certain aspects of globalisation, such as increased flow of capital, commodities, people and ideas
across borders have a profound effect on the environment in which terrorists
operate and on the means available to them. As already alluded to, the
impact of globalisation will be a recurrent theme throughout this book, as
its influences on more specific processes of change are explored. Globalisation has also altered the nature and ramifications of armed conflicts. In this
chapter, I will explore the most salient features of globalisation and armed
conflicts and suggest different ways in which they will shape the future of
terrorism.

The future of globalisation

Postulate: Globalisation in the sense of increased interconnectedness, interdependence and deterritorialisation will continue.

Possible implications for terrorism: The disruptive effects of globalisation will
generate more anti-Western anti-USA terrorism in the developing world. The
potential of distant conflicts to transform into transnational terrorism will
increase. The lethality of transnational terrorism will remain high due to a
continued decline of physical distance between socially alienated groups.
(Globalisation also has various indirect impacts on patterns of terrorism.)

Globalisation is one of the most used concepts in the growing body of literature that attempts to capture the essence of major socio-economic, political

and cultural changes in the post-Cold War age. Anthony Giddens noted back in 1999 that while the term was hardly used ten years earlier, by the end of the 1990s, the term was on everybody's lips: 'absolutely no one who wants to understand our prospects and possibilities at the century's end can ignore it.'[2]

Globalisation is a process that dates back to before the industrial revolution. There is little doubt, however, that the development has gathered pace since the Second World War, and its most prominent feature has been a progressive internationalisation of the world economy. Its consequences have come to be seen as one of the major determinants in any future socio-economic and political world order. With globalisation came worldwide interdependence and the consolidation of the free-market system, strengthening and spreading the ground rules for economic activity. Whereas trade in goods and services and the internationalisation of production are trends that date back to the nineteenth century, the greatly enhanced financial capital mobility is a novel development. Indeed, from being primarily an instrument for trade, currency is now primarily a trade commodity, making many national economies virtually hostage to the fluctuations and vicissitude of global financial markets.[3]

A simple description of globalisation is that 'events occurring on one part of the globe can affect, and be affected by, events occurring in other, distant parts of the globe.'[4] In the research literature, the term 'globalisation' is closely associated with increased transnational interdependence and trans-boundary movement.[5] According to Holm and Sørensen, a definition of globalisation is 'the intensification of economic, political, social and cultural relations across borders'.[6] The process of globalisation is facilitated through a technological revolution in the fields of telecommunication and transportation and in the formation of global financial markets made possible by geopolitical and political changes, first and foremost the collapse of the Soviet Union and its Communist satellite states.[7]

Hence, the increasing flow of information, products, people, money, technology and expertise across *national borders* and its consequences may be viewed as core aspects of the globalisation concept. It is a process of *deterritorialisation* and of expanding 'supraterritorial relations between the people', which take place in the world at large.[8] In this sense, globalisation can be described as 'a structural shift in the spatial organisation of socio-economic and political activity towards transcontinental or interregional patterns of relations, interaction and the exercise of power'.[9] A slightly different perspective of globalisation focuses on the transformation of perceptions of time and space produced by innovations of information technology. According to this view, key characteristics of globalisation are 'the speed of change and the compression of time and space, [produced by] electronic communication technologies and other means'.[10]

The impact of globalisation

Globalisation has wide-ranging political, economic, social and cultural implications. The globalisation debate has long extended beyond the confines of economy to cultural changes, such as the possible *evolution of a global culture*, on the one hand and, one the other, counter-responses to globalisation and *the growth of countercultures*, for example, the worldwide resurgence of Islamic militancy and the rise of anti-globalisation movements.[11] In recent years, there has been increased focus on culture and identity formation and identity conflicts, created *inter alia* by the globalisation process. The information revolution, cheaper transportation and the general growth of diaspora societies in the West have bolstered new transnationalist identities not only to substate clannish, tribal and local communities, but also allegiances to global entities, such as the Islamic *umma*. New and smaller claimants of sovereignty in the form of local and cultural autonomies have become more important for a growing body of people, although there is little chance that these 'deterritorialized and postnational communities' will supplant territorially bounded national polities.[12]

Much of the literature on globalisation, however, focuses on its economic aspects. The effects of a growing deregulation of international trade and finance markets and its effect on national economies are particularly in focus, especially the economic marginalisation of parts of the Third World.[13] A subtheme is the emergence of a private sector that is no longer geographically rooted, first and foremost, the growth of global transnational corporations (TNCs), whose annual turnover reaches the astronomic level of $100–200 billion, seemingly dwarfing the national economies of many countries in the world (see Chapter 4). Their economic power enables them to play a significant political role on the global scene. This illustrates another topic in the globalisation debate, namely the changes in the international state system brought about by the globalisation process, especially the challenge to *the state as an independent actor* in the international system. Although states respond to new transnational challenges by investing more resources in multilateral organisations, their course of action is being circumscribed by the institutional weight of the largest international organisations, such as the UN, EU, NATO, WTO, ASEAN, etc.

Another prominent challenge to the state comes from the increasing importance of transnational substate actors in international politics. The term 'transnationalism' was introduced precisely to fill a gap in the prevailing state-centric paradigm to 'denote interactions between non-state actors, that is, international interactions that are not directed by states', as it became clear that the scope and impact of such interactions were too great to be ignored.[14] The challenge to the traditional territorial nation-state and its prerogatives comes from both legal non-state actors, including global civil-activist networks such as the anti-globalisation movement, the International

Campaign to Ban Landmines (ICBL), as well as from illegal actors such as the Colombian drug syndicates and the global terrorist network of al-Qaida. The fact that following the 9/11 tragedy, the world's remaining superpower, the USA, formally declared war against a shadowy terrorist network and its supporters and not against a state or an alliance of states, illustrates the sudden rise to prominence of non-state actors in global politics. The prospect of strategic weapons, primarily biological, chemical and nuclear, in the hands of non-state actors has similarly shaken the classic state-centric paradigm, paving the way for an increased focus on transnationalism and transnational threats. The 9/11 attacks were a powerful demonstration of the ability of a substate organisation to effect profound changes in international politics.

As for the future evolution of globalisation, it is reasonable to assume that the process of increased interconnectedness, interdependence and deterritorialisation will continue. The CIA-sponsored *Global Trends 2015*, published in late 2000, revised its previous estimates by placing even more emphasis on globalisation 'as a more powerful driver' than previously anticipated.[15] It is indeed difficult to see how the process of growing interconnectedness and interdependency can be completely reversed on a global scale. The political and economic costs of doing so will be tremendous. Former president Bill Clinton noted following 9/11 that 'the world has grown increasingly interdependent and isolation is no longer an option'.[16] This was not simply a policy recommendation, but reflected also the basic fact that the physical ability to shut the door to the outside world is no longer there. Even if governments attempted, for example, to hermetically seal the borders for fear of terrorists armed with nuclear weapons or a new infectious plague, the impact would still be limited. Many governments in the Western world do not even have the manpower, let alone the infrastructure, to police their borders effectively. Furthermore, the proliferation of four-wheel-drive vehicles, beltwagons, small private airjets, speedboats, even privately owned submarines has made the notion of a hermetically sealed border an illusion. (Even the Israeli military closure of the Gaza Strip has never been watertight. In the mid-1990s, a UN police advisor in Gaza noted wryly that the only thing the smugglers could not get into Gaza was a Boeing 737![17]) Instead, a closure will dramatically increase the lucrative businesses along well-beaten smuggler tracks, where illegal immigrants, drugs, pirate copies and a host of other commodities are brought into the Western world on a daily basis. Furthermore, due to the new information technologies, everything that can be digitally or electronically transported will still continue to flow across national borders, even when airports, ship terminals, and land routes are all closed down. Ideas, information and news would still flow, e-business transactions and services would still be conducted, and transnational political and social contacts would still be possible.

On the other hand, one should be careful not to assume that the globalisation process is entirely irreversible in all its aspects. Economically, the process of globalisation is not 'complete' in the sense that a truly 'global economy' (satisfying Keynes's categories under conditions of globalisation) has emerged.[18] Furthermore, increasing global trade liberalisation may well be partly reversed by a protectionist backlash in parts of the world. For example, the strict restrictions on immigration to the Western world are already a powerful obstacle to the free movement of people. The spread of new contagious diseases, far more deadly than SARS and the Bird Flu, may give rise to a whole new set of barriers on cross-border trade, travel and transportation. Political instability and popular revolts against the economic disadvantages of globalisation may also give rise to new powerful regimes built on ideologies that challenge the current doctrine of market economy.[19] Finally, a deep and protracted economic recession in the USA, the lead-nation in the globalisation project, could severely slow down and possibly reverse economic globalisation, as happened during the Great Depression.[20] Still, none of these scenarios will necessarily lead to a serious long-term reversal of globalisation, but rather a slow-down and an adjustment. The political and economic costs of reversing globalisation are too high, and the technologies sustaining globalisation cannot be uninvented and removed.

While there is little disagreement that globalisation will continue to increase the world's interconnectedness, there is strong disagreement about the future impact of this development. One scenario is offered by the Spanish sociologist Manuel Castells in his widely acknowledged work *The Information Age*, where he describes the rise of 'the fourth world' composed of 'the black holes in informational capitalism'.[21] The social restructuring that globalisation has produced goes beyond the exacerbation of economic inequality and the diffusion of poverty. Today's dominant global economic system, which Castells labels 'informational capitalism', excludes entire peoples and territories and renders them irrelevant, hence the term 'black holes'. According to Castells, 'the territorial confinement of systematically worthless populations, disconnected from networks of valuable functions and people, is indeed a major characteristic of the spatial logic of the network society'.[22]

These black holes are socially excluded peoples, such as the large homeless population in American and European cities, or territorially excluded populations in sub-Saharan Africa and impoverished areas in Latin America and Asia. Black holes may be found, however, in literally every country and every city. They are made up of American inner-city ghettos, Spanish enclaves of mass youth unemployment, French suburbs inhabited exclusively by North Africans and shanty towns surrounding Asian mega-cities. Castells predicts that black holes 'are growing in number and increasing in visibility, the selective triage of informational capitalism and the political breakdown of the welfare state, intensify social exclusion'.[23] Castells' description of the effects of globalisation demonstrates the systemic changes in globalisation that produce social inequality, pauperisation and exclusion.

Possible implications for terrorism

The possible implications of globalisation for future terrorism trends will depend primarily on how globalisation shapes the intermediary factors that were outlined in the introduction, namely, state capacities, socio-economic inequality and armed conflicts. If Castells' predictions come true and globalisation continues to exacerbate socio-economic inequalities and increase their visibility, it is likely to give rise to more anti-hegemonic terrorism, directed against the foremost symbols of globalisation, namely the USA. Recent studies have found that globalisation, if measured along both economic and cultural dimensions, tends to increase anti-American terrorism.[24] Continued globalisation will probably sustain or possibly increase the level of anti-US terrorism. With a high-profiled and active European participation on the various fronts in the US war on terrorism, it is reasonable to assume that future transnational terrorism will remain not only anti-US but also anti-Western in a broad sense. Similarly, if globalisation continues to impact negatively on state capacity and weaken territorial states in the periphery of the international system, more of these regions may become prominent sources of transnational terrorism than is the case today. This might also be the case if a new wave of intrastate armed conflicts erupt, since globalisation creates a greater opportunity structure for internationalising conflicts and exporting the war to Western cities. Globalisation has greatly increased the potential of distant conflicts to transform into transnational terrorism by reducing the significance of physical distance.

Following Castells' thesis, one may argue that in the informational–capitalist society, the use of extreme violence against the key nodes in the system is a very efficient tool to establish global authority, power and influence, escaping from irrelevance, exclusion and marginalisation. Terrorism tactics are known to be 'contagious', and it alerts us to the possibility that al-Qaida's mass-casualty model will shape future terrorism, despite the fact that many contemporary terrorist and insurgent groups strongly disassociate themselves from such tactics. The extraordinary success of al-Qaida in establishing itself as a very influential global actor with the proven capability to shake global stockmarkets, provoke superpower invasions and change the course of history, will undoubtedly encourage other groups to attempt to emulate al-Qaida's success.

Another implication of globalisation can be found in theories on social distance[25] and mass-casualty terrorism. A sociological theory proposed by Donald Black predicts that destructive terrorism is more likely to arise under a certain 'social geometry' between victims, target audience and perpetrators, than in other settings.[26] Mass-casualty terrorism is more likely to occur in societies where adversaries are far apart in social space, for example, when they belong to different ethnicities and socio-economic classes and interact in very few arenas. It explains why terrorism is unlikely to occur in largely homogeneous tribal and peasant societies. It also explains why conflicts in modern industrialised societies where social collectives are relatively close lead to other forms of collective violence, such as riots and guerrilla warfare, or to less deadly forms of terrorism, such as assassinations and propaganda by deed-terrorism, not mass-casualty terrorism.

The presence of the right social geometry of pure terrorism is not sufficient to explain its occurrence. The physical opportunities need to be there as well. Violence requires physical proximity and contact, and, for much of human history, social distance has usually coincided with physical distance, making mass-casualty terrorism mostly impossible.[27] For example, native anti-colonial resistance groups on the African and Asian continent had grievances against their colonial masters in Europe, and there existed a social geometry for terrorism. And yet their violent protests could rarely manifest themselves in terrorism since there were very few European *civilians* in the neighbourhood, and Europe was too far away. Hence, anti-colonial violence usually involved assassinations, guerrilla warfare, bread riots, mutinies, but more rarely terrorism in its pure form. The exception was the settler-colonial states where European civilians lived in great numbers. Colonial Algeria is a case in point, where thousands of terrorist attacks were launched against the French settler communities, ranging from bombs placed in restaurants to killings of French civilians at their homes.[28] Similarly, terroristic violence grew steadily in 'Imperial Israel' after the 1967 war when Israel's settler-colonial character became more pronounced by the accelerated Israeli colonisation of the Occupied Territories. The implantation of Israeli civilian settler colonies in the Palestinian areas simultaneously removed the physical distance between the two communities, while at the same time deepening the vertical social distances between them, through military occupation, discriminatory laws, land confiscations and displacement, socio-economic domination, etc.

The theory of social geometry explains why terrorism is a modern phenomenon of the twentieth and twenty-first centuries, when the pre-modern barriers of physical distance were gradually overcome and socially very distant groups were brought much closer together in physical space. Similarly, it explains the growing recourse to mass-casualty terrorism during the contemporary age of globalisation, as new means of rapid and cheap transportation, new technologies of electronic communication and removal of political barriers for transborder interactions altogether have rendered physical distance less relevant. Globalisation has thus created more ideal conditions for mass-casualty terrorism. (This is also consistent with the terrorism trend projections made by *Global Trends 2015*, which predicts that 'terrorist tactics will become increasingly sophisticated and designed to achieve mass casualties.'[29])

Donald Black nevertheless contends that in the long term, globalisation, with its modern transportation and communication, will ultimately erode the specific social geometry of terrorism and remove the current conditions, which makes it prevalent:

> [Globalisation] increases global intimacy, cultural homogeneity, and other forms of human closeness – a multidimensional process that shrinks social space at the same time that it shrinks physical space. Technology thus makes terrorism easier and deadlier in the short term, but in the long term it destroys the social geometry on which terrorism depends.[30]

Thus, Black believes that terrorism in its pure form is doomed to 'sociological death'; it will only have a relatively short lifespan 'limited to the time of shocking implosion of physical and social space during the twentieth and twenty-first century'.[31] This optimistic view is, however, predicated upon a continuous shrinking of social space, through the intermingling of people and cultures and the fading away of differences, which polarise and collectivise violence. Many anthropologists and sociologists would probably disagree with this view. Globalisation often exacerbates differences, rather than diluting them, simply because it has a different impact on different societies: some prosper, others stagnate and yet others collapse. Economic development and modernisation promote secular-rational values and, ultimately, more tolerance, while economic decline and collapse 'propels societies in the opposite direction'.[32] The central role of identity in contemporary violent conflicts is a case in point. Increased intermingling also leads to a reassertion of identities, a reinvention of differences and a new consciousness of 'how different we really are'.[33]

The future of armed conflicts

Postulate: The total number of violent conflicts will probably remain the same, but more conflicts will become more internationalised than is the case today, and their implications will be more global in scope. A wider range of non-state actors will play a greater role in armed conflicts, and the political economies of conflicts will also become more transnational. New modes of 'deterritorialised' armed conflicts where the insurgents command authority and wield power without territorial control may become more widespread.

Possible implications for terrorism: The ideational basis and opportunity structures of terrorist and insurgent groups will expand, enhancing their influence and extending their reach. The lethality of transnational terrorism will remain high due to the likely emulation of al-Qaida's 'global civil war' model by future groups.

Terrorism usually occurs as part of broader socio-political conflicts, where many forms of collective political violence occur. In its international and transnational forms terrorism occurs perhaps most frequently as part of or as a by-product of armed conflicts. In an influential article in 2002, Michael Doran argues that transnational terrorism reflects a civil war taking place between a government and its opposition movements, while foreign nationals and interests are targeted because of their assumed politico-military alliance with, or intervention on behalf of, the government in question.[34] While the degree of spillover of international terrorism from domestic conflicts varies greatly, there is little doubt that armed conflicts have been a major source, both directly and indirectly.[35] Research in future patterns of armed conflicts is therefore helpful in assessing emerging trends in terrorism.

Throughout the 1990s, it was widely believed that civil wars, especially ethnic conflicts, were proliferating around the world, and that even if inter-state wars had declined, they were being replaced by a steadily growing number of civil wars.[36] This does not correspond to reality. According to Uppsala University Conflict Data Project, probably the best annual compilation of armed conflict, where the lower threshold for recording conflicts is twenty-five or more conflict-related deaths annually, there has been a relatively sharp, albeit uneven, increase in the number of armed conflicts from about 1960 until 1992.[37] During the past nine years, however, there has been a decline, pushing the number of armed conflicts well below forty every year. War between states, or 'inter-state armed conflicts', have been relatively rare since 1945; there have been only five or less conflicts of this type every year, and after 1991, the number has oscilliated between zero and two.[38] Civil wars and insurgencies, termed 'internal' or 'intrastate conflicts', have always been more numerous. By 1991, the number of such conflicts reached a record high of fifty-two, followed by a relatively steep decrease to twenty-six in 2002. Even if the Operation Iraqi Freedom in 2003 was a high-profile example of an inter-state war, it has become more and more unlikely for countries in the developed world to fight a state-to-state war. Future conflicts are most likely to be internal or intrastate with various international and transnational dimensions.

The rise in the number of conflicts until 1991 was in no small measure attributable to new state formations. The number of states expanded from sixty-six in 1946 to 187 in 1994, which contributed to inflating the statistics. Another factor skewing the statistics was the high number of states formally involved in certain international inter-state conflicts, without playing any significant military role, such as the first Gulf war in 1991. Together, these two factors suggest that the downward trend after 1992 is in fact even sharper.[39] Still, the declining numbers highlight not only success stories where conflicts have been settled, but are to some degree a reflection of the familiar pattern of today's conflicts. They 'tend to be long with extended periods of low-level conflict, punctuated by sudden eruptions of violence'.[40] As Wallensteen and Sollenberg have pointed out, armed conflicts often become institutionalised and reinforce their own existence. Most conflicts after 1989 have followed a general 'pattern of alternating escalation and de-escalation.'[41]

Where have most armed conflicts taken place? The world can be divided into 'zones of peace' and 'zones of conflict', to borrow an expression from Singer and Wildavsky.[42] There have been three important 'clusters' of conflict: first, from Central America to South America; second, another 'arc of conflicts' runs from the Balkans to the Middle East and to the Caucasus. The third cluster is in Africa. All these zones show signs of contraction, except for Africa where conflicts are spread more or less throughout the continent.[43]

In general, armed conflicts are about territory and access to resources, ranging from natural resources to education and power, as the means of administrating access to resources.[44] Still, competition for territory and power is seldom sufficient to initiate violent conflict. Particularly in multi-ethnic societies, the actual trigger is often a budding sense of insecurity, which is exacerbated by weakened state authority. Intercommunal violence erupts as the state fails to serve as the framework for a non-violent conflict-management mechanism and as the original guarantor of security. Lake and Rothchild maintain that '[s]tate weakness [. . .] is a necessary precondition for violent ethnic conflict to erupt'.[45] The strong linkages between weak states and violent conflict is illustrated by the observation that the majority of current wars are taking place in Africa, where the state system is weak, central governments frequently lack the means to police their territories, and de-facto authority on a local level often rests with other entities than the government bureaucracy.[46]

Fearon and Laitin have argued that today's civil wars 'are not temporary phenomena of the immediate post-Cold War world', but have 'structural roots' in the international system.[47] They are a result of two distinct processes: the proliferation of new military technology empowering insurgent armies and the decolonisation process between 1940s and the 1970s, which led to the proliferation of fragile states.

Armed conflicts are often unleashed as a result of so-called 'conflict entrepreneurs' who wilfully nurture tension and insecurity in order to polarise society and advance their own political role.[48] In deeply divided states where ethnic and religious cleavages are entrenched and the civic identity of the population is weak or eroded, it is possible to make a political carrier by promoting conflict. Former Yugoslav president Slobodan Milošević's decision to abolish Kosovar autonomy rule in March 1989 and Ariel Sharon's famous stroll on the Temple Mount in late September 2000 are two cases in point. Both moves served their respective political careers, at least temporarily, but plunged their societies into violent conflict. Sharon's Temple Mount visit triggered the second Palestinian uprising. Milošević's abolishment of Kosovar autonomy led to mass rioting, unrest, outbreaks of inter-communal violence, followed by a state of emergency in February 1990, and served as a prelude to the bloody Balkan wars.[49]

26

The rise of internationalised internal conflicts

A characteristic feature in current conflict patterns is the rise of so-called 'internationalised internal conflicts', previously labelled 'intrastate conflicts with foreign interventions', and is defined as internal conflicts in which both the opposition and the government receive support from other states.[50] This category has become somewhat more prevalent over the past five years. It numbered from one to six per year since the 1960s. Following a decline from 1989 to 1997, the past five years have seen at least four or more such conflicts every year. This number would have been much higher if conflicts with significant external *non-state* support to one or more of the warring parties were included. External support for the belligerents tends to prolong armed conflicts considerably. Internationalised civil wars have been extremely bloody. In terms of casualties, the Afghanistan liberation war, 1979–88, ranks as number four, only surpassed by the Korean war, the Iran–Iraq war and the Vietnam war, the three largest inter-state wars in the post-Second World War period.[51]

The rise of internationalised conflicts illustrates the impact of globalisation on armed conflicts in which a host of external actors (major powers, international agencies, neighbouring states, diaspora groups, arms salesmen, mercenaries and criminal networks) take part in one way or another.[52] It also explains perhaps why there is popular impression that armed conflicts in general and ethnic conflicts in particular are proliferating. The vast improvements in information technologies and media access, the steady increase of movements of goods and people across borders, the growth of diaspora communities, etc., all contribute in various ways to making distant conflicts matters of global concern, even if the overall number of conflicts are not necessarily spiralling out of control. Or, as Yahya Sadowski put it, it is 'one of those optical illusions that round-the-clock and round-the-world television coverage has helped to create.'[53]

International involvement in internal conflicts is increasing, spanning from humanitarian and development aid and overt or covert security assistance to direct military interventions. Although most conflicts indeed largely take place within a state's borders, they frequently spillover into neighbouring countries, either through refugee or arms flows, or by dragging border areas directly into the fighting. Geographically distant countries also become involved through the hostage-taking of their nationals, the assassination of their diplomats and the direct involvement in the conflict by their diaspora communities. Transnational criminal networks also make business from ongoing wars. Futhermore, conflict zones invite foreign interventions – political, diplomatic, or military – when terrorist attacks occur abroad in the name of one or another of the warring parties. Today's armed conflicts thereby defy the traditional classification of being either internal or inter-state.[54]

We may speak of two major types of violent conflict, where the second is a function of the first. First, there is the total, predominantly internal war that does not differentiate between soldiers and civilians and is fought as much for economic gain as for political or territorial reasons. Reviving eerily familiar terminology, Buse writes that '[t]he war of the future is a total war'.[55] Thus, the Clausewitzian concept of 'trinitarian' war with its distinction into the government, the armed forces and the general population seems obsolete.[56] Violence in today's intrastate wars is increasingly perpetrated by police, paramilitary units, mercenaries, rebel militias, self-defence leagues and non-uniformed personnel, rather than just conventional armies. It is also increasingly directed against civilians, underlining the uncivil and terrorist character of today's civil wars.[57]

Second, there are frequently international interventions in these wars that are usually conducted by multinational coalitions, operating under significant political constraints and driven by values rather than by strict military goals. The second type of conflict thus springs directly from the first one, due to the fact that globalisation has brought the world closer together, instilling both a sense of responsibility for world order and a fear of the consequences of inaction in members of the international community. The fact that conflicts are geographically remote is of diminishing importance, as their effects are felt across distances, as a result of economic and political interdependence and media coverage. As Ayres has correctly pointed out, the main new development since the end of the Cold War is not changes in the number and character of conflicts. It is rather the degree to which the developed world has allowed itself to take in more of the anarchy that has always been present in other parts of the world, but to which it previously did not pay much attention.[58] As the developed world listens more attentively than before, the utility of violence to further political agendas has increased and has opened up a host of new opportunities for insurgent and terrorist groups in pressuring and intimidating their governments and foreign intervening powers.

Illegitimate states, legitimate revolts

After the end of the Cold War, the nature of the state and its sovereignty changed; state sovereignty has become a more diverse concept in the face of globalisation and international co-operation, while the advent of humanitarian interventions in the post-Cold War era have strengthened the notions of individual sovereignty and human security.[59] Key factors in the assessment of the state are its ability to provide security for its territory and population, its monopoly on violence and its political legitimacy. Although this has not changed in principle, there are a growing number of weak states that either do not have the physical means or the political legitimacy to exercise effective control over their territory. According to Enriquez, the problem is not that the principle of sovereignty has been eroded, but 'rather that it has grown and unbundled', involving not simply a *de jure* territorial control and an army, but also more specific demands for regime legitimacy, economic performance and so forth.[60] As Rotberg has noted, 'more is required of the modern state than ever before. Each is expected to provide good governance; to make its people secure, prosperous, healthy, and literate; and to instill a sense of national pride.'[61] In the post-9/11 era, full de-facto territorial control, effective prosecution and suppression of international terrorist organisations and their support networks have been added to an already long list of requirements. Hence, states that prove unable to deliver on these increased demands risk international criticism, sanctions and ultimately external interventions. In many cases, this provides insurgents with a whole new leverage over the central government since heavy-handed counter-insurgency campaigns often trigger strong international reactions.

In other cases, governments also face the dilemma that if they move to reassert authority over semi-autonomous regions, in which international terrorist organisations are suspected to be operating, it upsets the traditional balance of power between the capital and the provinces. This often increases, rather than reduces the prospects for internal revolts and civil war. The Pakistani government's controversial campaign against Taleban and al-Qaida supporters in the autonomous north-west frontier provinces is a case in point.

A corollary of the challenges to the traditional notion of state sovereignty is the increased legitimacy of insurgencies and popular uprisings against non-representative and authoritarian regimes, perhaps most distinctly illustrated by the wide international legitimacy enjoyed by the Kosovo-Albanian insurgency in the late 1990s. Other armed opposition movements that have employed terrorist tactics against their governments have been greeted with tacit support and sympathy in many parts of the world. The widespread support for the Palestinian, Chechen and Iraqi resistance movements throughout the Arab world is an illustrative example. A wide array of terrorist groups also found safe haven and sanctuaries in the Western world throughout the 1990s, under the cover of being political dissident movements. The 9/11 attacks and the rise of al-Qaida as a global threat contributed to a partial reversal of this trend. The plethora of Islamist extremist groups in the West has come under much tougher scrutiny. Still, a number of insurgent groups such as the Liberation Tigers of Tamil Eelan (LTTE) and the People's Mujahidin (Mujahideed e-Khalq) of Iran, whose armed campaigns were almost exclusively local, continue to enjoy a surprisingly high level of international legitimacy. On a popular level in the diaspora communities in the West, the support for insurgent groups employing terrorist tactics is also far from neglible. This is illustrated, for example, by the ease with which they have been able to raise funds and secure material support among their supporters in Europe and the United States, where strong legal protection of freedom of speech and a history of tolerance for dissident movements have until recently allowed foreign insurgent groups to operate relatively freely. A good example is the Kurdish separatist group, PKK (now KADEK), in Germany where it was banned back in 1993, but where it still retains a relatively extensive political and logistical support network.[62] In the late 1990s, an estimated 50,000 Kurdish residents in Germany were believed to sympathise with the PKK, while nearly 10,000 were active members of the party or one of its front organisations.[63]

Al-Qaida and the rise of global civil wars

The character of al-Qaida's war on the USA and its allies has intrigued conflict theorists, given its global and deterritorialised nature. Its classification has posed serious problems. The Uppsala dataset on armed conflict has introduced a new term for the USA vs. al-Qaida conflict, namely an 'extrasystemic' conflict.[64] Others have suggested the terms 'a global insurgency', 'a globalised civil war' or 'a global civil war', which in themselves are contradictions in terms.[65] A conflict cannot be an internal conflict within a state and a global war at the same time; this is unless we are witnessing the rise of a global society within which this global civil war takes place. There can be no doubt that the conflict between the USA and al-Qaida is global in its character. In mid 2002 there were 536 detainees from more than forty nations in US military custody in Guantánamo Bay, and the 1,300 arrested extremists believed to be associated with al-Qaida had been arrested in more than seventy countries.[66] Since then the figures have increased. Furthermore, the level of casualties inflicted by al-Qaida and the military means with which the conflict is fought, make it difficult to classify the USA vs. al-Qaida conflict as yet another international terrorist campaign.

The steady flow of new recruits to al-Qaida and its associated groups is believed to be at least partly a result of grievances stemming from the ongoing armed uprising in Iraq, the festering conflict of militarised colonisation in the Israeli-occupied West Bank, Jerusalem, and Gaza, as well as other civil wars where Muslims suffer injustice, from Kashmir to Chechnya. Al-Qaida's resilience is also a product of its tremendous success in marketing its 'brand name'. Al-Qaida has had tremendous success in exploiting the global mass media's thirst of spectacular news and action, through unprecedentedly audacious operations, through its innovative use of terrorism and through its renunciation of all political-ideological barriers that terrorist groups previously have had with regards to mass-casualty attacks. Another factor is its reliance on cyberspace opportunities for propaganda and communication purposes, bringing together disparate communities of sympathisers and supporters, and facilitating contacts between operative cells across continents. It is now believed that al-Qaida, after Afghanistan, is 'metamorphos[ing] into a "virtual" network, depriving its enemies of a geographic target'.[67] By posting electronic libraries of ideological and theological literature as well as training manuals, tactical handbooks and weapon instructions in written, audio and video formats on the Internet, al-Qaida uses the web as 'an open university' in its effort at fostering an Islamist-jihadist nation in cyberspace.[68]

The most important factor in bringing al-Qaida to global prominence was perhaps not al-Qaida's own actions, but government responses to 9/11. Shortly after the attacks, the US administration declared the attacks to be not another act of terrorism, but 'an act of war'. The word 'war' was not used in the metaphorical sense such as 'the war on poverty' and 'the war on drugs', but with all its military and political implications. The notion of a 'declaration of war' as the distinguishing feature of whether or not a country is at war rests on the state-centred system and is historically a recent phenomenon. It has only been dominant for a century and a half. Before 9/11, it was sometimes argued that that phase of history was virtually over, after a period in which the two blocs had opposed each other in anticipation of the 'ultimate' declaration of war. The 9/11 attacks revived the term, but in a way that bypassed and weakened the state in favour of non-state actors. The famous *New York Times* columnist Thomas Friedman has lamented that the USA treated Osama bin Laden 'as though he were another nation-state'.[69] Referring to the US attacks with seventy-five cruise missiles at a cost of 1 million US dollars apiece against alleged al-Qaida bases in Afghanistan and Sudan following the bombing of the US embassies in East Africa in 1998, Friedman noted: 'That was the first battle in history between a superpower and a super-empowered angry man.'[70]

Given the magnitude of the death and destruction in Washington and New York, it was perhaps inevitable that al-Qaida's attacks would provoke a forceful counter-response. Terrorist groups have a long history of using violence precisely to trigger an overreaction from state authorities: in RAF's mind the German state's counter-response would unmask its 'true fascist face', and reveal 'the Auswitsz generation' among its leaders. Similarly, the Brazilian revolutionary ideologue Carlos Marighela hoped his urban terrorist campaign would lead to a militarisation of the conflict with the Brazilian government.[71] In this game, al-Qaida was extremely successful, triggering an invasion of Afghanistan and Iraq, as well as an expanded US military presence throughout the Muslim world. There is a growing realisation that the militarisation of the anti-terrorism campaign after 9/11 in general, and the invasion of Iraq in particular, has been a failed strategy. Richard Clarke, the former US counter-terrorism co-ordinator, noted in March 2004, that 'Osama bin Laden had been saying for years, "America wants to invade an Arab country and occupy it, an oil-rich Arab country" [. . .] [W]e stepped right into bin Laden's propaganda'.[72] Similarly, former UK foreign secretary Robin Cook observed in July 2004: 'I fear that by invading Iraq we have responded in precisely the way Osama bin Laden wanted and as a consequence we and the west will have to live with the violent consequences of this strategic blunder for a decade to come.'[73] The al-Qaida leadership has gloated much over this. In his video-recording in late October 2004, days ahead of the US presidential elections, Osama bin Laden noted that

> [It has been] easy for us to provoke and bait this administration. All that we have to do is to send two mujahidin to the furthest point east to raise a piece of cloth on which is written al-Qaida, in order to make the generals race there to cause America to suffer human, economic, and political losses without their achieving for it anything of note other than some benefits for their private companies.[74]

By inflicting mass murder and humiliation on the world's remaining super-power, al-Qaida was deemed worthy of being the US superpower's counter-part in a global war. It became the world's most well-known non-state actor, wielding an influence over global matters far beyond that of many states, triggering military invasions, shaking the stockmarkets by its statements and forcing governments to spend billions of dollars in extra security measures. By being elevated to a warring party in a global war, al-Qaida rose to global pre-eminence as the most potent symbol of a global anti-Western rebellion, attracting thousands of new followers, eager to join a winning party in 'the caravan of jihad'. Al-Qaida has not by itself introduced the global civil war, but the responses to 9/11 have made the new conceptualisation possible. The temptation to emulate al-Qaida, at least aspects of its modus operandi, will be hard to resist for future terrorist organisations.[75]

Beyond war: the globalised political economy of conflict

While the traditional notion of armed conflicts has been that legitimate *grievances*, such as socio-economic inequalities, discrimination and repres-sion, were the driving forces, economic *greed* as a motive of civil wars and armed insurgencies has received more attention in recent research.[76] The shift in focus is intimately connected to the end of the Cold War when military and financial assistance to local insurgent groups from the two superpowers largely dried up, and many guerrilla movements realised that they had to adopt 'a new, and more business oriented attitude', as Jean-Christophe Rufin has put it.[77] The greed interpretation emphasises the organisational momentum of the insurgent organisation. Over time, with dwindling external support, the mundane needs of its combatants override ideology and politics. Aided by the greed of its leaders, the insurgent movement is transformed into a criminal enterprise, offering hazardous but well-paid jobs to the unemployed masses. The revolution takes a back seat as war-fighting gives way to looting, hostage-taking and guards duties for drug cartels. Their sources of income involve everything from confiscation of civilian assets, 'taxes' levied on humanitarian aid, external funding from emigrant com-munities overseas and foreign-government aid to revenues from illegal trade in valuable commodities.[78] A number of insurgent groups are clearly more atuned to criminal business than their ideological programme. This goes for the Abu Sayyaf guerrillas in the Southern Philippines, the FARC rebels in Colombia, the UNITA movement in Angola and perhaps also some of the Protestant paramilitary groups in Northern Ireland. Had it not been for the rise of al-Qaida with its puritanical salafi-jihadist ideology and its global network of martyrdom-seeking fighters, one is tempted to agree with the assertion that 'there is virtually no war left in the world today, just crime.'[79]

Today's criminalised conflicts are not simply local conflicts. Instead, they are characterised by 'long-term and innovative adaptations to globalisation, linked to expanding networks of parallel (illegal) and grey (semi-legal) economic activity'.[80] This empowers and brings into focus a range of actors, including organised criminal groups, warlords or private security companies, in addition to the parties to the conflict.[81] The transborder activities of rebel groups are facilitated by the revolution in transportation, especially the dramatic reduction of container transportation rates for overseas import–export trade, the growing availability of private air transportation and, not least, the new communication technologies.[82]

Box 2.1 Transportation revolution and the globalisation of insurgency

In an important study on globalisation and the transformation of insurgencies, John Mackinlay has argued that the proliferation of old and new means of transportation has been crucial in empowering insurgents, in addition to information technologies (the Internet, mobile phones etc).[1] Rebel armies in remote districts of Third World countries are increasingly becoming connected to the global economy and have greater access to the outside world and to Western metropolises than before. New and more powerful cross-country vehicles have become increasingly accessible at much cheaper prices, even in desolated and geographically remote areas. After the end of the Cold War, logistics aircrafts, vessels and vehicles from the military surpluses were released on the global markets, at low prices. Strategic aircraft from the former Soviet fleet can be chartered, connecting small airfields in distant war zones directly to the international market, eliminating the government monopoly on such traffic. For shorter transportation purposes, a growing number of small privately owned aircraft such as *Cessna* and *Antonovs*, have increasingly become available for hire, with short take-off capability and capable of operating out of very primitive airfields.

Another important development is the containerisation in sea transportation, leading to a dramatically lower unit price for cargo, in addition to making international transportation much faster. This has enabled small entrepreneurs to transport illegal goods to international

---

markets with much greater ease than before. The previous monopoly of governments and international corporations regarding the extraction and export of natural resources from developing countries has been broken. Illegal substate actors are cashing in on increased profits due to the lower transportation rates. The term 'portable resources' is changing as the export of a wider variety of goods is becoming possible even for small private entrepreneurs.[2] The huge size of the international container traffic ensures anonymity and facilitates the global trade in illegal merchandise, supplies and arms. Any attempt to screen a substantial portion of containers has so far remained unfeasible. (The magnitude of the problem can be illustrated by the fact that the USA relies on ocean transportation for 95 per cent of the cargo tonnage that moves in and out of the country, while more than 7,500 commercial vessels make about 51,000 port calls annually. The total figure of containers entering US ports each year is about 6 million.)[3]

Notes
[1] Mackinlay, *Globalisation and Insurgency*, pp. 15–20.
[2] ibid., pp. 19–20.
[3] Information given in 'Transportation Issues', by Congressman Rob Simmons, *E-letter* 31 March 2002, <http://www.reformpartyct.org/simmons040302. html>. Accessed September 2004.

The transnational and criminal dimensions of contemporary conflicts have a number of implications. They allow for the expansion of transnational criminal enterprises, which export illegal refugees, drugs, diamonds, gemstones, jade, protected antiques, ivory, precious wood, oil, pirate-copy products, etc., from conflict zones, and ship weapons, supplies and mercenaries back. The proliferation of small arms is particularly significant. The availability of arms has increased as the end of the Cold War released a tide of war material and weapons to global markets.[83] The criminal character of conflicts also ensures their longevity. The warring parties do not run out of supplies, and they make sure to keep the conflict at a low level of intensity for significant periods of time. Hence, such conflicts are characterised by periodic eruptions of violence and no clear dividing line between the state of war and the state of peace.[84]

The consequences for international terrorism are evident. Transnational crime networks and the services they provide aid terrorist networks in expanding their assets, diversifying their sources of income and supply and their access to weapons, false identification papers, etc. In this way, the new globalised political economy of conflict is linked to the rise of transnational private support networks for terrorist organisations. These networks have arguably eclipsed the role of states in underpinning international terrorism.

The emergence of a global guerrilla state authority?

In weak states economic interests, often of a criminal nature, flourish in the absence of authority, and various forms of private-security entities step in where the state government has abandoned control, or where there is a 'perceived shortfall' in the maintenance of order in society.[85] Local community committees, self-styled vigilante squads, warlords and clan and tribal structures often become 'the police' and final arbiter on the local level, blurring the line between legitimate policing and vigilantism as well as between taxation and racketeering. While many have pointed to economic agendas and criminal greed when explaining insurgents' preoccupation with other businesses than strictly war-fighting, there is a clear logic in the insurgents' prioritising of vigilantism/'policing' and extortion/'taxation'. Separatist insurgent groups in ethnically divided societies often make determined attempts at asserting themselves as the only legitimate authority through a mixture of paramilitary coercion and genuine community policing. By doing so they succeed in reducing the population's contact with the government's police and security forces, prevent the recruitment of informers, and gained communal legitimacy for being harsh on crime.

Box 2.2 Insurgents and policing

The PLO's Fatah in the occupied territories during the first intifada, 1987–93, and the Provisional Irish Republican Army (PIRA) in Catholic working-class districts in Northern Ireland since the ceasefire in 1994 are two examples of how insurgent/terrorist groups engaged in vigilantism/'policing'.[1] Both meted out public punishments to suspected collaborators, but they also investigated and punished non-political crimes and enjoyed at times significant popular support. To some degree they also collected taxes, while using a mix of encouragement and enforcement to promote a tax boycott of the Israeli or British authorities.

In the Palestinian case, it was clearly understood that insurgent policing was nothing more than an interim emergency measure. As a former 'Fatah Hawk', a member of Fatah's paramilitary organisation in Gaza, noted in an interview with this author, the purpose of their policing and arbitration services was not to provide final solutions to social problems. These measures were simply an 'anaesthetic' to contain internal conflicts and preserve unity, until such problems could be settled in more conducive circumstances in an independent Palestinian state.[2] Indeed, the harsh methods applied, especially against suspected collaborators, and the spiralling cycle of violent collaborator executions in the so-called 'red squares' in Gaza's refugee camps, made people

---

question the wisdom of abaondoning the official police. The traditional authority of families and clans had been usurped by young bands of armed militants who asserted the right to execute any suspect of collaboration. Implicit in these policing efforts lay a state building logic, namely the construction of a 'guerrilla state authority', which was impenetrable and steadfast vis-à-vis the Israeli occupation.

Notes

[1] For a case study of informal policing and vigilantism in the West Bank and Gaza during the first Intifada, see Brynjar Lia, *A Police Force Without a State: A History of the Palestinian Security Forces in the West Bank and Gaza* (Reading: Ithaca Press, 2005), Chapter 2. For PIRA in Northern Ireland, see Andrew Silke, 'Lords of Discipline: The Methods and Motives of Paramilitary Vigilantism in Northern Ireland', *Low Intensity Conflict* and *Law Enforcement* 7 (2) (autumn 1998), pp. 121–56.

[2] Author interview in Khan Yunis, September 1998.

The importance of vigilantism in armed conflicts is often overlooked. It is usually conceptualised as a state-sponsored counter-insurgency strategy, by delegating policing powers to collaborationist militias, local warlords and loyal tribes. Vigilantism by insurgents has been subsumed into other political-violence categories, either as outright terrorism, as ethnic strife or simply as intra-communal violent crime. Low-intensity conflicts between a government and an insurgent organisation often revolve around the very idea of authority, namely, who commands the population's generalised obedience. Hence, the strategy of insurgent vigilantism assumes particular importance. As future conflicts will increasingly be influenced by the logic of informational capitalism, where authority can be exercised through nodes in global transnational networks, and less by territorial control, it is reasonable to expect that insurgents may be able impose their authority on scattered deterritorialised communities across national borders. An indication that this future scenario is coming to fruition is the phenomenon of extortion or 'taxation' carried out by various terrorist and insurgent groups in several European and North American diaspora communities. Attempts at exercising some political control is also done through various forms of intimidation against critics of the insurgents' policies.[86] The growing size of immigrant communities in the West has led terrorist groups from around the world to establish political and financial support networks in the diaspora. For example, back in 1998, Canadian Security Intelligence Service (CSIS) investigated more than fifty organisational targets and about 350 individual targets. According to the CSIS Director there were terrorist groups present in Canada, 'whose origins lie in virtually every significant regional, ethnic and nationalist conflict there is'.[87]

The prospect of insurgent groups extending their authority over transnational communities in the developed world has also gained more credence by the rise of al-Qaida, which exemplifies the first truly global terrorist organisation, with global recruitment, global goals and a global scene of operation. Even if al-Qaida cannot be said to be a global insurgent group, with the ambition and means to command state-like authority over large constituent communities, the remarkable resilience of its support networks, the steady recruitment to its operational cells and the global reach of its operations suggest that it commands considerable authority beyond the extremist fringes of the jihadist communities. While its empowerment stems from its method of warfare, namely mass-casualty attacks on mostly Western high-quality targets, this also sets limits for its further empowerment as a political entity and prevents its transformation into a more mundane mass-based political-minded organisation with negotiable goals.

Still, the proliferation of al-Qaida's and like-minded jihadist ideologies has reached a point where the potential for new local self-declared 'Islamic emirates', ruled by jihadist clerics and their supporters is no longer conceivable only in a few well-known hot spots in the Muslim world, such as the Imbaba district in Cairo, the Sidi Moumin slum in Casablanca, the tribal areas in north-western Pakistan, the rugged Yemeni mountains or the rebel-ruled Iraqi town of Faluja. In light of the growth of transnational identities in general and the spread of radical Islamist ideologies in particular, future 'Islamic emirates' may also appear in shanty towns on the outskirts of Western cities, where racism, alienation and social exclusion create fertile ground for the jihadist message, propagated through sleek multimedia shows of heart-breaking sufferings of Muslims under the combined Western–Russian–Israeli assault on Islam. Indeed, in some of the vast *banlieue*, the suburban ghettos of Paris where crime, inequality, ethnic alienation and Islamic extremism have converged in an angry subculture, Islamist extremists have occasionally attempted to form their own local emirates through maintaining discipline and fighting crime.[88] The war of ideas will be decisive in these coming battles for hearts and minds. At the end of the day, the notion of sovereignty and territorial control would mean little if mini-emirates pop up in the Western shanty towns, policed by militant youth under the guidance of a jihadist clerics, known only to the initiated. In the early 1990s, Egypt sent 14,000 troops, backed by tanks and heavy weapons to retake the 'Islamic emirate of Imbaba' in the middle of the Egyptian capital.[89] A similar scenario in a Western city would obviously be hailed as an immense victory for the jihadist movement.

Conclusion

The purpose of this chapter has been to offer perspectives on how globalisation and armed conflicts are likely to influence the occurrence and patterns of terrorism in the future. Pulling these various threads together in a brief conclusion, I argue that in the future armed conflicts are likely to be characterised by multiple asymmetries, tilting the balance in favour of non-state actors. As has been demonstrated in this chapter, various trends come together to strengthen the means and conditions for insurgents, while weakening the material and ideational basis for states' counter-responses. The rise of internationalised internal conflicts implies an increased involvement of external actors, complicating any efforts at a unilateral state-imposed military solution. The unbundling of state sovereignty provides new legitimacy of popular revolts; in order to be a state, it is no longer sufficient to have a flag and an army. Due to the globalisation of parallel trade and civil-war economies, insurgents are able to gain supplies and resources on a scale previously unheard of. The new information technologies and the growth of diaspora communities offer new hitherto-unthinkable opportunities to global insurgents to extend their influence across borders and to wage a global civil war on their enemies, with little or no concern for territories or national borders.

3

INTERNATIONAL RELATIONS AND POLITICS

> Enemies in the past needed great armies and great industrial capabilities to endanger America. Now, shadowy networks of individuals can bring great chaos and suffering to our shores for less than it costs to purchase a single tank. Terrorists are organised to penetrate open societies and to turn the power of modern technologies against us.[1]
>
> (The White House, September 2002)

International terrorism has long been an integral part of international politics, even if its perpetrators are illegal actors and their acts are roundly condemned by most states in the world.[2] Terrorist incidents are frequently international in the sense that they relate to events or conflicts taking place in another country or region. Furthermore, the very character of the international system itself and the foreign policies of states influence the occurrence of terrorism, for example, by generating more conducive or more prohibitive circumstances for terrorist organisations. Following the framework outlined in the introduction, the present chapter examines seven different trends or processes of change in the international state system. Drawing upon relevant causal relationships outlined in the introduction, I discuss their implications for future patterns of terrorism. This is the primary objective of the present chapter.

The world order

Postulate: During the next two decades, the world system will remain basically unipolar, although there is a possibility that regional power centres will grow stronger and contribute to a relative decline in the US global hegemony. Any return to an intense bipolar military and ideological rivalry is unlikely, as is the rise of a truly multipolar world order.

Possible implications for terrorism: State-sponsored terrorism will not increase but will remain a factor in regional conflicts. Anti-hegemonic transnational terrorism will continue and possibly increase.

We have previously reviewed literature suggesting that the character of the international system is significant in accounting for the level of international terrorism. An assessment of the future development of the world order, and of hegemony in global politics in particular, is therefore a useful avenue to predict future patterns of international terrorism.

Since the collapse of the Soviet Union, the USA has enjoyed a period of unparalleled global preponderance, controlling a greater share of global power than any other state in modern history.[3] John Ikenberry has noted in the introduction to his recent book, *America Unrivalled*, that 'the pre-eminence of American power today is unprecedented in modern history. No other great power has enjoyed such formidable advantages in military, economic, technological, cultural or political capabilities. We live in a one superpower world and there is no serious competitor in sight.'[4]

The classical realist tradition in political science postulates that a unipolar state system is inherently unstable and will sooner or later lead to the rise of new global powers, which challenge the hegemonic power and restore the balance of power and hence, the equilibrium of the system. Classical realism, however, may be less accurate in describing and predicting the behaviour of states in the contemporary international system. The latter is characterised by increasing economic interdependence and a rapidly expanding web of economic and political relations, treaties and regulations, often embedded in permanent multilateral institutions. The urge to restore the balance of power and challenge the global hegemony of the United States may therefore be weaker than the realist tradition leads us to believe.

For the same reasons, the chances of the United States retreating as a major player on the global scene through the first part of the twenty-first century are also slim. The United States is tied into a dense and growing web of commercial, political, military and cultural ties with other countries. Still, its dominance often proves offensive to the rest of the world, even at times when it has attempted to exercise its power with care. As a Rand Corporation report explained, 'its sheer pervasiveness and prominence make the United States the globe's 500 pound gorilla whether we like it or not'.[5] The prevalent perception among most segments of the US political elite that a continued major US role in world politics is a historical necessity will probably continue to make US isolationism and US withdrawal from world politics a distant possibility at best.[6]

There are several reasons to expect a gradual decline of US hegemony as regional powers develop their economies and seek to assert their influence, and as American unilateral power politics prove prohibitively costly. Long before the US military overstretch in Iraq and Afghanistan became apparent and its current budget deficit reached an unprecedented 520 billion US dollars for the fiscal year of 2004, observers pointed to structural factors challenging the US global hegemony, especially in the economic field.[7] For example, Bornschier and Chase-Dunn argued back in 1999 that 'the US economic hegemony is declining'.[8] The fact that the dollar is the world's primary reserve currency, especially with regards to the oil trade, is often said to allow the US Central Bank to 'print gold', ensuring the US position as the world's predominant economic power.[9] There is undoubtedly a net advantage to the USA of the dollar hegemony, but it should not be exaggerated. There is a slight chance that the dollar might be replaced by another dominant currency. If a sufficient number of countries should decide to switch to euro as the medium of exchange for purchasing oil, as the former Iraqi president Saddam Hussein did in 2000, the US economic dominance would be significantly affected.[10] In October 2003 Russia's president Vladimir Putin stated that Russia was considering pricing its crude oil in euro rather than dollars, while Iran, the second largest OPEC producer has also discussed switching to euro for its oil exports. For various technical reasons, the shift away from dollars towards, for example, petroeuro seems unlikely, however, at least in the short term.[11]

The long-term challenge to a continued US hegemony also comes from the expectation of a continued sharp economic growth of the Asian economies. Over the past decades, the providers of military hardware and technologies are increasingly private, and sometimes even transnational, military companies, not state-owned industries monopolised by governments. Hence, economic power can more easily be converted into military force capabilities than was the case fifteen years ago. As for the Asian economies, the World Bank and the OECD have previously predicted that by 2020, China will have the world's largest economy.[12] According to a policy report by the OECD Secretary-General on future economic developments, economic growth is expected to 'be far more dramatic in the non-OECD world' and their real GDP in 2020 would be around 270 per cent above the 1992 level. As a result of higher growth in the non-OECD area, there would be a global shift in economic weight towards Asia.[13] CIA's *Global Trends 2015* also expected emerging Asia to 'be the fastest growing region' in the world, led by China and India.[14]

By 2004, these predictions were less certain. True, China's and India's growth rates have remained very high, despite the 1997–8 financial crises, and China's economy was expected to be double the size of Germany's by 2010.[15] The numerous structural problems accumulating from China's rapid economic transformation had become more evident, however, leading analysts to the conclusion that China would not become 'the new hegemon, or even a superpower, any time soon'.[16] Other studies have noted that economic growth rates tend to converge when states approach the US level of per capita GDP.[17] Hence the above-mentioned OECD prognosis of China's economy in 2020 is probably too optimistic. Canada' *Strategic Assessment 2003* also allows for the possibility that 'five years from now China will be wealthier and able to exert increased economic, demographic and strategic weight'.[18] At the same time, it questions whether structural reforms can be continued without incurring serious problems of social instability. The Chinese economy undergoes 'an uncomfortable transition', manifesting itself in a growing national debt, pervasive corruption, lack of transparency and good corporate governance, the loss of income security, unemployment and the spread of social unrest. At the core of the transition problem is 'the growing disconnect between an increasingly pluralistic economy and one-party rule'.[19] There is a significant potential for political instability as demands for greater political freedom are likely to rise.[20] In this perspective, the long-term economic growth potential of India, which already has a relatively robust democracy, might be better, while China remains extremely vulnerable if or when it decides or is forced to abandon its one-party Communist rule.

As Asian economies expand, political influence and ambitions are likely to grow, and one may expect an increasing Asian assertiveness in global politics. The European Union's expansion, its continued economic growth and moves towards an even closer integration also signals its transformation into a more global power, more willing to disagree with and challenge the United States. The Iraqi conflict was an important showcase and the difficulties in healing its wounds have alerted some observers to the possibility of a fundamental remaking of transatlantic relations. Still, even if new economic muscles may allow for greater diplomatic assertiveness and open new avenues for exercising influence on a global arena, they do not necessarily translate into military power capable of truly challenging US hegemony. In the military field the USA currently has a tremendous technological edge and spends more money on the military than the next dozen or so largest industrial countries combined. At least in the coming decade, it is very unlikely that any new regional power will be able to challenge the United States as the only truly global military power. Since military power depends on highly advanced and extremely expensive technologies, and economic growth depends more and more on open economies and integrated markets, the rise of a new global Soviet-style military challenger to the United States based on an efficient introverted state-run economy remains highly unlikely.

Judged only by Cold War military standards, the world will remain highly unipolar. In many areas, however, the world has already moved towards a looser system, less constrained by the dominant powers compared to the Cold War era. We are witnessing the rise of a hybrid system, what Samuel Huntington has termed a 'uni-multipolar world', in which there is one superpower and several major powers. In this system, there are also 'important regional dynamics that are independent of the United States'.[21] Below 'the lonely superpower' Huntington identifies a second tier of major regional powers including the German–French axis in Europe, Russia, India, China, Iran, Brazil, South Africa and Nigeria, followed by a third tier of 'secondary regional powers whose interest often conflict with the more powerful regional states', including states such as Great Britain, Ukraine, Japan, Argentina, Saudi Arabia and Pakistan. The latter states seek closer relations with the hegemon, the United States, as a counterweight to the major regional powers.[22] In contrast to the bipolar system of the Cold War, the new uni-multipolar world system is inherently unstable as the United States would prefer a unipolar order, while the major regional powers strive to create a truly multipolar system, as they feel threatened and constrained by the US global hegemony. Huntington predicts that global politics 'is now passing through one or two uni-multipolar decades before it enters a truly multipolar twenty-first century.'[23] On the other hand, if the United States chooses to pursue its policies through multilateral institutions relying more on soft power than on its mighty war machine, it is more likely to avoid provoking anti-hegemonic power-balance responses from regional powers. If that happens, the current uni-multipolar system is more likely to last.

Although the post-Cold War world has demonstrated the utility of 'soft-power', the power of persuasion rather than coercion, the United States will remain incapable of fully exploiting those new avenues.[24] Instead, the entrenched image of the United States as an empire will remain and possibly be reinforced, as it seeks to confront emerging transnational threats with military force through its 'war on terror'. Despite the many warnings that 'nothing is more dangerous for a "hyperpower" than the temptation of unilateralism', US foreign policy, even with a possible reorientation after President George W. Bush Jr., is doomed to be seen as unilateralist, arrogant, interventionist, exploitative, hegemonic, hypocritical and colonialist.[25] After 9/11 Washington sees US foreign-policy matters far more single-mindedly than before through the lenses of national security whose primary tenets cannot be subject to negotiations with other nations. The image of the United States around the world has suffered tremendously as a result of the Iraqi war. Being viewed increasingly as an imperial power, it attracts opponents rather than allies and friends.[26] Long before 9/11, however, there was already a globally entrenched and pervasive anti-Americanism embracing many, if not most, of the world elites. A 1997 Harvard conference studying elite perceptions of the United States found that the elites in China, Russia, India and the Arab and Muslim world viewed the United States as 'the single greatest external threat to their societies', and unanimously agreed that American hegemonic unilateralism must be resisted.[27] Against this background, there are good reasons to assume that in the future US long-term hegemony will increasingly be challenged on multiple levels, and that anti-US anti-hegemonic movements will continue to find supportive global audiences.

In the more distant future, it is possible that global hegemony may change more fundamentally. Bornschier and Chase-Dunn have suggested that the nature of global hegemony may be entirely restructured around other entities than the state. Global hegemony may be based on, for example, 'a new powerful and increasingly integrated global capitalist class', or 'a new form of hegemony based on transnational alliances among the world's largest firms'.[28] Furthermore, the arena for hegemonic rivalry may also move from the peripheries to the core itself, which is expanding by incorporating new members from central Europe and east Asia. In other words, one may see the rise of 'hegemonic rivalry within a system of shared institutions and beliefs'.[29]

Consequences for the future of terrorism

In none of the assessments above should one expect a sharp rise in state-sponsored international terrorism. Volgy, Imwalle and Corntassel have shown that a system characterised by strong bipolar hegemony and a high level of bipolar conflict in world politics appears to be more prone to international terrorism than a more unipolar or multipolar system.[30] Since a return to a Cold War-type of global military confrontation seems very unlikely, international terrorism would not become an instrument of war between two global rivals. For example, during the Cold War 'members of the German Red Army Faction found refuge in East Germany' which also provided 'extensive training facilities' for members of various leftist guerrilla organisations operating in sub-Saharan Africa.[31] After 1991, however, it has progressively become more difficult and costly to overtly host and sponsor terrorist organisations. True, cross-border terrorism remains an important factor in regional conflicts, such as the Indian–Pakistani conflict, or the Israeli–Syrian stand-off over the Sheba farms in Southern Lebanon. A development towards more assertive regional powers may lead to greater rivalry between major regional powers and secondary regional powers allied with the United States, creating a certain basis for state-sponsored terrorism. Still, the overall trend will be a continued low level of state-sponsored international terrorism. This is consistent also with the predictions in the CIA's *Global Trends 2015*.[32]

The theory of bipolarity and terrorism does not predict that the decline in international terrorism that followed the end of the Cold War will continue. The rise of al-Qaida and its associate groups has demonstrated that a number of terrorist organisations have become more transnational and less dependent upon state sponsorship. A tentative model by Bergesen and Lizardo on world systems, hegemony and transnational terrorism suggests that a unipolar international system will encourage anti-empire, anti-hegemonic transnational terrorism, especially at times when the hegemon is in decline. This type of terrorism will primarily originate from semi-peripheral zones of the international system.[33] Even with a gradual movement towards greater multilateralism, the character of the world system will remain unilateral for many years to come. There will probably be a strong US military presence and visibility in the semi-periphery, primarily in the Middle East, as well as in central – and south-east Asia. Hence, one may anticipate a continuation and possibly an increase in transnational anti-hegemonic terrorism.

Another argument supporting this thesis is the dialectic relationship between terrorism and counter-terrorism as discussed in a number of studies.[34]

Anti-hegemonic transnational terrorism inevitably strengthens the perception of the USA as an empire. Boggs has argued that 9/11 must be understood 'as part of a larger dialectic linking US militarism and what has become global terrorism'.[35] Terrorism in its different manifestations 'amounts to both a striking back at US empire [. . .] and to the unintended relegitimation of this empire as it helps to bolster the war economy and security state'.[36] While this may be a harsh criticism, it underscores the point witnessed in many other terrorist campaigns, that countermeasures have the unintended effect of reinforcing motivations for continuing attacks.

Weapons of mass destruction

Postulate: There will be more nuclear powers in the world. Nuclear, biological and chemical-weapons programmes will continue, primarily in the Middle East and North Korea. Technological advances in biotechnology, medicine and in the pharmaceutical industries will broaden the spectrum of risk agents. Countermeasures in this field will remain very significant, however.

Possible implications for terrorism: The likelihood for WMD proliferation to terrorist groups will remain significant and possibly increase, as new and more complex proliferation risks steadily emerge, undermining the overall impact of countermeasures.

Studies of the relationship between technology and terrorism have tended to dismiss a direct causal link between availability of weapons and their use by terrorists, underscoring the conservative nature of terrorist groups when it comes to weapon of choice.[37] It also remains true that most terrorist groups still employ violence in carefully choreographed settings designed to impress rather than to kill. The rise of al-Qaida and other mass-casualty terrorist groups have nevertheless demonstrated that one can no longer assume that terrorist groups have political-ideological barriers or moral constraints regarding the use of WMD or do not find these weapons useful. This growing minority of terrorist groups favour mass-casualty attacks, and will probably seek to employ the most deadly weaponry they can acquire, including WMD.[38] Since there is no longer a motivational factor in the equation, the future of the WMD terrorism threat will be determined by technological barriers and weapons availability.

The deadly anthrax-laced letters, which killed five people, injured many more and disrupted the postal system in the United States in late 2001 was a watershed in the history of WMD-terrorism, almost as important as the sarin-gas attacks by the Japanese religious cult Aum Shin-rikyo in Tokyo six years earlier. The anthrax letters were highly significant because for the first time in recent history people were being killed by non-state bioterrorists. For the first time military-grade biological weapons were being used by a non-state actor for the purpose of terrorism. At the time of writing, the FBI investigation is still ongoing, but essentially no new information has emerged over the past two and a half years.[39] A prevailing theory is that the anthrax letters were the work of a US scientist with access to military-grade anthrax from a US military facility. If it turns out that one or several US insiders were the perpetrators, it highlights the inherent proliferation risk of state-run WMD-programmes, as it demonstrates that not even the United States is capable of providing absolute security around its WMD arsenals.

On the other hand, if the highly sophisticated military-grade anthrax used in at least one of the anthrax-laced letters originated from a private-owned laboratory, it undercuts the commonly accepted wisdom since Aum Shin-rikyo's attacks in the mid-1990s, that terrorist groups are only technically capable of producing limited amounts of crude chemical, biological, and radiological weapons, not 'weapons of mass destruction' in the real sense of the word.[40] Despite the frequent hyping of the WMD threat in much of the terrorism literature, the most reliable analyses demonstrate that CBRN terrorism has been extremely rare and it hardly ever succeeds. Most reported incidents of 'WMD terrorism' incidents turned out to be unreliable, fictitious or involved non-lethal material.[41] The real WMD terrorism threat seems to be limited to three distinct scenarios: the possible terrorist acquisition of ready-made military biological, chemical and nuclear weapons; the production of a crude chemical weapon with a simple dispersement device, to be used in a crowded confined space; and the acquisition of weapons-grade highly enriched uranium (HEU). The construction of a crude nuclear device using weapons-grade HEU is believed to be relatively simple and might be within the reach of terrorist groups.[42] Without these elements, the threat is reduced to the prospect of undoubtedly scary, and possibly lethal 'mass disruption' attacks, but not 'mass destruction' beyond what conventional terrorism can achieve with large amounts of conventional explosives. A review of available information on al-Qaida's pursuit of WMD capabilities (see Box 3.1), seems to confirm the assessment that while a few terrorist groups are capable of producing simple radiological devices and crude chemical weapons, they are still far away from developing their own WMD capability. Hence, the future WMD terrorism threat must first and foremost be evaluated by examining the future of state-run weapons programmes and the proliferation risks involved.

Box 3.1 Al-Qaida and its WMD ambitions

It is an undeniable fact that the overwhelming number of accomplished and attempted al-Qaida-related attacks so far have been conventional in nature and are entirely unrelated to CBRN terrorism. Reporting on al-Qaida's WMD programmes is very hard to verify; international media

---

have reported a large number of incidents of al-Qaida attempts to acquire such weapons. Press reports from uncorroborated sources have even suggested that al-Qaida possesses various types of WMD, including portable nuclear arms. This appears very unlikely. There is little doubt, however, that the network has made determined efforts at researching WMD in order to develop a capacity for unconventional attacks, either with a crude radiological device, by crashing an hijacked airliner into a US nuclear facility, or by using improvised poisons and toxins, such as cyanide, ricin, botulinum toxin and salmonella, or by acquiring or developing anthrax.[1]

Judging by documents recovered in Afghanistan, al-Qaida also possessed 'crude procedures for making mustard agent, sarin and VX'.[2] It had several laboratories at its disposal and made various experiments with poisons and toxins in the Afghan camps prior to 9/11; the equipment found in one such laboratory near Kandahar indicated a possible capacity for producing limited quantities of crude CBW agents.[3] Al-Qaida was also believed to have 'well-advanced plans to produce anthrax' and had recruited skilled scientists for this purpose. Papers and computer hard drives recovered during the capture of the al-Qaida leader Khalid Shaykh Mohammad in March 2003 included, for example, orders to obtain *Bacillus anthracis*, as well as detailed production schedules and inventories of necessary equipment.[4] There is no evidence that al-Qaida managed to weaponise biological agents. Indicatively of the rudimentary stage of al-Qaida's WMD programme, the anthrax strain sought by Khalid Shaykh Mohammad was not the most virulent one. Judging by the uncovered documents, Khalid Shaykh Mohammad lacked knowledge of the specialist milling techniques required for military-grade air-borne anthrax.[5] The capacity to produce and operate crude toxins and poisons may be within al-Qaida's reach, however. Equipment for the manufacturing of ricin has been discovered in a house occupied by al-Qaida-affiliated Islamist militants in the 'Little Algiers' district in London.[6] In 2002, planned cyanide-gas and ricin attacks by suspected al-Qaida militants in Rome, London and Paris were reportedly uncovered.[7] One of these conspiracies involved depositing ricin on the handrails in subway stations in London and Paris, according to Italian investigators.[8] In 2004 new reports emerged of a makeshift laboratory in Lyon where ricin and botulinum toxin were being manufactured. 'Dozens of small containers' of ricin had reportedly been produced by al-Qaida-associated militants and had gone missing despite their arrests.[9]

With regards to al-Qaida's plans for nuclear and radiological weapons, there are witness reports from the trial following the al-Qaida bombing of the US embassies in east Africa corroborating previous reports that al-Qaida had been trying to acquire fissile material since the early 1990s. The CIA has also uncovered 'rudimentary diagrams of nuclear weapons inside a suspected al-Qaida safehouse in Kabul', but the diagrams were apparently technically inaccurate.[10] In 2003 interrogations of senior al-Qaida commanders, including Abu Zubayda, and a closer examination of the material discovered in Afghanistan led US authorities to believe that a dirty bomb plot was within al-Qaida's grasp. British authorities confirmed they had evidence that al-Qaida already had constructed a small dirty bomb in the Afghan city of Herat, using radioactive isotopes from medical equipment. No ready-made bomb was ever found, however.[11] Reports of al-Qaida's alleged possession of nuclear arms procured from the former Soviet Union in 1998 remain uncorroborated.

Notes

[1] The CIA has published a brief unclassified report on its web site, containing a summary of 'typical agents and CBRN devices available to al-Qaida', see CIA, *Terrorist CBRN: Materials and Effects*, CTC-2003-40058, June 2003, <http://www.cia.gov/cia/reports/terrorist_cbrn/CBRN_threat.pdf>. Accessed April 2004. See also Chapter 3 of the British parliamentary report 'Review of Intelligence on Weapons of Mass Destruction', House of Commons, Report of a Committee of Privy Counsellors, Chairman Lord Butler of Brockwell, London, 14 July 2004, <http:// www.official-documents.co.uk/ document/deps/hc/hc898/898.pdf>. Accessed October 2004.

[2] CIA, *Terrorist CBRN*, p. 2.

[3] Gary A. Ackerman and Jeffrey M. Bale, 'Al-Qaida and Weapons of Mass Destruction', Center of Non-Proliferation Studies, Monterey, December 2002, <http://cns.miis.edu/pubs/other/alqwmd.htm>. Accessed April 2004.

[4] David Rennie, 'Al-Qaeda Close to Making Anthrax, Says US', *Daily Telegraph* 24 March 2003.

[5] ibid.

[6] Sarah Lyall, 'Arrest of Terror Suspects in London Turns Up a Deadly Toxin', *New York Times* 8 January 2003; Jon Henley, 'Terror Fear After Ricin is Found in Paris', *The Guardian* 21 March 2003; Tim Radford, 'Terror Weapon from a Humble Bean: The Background: Ricin', *The Guardian* 8 January 2003; and 'Terror Cells Plotting Random Poisonings', *New Zealand Herald* 13 January 2003.

[7] Ackerman and Bale, 'Al-Qaida and Weapons of Mass Destruction'.

[8] According to Stefano Dambruoso, former counter-terrorism team chief in Milan, Italy. See his article: 'Milan-Tbilisi (via Baku): Route of Fear [in Italian]', *Milan Panorama* 16 September 2004, pp. 42–3.

[9] Jon Henley, 'Al-Qaida Terror Plot Foiled, Say French Police', *The Guardian* 12 January 2004; and Jason Burke, 'French Warn that "Lost" Terror Ricin may be in Britain', *The Observer* 20 June 2004.

[10] Ackerman and Bale, 'Al-Qaida and Weapons of Mass Destruction'; and CIA, 'Unclassified Report to Congress on the Acquisition of Technology Relating to Weapons of Mass Destruction and Advanced Conventional Munitions, 1 January through 30 June 2003', <http://www.cia.gov/cia/reports/721_reports/jan_jun2003.htm>. Accessed April 2004.

[11] Eric Lichtblau and David Johnston, 'Confidential Advisory Warns of Rise in Possible Terror Threats', *New York Times* 5 February 2003; Josh Meyer, 'Al Qaeda Feared to Have "Dirty Bombs" ', *Los Angeles Times* 8 February 2003; and 'BBC Says Al Qaeda Produced a "Dirty Bomb" in Afghanistan', *Associated Press* 31 January 2003.

Nuclear proliferation risks

The nuclear tests by Pakistan and India in 1998 may be seen as the last chapter in the uneven but gradual spread of nuclear arms since 1945. Acquiring a nuclear capability is not a policy objective for the overwhelming majority of countries in the world. Nevertheless, there are very few examples of countries that have renounced their nuclear arsenals as South Africa did in the early 1990s and Ukraine did in 1996, although since 1945 a number of countries have terminated nuclear weapons *programmes* either willingly, such as Sweden in 1968, or under heavy international pressure exemplified by Libya's recent decision to declare and dismantle its nuclear programme. While it is safe to assume that most countries capable of producing nuclear arms will desist from this opportunity, there are good reasons to assume that some states will continue their efforts at building nuclear arms, even at high political costs including sanctions and international isolation. The possession of nuclear arms is regarded as a sign of national prestige and has a valuable deterrent effect on foreign adversaries.

After Pakistan and India became nuclear powers, the incentives for regional powers in the developing world to acquire weapons of ultimate deterrence may have increased. During the 1970s and 1980s, both Argentina and Brazil embarked on nuclear-weapons programmes, but they renounced these ambitions in the early 1990s through a series of agreements.[43] Still, Brazil's recent launch of an independent uranium-enrichment program, its plans for establishing several nuclear-energy plants, talks of expanding nuclear co-operation with China and recent public statements by Brazilian politicians about the need to know how to build nuclear bombs, suggest that the idea of reviving the military nuclear programme is alive and well.[44]

The US adoption of the doctrine of pre-emption, and the expanded range of its military interventions have highlighted the weakness of state sovereignty based on international law, and may encourage regional powers in the Third World to develop nuclear capabilities. In 2003 North Korea announced to US officials that it already possessed nuclear weapons and threatened to build a nuclear deterrent force.[45] The country is expected to expand its programme and perhaps also to establish relations with other nuclear-capacity-seeking countries to deflect attention from its own programme and provide a to counterweight to the United States. The current status of Iran's nuclear programme is not clear. Traces of HEU have been found by International Atomic Energy Agency (IAEA) inspectors at Iranian sites, 'raising concerns that the country's alleged nuclear weapons programme is much more advanced than suspected'.[46] Iran is a probable candidate for the nuclear club in the coming decade, although the political and economic cost of going down that path will be staggering. An Iranian nuclear capability may push Israel to expand and diversify its nuclear arsenal further. Israel may also launch pre-emptive strikes against Iranian nuclear reactors similar to its raid on the Osirak reactor in Iraq in June 1981, which would probably only strengthen Tehran's resolve to build atomic bombs.[47]

If the regional tensions increase sharply, Israel may also decide to become a declared nuclear state and wield its nuclear weapon more openly vis-à-vis the Arab states, and thereby encourage more determined efforts at building a nuclear capacity in the Arab world. If Iran seems close to building nuclear weapons, its regional rivals, Saudi Arabia in particular, might attempt to follow suit. This will not only serve as a counterweight to Iran and Israel, but also lessen Saudi dependence on the United States. Saudi reliance on foreign technical expertise in its arms industry makes this an unlikely scenario. It has been pointed out, however, that the Saudi Defence Minister took great interest in Pakistan's nuclear programme and visited Khan Research Laboratories (KRL), where Pakistan's nuclear weapons were developed, before the proliferation scandal erupted in February 2004.[48] Future proliferation risks in the region may also come as a result of increased external supply of advanced military and nuclear technology. In view of the fact that east Asian states are expected to become more dependent on Middle Eastern oil supplies than they are today, it is expected that they will take greater interest in oil-producing regions. US analysts have predicted that this dependence might translate into a greater Asian willingness to enter into closer military co-operation with the states in the region and that this collaboration might well include the supply of sensitive WMD-related technology.[49]

There are numerous risks of nuclear proliferation to terrorist organisations in relation to state-run WMD programmes. Although the chances that governments deliberately will provide terrorist organisations with chemical, biological or nuclear weapons are very slim, state-controlled WMD programmes nevertheless represent a serious proliferation risk to terrorist organisation. One reason for this is that states, when pursuing internationally proscribed weapons programmes, must seek the technology and material they need covertly and must often rely upon various shadowy trafficking networks. An illicit underground proliferation market is thus created, involving international criminal networks where state control and oversight is minimal. It is likely that certain terrorist organisations will continue attempts to tap into this illicit trade and acquire material, technology and expertise contacts, which ultimately will bring them closer to acquiring a crude nuclear weapon. There are several examples that al-Qaida have attempted to do so in the past.[50]

The example of the illicit nuclear-trafficking network of Abdul Qadeer Khan, the father of the Pakistani nuclear bomb, is telling. Due to international restrictions on sales of nuclear and dual-use technologies, the Pakistani nuclear programme was pursued in a covert manner, without much government oversight and transparency. Via Khan's global web of suppliers and intermediaries in a host of countries, probably including all of Pakistan, Malaysia, South Korea, Japan, Dubai, Spain, Germany and the Netherlands, other nuclear-seeking states such as Libya, North Korea and Iran were able to obtain nuclear technology. According to witness statements, the global black-market network run by Khan provided nuclear centrifuge parts to Iran in the mid-1990s and enriched uranium as well as centrifuge units to Libya in 2001.[51] What was revealed in the Khan case was literally a 'proliferation supermarket', in the words of the IAEA director, Mohamed El Baradei, involving not only states but also private intermediaries with dubious contacts to the criminal underworld, religious extremists and international terrorists.[52] There was apparently very little government oversight and control of the various activities and contacts of Khan. His research agency, Khan Research Laboratories (KRL), the main Pakistani nuclear-research centre, has produced around 1,000 kilograms of enriched uranium, and following the revelation of the scandal in February 2004 nobody could say for sure that all of this material was safe and secure.[53] A relatively small amount (a few tens of kilograms) of weapons-usable HEU might be sufficient to make a crude nuclear device. Since the major technological barrier for terrorist acquisition of a nuclear bomb is believed to be the acquisition of the critical mass of weapons-grade HEU, not the construction of the bomb itself, the black-market availability of HEU is indeed a serious global terrorist threat.[54] On the other hand, the HEU enrichment needs to be very high, otherwise much larger amounts of HEU is needed and the construction of a nuclear device becomes very complicated. Material classified as HEU has minimum 20 per cent enrichment (which refers to the content of the isotope U-235), and is not necessarily weapons grade uranium, which preferably has higher than 90 per cent enrichment. Since a number of submarines and research reactors still use HEU with very high enrichment as fuel, one has to assume that the availability of weapons-grade HEU is not limited to the strategic nuclear-arms facilities.[55]

Another serious risk of state-run WMD programmes is that disloyal insiders, acting on psycho-pathological obsessions, economic needs or terrorist motivations, may steal small quantities of HEU or lethal biological weapons and try to sell it on the black market. With regard to nuclear material, this is no longer a theoretical possibility. A recent study by researchers at the renowned Center for Non-Proliferation Studies at Monterey, warns that 'substandard security at nuclear facilities in Europe, central Asia, Russia, and Pakistan increases the risk of terrorists seizing highly enriched uranium to make crude, but devastating, nuclear explosives'.[56] The state of government control over Russia's WMD capabilities has long been the primary object of concern. The causes for this concern range from the pervasive networks of organised crime in Russia, the many internal problems facing the Russian military, such as drug abuse, *dedovshchina* or bullying of new recruits, and economic hardship, to the fact that Russia's nuclear-security measures are still designed to face external threats, not 'the pre-eminent threat faced today – an insider who attempts unauthorised actions.'[57]

Most material seized from the illicit trafficking in nuclear material originates in the former Soviet republics. While existing nuclear arms sites are heavily guarded, this is not necessarily the case of many sites where HEU is stored. (It is most certainly not the case with regards to most facilities where other types of radiological material are stored that may be used for a so-called 'improvised radiological dispersion device' or 'dirty bomb'.) According to IAEA statistics (see Figures 3.1 and 3.2), there have been as many as 214 confirmed incidents involving illicit trafficking of radioactive and nuclear material since 1993. These numbers include ten confirmed incidents involving small amounts of HEU.[58] It is uncertain how many of these incidents involved weapons-grade HEU, but researchers at the Center for Non-Proliferation Studies at Monterey have reported that 'a close examination of open source evidence reveals 14 confirmed cases of theft or attempted theft of weapons-useable material' from facilities in the former Soviet Union between 1991 and

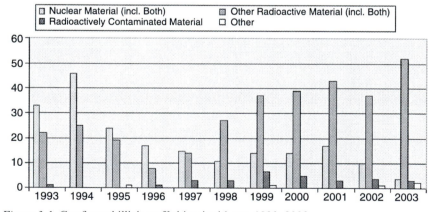

Figure 3.1 Confirmed illicit trafficking incidents, 1993–2003.

Source: IAEA illicit trafficking database (ITDB), the International Atomic Energy Agency, <http://www.iaea.org/newscenter/features/radsources/chart1.html>.

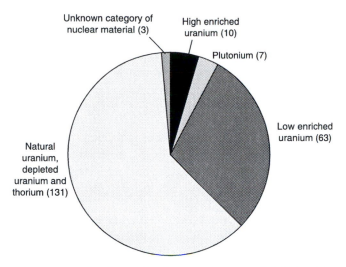

Figure 3.2 Distribution of incidents involving nuclear material, 1993–2003.

Source: IAEA illicit trafficking database (ITDB), the International Atomic Energy Agency, <http://www.iaea.org/newscenter/features/radsources/chart2.html>.

2001.[59] As far is is known, none of the incidents involved amounts beyond the critical mass needed for a nuclear device.

Many nuclear-trafficking incidents in the former Soviet Union have involved poorly paid workers at nuclear facilities or plants where radioactive materials are used and stored. In 1994 a Russian naval officer was arrested as he sought a buyer for nearly five kilograms of HEU that had been stolen from a military shipyard.[60] According to Viktor Kuznetsov, Russia's top nuclear-safety inspector in the 1990s, the number of actual thefts and attempted thefts of nuclear material from high-security facilities in the former Soviet Union are probably considerably higher since Russian authorities have hushed up a number of such incidents.[61] Despite significant international efforts at securing Russia's WMD facilities since the early and mid-1990s, security will probably continue to remain relatively lax at sites where potential WMD material is stored. Kuznetsov noted for example that most Russian nuclear facilities were not equipped with technology capable of detecting whether a worker is smuggling out nuclear or radioactive material.

CBW-proliferation risks

CBW programmes are banned by international treaties signed by most of the UN's member states. Such activities must therefore be pursued covertly. The fact that significant CBW arsenals still exist in the former Soviet Union, the revelation that Soviet BW-programmes had continued up to the 1990s, as well as growing concerns about bioterrorism apparently induced the US government to intensify research efforts on bioterrorism defence, including activities which might have violated the bioweapons treaty.[62] This research also involved producing small amounts of B-weapons. During the US investigation into the anthrax letters in October 2001, the US army disclosed that researchers at the Dugway Proving Ground in Utah 'had been producing small quantities of anthrax powder, similar to the type found in the letters, for use in testing military equipment'.[63] This obviously raises the prospect that the military-grade anthrax spores used in the deadly letters might have been stolen from Dugway's supply. In other words, the United States 'had an ongoing programme to produce dried, weaponised anthrax spores for defensive testing', and the total production was estimated to have been 'in the 10s or 100s of grams of dried anthrax spores'.[64]

Russia's CBW weaponry has long been a source of concern in light of the formidable extent of the Soviet Union's research, development and large-scale production of a wide variety of bioweapons. The Soviet programme was reportedly the largest in the world, employing some 60,000 people in the late 1980s.[65] Not only are there still storage sites where CBW agents are not properly stored and guarded, but there is also concern about the proliferation of Russia's extensive CBW expertise. Kenneth Alibek, who worked on the Soviet CBW programs until the early 1990s, cited in 1998 several examples of Russian renegade scientists who offered 'to sell their genetic engineering knowledge to anyone' via private companies:

> I have a copy of a flier advertising the wares of a company called 'BIOEFFECT Ltd', with offices in Moscow and Vienna. [. . .] The flier offers recombinant Francisella tularensis bacteria with altered virulence genes. [. . .] The authors of the flier also express willingness to form co-operative ventures to which they will contribute their genetic engineering knowledge.[66]

Apart from Russia, a number of countries probably still have ongoing CBW activities of some sort, including storage sites of CBW agents, which in itself constitutes a proliferation risk even if their governments have no intention of using them. This is in large part due to the worldwide spread of such weapons programmes during the past century. Five countries have declared past or present BW programmes under the Biological Weapons Convention (BWC) confidence-building measures. These include Canada, France, Russia, the United Kingdom and the United States. Thirteen countries have declared past or present CW programmes: Albania, Bosnia-Herzegovina, France, China, Iraq, Russia, India, Iran, Japan, South Korea, the United Kingdom, the United States and Yugoslavia.[67] A number of other countries are believed to be pursuing covert programmes as can be seen from Table 3.1.

Table 3.1 Weapons of mass destruction capabilities in the Mediterranean region and eastern Asia: proliferation patterns[1]

Country	Nuclear	Biological–toxicological	Chemical
North Korea	Weaponisation	Research	Probable
Iraq	Dismantling	Dismantling	Dismantling, CW used in 1983, 1987–8 against Iran and the Kurdish village of Halabja
Iran	Development	Development	Deployed, CW used in 1984–8 against Iraq
Saudi Arabia	None?	None	None?
Syria	Research	Development?	Deployed Presumably the largest and most advanced CW capability in the Middle East
Israel	Deployed *c.* 100–200 warheads	Production capability	Production capability
Egypt	Research	Development	Stockpiled, used in 1963–7 (during the Yemeni civil war)
Libya	Dismantling? Announced full disclosure in 2003	Dismantling? Announced full disclosure in 2003	Dismantling? Announced full disclosure in 2003, CW used in 1987 against Chad
Algeria	Research	Research	Development?

Notes
[1] Data from 1999, except the Libyan and Iraqi entries. Source: Monterey Institute of International Studies' Center For Nonproliferation Studies, <http://cns.miis.edu/research/wmdme/index.htm>. Accessed April 1999.

Explanation of terms: 'Deployed': nuclear, biological, or chemical (NBC) weapons integrated into military forces and ready for use in the event of conflict. 'Stockpiled': produced significant quantity of NBC weapons, but these are not stored in close proximity to military units that would employ them. 'Weaponisation': in the process of integrating nuclear explosives or CB agents with delivery systems, such as aerial bombs, missile warheads, etc. 'Production capability': able to produce significant quantity of fissile nuclear material or CB agents, but not known to have done so. 'Development': engaged in laboratory- or pilot-scale activities to develop production capability for fissile material or CB agents. 'Research': engaged in dual-use research with peaceful civilian applications, but that can also be used to build technical capacity and/or infrastructure necessary for NBC development and production. 'Dismantling': removing NBC weapons from deployment to storage areas and destroying agents and munitions. 'Terminated': produced WMD, but subsequently ended and dismantled program. 'None': no confirmed open-source evidence of capability.

The pursuit of CBW programmes already involves very high political costs. The international pressure against states suspected of involvement in such activities will probably continue to increase in the near future, forcing states to abandon their CBW ambitions. Still, as the Iraqi programmes until the 1990s demonstrated, states are quite capable of eluding current surveillance and monitoring mechanisms of CBW proliferation. A whole range of new intrusive measures have been put in place after 9/11 to limit the access to and proliferation of sensitive WMD-related information and technologies. The US-led Proliferation Security Initiative (PSI) is one example. Launched in May 2003, the PSI outlines a set of 'interdiction principles' agreed upon in September 2003, which commit participating countries to undertake effective counter-proliferation measures in a number of specific areas, in particular with regards to 'interdicting the transfer or transport of WMD, their delivery systems and related materials to and from states and non-state actors of proliferation concern'.[68]

In the future, WMD-related information and technology may still be quite accessible. The control of dual-use technology proves increasingly difficult in a more global and open economy. Arms-control advocates contend that it is still possible to slow down the spread of these dual-use technologies, while others have argued that efforts to restrain dual-use exports are doomed to failure on the grounds that they can never be fully effective and hamper legitimate commercial activity.[69] Proliferation risks are rooted in systemic factors such as the increased level of education in areas like physics, chemistry and biology, and the difficulties in controlling available information on WMD, whether on the Internet, in public libraries or in research institutions. Efforts at placing greater restrictions of WMD-related information run against an economically-driven global development towards greater transparency and more rapid diffusion of knowledge and technology. Other global developments such as increased transborder parallel trade and the spread to private actors of advanced information technologies, including spyware and surveillance, will make it harder and harder for governments to keep WMD technologies secret.

Another serious proliferation risk, inherent in state-run WMD programmes is the prospect of total or partial state collapse in countries with some WMD capabilities. A collapsed state situation, partially or totally, may be caused by an external military intervention, or the implosion of the state may come as a result of an internally generated upheaval. The net result may be the same, namely the 'privatisation' of the states' coercive capabilities, including its WMD programmes. The combination of state failure and WMD programmes is therefore highly risky. Deadly weapons arsenals will end up in the hands of individuals and non-state actors, similar to the events in Albania in 1997, and serve as a nearly inexhaustible source of weapon supply for insurgent groups, militias and organised criminal networks.[70] Failed-state situations may also attract international terrorist organisations, willing to purchase and then use the deadly arms against targets beyond the conflict area.

It is one of the great ironies that the current US-led efforts to topple 'rogue regimes' have inadvertently also created collapsed-state situations in which all kinds of weaponry have flown into private hands and thousands of scientists specialised in the manufacture of various kinds of WMD are out of work and are likely to sympathise with anti-US resistance groups. The long-term consequences of this are yet not obvious. Given the anarchical situation in post-Saddam Iraq there are considerable uncertainties with regards to the vast Iraqi WMD expertise and materiel. Even deployable WMD is still a cause of concern. In May and June 2004 US and Polish troops reportedly found more than a dozen missiles with warheads containing mustard and sarin gas in Iraq, in addition to a 1991 Gulf war-era mortar round with mustard gas and a 155 mm artillery round testing positive for sarin gas. Both rounds had been rigged as a roadside bomb, the major and most effective insurgent weapon against the Coalition forces in Iraq.[71] The chemical-filled artillery shells and missiles were leftovers from Iraq's pre-1991 stocks, and due to their age no chemical injuries were reported. US forces have found fifty-three decaying chemical-filled shells or artillery rockets that probably were looted from unguarded ammunition bunkers or other sites.[72] More disturbing is the revelation that several insurgent groups have recruited a number of Iraqi scientists with access to laboratories with a view to developing chemical and biological weapons. A recent CIA report leaked to the press in October 2004 details the efforts by Iraqi rebels at developing 'their own crude supplies of such deadly agents as mustard gas, ricin and the nerve gas tabun' to be used against coalition forces.[73]

There are many potential candidates for state failure. Prime suspects are those that combine authoritarian rule with a faltering Communist or state-capitalist economy and an isolationist regime. Some of these states also have or have had WMD programmes, such as Iraq, North Korea, Syria and Iran. A paper on east Asia presented as part of the CIA-sponsored *Global Trends 2020* project singled out North Korea as 'the most likely candidate for state failure'.[74] A collapsed state situation in parts of the Russian federation cannot be ruled out entirely either. In addition to the collapsed-state scenario, various versions of weak state scenarios in states possessing WMD programmes are equally fraught with risks. The presence of thousands of experts on WMD in the former Soviet Union and Pakistan remains a major concern, as ideological convictions or a lack of socio-economic prospects may prompt some of them to sell their WMD expertise to other states or to terrorist organisations. With Iraq joining the club of nations with large contingents of unemployed and dissatisfied WMD experts, there is undoubtedly a future potential for terrorist recruitment of WMD scientists. The various reported contacts between al-Qaida, Pakistani nuclear experts, and various nuclear traffickers in former Soviet Union over the past few years underscore that this is a real possibility.[75]

While the chances that a terrorist organisation would acquire its own WMD capability through in-house research and development efforts were previously considered to be minimal, the Aum Shin-rikyo case was a wake-up call, first and foremost with regards to chemical weapons. Aum's production of considerable amounts of various nerve gases, sarin in particular, and the ease with which it acquired the necessary equipment and materials for its CBW programmes illustrates the new proliferation risks ahead. With more inventive or advanced dispersion mechanisms, future terrorist groups would probably do better than Aum in turning lethal chemical agents into effective weapons. Various expert assessments point to the fact that rapid technological advances in commercial chemical and pharmaceutical industries result in the emergence of many new chemicals and biochemicals each year, some of which may be considered potential CW agents. The threat spectrum is not only widening but also deepening as new types of threat agents are emerging with high toxicity.[76] At the same time, the know-how and material technologies needed to construct a chemical weapon, including an effective dispersion device, are also becoming more available throughout the world, making effective anti-proliferation efforts an almost impossible task.

The future terrorist threat from biological and toxic[77] agents must be seen in the context of technological advances, especially the emergence of new genetic technologies over the past years, and the rapid diffusion of these technologies. While the human genome has already been sequenced, analysed, but not yet completely mapped, many research efforts in biology are now going into the mapping of the genomes of various microbes, providing a well of information on functions and vulnerabilities. This research also opens up a plethora of possibilities for producing new threat agents. It is already possible to synthesise simple viruses due to their small genomes. It is possible to produce viruses that are more stable and virulent than already existing ones, which may pose an increased threat.[78] Genetic modification of existing pathogens may also enhance their virulence or enable them to produce more lethal toxic substances. (According to the Soviet defector Kenneth Alibek, the former Soviet bioprogrammes conducted research on enhanced virulence of BW agents.[79]) Similarly, the detailed knowledge of the humane genome raises the possibility of developing 'weapons of mass extermination' aimed at ethnic or racial groups.[80] Such weapons are a distinct possibility, since there are known racial differences with regard to sensitivities to various infectious diseases. New threat agents may also emerge from bioengineered toxin production, which are far more toxic than previously known agents. These may also resist protective equipment, and are easier to mass produce for unsophisticated non-state actors.[81]

As the new generation of terrorist networks seek mass-casualty attacks through innovation of tactics, their interest in biological weapons, which so far has been limited, will increase substantially if technological breakthroughs create a situation where effective weapons can be produced from commercially available material. If the diffusion of genetic technologies continues unabated, it may become within the reach of non-state actors to genetically modify contagious diseases, for example by turning an innocent flu into a deadly contagious disease, capable of spreading far more death, disruption and fear than the recent outbreaks of SARS and Bird Flu. Indeed, the breakthrough in genetics has the potential of radically expanding the very notion of bio-logical weapons. It is also hard to see how governments should be able to prevent the spread of knowledge for genetic manipulation without extremely intrusive security measures.

In light of what I have said so far, it is reasonable to assume that despite the new counter-proliferation measures taken over the past few years, the chances for WMD proliferation to terrorist groups in the future will remain significant. While at least two potential WMD suppliers, Iraq and Libya, for the time being no longer are considered 'rogue states', several states combin-ing WMD programmes with state involvement with insurgents and terrorist organisations remain. Among these are Syria, North Korea, Pakistan and Iran. More disconcerting is the prospect of deteriorating failed-state situ-ations in countries possessing WMD weaponry and WMD expertise. A total state collapse in North Korea cannot be excluded either, while weak govern-ment control over WMD facilities in the Russian federation will remain a serious source of concern for years to come. Although there have been a number of positive developments in terms of dismantling of WMD pro-grammes, the trends reviewed above strongly suggest that the WMD terror-ism threat will not diminish in the future. While terrorist incidents involving crude weapons made out of CBRN material are far more likely, WMD terror-ism in the true sense of the word will continue to remain a low probability but high-risk event.

Democratisation processes and the spread of illiberal democracies

Postulate: The number of states in transition to democratic rule or which are neither autocracies nor fully fledged democracies will remain high and possibly increase.

Possible implications for terrorism: A growing number of semi-democratic states will cause heightened risks for state collapse, intrastate conflicts and civil violence. Higher levels of domestic terrorism in some of these states are likely. New sources of international terrorism may also emerge as a by-product of these conflicts, especially if they cause state collapse.

While there is no clear-cut direct relationship between democracy and terror-ism, theories of democratisation, state legitimacy and terrorism argue con-vincingly that semi-democratic countries and states in democratic transition are more exposed to domestic terrorism than totalitarian states and 'old' fully fledged democracies. States that are neither authoritarian nor perfect democracies vary greatly and have many names: 'illiberal democracies', 'anocracies', 'semi-autocracies', 'demonstration democracies'. A common denominator of these regime types is that they 'are far more likely than autocracies or democracies to be challenged by armed conflict, and are less likely to be able either to repress or settle it'.[82] Studies also show that this relationship is valid for terrorist violence as well. Hence, one may establish qualified predictions about the future of terrorism by looking at future trends in democratisation, in particular the possible growth of anocracies versus totalitarian states and fully fledged democracies.

The community of democratic states has expanded significantly over the past two decades. Samuel Huntington described these sweeping political changes as 'the third wave of democratisation'.[83] This process began with the introduction of democracy in Greece, Spain and Portugal in the mid-1970s. Later, a number of democratic governments came to power in Latin America and Asia. The process of democratisation then reached eastern Europe in the early 1990s. Hence, the collapse of the Communist bloc, and the ongoing democratisation processes in Africa and Asia have been the latest stages in the uneven, but gradual, expansion of states undergoing a transition to democracy. The Middle East has remained the most enduring bastion of authoritarian rule, but even here a number of states have experimented with more representative and democratic forms of government.[84]

Even if there appears to be a broad historical evolution towards democratisation worldwide, the process towards global democratisation is by no means inevitable. Nor is there any guarantee that democratising states will reach the stage of fully fledged democratic systems. In fact, studies show that the number of semi-democratic/semi-authoritarian states, or 'anocracies' has grown significantly since the mid-1970s and became more numerous than autocracies for the first time in 1994, while the number of autocracies has declined sharply since the mid-1980s.[85] Theories on democratisation processes are complex and offer no clear-cut answers on the future of global democratisation. There is relatively broad agreement, however, that various aspects of today's globalisation processes will probably contribute to putting greater pressure on autocratic regimes, forcing them to at least pay lip service to democratisation and human rights. Leading global powers, including the United States, have at least in principle adopted global democratisation as one of their major foreign-policy objectives, based on the assumption that democracies rarely wage war against each other. Authoritarian regimes have also come under greater pressure from a growing transnational community of non-state actors, including human-rights activists, pro-democracy movements and other advocacy groups, which wield far more influence in world politics today than was the case twenty years ago.[86] Also, due to the revolution in information and communication technology, it has been argued that 'governments have lost their ability to control transnational communication

[. . .] and the transnational relations of their citizens'.[87] Although there is no real consensus that the rise of the Internet has had or will force authoritarian regimes to introduce political democratic reform, it seems clear that the power to control information flow and political life inside a single country is decreasing.[88] Restrictions can be imposed but only at high political and economic costs. Countries with poor democratic records where the rule of law is absent will fail to attract foreign investments, which, in a more global economy, will become an increasingly important determinant of economic performance and political legitimacy. That is not to say that foreign investments will be systematically channelled away from authoritarian states. There is nevertheless a significant tendency that transnational companies (TNCs) are increasingly put under pressure to pay more attention to human rights, democratic standards and transparency in their foreign-investment policies, and this trend is likely to continue.

Globalisation and growing economic interdependence are often assumed to provide incentives for democratisation, although there is no real consensus as to the impact of economic globalisation on democratic governance and human-rights compliance.[89] Many scholars argue, however, that economic globalisation has the potential to alter the interests of social forces (labour and capital) to favour democratisation. As Eva Bellin has pointed out, labour and capital are most likely to champion democracy when their economic interests put them at odds with the authoritarian state.[90] In the case of democratisation in late developing countries, a number of factors, such as extensive state sponsorship, the structural weakness of social forces and pervasive poverty, 'have led capital and labor to ally with authoritarian states rather than championing democratisation'.[91] On the other hand, since the political disposition of capital and labour appears to be largely governed by interest, these interests and alliances may change. Bellin therefore predicts that

> [t]he logic of international economic integration may force the state to reduce its sponsorship of social forces. Or robust growth may eliminate mass poverty and the pervasive sense of fear within the propertied class. Under these conditions capital and/or labor may perceive democratisation in a new light and choose to embrace it.[92]

Although the post-Cold War period witnessed a wave of democratisation, some empirical studies are rather sceptical as to whether there has been any global improvement in human rights after the Cold War ended, except perhaps in the fields of detainment of political prisoners.[93] The improvement in this particular field is a manifestation of what Cingranelli and Richards have termed 'demonstration democracy', namely, limited political liberalisation to counter international criticism and domestic pressure, without aiming at introducing a fully fledged democratic system.[94] One is witnessing the proliferation of so-called 'illiberal democracies', a term used by Fareed Zakariya, highlighting a trend towards a growing number of states in limbo between authoritarianism and fully fledged consolidated democracies.[95] It is increasingly clear that the democracy–dictatorship dichotomy is no longer valid; democracies cannot be treated as 'a uniform category, which exists only in relation to its antithesis, non-democracy or autocracy'.[96] This alerts us to the possibility of the spread of types of democracies with more violent conflict participation. Anita Schjølset finds, for example, that unitary states, presidential countries and majoritarian democracies appear to pursue more violent conflict participation than federal states, parliamentary countries and consensus democracies.[97]

Zakariya's prediction on the rise of illiberal democracies has been challenged by Karatnycky, who argues that the substantial increase in electoral democracies since 1987 has been followed by 'a growing respect for civil liberties in a number of electoral democracies'.[98] In the latter half of the 1990s, the Comparative Survey of Freedom recorded 'an increase in the number and proportions of the world's electoral democracies that are also liberal'.[99] Other reports paint a less optimistic picture, however. The National Defense Council Foundation's annual reports on global conflicts have recorded a setback for democratisation processes in a number of countries and predicted that such setbacks would slow down the long-term development towards global democratisation.[100] A number of the new democracies that emerged from the third wave between 1972 and 1996 struggle with weak economies and high levels of organised crime, while their police and judicial institutions remain abusive, corrupt and ineffective. To combat crime, state authorities have reinstated emergency laws, deployed military forces for law-enforcement tasks and curtailed civil liberties, raising fears of a backsliding into semi-authoritarianism.[101] Post-9/11 developments also suggest a serious reversal of international efforts at promoting democracy, human rights and liberal rule, according to the UN and human-rights advocacy groups. According to Amnesty International Report 2004, the 'war on terror' has impacted negatively on human-rights compliance around the globe.[102]

It appears that the third wave of democratisation has peaked, and there are ominous signs of a reversal. The global democratisation record is relatively optimistic in certain regions were strong clusters of democracies are formed and reinforce one another. Regional democratisation is a key factor in consolidating democracies.[103] Europe's periphery offers a gloomy picture in this regard. In the former Soviet Union, there have been a number of setbacks, and a number of countries are growing into dictatorships.[104] Apart from the Baltic states, the post-Soviet states have become what one commentator described as 'a democratic wasteland', with some very harsh authoritarian regimes in some countries and seriously backsliding leaders in others.[105] In Turkmenistan, the authoritarian character of the regime has assumed absurd proportions as the President Saparmurat Niyazov not only has appointed himself president for life but also had himself hailed as 'a prophet' due to his 'divine abilities'.[106] Uzbekistan, under its president Islam Karimov, has also gone far in installing a harsh dictatorship, with thousands of political prisoners and widespread use of torture, especially with regards to the growing number of Islamic activists in the country. Its harsh repression of the hirtherto non-violent Islamist movement, Hizb al-Tahrir al-Islami (HTI) has prompted observers to warn, 'sooner or later the peaceful jihadis may exchange the pamphlet for the bomb'.[107] The recent bombings in Tashkent in April 2004 have given analysts ample reasons to predict that violent Islamic radicalism is on the rise in Uzbekistan. The emergence of radical HTI offshoots is also a trend in neighbouring Kyrgyzstan.[108]

Europe's southern periphery is characterised by a near absence of democracies and a growing number of semi-authoritarian states. The Middle East and north Africa remains the regions in which the roots of democracy are weakest. According to the Comparative Survey of Freedom, the region had in 2004 only one 'free' country (Israel[109]) and six 'partly free' states (Turkey, Kuwait, Jordan, Morocco, Bahrain and Yemen); the rest are described as 'not free'. Among the eight most repressive countries in the world, four were in the Middle East in 2004: Iran, Saudi Arabia, Syria and Libya.[110] The democracy record is still better in 2004 than it was in 1998 when there were only four 'partly free' countries in that region and five Middle Eastern regimes were in the 'most repressive' category.[111]

There are few signs of genuine democratisation in the Middle East and north Africa. Many regimes have moved towards semi-authoritarianism, and more will probably do so in the near future. The obstacles to democratic consolidation, however, remain formidable. To the rulers in the region, the bloody internal conflict and massacres unleashed by the aborted democratic transition in Algeria in 1991–2 is still a powerful reminder of the perils of democratisation.[112] Despite the negative lessons from Algeria, the pressure to democratise will continue and possibly increase in years to come. In the late 1990s, a negotiated transition to democracy was thought to be underway in several Arab countries.[113] By 2004 this no longer seem to be the case as reforms have been limited and adaptive and designed to ensure the regimes' survival and relieve growing popular pressure for particiation from below. While political liberalisation can be expected to advance slowly, democratisation will remain limited in the near future.[114]

The recent US initiatives to promote democracy in the Arab world in order to tackle the underlying causes of terrorism probably have slim chances for success, because the US credibility is at a record low following the Iraqi invasion, the revelation of its widespread abuses of Iraqi prisoners and the continued deepening of the bipartisan consensus in Washington around a strongly pro-Israeli foreign policy. The US Advisory Group in Public Diplomacy revealed in a shocking report in October 2003 how deeply resented the United States were in the Middle East, even among its supposedly closest allies, Kuwait and Saudi Arabia. The countries in the region also lack strong domestic pro-democracy movements that might stage large-scale demonstrations and put effective popular pressure on autocratic regimes.[115] There are, in other words, few prospective partners with whom the United States or its European partners can work to promote democracy in the region, apart from working with the regimes themselves. Furthermore, the expressed hope of the Bush administration that the toppling of Saddam Hussein's dictatorship would somehow promote democratisation in the neighbouring states has not materialised. Given the strength of the Iraqi insurgency movements, it is not even certain that a democratically elected Iraqi government, or the Iraqi state for that matter, will survive without continuous and direct US military interventions. With its history of brutal repression, armed insurgencies and ethnic divisions and its petroleum-dependent economy, it is unlikely that a democratic system will be fully established in Iraq over the next decade.[116] In sum, the future probably holds few changes with regards to democratisation in the Middle East. The stage is set for limited reforms, perhaps pushing more regimes towards semi-authoritarian or semi-democratic rule, while the prospect of fully fledged liberal democracies in the Arab worlds will remain remote.

While all twenty-five EU member states are considered fully fledged democracies, the Mediterranean is, and will probably remain, one of the world's sharpest fault-lines in terms of political regime differences. The situation in the Americas is less stark. The US–Mexican border is more a socio-economic fault-line than a political one. The Latin American countries have progressed further towards consolidated democracies than their Middle Eastern counterparts. Despite serious regional implications of the civil war in Colombia, the drug wars in the Brazilian favelas, and remaining Marxist rebel groups, there are good prospects for economic growth and strengthening of state institutions, which will reduce the vulnerabilities of newborn democracies and foster a deepening of democratic rule in this region. Still, as Monty G. Marshall has noted, several Latin American countries have oscillated back and forth between military autocracies and civil democratic rule in response to recurring crises and 'may continue to do so in the foreseeable future.'[117]

As is evident from the assessment of democratisation trends, the number of semi-democracies will probably increase in the future. With less information control, weaker economic performance and increased international pressure, authoritarian states will find it increasingly difficult to withstand the pressure for political liberalisation. Hence, one will continue to see a relatively large group of states in some kind of political transition from highly authoritarian rule to more democratic forms of government. There may be a certain growth in the number of consolidated democracies, but this trend is less clear. The number of anocratic, semi-authoritarian and illiberal regimes will remain relatively high and probably increase further.

The very existence of so many semi-autocratic states bodes ill for the fight against terrorism and the spread of armed conflicts, since this regime type appears to experience more terrorism than others. One of the great conundrums of democratisation is that while 'old' consolidated democracies have all kinds of virtues, including low levels of domestic terrorism, the process of getting to 'perfect' democracies is fraught by a whole series of dangers, from political instability, chaos and secessionism to armed insurgencies and terrorism. The upsurge of terrorism in the former Soviet Union seems to confirm these predictions. In the era of Soviet totalitarianism, there was hardly any substate terrorism on Soviet territory. By contrast, ten years after the collapse of the Communist bloc, Dennis Pluchinsky noted that 'The emergence of terrorism, in its criminal and political forms, is one of these problems [which] the fifteen newly independent states of the former Soviet Union (FSU) have encountered [. . .] on their road to democracy and free market economy.'[118] In 1999 the southern Russian republics of Daghestan, Chechnya, Ingushetia, North Ossetia, Georgia, Azerbaijan and Tajikistan were in fact judged to have the potential of 'replacing the Middle East as the primary generator of [. . .] international terrorism'.[119] Similarly, the democratisation of Indonesia since the late 1990s has been accompanied with a serious upsurge in domestic and international terrorism, as well as outbreaks of ethnic violence and intensifying civil wars.

Trends in state formation and state failure

Postulate: The number of states will continue to increase. Many states will be weak states, and a few will also be failed or collapsed states incapable of exercising any control over their territories.

Possible implication for terrorism: State formation processes are often accompanied by widespread organised violence, including terrorism. New states often have legitimacy problems, which may cause intrastate conflicts and domestic terrorism. A further proliferation of weak and collapsed states will generate more transnational terrorism as weak states are incapable of suppressing insurgents and terrorists present on their territories and denying them sanctuary or transition. Even the continued existence of a relatively small number of weak and collapsed states will ultimately cause higher levels of transnational terrorism. This trend may be reversed by greater international political will to assist in restoring legitimate state authority.

Trends in state formation and state performance are useful indicators of future patterns of terrorism. Political instability, economic disruption and new intrastate violent conflicts are all familiar features of the painful processes associated with the creation of new states in the twentieth century. New states usually go through a long period of state-building and internal consolidation. Their fledgling political institutions are fragile, their economies have often been disrupted either by war or by the fact that the newly erected borders deny or reduce access to international transportation and communication links and interfere with former patterns of trade and commerce. Most new states are also small, lack resources and are plagued by political unrest and civil violence. In particular, the policing of their newly erected national borders presents a serious challenge for new states. Weak and non-existent policing of borders makes it much easier for transnational terrorists to operate. The rise of the Islamic Movement in Uzbekistan is a case in point. In the latter half of the 1990s its fighters, operating out of bases in Tajikistan, launched repeated spring campaigns across Central Asian borders, attacking almost at will and exposing the inability of Uzbekistan and its neighbours in policing their territories.[120]

New minority conflicts often arise as a result of the new borders and perceived unsatisfactory outcomes of past conflict. If state formation is the outcome of negotiated settlements, future instability is likely. As has been observed by Roy Licklider and others, negotiated settlements after civil wars are inherently unstable and are rarely sustainable.[121] Hence, even if state formation does end a protracted secessionist conflict and removes a main source of ethnic-separatist terrorism, more often, however, the redrawing of borders creates new patterns of conflict, reshaping, rather than removing, sources of ethnic strife, creating lingering legitimacy problems for the new government. Studies show that state legitimacy problems, in particular a lack of continuity of the political system, are key factors in explaining the occurrence of domestic terrorism.[122] Since the formation of a legitimate political order in newly created states is such a time-consuming process, it follows that new states are likely to be more exposed to domestic terrorism than their older cousins. A persistent growth in the number of states will therefore not only widen the opportunity structure for transnational terrorism, but also exacerbate underlying factors behind terrorism.

Irrespective of states' longevity and maturity, their performance also appears to have an impact on patterns of terrorism. Although the relationship between terrorism and the existence of weak and failed or collapsed states is not so straightforward and direct as some of the recent terrorism literature has suggested, there is little doubt that lawless ungoverned territories have the potential of becoming safe havens and sanctuaries for transnational terrorist networks. Furthermore, most collapsed states did collapse in the first place due to the outbreak of civil wars, which often attract a host of unsavoury elements from international mercenaries, traffickers in valuable commodities and mafia organisations to rebel groups and transnational jihadists. Protracted civil wars have sometimes become important sources of international terrorism. Assuming that these explanations are valid, and that state-formation and state-collapse processes are likely to be among the driving forces in future terrorism, one should investigate two separate trends: will state formation processes remain a dominant feature in the future and is the ongoing proliferation of weak and collapsed states likely to continue? These two trends would give us an idea of the patterns of future terrorism.

State formation

The number of new states grew considerably in the twentieth century. The demise of the Ottoman empire, the Habsburg empire and Czarist Russia during and after the First World War, 1914–18 gave birth to a host of new states, many of which were plagued with internal strife, instability and weak political institutions. Another wave of state formation occurred when former European colonies gained independence in the 1950s and 1960s. Three decades later, the dissolution of the Soviet Union and of Yugoslavia created the third large wave of new states during this century. Between 1946 and 2000 the number of states increased from 66 to 194. Compared to this impressive historical record of state formations, there have been very few examples of state merger.[123]

There are many entities today seeking statehood and independence. The Unrepresented Nations and Peoples Organisation (UNPO) in The Hague has had a steadily growing membership since its foundation in 1991, reaching some fifty-six members by 2004, all with their own flags, national symbols and aspiration for statehood or some sort of autonomy.[124] While these minorities are the most vocal ones, the UNPO estimates that 'there are almost 6,500 nations, peoples, minorities and indigenous peoples in the world'.[125] Judging by the UNPO's assessment, the potential for future minority conflicts is high:

> [M]any of these unrepresented nations and peoples do not recognise these oppressive state-governments as their legitimate representatives. Very often state-governments have no qualms using any means available to suppress and control them. Standard mechanisms within the UN and OSCE system for preventing conflicts are generally not available for the unrepresented nations and peoples. [. . .] As a result, many unrepresented nations and peoples in the world have lost faith in the international community's ability to be fair and just in solving their problems. Most of them feel deceived, abandoned and betrayed by the international community. In their hopelessness, frustration and desperation many unrepresented nations and peoples are gradually abandoning the path of nonviolence in order to draw the attention of the international community, because the international community only reacts when conflict breaks out.[126]

The success of separatist movements and rebellious ethnic minorities in achieving formal independence during the latter decades is striking.[127] Their success will probably continue to motivate disaffected and disgruntled minorities for years to come. One may assume, therefore, that the number of states will also grow in the future, as the rate of 'state death' over the past century has been much lower. The disappearance of states through conquest and occupation has virtually ceased after the Second World War.[128] Instead, multinational and multi-ethnic states, in particular, will come under increased pressure to grant autonomy and independence to rebellious and assertive minority groups. Compared to the relatively recent collapse of the Soviet Union and Yugoslavia, it seems far-fetched to predict a similar large-scale wave of state formation. Noting the remarkable 20 per cent increase in the number of states since 1990, the CIA's *Global Trends 2015* predicts that the number of states 'is likely to increase at a slower rate through 2015'.[129]

While this prediction seems safe, there is less agreement about which region will experience most state formations in the near future. *Global Trends 2015* expects that new states will emerge from 'remaining cases of decolonisation and to communal tensions leading to state secession, most likely in sub-Saharan Africa, central Asia, and Indonesia'.[130] One might also argue that the intensification of internal conflicts in many of Asia's multinational states, such as Indonesia, India, China and the Philippines, as well as in the Russian federation should alert us to the possibility of new state formations in those regions. Pavel Baev has observed in a recent study of secessionist conflicts in central and eastern Europe in the 1990s that 'few if any of the violent secessions have found satisfactory resolutions'.[131] As the shape of the future Europe is still undetermined and a host of ethnic secessionist conflicts remain unresolved in the periphery of the EU, it seems safe to conclude that the 'rise of secessionist movements [in OSCE Europe] is far from exhausted.'[132] Menon and Fuller agree, arguing that the fighting in Chechnya is leading dissatisfied nationalities in the Russian federation to rethink their options and their dependence on Russia. While Chechnya was the first to rebel, it 'will not be the last'.[133]

Not every region is as plagued with secessionism as the European periphery. There have been relatively few violent secessionist movements in the Americas, such as the Puerto Rican FALN, and the FLQ in Québec, Canada.[134] Eric Hobsbawm noted in 1995 that the 'only signs of significant separatism in Latin America comes from the richest state in Brazil, Rio Grande do Sul.'[135] This is not the case of Africa and south-east Asia where ethnic separatist conflicts persist in a number of countries, from west Sahara, Sudan and Somalia to Sri Lanka and several provinces in Indonesia. These protracted conflicts will ensure that the state formation process will not come to an end and will continue to take its toll in terms of more domestic and international terrorism.

Failed and collapsed states

Under certain circumstances, weak states may become 'failed' or 'collapsed' states. Such states share a number of characteristics, such as a rise in criminal and political violence, a loss of control over their borders, civil war, weak institutions, high levels of corruption, collapsed health, education and welfare systems, basic food shortages, etc. What concern us here are states failing in upholding the Weberian definition of the state, namely failure to sustain a central government authority that controls and polices all of its territory. While failed states usually have lost control of some of their territory, collapsed states are typified by a more or less complete absence of government authority: 'a shell of a polity', of which Somalia is the classical example.[136] The phenomenon of partial breakdown of state authority, that governments are incapable of controlling parts or most of their territories, is much more widespread.

The 1990s witnessed an increase in states suffering partial breakdown of their authority, usually in conjunction with internal armed conflicts, corrupt governance, or both.[137] In Europe's recent history, the most prominent example is Bosnia-Herzegovina, which quickly descended into civil war after being hastily created in the wake of the demise of Yugoslavia and was uneasily restored as a state by the UN, NATO and the EU in the second half of the 1990s. A quite different example was the temporary collapse of the central authority in Albania in 1997, also prompting European intervention to assist in re-establishing the state. In Eurasia, Tajikistan has experienced internal regional fragmentation and civil war (1992–7). In the Caucasus, Chechnya came under the spell of warlords after the Russian defeat in the mid-1990s. Georgia lost control of large territories to various ethnic separatists. In Asia's civil-war zones in Nepal, Indonesia, the Philippine Islands and Sri Lanka, large swathes of land are de-facto rebel-controlled. In Africa, a number of countries can be classified as failed states in which insurgents control significant parts of the country. These include DRC, Sudan, Angola, Somalia and Liberia.[138]

In North Africa, Algeria witnessed an unprecedented surge in political violence and massacres after the outbreak of the civil war in 1992, and significant territories were lost to the Islamist insurgents. The rebels controlled much of the so-called 'triangle of death' (Medea and the Mitidja Plateau) for nearly three years until the Algerian military managed to recapture it in 1995–6.[139] In the Middle East, Lebanon was very much a failed state, controlled by local warlords, intervening powers and Palestinian guerrilla armies during the civil war from 1975 to 1989. In its reconstructed form under Syrian hegemony, Lebanon still has pockets where non-state actors hold sway. The largest Palestinian refugee camp Ayn al-Hilwah is beyond the control of Lebanese police and security forces. Inside the camp, armed Fatah fighters and other militias are de-facto the authority for the 70,000 or so Palestinian refugees.[140] The most notorious group operating in the camp since the late 1990s was Asbat al-Ansar (Band of Partisans), an al-Qaida-affiliated group of some 300 fighters, which has been implicated in a number of violent attacks in Lebanon in recent years.[141] In mid-2004, six to eight

Iraqi cities, most of them in the so-called Sunni triangle, were reportedly under the control of various Iraqi resistance groups, including al-Qaida-affiliated groups and foreign Islamist fighters. This raised the disturbing possibility that Iraq was on the verge of becoming a second Afghanistan, where Muslim youth received weapons-training and combat experience and were converted into die-hard fighters and global jihadists, in short al-Qaida's next generation.[142]

While these states are all very different and may not be failed or collapsed along all dimensions, a common trait is that the central government authority lacks both sufficient coercive power and political legitimacy to establish a monopoly on the use of force, hence its capacity to function as a state comes into question. The recent rise in the number of failed states is partly due to superpower withdrawal following the collapse of the Soviet Union and the bipolar world order. Without superpower backing in terms of military and economic assistance, a number of client regimes came under pressure and some succumbed. The post-Cold War period has also brought more pressure to bear on authoritarian governments to democratise. Since democratising states are more likely to experience armed conflicts and internal disintegration, the external and internal pressure to democratise may have increased the scope for state failures. Another possible explanation is that globalisation has created a greater potential for lucrative illegal or semi-legal transnational trade, which weakens the state economically vis-à-vis substate actors.[143] Thus, economic incentives add to other grievances and strengthen the centrifugal forces inside weak states or, alternatively, the state may be transformed into inherently unstable criminal state entities or warlord-dominated zones of influence. Such patterns of trade sustain the political economy of internal wars and perpetuate situations of state failure. This is part of the expansion of what Timothy Luke and Gerard Toal have termed 'contraband capitalism', a pattern of interaction between markets and states in conflict zones where the world political map is 'fraying' and coming undone.[144]

In many parts of the world there are numerous areas where central governments exercise either limited or virtually no control. Several African countries exercise very limited authority beyond the capital and the largest cities. The Pakistani central government exercises little formal authority in the tribal areas in the North-West Frontier Province. Lawless coastal areas in the archipelagic states in south-east Asia have fostered the proliferation of numerous professional pirate gangs, turning the area into the 'the world's most pirate-infested waterways, where almost one-third of all reported pirate attacks take place'.[145]

In Latin America, there are fewer black holes. Colombia, with its deadlocked civil war, is the major example. Even if Colombia is not a failed state in the classical sense, large swathes of its territory, nearly 40 per cent according to some estimates, are rebel-controlled territory, and enormous revenues are generated through kidnapping and the drug trade.[146] Widely regarded as the wealthiest rebel organisation in the world, the FARC is reported to have collaborative relationships with a number of other terrorist organistions, in Europe as well as in Latin America. Its political wing, the Bolivarian Movement, claims to have established cells in Peru, Argentina, Venezuela, Ecuador, Chile and Bolivia.[147] Other significant pockets of unpoliced areas include the triborder region in South America, where Hizbollah and other militant groups from the Middle East have established a foothold, and the remote Peruvian highlands where remnants of the once 10,000-strong Sendero Luminoso (Shining Path) rebel army still hold sway.[148] These rebels may experience a renaissance due to increased sponsorship from the wealthy Colombian FARC guerrillas, who provide money and new direction for their Peruvian cousins.[149] The unruly Brazilian *favelas* harbour another type of lawlessness where the combination of poverty, immigration, government neglect and the lucrative drug trade have turned the slum communities into virtually no man's land, governed by feuding druglords and thugs. They also apparently attract terrorist organisations. FARC instructors have reportedly trained guerrilla-warfare techniques to various local drug kingpins in the Brazilian favelas.[150] Haiti has experienced recurrent collapses of the central government. Political disturbances, civil violence and endemic poverty in many Latin American countries also indicate that areas of weak government and state failure will not diminish in the foreseeable future.

In Europe's periphery, the potential of new failed and collapsed states may be most imminent in some of the southern Mediterranean countries, in the Caucasus region and central Asia. Most Middle Eastern and some African regimes rely heavily, and in some cases exclusively, on petroleum exports for their foreign-currency earnings and thus food imports.[151] A sudden and dramatic drop in the price of petroleum products, caused for example by new revolutionary energy technology, will therefore put severe and unprecedented strains on these regimes, dramatically increasing the prospects of state failure. Bad governance, weak state institutions and growing internal pressure for change may precipitate new violent conflicts.[152] Several analysts have stressed the 'dysfunctionality' of the states in the Middle East and the southern Mediterranean and their inability to provide basic services to their populations as a major factor for the eruption of internal wars in the region during the 1990s.[153] The economic crisis is compounded by a profound crisis of legitimacy, due to corruption, mismanagement, weak economic performance and the widespread abuse of power. Human-rights abuses are rampant in virtually all states in the Middle East and north Africa, even if there is a significant difference between the 'benign authoritarianism' of Morocco and Jordan and the totalitarian cult-of-personality regimes of Syria and Libya. Torture and extrajudicial killings by the state's security apparatus are frequently the direct cause of unrest and popular riots, and histories of torture figure very prominently in the biographies of the new generations of Islamist jihadists from the region.[154] In the wake of 9/11, the US and Israeli governments have hinted to the need for toppling or at least undermining several of the regimes in the region, including Syria and Iran, and perhaps also Saudi Arabia. If they were to act upon these threats, it might exacerbate the potential for state failure in the region, although the price tag of the Iraqi invasion, politically, economically and militarily, may have reached such proportions that it will probably deter future US interventions in similar scenarios.

In sum, there appears to be a significant likelihood of new failed and collapsed states in the future, while many existing failed states show little sign of recuperating. Even without any increase in the number of failed states, the globalisation process will probably aggravate rather than ameliorate the consequences of existing failed states due to the broadening scope for transportation and interaction across borders and geographical distance. Breakdown of state authority – in the frequently encountered local version as well as in the rarer form of a nationwide implosion – are likely to cause increased levels of transnational terrorism in the foreseeable future.

The prospect for countering this trend is quite good, however. The fact that failed states have become so closely associated with transnational terrorism in view of al-Qaida's training bases in Afghanistan has increased significantly the international will to forestall and prevent state failures. Not only have national authorities become more determined to prevent lawless areas from turning into terrorist sanctuaries, but the international community also seems more willing to assist governments in restoring state control throughout their territory. This might mitigate the worst effects of new state failures.

Trends in peacekeeping and military interventions

Postulates: Peacekeeping activities will remain on a high level or possibly increase. There will be many new international military interventions, including US-led operations, in armed conflicts. Non-Western countries may become more prominent in peacekeeping, but Western countries are also likely to become involved in new military interventions in the Islamic world.

Possible implications for terrorism: A high level of muscular peacekeeping and military interventions in conflicts will cause many incidents of transnational terrorism, at least in the short run. In the long run, however, there is a reasonable possibility that greater peacekeeping involvement will reduce the scope for terrorism as the outbreak of new conflicts are prevented, collapsed state situations are averted and internationalised armed conflicts are brought to a close. This depends on the success of these interventions. Protracted and faltering peace processes are likely to sustain, or in some cases, precipitate more terrorism, at least on a local level, while new US-led military interventions in the Islamic world will most certainly be accompanied with new incidents of transnational terrorism. Due to the current power structure of the international system, there is a tendency that Muslim nations are more likely to be pressured to accept peacekeeping interventions than non-Muslim powers with large Muslim minorities. This regrettable fact will continue to fuel jihadist ideologies, which propagate that the Islamic nation is under siege and a war must be launched on the 'Crusaders'.

Armed conflicts are a key source to transnational terrorism. Militant groups have employed violence to protest not only against forgotten wars, but also, far more often, against external military involvement in wars in which the intervening parties are perceived to favour one party over the other. Although the various causal relationships between armed conflicts and transnational terrorism need to be explored further, there is little doubt that a reduction of ongoing armed conflicts serves to reduce the potential for terrorism, both in its domestic and transnational form. Conversely, multilateral military interventions in conflicts, especially if they are led by the United States, are often accompanied by transnational terrorism against the participating countries' interests. This does not seem to be the case with regard to multinational UN peacekeeping, however, where in-theatre violence is rarely accompanied by terrorist attacks on participants' interests elsewhere.[155] If these explanations are correct, they provide an avenue to explore the future of terrorism by looking at prospects for future international involvement in peacekeeping and peace-making. Are states moving away from involvement in armed conflicts, or are they likely to build greater capacities for engaging in such efforts in the future? Are non-Western regional actors assuming a greater responsibility in peacekeeping? What are the future directions in US-led military interventions?

Peacekeeping

After the end of the Cold War, there was a general belief that the United Nations should assume a greater role in resolving international conflict. To deal with the predominantly intrastate nature of post-Cold War conflicts, new types of peacekeeping operations evolved. Hence, the 1990s witnessed a significant shift in the development of peacekeeping (now usually referred to as 'peace operations') in terms of the types of tasks and the spectrum of actors involved as well as the mandates and the level of force used in peacekeeping operations. More importantly, there has been a gradual, controversial evolution towards relying on the use of military force to enforce a ceasefire between parties in internal conflicts, and to bring about a peace settlement. The concept of 'peacekeeping with muscle' gained considerable ground.[156] Furthermore, the willingness to accept sustained involvement lasting for many years rather than six to twelve months has been the outcome of a learning process in peacekeeping from the Balkans, where the United States deployed troops as part of SFOR, a NATO peacekeeping force in Bosnia-Herzegovina in 1995, with a declared objective of pulling out after one year only. Later, nation-building became a buzzword, illustrating the new ambitions and the longer time perspectives.

A number of non-Western states have been critical of the new interventionism, objecting to what they perceive as a dilution of the principle of non-interference in the domestic affairs of states. For example, China has lamented the NATO intervention in Kosovo as an 'ominous precedent', especially in view of the lack of an explicit UN Security Council mandate for the operation.[157] Still, compared to the experiences during the Cold War, when humanitarian concerns were hardly ever mentioned in the UN Security Council, there has been a sea change in political thinking among major powers about the international community's role in intrastate conflicts and the duty to intervene to sustain humanitarian objectives.[158] As Glennon has observed, 'the anti-interventionist regime has fallen out of sync with modern notions of justice' and we now have 'a vague new system that is much more tolerant of military intervention'.[159] The concept of human security has become more established, underlining the responsibility to protect and ensure security for the individual, even if that means stepping on state-sovereignty sensibilities. Most recently, the emphasis on the dangers of failed states as terrorist sanctuaries has reinforced trends towards increased and long-term commitment to reshape conflict areas through various forms of external assistance and engagement, including multilateral interventions. Fearon and Laitin observe that '[m]ajor international interventions to prop up and rebuild failed states are not a temporary aberration in the course of international politics. Rather, they reflect more durable, even structural characteristics of the present international system'.[160]

The shift in political thinking on state sovereignty and military interventionism has been accompanied by a significant restructuring of Western armed forces towards overseas interventions, be it in peacekeeping scenarios or in more muscular enforcement operations, emphasising smaller, more mobile and flexible expeditionary forces over large standing armies and heavy infantry. The process towards a common European security and defence policy has been motivated largely by the need for an independent European military capacity for such military contingencies. The NATO intervention in Kosovo in 1999, 9/11 and the intervention in Afghanistan also lead to greater emphasis on special operations and rapid reaction forces capable of a wide variety of high-risk missions. Despite disagreements over Iraq, EU member states have agreed that their military forces, to a considerable extent, will be deployed and used 'out of area', i.e., outside the territory covered by EU and NATO member states, for peacekeeping or peace-making purposes, with a significant enforcement component. While such involvement was deemed most likely in conflict areas in Europe's geographical periphery, there is a growing acceptance of intervention in more distant areas, including African and Asian conflict areas. The NATO International Security Assistance Force

(ISAF) in Afghanistan and plans for a NATO role in Iraq are illustrative of this new thinking. Similarly, the deployment of the Interim Emergency Multinational Force (IEMF), an EU-led peacekeeping force, in the DRC in June 2003 underscored the new commitment to peacekeeping in Africa. Code-named Operation Artemis, IEMF was the EU's first fully autonomous crisis-management operation outside Europe and included some 1400 troops deployed in Bunia in the North-eastern Ituri region in DRC with a UN mandate and with France as lead nation.[161]

Recent NATO and EU interventions illustrate a trend towards greater involvement of regional organisations in peace operations.[162] The United Nations has repeatedly called upon regional organisations to assume a greater share of the burden of peacekeeping.[163] In part, this is a result of the strategic thinking in the Brahimi Report in August 2000, which reflected experiences from the mid-1990s when the United Nations was seen to have overextended itself in demanding peacekeeping missions. The organisation wanted to refocus its peacekeeping activities around its traditional competencies and avoid direct UN peacekeeping engagement in ongoing conflicts without a stable ceasefire in place. It recognised that the United Nations is not suited to dealing with the demands of peace enforcement, and that such operations should be deferred to coalitions of willing states and regional organisations.[164]

The degree to which regional organisations have conducted or authorised peace operations varies considerably, but the experiences gained over the past fifteen years have increased the belief in the need for peacekeeping capacity on a regional level. In 2004 UN officials spoke of a 'growth of support for peacekeeping', in Asia, Africa, Europe and Latin America.[165] Africa has been plagued by the most violent, extensive and long-lasting conflicts and has also seen the most autonomous peace operations, primarily through the Economic Community of West African States (ECOWAS), which first deployed peacekeeping troops into Liberia in 1990. ECOWAS has become the foremost example of an organisation willing to engage in military peace operations. Using its own military intervention force, ECOMIL, ECOWAS deployed mostly Nigerian peacekeepers to several of its member states, including Sierra Leone, Ivory Coast and Liberia, albeit with mixed success.

The African Union (AU, formerly Organisation of African Unity [OAU] has also introduced military peacekeeping among its activities, following 'significant changes' and 'remarkable progress' in the organisation's willingness to engage in conflict prevention and conflict management since the 1990s.[166] The AU's Constitutive Act of 2000 mandates the organisation to intervene in cases of war crimes, genocide and crimes against humanity, in itself a new development compared to the previous OAU Charter where much emphasis was on the principle of non-interference in other states' internal affairs. Despite weak financial and operation capabilities, the AU has begun to engage in military peacekeeping. It deployed a peacekeeping force in Burundi in 2003 and is developing plans for the formation of an African standby force by 2010.[167]

Africa is where most bilateral and multilateral initiatives have been launched to enhance indigenous peacekeeping capacity over the past decade, such as the US-sponsored African Crisis Response Initiative, and the European Union's Peace Facility for financing of African peace-supporting operations and building an African institutional capacity for peacekeeping.[168] The latter has a proposed budget of 250 million euro and is expected to be operational by the end of 2004. The European Union has also agreed to finance the ECOWAS Mechanism for Conflict Prevention, Management and Resolution, and other peacekeeping efforts by regional organisations on the African continent. These initiatives expand previous assistance programmes such as EU aid to an African peacekeeping force in Liberia in 1994–7. Lacking the institutional structures and the financial means to mount effective military operations, the AU and ECOWAS have been in dire need of this assistance. Another African regional organisation, the South African Development Community (SADC) has been less involved in peacekeeping partly due to internal divisions, but it receives financial support from the European Union for its efforts at finding a peace settlement in Burundi and DRC.[169]

From being a marginal contributor to peacekeeping missions in the past, the United States has over the past decade come to view the strengthening of UN and NATO peacekeeping capacities as a priority task.[170] The heavy US involvement in the Balkans was a turning point in US participation in peacekeeping operations. Since the mid-1990s the US State Department has funded various training-assistance projects to boost the peacekeeping capabilities of African states, such as the African Contingency Operations Training and Assistance and the Enhanced International Peacekeeping Capacities programmes, but these have not been well funded. More recently, in April 2004 the Bush administration has unveiled plans for significantly expanding funding for UN peacekeeping capacities. Under a five-year programme labelled the Global Peace Operations Initiative (GPOI), the United States pledged to spend 660 million US dollars on peacekeeping assistance.[171] The GPOI initiative was announced at the G8 Summit in Sea Island, Georgia, June 2004 where the United States committed itself to 'train and, where appropriate, equip a total of approximately 75,000 troops worldwide by 2010'.[172] Although the GPOI's focus was African peacekeepers, it would also build peacekeeping capabilities in other regions as well and would work with interested parties to develop 'a transportation and logistics support arrangement' in order to put in place a more effective peacekeeping deployment capacity.[173]

In the former Soviet republics, Russia has undertaken various peacekeeping missions in the name of the Commonwealth of Independent States (CIS), deploying troops in various trouble spots, including Tajikistan, Moldova and

Georgia. These were mostly unilateral Russian deployments in accordance with bilateral agreement, while the mandate was only subsequently approved by the CIS council of heads of states.[174]

The Association of south-east Asian Nations (ASEAN) has traditionally pursued a well-honed approach of quiet diplomacy, dialogue and non-confrontation. Previously, it has been reluctant to venture into more hard-core security issues and has preferred to focus on economic co-operation and cultural issues. However, at a top-level meeting in February 2004, Indonesia launched preliminary discussions on an ASEAN peacekeeping force, proposing *inter alia* the creation of a standby force by 2012. This was part of a wider effort to establish an ASEAN security community by 2020, endorsed by the member states in 2003.[175] While the standby force proposal has been surrounded with controversy, the idea of improving regional peacekeeping, conflict prevention and crisis-management capacity has gained ground.[176] Since the 1990s, Asian countries have assisted in mediating and monitoring efforts in local conflicts. In 2003, the Philippines sent unarmed monitors to the troubled Indonesian province of Aceh along with Thailand under UN mandates. In 1996 Indonesia sent military observers to Mindanao in the southern Philippines in 1996 to oversee a peace settlement with the separatist movement Moro National Liberation Front (MNLF). More recently, Malaysia also has commited itself to sending an observer team to Mindanao to monitor the government's ceasefire accord with the Moro Islamic Liberation Front (MILF), an Islamic offshoot of the MNLF.[177]

Similar to ASEAN's traditional role, the Organisation of American States (OAS) has frequently played an important diplomatic and mediating role in conflicts within its region. The OAS continuous efforts to assist in resolving the crises in Haiti since 1991 are a prime example of this role. Conducting military operations, however, has been absent from the OAS agenda for several reasons. First, the legacy of military rule throughout Latin America has left the member states reluctant to launch military interventions in third countries. Second, aside from Haiti, the challenges in the region require less military and more political and economic attention. Still, even in the OAS there is a move towards greater interventionism, even if not with military means. This was reflected in the fact that Article 20 of the Inter-American Democratic Charter, which allows the Permanent Council to consider measures even without the consent of the stricken state, was invoked for the first time to condemn the April 2002 coup in Venezuela.[178]

Studies in settlements of violent internal conflicts indicate that one of the most decisive factors for a successful outcome is sustained outside involvement throughout the peace process. In a quantitative analysis of peacekeeping after civil wars, Fortna finds that it makes 'an important contribution to the stability of peace'; although not a silver bullet, peacekeeping 'does tend to make peace more likely to last, and to last longer'.[179] Hampson has argued that conflict settlements that 'enjoy high levels of third party assistance and support during the entire course of the peace-making and peace building process are arguably more likely to succeed than those that do not.'[180] According to a study by Lake and Rothchild, the failure of a number of peace agreements 'is partly attributable to the unwillingness of the international community to provide mediators with economic, logistical, police and military support needed to oversee the process of disarmament, integration of the armed forces, repatriation of refugees, and holding of general elections'.[181] This suggests that if the international community is more willing to use resources, including a sustained international military deployment, for intrastate conflict resolution, the chances of a peaceful settlement will become better. There is a widespread recognition among policy-makers, academics and advocacy groups that sustained engagement is critical to any international intervention. This recognition has gradually evolved and been strengthened as a result of the experiences in peace operations since the mid-1990s.

Popular commentary has erroneously described the post-Cold War era as one of unabating proliferation of ethnic conflicts. Data on endings of violent nationalist conflicts strongly suggest otherwise, however, despite the resurgence of internal wars in Europe's eastern and south-eastern periphery.[182] Studies of the way recent ethnic conflicts ended (defeat or agreement) suggest that the end of the Cold War, in addition to contributing to some new nationalist conflicts, has brought about a wave of peace-making by means of negotiations rather than defeat on the battlefield. There have been three major waves of conclusions to violent nationalist conflicts in the post-war era: late 1940s and early 1950s, a small group in the 1970s and a third (and largest) in the late 1980s and early 1990s. The conflict endings in the latter period were resolved more frequently by agreements than defeat compared to earlier periods. While twenty-two violent conflicts began from 1985 to 1996, twenty-five conflicts ended during the same period. Against this background, one scholar has argued that we are witnessing a 'new era of nationalist peace'.[183] Although this seems overly optimistic in view of the more than thirty or so ongoing armed conflicts today, a new international order has evidently emerged, which is more capable of dealing with internal armed conflicts and bringing these to a negotiated settlement. Since armed conflicts clearly contribute to increase the prospects for transnational terrorism, this bodes well for the future, at least in a long-term perspective. In the short run, new peace processes will undoubtedly generate much terrorism by spoiler groups.[184] These are usually marginalised, however, when the peace settlement is consolidated and capable and legitimate governments are formed.

Military interventions

Military interventions often create powerful incentives for terrorist attacks against the interests of the intervening powers, which are often seen as invaders, occupiers and Crusaders, even in cases where there is a legitimate UN mandate for the intervention. During the Cold War era, there were several hundred military interventions, around the world, nearly all of them unilateral, and often carried out by the great powers, or with their blessing, with the purpose of serving national goals or geopolitical goals. In this regard, the post-Cold War period ushered in a new era as military interventions increasingly became multilateral operations carried out, or approved, by the international community, and served conflict prevention goals, not simply narrowly defined national interests.[185] The survey provided in Box 3.2 illustrates the significant scope of multilateral military interventions today. In April 2004, the United Nations oversaw as many as 50,000 troops in fourteen places, a number that was due to increase by about 20,000 if the projected operations in Haiti, Burundi, Sudan and Cyprus were to take shape.[186]

Box 3.2 International military interventions worldwide

US-led military interventions:

- Operation 'Iraqi Freedom': coalition forces and the Iraqi stabilisation force, consisting of a total of 150,000–160,000 forces as of March 2004, from more than thirty states. More than 90 per cent of the forces from the United States and the United Kingdom.[1]
- Operation 'Enduring Freedom' in Afghanistan, consisting of 11,000–20,000 US forces and more than 2,000 troops from allied countries as of spring 2004.[2]
- Proliferation Security Initiative (PSI), maritime counter-proliferation operations by a US-led coalition of fifteen core nations.[3]

Current NATO out-of-area operations involving significant military forces, drawn from more than thirty states, both inside and outside NATO:

- NATO Stabilisation Force (SFOR) in Bosnia, numbering c.12,000 as of August 2003.[4]
- NATO Kosovo Force (KFOR) in Kosovo, numbering c.18,000 as of August 2003.
- NATO's International Security Assistance Force (ISAF) in and around Kabul, Afghanistan, numbering 6,536 as of April 2004.
- NATO's Active Endeavour in the Mediterranean to combat terrorism at sea. The task force consists of a squadron of eight to ten vessels and submarines. Between October 2001 and April 2004 it had monitored some 42,000 vessels.[5]

Current UN peacekeeping operations involving significant military forces. (All troops figures as of 31 March 2004.):[6]

- UNAMSIL in Sierra Leone, established in October 1999, 11,274 troops and 255 observers.
- UNMIL in Liberia, established 19 September 2003, 13,808 troops and 137 observers.
- UNOCI in Ivory Coast, established in April 2004, 6,240 military personnel.
- MONUC in DRC, established on 30 November 1999, 10,184 troops and 551 observers.
- UNMEE in Ethiopia and Eritrea, established on 31 July 2000, 3,804 troops and 214 observers.
- UNMISET in East Timor, established on 20 May 2002, 1,660 troops and 77 military observers, 302 civilian police.
- UNIFIL in Lebanon, established in March 1978, 1,987 troops and 50 military observers.

Notes
[1] Perspectives of World History and Current Events, 'Coalition of the Willing', <http://www.geocities.com/pwhce/willing.html>. Accessed May 2004, citing *The Australian* 17 March 2004. According to Reuters, there were '138,000 US Troops and Nearly 25,000 Allied Troops', in Iraq in April 2004, see Will Dunham, 'U.S. General Wants Iraq Troops from Muslim Nations', *Reuters* 30 April 2004. See also 'US Forces Order of Battle – 13 May 2004', *Global Security*, <http://www.globalsecurity.org/military/ops/iraq_orbat.htm>. Accessed May 2004.
[2] Will Dunham, 'U.S. General Wants Iraq Troops from Muslim Nations', *Reuters* 30 April 2004.
[3] NATO, 'Combating Terrorism at Sea'.
[4] The following figures are taken from UNMIK Division of Public Information, Media Monitoring, 'Kosovo News', 26 August 2003, <http://www.unmikonline.org/press/2003/wire/Aug/imm260803PM.htm>. Accessed May 2004.
[5] Information from NATO, 'Combating Terrorism at Sea'.
[6] The following figures are taken from UN Department of Peacekeeping Operations web site, <http://www.un.org/Depts/dpko/missions>. Accessed May 2004.

Even as multilateral military interventions become more common, countries continue to intervene militarily in other countries in numerous ways. A number of states have deployed military forces overseas in conflict areas with and without UN mandates, multilaterally or unilaterally, either for peacekeeping and humanitarian reasons or for anti-terrorism purposes, or both. British and French interventions in west Africa and Australia's early deployment to

East Timor were examples of the former, while the latter motive underlies the post-9/11 deployment of US military personnel to Georgia, the Philippines, Yemen, and Djibouti, in addition to its military occupation of Afghanistan and Iraq. Other states intervene in internal conflicts abroad either out of national self-interest and hegemonic ambitions, such as Russia in its 'near abroad' republics or out of security concerns and 'self-defence' such as Israel in Lebanon. Finally, military interventions may assume a covert character through the infiltration of agents and special forces, backed up with financial support, such as the operations by the US CIA and the Pakistani Inter-Service Intelligence (ISI) in Soviet-occupied Afghanistan in the 1980s or Iran's Revolutionary Guard Corps (IRGC) in Lebanon during the 1980s and in post-Saddam Iraq.

Interventionism has many faces, but its legitimacy hinges on UN mandate and wide international support and participation. The US-led intervention in Afghanistan in October 2001 and the US-led Operation Iraqi Freedom in Spring 2003 introduced a new discourse on the legitimacy of military interventions, dominated by the new US doctrine of pre-emption and its emphasis on national security and self-defence, not collective security and humanitarianism. The US-led war on terror, especially after the Iraqi war, seems to have weakened the legitimacy that interventionism gained during the 1990s, punctuating the evolution towards a growing international consensus on the principles for military intervention in internal conflicts.

Islamist responses to Western interventions

A key aspect of interventionism in the post-9/11 world, is the growing US-led interventions and engagements in local conflict zones, militarily or otherwise in the Islamic world, in which the underlying motive is Western security interests and self-defence, not altruism and benign humanitarianism. Given the authoritarian character of many governments in this part of the world, these interventions have strengthened the sense of Western responsibility and complicity in repression, atrocities and abuses occurring in these zones of conflict. In recent years, armed conflicts in the Islamic world have occurred in a large number of countries and provinces, including Nigeria, Morocco, Algeria, Somalia, Sudan, Egypt, Lebanon, Yemen, Saudi Arabia, Palestine, Iraq, Kosovo, Bosnia-Herzegovina, Macedonia, south-eastern Turkey, Chechnya and Dagestan, Azerbaijan, Afghanistan, Uzbekistan, Tajikistan, Kashmir, Xinjiang, the southern Philippines and Indonesia. Many of these conflict zones have pitted Muslims against non-Muslims giving credence to Huntington's thesis of a 'clash of civilizations' and 'Islam's bloody borders'.[187]

This perception has been further reinforced in the age of increased peacekeeping and humanitarian interventionism, precisely because the very *selectivity of interventions* often has left Muslim populations to fend for themselves. Even if 'Muslim' Kosovo was eventually was saved by the 'Christian' NATO, the image of Western interventionism in the Muslim world was by then already shaped by Europe's inability to stop the slaughter of Muslims in Bosnia. A pattern of Western inaction over atrocities against Muslims undercut the credibility of the new discourse of humanitarian interventions: the West has done little to stop Russian atrocities in the Chechen wars, Israel's brutal counter-insurgency campaigns in the West Bank and Gaza, the massacres of civilians taking place under the noses of the French-supported secular junta in Algeria, Chinese actions against Muslim separatists in Xinjiang, India's heavy-handed 'war on terror' in Kashmir and the harsh Philippine counter-insurgency campaign in its Muslim provinces in Mindanao.

The perception of Western double standards with regards to humanitarian interventions has been further reinforced by the swift and tough international response vis-à-vis Indonesia and Sudan, both Muslim-majority states with rebellious non-Muslim minorities. Jakarta came under heavy international pressure to accept an Australian-led coalition force in East Timor, which in turn paved the way for East Timorese independence. At present, Khartoum is being subjected to considerable arm-twisting to accept a peacekeeping force in the Darfur region, and it has previously been pressured to accept a peace agreement with the SPLA-separatist guerrillas in the Christian-dominated southern part of the country. The apparent pattern of selectivity fuels radical Islamist ideologies, which portray today's humanitarian interventions as manifestations of Christian colonialist 'Crusader' ambitions. Forcing Indonesia to part with East Timor has often been described in Islamist literature as 'the tearing away of a limb from the Islamic nation' to create a Christian statelet, subservient to the West. Osama bin Laden made specific reference to his previous warnings to Australia to end its support for East Timor independence in an audio tape aired on the Arab television channel al-Jazeera in October 2002, only days after the Bali bombings where nearly 200 people were killed: 'We warned Australia before not to join in [the war] in Afghanistan, and [against] its despicable effort to separate East Timor. It ignored the warning until it woke up to the sounds of explosions in Bali. Its government falsely claimed that they [the Australians] were not targeted.'[188]

There is little doubt that the major powers continue to enjoy a much higher level of immunity against foreign interventions than smaller nations.[189] Even if the underlying cause is power politics, not religion, the relative absence of Islamic nations among the major powers will continue to disfavour Muslims. There are, for example, no Muslim countries in the G-8 group, or among the veto powers in the UN Security Council. Even if the council is expanded, it is far from certain that any of the Muslim regional powers, Pakistan, Indonesia, Turkey, Iran and Saudi Arabia, will qualify for a permanent seat, even if Muslims constitute nearly 20 per cent of the world's population.[190]

Hence, in view of this structural 'imbalance' in today's international order, international interventions will continue to be perceived as fundamentally biased; they assist rebellious non-Muslim minorities to dismember the Islamic nation but will not save Muslims under siege in a non-Muslim country. These perceptions will probably carry more weight in the future than today, as the revolution in communication and transportation and the rise of transnational identities constantly reinforce the perception of proximity and immediacy to conflict zones. It is likely to increase the prospects for violent activism against military interventions. The recent protest campaign by the Islamist Hizb al-Tahrir movement, which has an active presence throughout the world, against the US peacekeeping training programme and plans for a UN peacekeeping operation in Sudan underscores this point. Referring to the US role in mediating in the Sudanese civil war and its plans for training 75,000 African peacekeepers, Hizb al-Tahrir has little doubt about what the ultimate US plans are:

> they are, in reality, preparing for the invasion of Sudan. The outcome will be just as it was in Iraq where they spread corruption, tortured and frightened away thousands of Muslims, exploited the resources, disgraced mosques, destroyed houses, and abused prisoners with the most horrific and disgraceful physical treatment, and continue to do so.[191]

Even if UN peacekeeping has experienced a new renaissance by its extensive deployment in African conflict zones, there is a perception that humanitarianism has given way to hard security and that the Western world only gives priority to controversial NATO-led and US-led enforcement operations. In September 2000 an International Commission on Intervention and State Sovereignty (ICISS) was established by the government of Canada to respond to the challenge of forging consensus around the basic principles of when interventions should occur, under whose authority and how.[192] And yet, in the post-Iraqi era, any broad international consensus on the principles for intervention seems remote. Furthermore, the high level of violence in contemporary interventions undercut domestic political support in participants' home countries.

Presumed weaknesses in the intervening coalition due to policy differences between main participants are perhaps the coalition's most vulnerable points.[193] This vulnerability has not passed unnoticed. The multiple bombings of commuter trains in Madrid on 11 March 2004, killing 192 people and injuring more than 1,600, is a case in point. These terrorist attacks, which led to the Spanish decision to pull out of Iraq, prompting Honduras and El Salvador to follow suit, were specifically aimed at breaking the US-led coalition by targeting the country where domestic opposition to the Iraqi war was greatest. The timing of the attacks – just days ahead of the Spanish elections – was a deliberate attempt to influence the Spanish electorate, since the socialist party ran its election campaign on a foreign-policy decision to pull its forces out of Iraq (see Box 3.3).

Box 3.3 International military interventions and terrorism responses: the case of Madrid

The strategy of exploiting differences between the countries making up the Coalition force in Iraq, with a view to breaking the alliance and undermining US will to stay on in Iraq, was outlined in great detail in an al-Qaida document uncovered by this author on a radical Islamist web site in December 2003.[1] Dedicated to the well-known Saudi al-Qaida communicator Shaykh Yusuf al-Ayiri and addressing an audience of international jihadist militants, the document highlighted the military, political and economic weaknesses of the US-led Coalition, ranging from the skyrocketing financial costs and mounting human casualties to the growing domestic opposition to the war. Written in a mostly secular-style 'strategic studies' genre and mixed with jihadist rhetoric, the document analysed various options for the jihadist movement, emphasising that the outcome of the battle over Iraq will be decisive for the future of the jihadist movement. A victory in Iraq will provide the jihadists with 'an advanced base' close to the heartland of Islam in Mecca, Media and Jerusalem, while a US military victory 'will hurt the Islamic renaissance in the entire region, at the heart of the Islamic world'.[2] It provided specific policy advice for the jihadist movement in Iraq such as striking at oil installations and establishing jihadist fighting cells in the Shiite-dominated south.

As for the Coalition partners, the document gave a detailed analysis of domestic politics in the three major Coalition partners, the United Kingdom, Poland and Spain. Poland was considered unlikely to withdraw from the Coalition because of its political consensus on foreign policy and its alleged high tolerance for human casualties, while the United Kingdom was deemed somewhat easier to force out, due to the popular opposition to the war and the occupation. However, the author believed that Britain would only withdraw from Iraq in one of two cases: 'if Britain suffers huge human casualties in Iraq or if forces of other countries, such as Spain and Italy are withdrawn'.[3] Spain on the other hand was judged to be very vulnerable to attacks, primarily because of domestic opposition to the war. The author therefore identified Spain as the weakest link in the Coalition:

'Therefore we say that in order to force the Spanish government to withdraw from Iraq the resistance should deal painful blows to its [i.e. the Spanish] forces. This should be accompanied by an information campaign clarifying the truth of the matter inside Iraq. It is necessary to make utmost use of the upcoming general election in Spain in March next year. We think that the Spanish government could not tolerate more than two, maximum three blows, after which it will be forced to withdraw as a result of popular pressure. If its troops still remain in Iraq after these blows, then the victory of the socialist party is almost guaranteed, and the withdrawal of the Spanish forces will be on its electoral programme. Lastly, we are convinced that a withdrawal of the Spanish or Italian forces from Iraq will put huge pressure on the British presence [in Iraq], a pressure that Tony Blair might not be able to withstand. In this way, the domino tiles would fall quickly, but the basic problem of making the first tile fall still remains.'[4]

Notes

[1] The full Arabic title is Iraq al-Jihad – Amal wa Akhtar: Tahlil al-Waqi' wa Istishraf lil-Mustaqbal wa Khatawat Amaliyyah ala Tariq al-Jihad al-Mubarak [Jihadi Iraq – Hopes and Risks: Analysis of the Reality, Overview of the Future and Practical Steps on the Way of the Blessed Jihad]. The Arabic original is available on <http://www. mil.no/multimedia/archive/ 00038/_jihadi_iraq_hopes_38063a.pdf>. An analysis of the document and its importance in given in Brynjar Lia, and Thomas Hegghammer, 'Jihadi Strategic Studies: The Alleged al-Qaida Policy Study Preceding the Madrid Bombings', *Studies in Conflict and Terrorism* 27 (5) (September-October 2004), pp. 355–75. See also Jay Tolson, 'Cracking al Qaeda's Code', *U.S. News and World Report* 17 May 2004.

[2] Iraq al-Jihad, p. 2.

[3] ibid., p. 28. (The passage is underlined and in bold types in the Arabic original.)

[4] ibid., p. 33. (The passage is underlined and in bold types in the Arabic original.)

Implications for terrorism

The effects of greater international interventionism in violent conflicts on the occurrence of terrorism are complex. International terrorism has often been a by-product of protracted armed conflicts, which have been left to fester for years or even decades. By improving its ability to reduce and mitigate armed conflicts, the international community may prevent them from becoming important new sources of transnational terrorism. One good example of this is the Balkan wars during the 1990s, which generated very few significant incidents of transnational terrorism. There were several 'protest attacks', however, such as a hijacking episode by a Bosnian refugee in Norway in 1994, demanding that European governments paid more attention to the siege of Sarajevo and Bihac.[194] The potential for much more widespread terrorist attacks was probably there, if Western governments had not taken as firm action as they finally did in Bosnia and later in Kosovo. In 1994 many analysts warned that the likelihood of terrorist attacks in Europe would increase significantly if the plight of the Bosnian Muslims was not resolved. The theme was that 'another Palestinian disaster' was about to happen in the European heartland with severe long-term consequences.[195] One also feared the emergence of an Iranian-supported irredentist and possibly fundamentalist Bosnian mini-state in the Balkans. The forceful intervention of NATO in 1995 and the subsequent long-term commitment of Europe and the United States to resolve the conflict in the Balkans probably prevented such an outcome.

Despite a possible long-term inhibitive effect of peacekeeping interventions, there are several reasons why terrorism may indeed increase in the short run as a result of more muscular peacekeeping operations. Stedman's thesis on spoiler problems in peace processes, theories on democratisation and terrorism as well as theories on terrorism and state legitimacy all strongly suggest that terrorism tends to increase in times of societal upheaval and transition.[196] Furthermore, foreign military interventions, including those which are multilateral and bestowed with UN mandates, often trigger violent counter-responses, in which terrorism is used as a tactic both in the conflict area and outside. For example, the level of domestic terrorism in Europe increased during the Gulf war in 1991.[197] A recent study of five US-led multilateral interventions between 1982 and 2003 shows that all interventions triggered out-of-theatre terrorist attacks against the Coalition partners. Furthermore, the scope and lethality of the attacks have increased over time, making the war in Iraq the worst case to date.[198] We should therefore expect many new incidents of transnational terrorism as Western countries increase their military involvement in distant wars. If these engagements are successful in consolidating peace settlements, the long-term effect of some of these operations is likely to be lower levels of terrorism. This positive net effect is going to be offset, however, by a significant number of terrorist attacks directed against future peacekeeping or military interventions in the Islamic world, in which Western countries are likely to be involved. Due to the current power structure of the international system, there is a tendency that Muslim nations are more likely to be pressured to accept peacekeeping interventions than non-Muslim powers with large Muslim minorities. This regrettable fact will continue to fuel jihadist ideologies, which propagate that the Islamic nation is under siege and a war must be launched on the 'Crusaders'.

Trends in multilateralism

Postulate: Multilateral institutions, international treaties and regimes will play an increasingly more important role in regulating relations between states as well as internal politics inside states.

Possible implications for terrorism: The attractiveness of international terrorism as a foreign-policy tool will be reduced. Furthermore, the opportunity structure for transnational terrorism will diminish, as states and multilateral institutions move towards closer counter-terrorism co-operation. These gains may be reduced, however, by unintended consequences of greater economic and political integration.

The international system as anarchy has been the dominant view in the writings of Waltz, Mearsheimer and other classic realist works in the international-relations literature. Anarchy, the struggle for power and relative gains are the most important features in the realist approach to international relations. The realist school has been much criticised for underestimating the significance of multilateral institutions, international regimes and international treaties in contemporary international politics. These international arrangements modify the ways in which states relate to each other. They provide 'persistent and connected sets of rules (formal and informal) that prescribe behavioural roles, constrain activity, and shape expectations'.[199]

Europe is a prime example of the inadequacy of the realist school. The prevailing tendency in present-day Europe is not anarchy but hierarchy where relations between states have been domesticated through an expanding web of multilateral institutions and co-operative arrangements. Europe has moved towards a system of institutions and highly regulated treaties on how states, firms and persons shall relate to each other. The result has been a more 'universal type of system', with common policies in an increasing number of key areas in which governments have previously been very reluctant to relinquish full control.[200] European security and defence policy is increasingly based upon integration among states, which indicates a progressive 'Europeanisation' of European security. The very concept of 'national security' is being modified by the concept of 'European security'. This progressive integration, incorporating now twenty-five states, is set to continue despite the disagreements over the Iraqi war and a greater diversity among the member states.

Integration through multilateral institutions will probably continue to grow in importance not only in Europe, including central and eastern Europe, but also other parts of the world. The European model has already many parallels on other continents, albeit with less ambitious integration schemes. ASEAN, formed in 1967 by Indonesia, Malaysia, the Philippines, Singapore and Thailand, has moved from economic co-operation to greater emphasis on regional security issues. Its membership has gradually expanded to ten countries, including Myanmar, Brunei, Laos, Vietnam and Cambodia, while the ASEAN Regional Forum also includes China, India, Japan, Mongolia, South Korea, North Korea, Papua New Guinea, Russia, Australia, New Zealand, Canada, the EU and the USA.

Other examples are the North American Free Trade Agreement (NAFTA), signed in 1992 by the governments of Canada, the United States and Mexico; the South Asian Association for Regional Co-operation (SAARC), established in 1985 by Bangladesh, Bhutan, India, the Maldives, Nepal, Pakistan and Sri Lanka; and the South African Development Community (SADC), formed in 1992, comprising Angola, Botswana, DRC, Lesotho, Malawi, Mauritius, Mozambique, Namibia, the Seychelles, South Africa, Swaziland, Tanzania, Zambia and Zimbabwe.

Various problems have hampered regional integration efforts. The North African Arab Maghreb Union (AMU), created in 1989, has been hamstrung by the conflict over Western Sahara, political unrest in Algeria and the international embargo against Libya. Still, it has scored progress in substantially increasing economic trade between member states.[201] In Africa, efforts at regional economic integration have a long history, back to the early twentieth century. Today there are approximately ten regional economic groupings in Africa, while attempts at establishing continent-wide organisations culminated with the formation of the African Economic Community treaty (or the Abuja treaty) in 1991, entering into force in 1994. These integration schemes have not been an unqualified success. Still, a recent study has observed that 'there seems to be a new momentum to invigorate the process of integration of African economies'.[202] Many developing countries have long been under pressure from the Bretton Woods institutions to liberalise trade. The formation and the strengthening of regional blocks in other parts of the world have also created a new sense of urgency about moving towards regional integration. Further economic integration is expected on a regional as well as a global level. In a 1997 report, the OECD predicted that 'there would be a deepening and widening of economic integration among all economies [. . .] trade would rise from 30 per cent of world GDP today to almost 50 per cent in 2020, stimulating growth in all countries'.[203]

The expansion of regimes and international regulations is motivated largely by the intensification of economic interdependence. Globally, economic regimes and regulations have made significant advances. The former free-trade regime, the General Agreement on Tariffs and Trade (GATT), signed in 1947, initially included only some twenty states. It was subsequently superseded by the World Trade Organisation (WTO), which has a membership of more than 130 states. After China's entry into the WTO, the organisation encompasses virtually the entire world economy. As a symbol of economic globalisation, WTO meetings have become the focal point of protest for a broad multifaceted anti-globalisation movement with a number of militant elements. Even if some commentators fear that an emerging north–south rift in the WTO will reduce the organisation to irrelevance, others have hailed the recent WTO meeting in Cancun as 'one of the most successful international meetings in years because it redefined how trade can benefit the poor and how the developing world can be real players in these negotiations'.[204]

Also in the field of political and military affairs, multilateral institutions have come to play an increasingly important role. True, the UN Security Council has often been hamstrung by disagreements between member states, in particular the veto powers. Nevertheless, as the previous section illustrated, the growth in peacekeeping and humanitarian interventions over the past decades both in terms of participants, the scope of the missions and their overall cost, suggests that there is a trend towards increased multilateralism in global security issues also. To a significant extent – though not exclusively, the USA is likely to conduct foreign policy through multilateral institutions. There has been a strong unilateralist tendency in American foreign policy during the past years, illustrated by recent events like the non-ratification of the Comprehensive Test-Ban Treaty (CTB), the non-participation in the International Criminal Court (ICC) and the launching of the Iraqi war without a UN mandate. These steps have provoked forceful responses, however. There have been intense and massive international protests against the most explicit manifestations of US unilateralism, in particular the Iraqi war. The anti-war protest campaigns in 2003 were joined by tens of millions of people worldwide, including tens of thousands in the USA itself. It also deeply impacted on important transatlantic relations. Some of its closest allies in Europe, Germany and Turkey turned their backs on the USA at this critical juncture. The Iraqi war also threatened to unravel important anti-terrorism co-operative arrangements, which the USA succeeded in establishing following 9/11.

The global responses to the Iraqi war highlighted the high political costs of a strongly unilateralist policy and the growing ideational basis for a multilateralist model for global governance. The USA is knitted into the global international economy in such a way that it cannot control the international system alone. Its dependence on allies for sharing the burden of policing the world was underscored during the aftermath of 9/11 and the staggering costs of ruling and rebuilding Iraq. These developments indicate that the USA will have to put more efforts and resources into managing international challenges through multilateral institutions and regimes and into coalition with other states. Even if the US administration will continue to threaten to 'go it alone' if it feels its security threatened, the lessons of Iraq will not be forgotten.

The US hegemony and unilateralist policies have created an important impetus for strengthening multilateralist institutions worldwide and investing them with new security tasks. Regional great powers feel constrained by the US exercise of power and seek counterweights in regional institutions and alliances. China is a case in point. Since the late 1980s, the People's Republic of China has increased its participation and profile in multilateral security processes, viewing multilateralism 'as a proven technique [. . .] to enhance its own security and temper US influence while soothing smaller neighbours' concerns'.[205] In 1996 China took part in launching the 'Shanghai process' for co-operation and confidence-building in central Asia together with Russia. This initiative became institutionalised as the Shanghai Co-operation Organisation (SCO) in 2001. The SCO comprises China, Kazakhstan, Kyrgyzstan, Russia, Tajikistan and Uzbekistan, and involves co-operation against terrorism, joint military exercises, etc. China has also agreed to give the ASEAN Regional Forum a security dimension; it has sought formal dialogues with NATO and the EU and has also promoted multilateral processes to deal with specific regional security issues, the North Korean nuclear programme particular.[206]

Implications for terrorism

While there is no theory linking multilateralism directly to the prevalence of terrorism, literature on state sponsorship of terrorism and the impacts of hegemony and bipolarity on international terrorism provide some answers. State sponsorship becomes less useful and more costly in a world dominated by multilateralist organisations, especially if there is a hegemonic power to enforce sanctions against state sponsors. This was the situation following the end of the Cold War, and the successful application of sanction regimes against Libya and Sudan forced these countries to comply with international demands to cease offering support and sanctuary to terrorist organisations. Increased dependence on multinational organisations for trade and other co-operative arrangements will also reduce the attractiveness of international terrorism as a foreign-policy tool. As an increasing number of the global and regional organisations expand their co-operative arrangements to the field of security, law enforcement and anti-terrorism, the opportunity structure of transnational terrorism will diminish. Nearly all of the dominant multilateral organisations based in the Western world, the UN, NATO, EU, OSCE and G8, have made anti-terrorism a key policy objective. In the post-9/11 era, the UN has greatly broadened its activities in the field of counter-terrorism through the establishment of the Counter-Terrorism Committee (CTC) where it wields considerable power through its continuous monitoring and assessment of member states' compliance with the United Nations Security Council (UNSC) resolution 1373. The resolution has a far broader scope than any previous UN anti-terrorism resolution, ranging from domestic legislation and internal executive machinery to international co-operation.[207] Many other regional organisations have also sought to make a greater contribution in the field of anti-terrorism and implement more effectively the numerous existing conventions for combating terrorism.[208]

It is possible that the trend towards greater multilateral co-operation and integration may not be very effective in countering terrorism. Even if expanded anti-terrorism co-operation clearly will reduce the threat level, greater economic and political integration, which inevitably means less border-control, more flow of persons and goods across borders, etc. also makes terrorism prevention more difficult. As multilateral institutions tend to foster increased co-operation through liberalisation, economic transaction and freer movement of people and goods, they inadvertently create new opportunities for transnational terrorists operating across national borders. The EU experience illustrates that there is an immense time lag between the early stages of economic integration and the achievement of real and effect-ive co-operation on foreign-policy issues, let alone sensitive internal-security issues. In the field of anti-terrorism co-operation, especially in the field of intelligence-sharing, the obstacles to effective co-operation are formidable, even among close allies. Although there has been a growing awareness of the importance of such co-operation and a significant institutional progress in this field over the past years, many counter-terrorism officials continue to complain about vital information not being shared.[209] Sensitive intelligence is shared mostly via bilateral channels while multinational institutions are seen as too unreliable for such sensitive matters. Hence, multilateral organisations do not yet play a key role in certain key anti-terrorism areas.

The proliferation of non-governmental organisations

Postulate: International non-governmental organisations (INGOs) and other transnational non-state interest groups will continue to grow in numbers, and their importance in international politics might also increase.

Possible implications for terrorism: The existence of a large number of poorly regulated INGOs in many countries, especially in civil-war zones, greatly expands the opportunity structure for transnational terrorism by facilitating financing, logistics, propaganda efforts and recruitment of fighters, as well as by expanding the ideational basis for transnational expressions of protest and resistance. On the other hand, the growing NGO community may con-tribute to diminishing the prospects for revolutionary terrorism by providing a powerful alternative channel for advocating rights and voicing peaceful protest.

As discussed in several studies, INGOs may have a facilitating effect on terrorism, in terms of providing support networks for insurgent groups and transnational terrorists. For example, a long list of Islamic NGOs, mostly charities, figures as terrorist or terrorism-supporting entities on the US Treasury Department among the 374 individuals and entities, which were designated (by June 2004) under the President Bush Executive Order aimed at freezing the assets of terrorists and their supporters after 9/11. According to one study, as many as 'one-fifth of all Islamic NGOs worldwide have been unwittingly infiltrated by al-Qaida and other terrorist support groups'.[210] On a more general level, INGOs expand the ideational basis for transnational expression of protest and resistance by linking local grievances to global injustices. INGOs are 'primary institutional carriers and diffusers of world cultural models', and constitute an important international infrastructure for non-state groups working to change the status quo.[211] The evolution of the NGO community is therefore a possible determinant for future trends in terrorism.

It is increasingly acknowledged that global politics can no longer be ana-lysed from only a state-centric point of view and that non-state actors play an increasingly important role in a number of areas. These include legal non-state actors such as multi-billion dollar transnational companies, the expanding business of private-security companies and a plethora of non-profit NGOs, as well as illegal organisations such as organised criminal net-works, transnational terrorists and national guerrilla movements.[212] The word 'transnational' has been coined by academics in order to illustrate that 'international relations are not limited to governments'.[213]

Several of these non-state actors are growing in importance, the NGOs in particular. NGOs can be defined as 'privately organised and privately financed agencies, formed to perform some philanthropic or other worth-while task in response to a need that the organisers think is not adequately addressed by the public, governmental or United Nations efforts'.[214] NGOs frequently focus their work on issues beyond the borders of their country, such as alleviating human suffering and philanthropic work in Third World countries. Many INGOs are involved in humanitarian emergency aid, long-term social and economic development in the Third World, promoting and monitoring respect for fundamental human rights, peace-building activities (reconciliation, negotiation techniques, conflict settlement, non-violence, etc.) and support for liberation movements, oppressed groups and minorities.[215]

Over the past fifteen years, there has been a remarkable increase in the num-ber and size of NGOs. According to one study, the number of large INGOs has grown steadily from 469 in 1971 to 893 in 1990 to 1,995 in 2000, which is more than 100 per cent increase in ten years![216] Using other criteria of clas-sification, another study found a total of 37,281 INGOs in 2000, which was a 19.3 per cent increase since 1990.[217] Judging by these numbers, INGOs are not only growing quickly in numbers. They are also growing in size. One of the reasons for this is probably that both Western and non-Western development funds and humanitarian aid increasingly flow through NGOs.[218]

The example of the International Campaign to Ban Landmines (ICBL) highlights the new-found effectiveness of networking NGO activists in mobilising a global opinion and forcing the great powers to change their policies. The growing importance of NGOs in global politics can also be illustrated by the fact that NGOs, particularly trade unions and campaigning groups in the fields of human rights, women's rights and the environment, have their membership measured in millions, whereas thirty-seven countries in the world have populations of less than one million. The expanded role of the NGO community is nevertheless largely contingent upon the benefits that Western states derive from their activities, primarily in terms of foreign-aid policy. Notwithstanding the term '*non-governmental*' organisation, much NGO funding, especially in the relief and development sector, still originates from the budgets of Western governments. Despite persistent claims that NGOs reflect only a tiny segment of the populations of their members' states, and that they represent only mostly developed countries,[219] there has been a tremendous proliferation of NGOs in the Third World too. Many of these NGOs are locally funded. Egypt, the most populous Arab country, claims an estimated 17,000 NGOs, according to official newspapers.[220] In Jordan, the number of NGOs has also increased significantly from sixty-two in 1960 to over 750 in 1997. In Latin America, the number of NGOs 'exploded onto the scene in the mid-1980s' when a dual political-economic transformation led to a retreat of the state and paved the way for foreign-funded development aid through NGOs.[221] The growth of NGOs has been far slower in states with limited democracy and an ever-present state, such as Mexico under the Partido Revolucionario Institucional (PRI) one-party rule, which lasted until 2000. The Mexican government played a very strong role in upholding welfare and public services, particularly among the most disadvantaged sectors.[222]

The expansion of NGOs in the developing world is rooted in the shift towards the liberal economic-development model, the weakening of state capacities in the face of the mounting challenges of modernisation, exposing their shortcomings in providing welfare and services for the population. Robert Milano predicts a growing need for such organisations: 'As poverty trends show no signs of decrease in the decades to come, and governments lack the capacity to ensure their citizens' basic rights and services; there will be an increasing need to turn to organizations outside the state for alternative solutions in the provision of social services.'[223]

The NGO-sector is characterised by an increasing diversity, but their involvement in humanitarian work in conflict areas is perhaps their most visible and controversial engagement. Compared to UN humanitarian organisations, the NGO contribution today is much larger than some fifteen years ago. During the 1990s, a large number of NGOs have been present and active in the field in conflict zones alongside international peacekeepers. In Kigali in 1994, some 175 international NGOs operated, while there were 200 in Zagreb, 200 in Mozambique and 600 in Bosnia-Herzegovina in the autumn of 1997.[224] By 2003 the number of NGOs in war-torn Afghanistan had grown to an estimated 500, and 150 of these were considered 'internationally-based NGOs with credible mechanisms for delivering humanitarian assistance'.[225]

Implications for terrorism

In principle, there are at least three relevant effects of the transnational community of NGOs and advocacy groups with regard to the occurrence of terrorism. Theories of democratisation, state legitimacy and terrorism provide a strong argument that integration problems and the lack of channels for political expression available to disaffected groups tend to encourage terrorism, in particular ideological terrorism. In this light, NGOs, especially the various advocacy groups, constitute a powerful mouthpiece for disaffected groups and represents a valuable alternative channel for voicing political and economic grievances, which may otherwise have produced political violence. NGOs are also believed to play an increasingly important role in conflict settlements, thereby undermining some of the driving factors behind transnational terrorism.[226] Hence, the existence of a vibrant NGO community may indeed contribute to diminishing the prospects for revolutionary terrorism. The role of INGOs in voicing the cause of the Indian Chiapas during the mid- and late 1990s played a key role in prodding the Ejército Zapatista de Liberación Nacional (EZLN) 'Zapatista' guerrilla uprising in 1994 towards a political dialogue, and turning the initially Marxist–Maoist inspired rebels towards non-violent political activism focused on demands for improved indigenous rights.[227]

On the other hand, there are several examples of single-issue and ideological terrorist groups growing out of a radicalised activist community around one or several NGOs. Advocacy groups have also served as front organisations and auxiliaries for guerrilla and terrorist organisations. During the Intifada, for example, the Palestinian Prisoners' Welfare Association was widely seen as a PLO/Fatah-controlled institution, and shortly after the signing of the Oslo peace accord in September 1993, their offices were turned into local PLO headquarters in the Occupied Territories.[228] A number of Australian government-funded NGOs were closely involved with liberation movements in the Indonesian provinces of Aceh and West Papua, causing serious rifts between the two countries' governments in 2002.[229] Norwegian People's Aid has repeatedly incurred criticism for its very close co-operation with the South Sudanese guerrilla movement SPLA.[230]

Over the past years, INGOs and charitable organisations, especially Islamic charities, have recently come under scrutiny following a number of investigations of terrorist financing through INGOs. There have been many examples of INGOs acting as front organisations or as advocacy groups for groups defined as terrorist by the United States. This should not come as a surprise. It is exactly the action-oriented transnational network model of INGOs, which has proved so useful for the new jihadist organisations and their support networks during the recent decade.[231] Many jihadist groups have nurtured close links with the growing number of Islamic INGOs. Al-Qaida, in particular, has used such organisations for multiple purposes, from fund-raising and fund transfers to logistical support purposes. For example, al-Qaida used the International Islamic Relief Organisation (IIRO) as an instrument to funnel money to its affiliate groups in Asia, such as the Abu Sayyaf and the MILF.[232]

On a more general level, the proliferation of INGOs has enabled the spread of new transnational collective identities. This was the case of pan-Slavism in the nineteenth century, and pan-Indigenism in Latin America and pan-Islamism in the Islamic world today.[233] The linkages between disparate groups of leftist and Marxist movements during the 1970s and 1980s were also forged through the works of various INGOs. These transnational links, built around a shared sense of trust, collective identity and, not least, a commitment to a radical internationalist ideology have been essential in transforming terrorism from a local to an international and transnational mode of action.

The extensive involvement of INGOs in conflict areas also contributes to establishing closer links between rebel groups and the outside world. Hence, the presence of INGOs in these areas may provide an institutional infrastructure for bringing funds, supplies, equipment, recruits, etc., to the rebels, while video footage of the horrors of war, martyr stories and war veterans are brought back. In many cases, a growing access to a worldwide NGO community, sympathetic to their causes but not their means of struggle, may well encourage some insurgent groups to pursue a political track and desist from engaging in international terrorism. In other cases, local civil wars provide opportunities for the mobilisation and recruitment for a war of transnational terrorism, exemplified by the international jihadist movements associated with al-Qaida. For these groups, the plethora of poorly regulated INGOs with branches all over the world has been a very useful instrument in their war. A recent Rand study on external support for insurgencies argues that diasporas whose political organisations are usually centred around various local and international NGOs 'may become more important in the future' since insurgent groups view them as more reliable and less controlling than states.[234]

Hence, it is not a question of whether NGOs are a much-needed mouthpiece for disaffected groups or a front organisation for terrorists. They are obviously both. The mouthpiece function is perhaps less measurable and will in many cases only have a long-term effect via conflict prevention and via the promotion of non-violence as the preferred form of activism. The front-organisation effect, however, is more immediate and direct, although it might be reduced over time as regulations and anti-terrorism measures are tightened. Hence, the expected expansion of INGOs in the future will have an ambiguous impact on patterns of transnational terrorism. Despite the admirable work done by the overwhelming majority of the world's INGOs, transnational terrorist networks will probably benefit considerably from their future expansion.

4

THE GLOBAL MARKET
ECONOMY

> The 11 September raid marked the beginning of the collapse of the US empire. These strikes proved that the foundation of US power is fragile. The economy, which is the most important part of the foundation, is based on usury, fraud, and consumerist avarice. When these ebb, the economy suffers. [...] the US economy's losses in the airline transportation sector alone after the attacks reached $100 billion and led to the loss of some 100,000 jobs. All told, total losses came to $1 trillion.[1]
>
> (Al-Qaida propagandist Abu Ubayd al-Qirshi, August 2002)

Even if terrorism is often seen as a distorted response to present or past grievances of a political nature, socio-economic factors are far from irrelevant. Indeed, a great number of terrorist organisations have seen their struggle as part of a global struggle against an economic system, capitalism, whose inherent dynamics caused the oppression of the masses and the dispossession and colonisation of the Third World. During the heyday of Marxist–Maoist inspired terrorist groups in the 1970s, economic interests, such as corporate banks and transnational companies, were often considered important and legitimate targets. Big business became the victim of leftist terrorism *inter alia* due to its alleged imperialist and exploitative role in the Third World. The Weather Underground in the USA, for example, targeted the AT&T Company in the 1970s for its alleged involvement in the US-supported military coup against the Allende government in Chile.

Today, the al-Qaida network has declared US and Western economic targets a priority, acting on the premise that the US economy is the mainstay of its military power. Pro-al-Qaida jihadist magazines have extolled the destruction of the World Trade Center (WTC) on 11 September, 2001 by listing trillion-dollar estimates of the overall economic losses suffered by the United States due to the attacks.[2] The suicide-bombing of the French-owned *Limbourg* oil tanker in October 2002 was justified by the need to cut 'the umbilical cord and lifeline of the Crusader community'.[3] Similarly, the hostage-takings and massacres of residents of a foreign housing compound in the northern Saudi port city of Khobar in late May 2004 were part of the campaign to drive foreigners out of the peninsula and cause a collapse of Saudi oil exports.[4] US financial centres such as the Prudential building in Newark, the New York Stock Exchange, the Citigroup building in Manhattan and the International Monetary Fund headquarters in Washington were also meant to be targeted by the al-Qaida network, judging by the reconnaissance reports found in the possession of al-Qaida suspect Dhiren Barot in 2004.[5]

None of this is to say that the economy is the sole issue of concern but instead that economic considerations have played and continue to play an important role in facilitating and motivating terrorist operations. Similarly, one finds that socio-economic conditions on local, national and international levels appear to have an impact on violent conflicts of which terrorism is a part.[6] Väyrynen reminds us that '[c]ollective violence is, almost by definition, embedded in social and economic structures'.[7] Poverty is an important context for violent conflicts, as well as for terrorism, especially in combination with other aggravating factors.[8] High levels of socio-economic inequality also tend to promote ideological terrorism, in particular when inequalities are not only vertical, but also horizontal, involving systematic discrimination of culturally distinct groups. All in all, economic conditions do have an impact on terrorism, and one may learn more about the future of terrorism by studying how certain key economic parameters are expected to change.

In this chapter, I will review future patterns of income inequality, future trends in the power relationship between politics and big business, trends in transnational organised crime and, finally, the future of Middle East oil dependency. The main objective is to identify whether the future holds significant changes with respect to factors known to influence patterns of terrorism.

Trends in economic inequality

Postulate: Socio-economic inequalities inside states will remain or become larger. Inequality between rich and poor countries is likely to continue to grow. Disparities in wealth will become more visible, and in many Western countries, inequality patterns will have a more pronounced ethnic dimension.

Possible implications for terrorism: Persisting socio-economic inequalities may provide the basis for a resurgence of militant leftist anti-globalisation ideologies, which might translate into transnational terrorism. Domestically, increased inequalities are likely to generate more civil violence, possibly including terrorism, especially in conjunction with other aggravating factors, such as ethnic discrimination. The growing ethnic diasporas in the Western world will reinforce the 'horizontal' dimension of current inequality patterns. This is likely to become a more serious source of domestic as well as transnational terrorism.

One of the most characteristic features of the modern world is the enormous socio-economic inequality between and inside countries. The numbers are dramatic. A recent study observes that on a global level '1 per cent of the richest [population] have an income equal to that of 57 per cent of the poorest', which means that 'less than 50 million of the rich receive as much as do 2.7 billion of the poor'.[9] A UN report using a three-tier system, where the upper 20 per cent are defined as the 'rich' countries, 'middle-income countries' are the middle 60 per cent and 'poor' countries make up the bottom 20 per cent, finds similar results: the upper tier accounts for 86 per cent of the world's GDP, while middle-income countries account for only 13 per cent, and the poorest tier only represents 1 per cent.[10] This inequality is not only a moral issue: it also brings with it a host of security-related problems, including illegal migration, organised crime and political instability.[11] Furthermore, wealth disparities of this magnitude will have greater and greater repercussions in an interwoven world where isolation and disengagement are no longer an option.

Apart from the first half of the twentieth century, when income inequality within states experienced an average decline, wealth disparities have grown steadily since the nineteenth century. A study by Bourguignon and Morrison, based on data for the period between 1820 and 1992, demonstrates that inequality between countries has grown considerably throughout the whole period, while in-country inequality has risen steadily since 1950. If in-country and between-country inequalities are measured together ('global inequality'), seeing the overall population in the world, one also finds a continuous rising trend throughout the two past centuries, but with a flat slightly oscillating curve for the first part of the twentieth century.[12] The relationship between intra- and international inequality trends is uncertain, but studies suggest that they are connected and tend to move together.[13]

There is little disagreement that the modern world has a history of growing inter-country inequalities. With regards to developments over the past three decades as well as for in-country inequalities, the trends are perhaps not as obvious or uncontested. Various methods of calculating inequality also yield different results.[14] Glenn Firebaugh and others have measured 'global inequality' by weighting countries based on their population size, and by using income adjusted for purchasing-power parity. They find that 'income inequality across nations peaked sometime around 1970 and has been declining since'.[15] The validity of these findings is contested, however.[16]

Regional trends are also very different, with regards to both in-country and between-country inequality. As for the latter, there seems to be a mixed trend with some groups of countries coming closer to the mean income of the OECD countries, while others have fallen further behind. The South Asian and Pacific countries, in particular China, have greatly improved their record; so has India, but to a lesser extent, whereas sub-Saharan Africa worsened significantly. Latin America, the Caribbean and the Arab states performed much better but are still slowly falling behind the mean income of the OECD.[17] These regional trends will most probably not follow a linear development in the future but will evolve and change under the influence of a host of parameters. Dicken is probably correct in his description of the global economy as 'a mosaic of unevenness in a continuous state of flux'.[18]

As for in-country disparities in wealth, there is also a mixed record.[19] For example, between 1976 and 1996, Mexico experienced an increase in income inequality, while Brazil a decline. China, despite being a main contributor to reducing inequality between countries, has experienced a significant rise in economic inequalities internally, with a record high wealth gap between its 900 million peasants and its privileged urban citizens.[20] On the whole, however, countries in the South have a higher degree of in-country inequality than the OECD countries.

Predicting the future based on an extrapolation of current inequality trends is not simple, not least because of the uncertainties about past patterns, but also because regional trends vary a great deal. One possible avenue to greater insight into future developments is to examine the driving forces behind increased inequality. Various theories have been advanced. One point of departure is that rapid modernisation is often accompanied by increasing inequalities for a variety of reasons. Developing countries often embark on geographically located experimental pilot projects with a view to attracting foreign investment and industrial production for an export market. This process inevitably generates inequalities, as employees in these privileged zones, especially those employed in transnational corporations (TNCs), usually earn more than the average worker in traditional manufactural and agricultural sectors. China is a prime example. Enormous inequalities have emerged in Communist China, a state still ideologically committed to social equality and justice. This inequality is generated in part by the economic restructuring programmes, the loss of income security, including social programmes, and the establishment of privileged zones and developmental cities, while the rural population in the countryside falls behind.[21]

A more general explanation is that 'the very logic of capitalism does not favor social justice', and that economic globalisation is a 'formidable cause of inequality among and within states'.[22] Even if globalisation may well produce domestic trends conducive to inequality, state authorities have means to mitigate these, and often do so when they can, that is if the state is strong and the elites are non-predatory.[23] This is not always the case in many developing countries, to put it mildly. But even developing countries with good governments fail to uphold social welfare. Recent studies have shown that while the welfare state has demonstrated resilience in the face of globalisation in developed countries, this is not the case in less developed countries (LDCs). While the former have, for the most part, expanded welfare-spending and safety-net arrangements, the opposite has happened in the developing world, due to the weakness of labour unions in countries with large pools of low-skilled and surplus workers.[24] Growing inequality is therefore the result. Between-country inequality is also negatively affected because robust economic growth depends on a strong state that can enforce laws, and most developing countries have dysfunctional instutitions and weak state capacities.[25]

Globalisation advocates have argued that open economies benefit the poorest countries, because they lead to increased investments and trade, which in turn generate growth and development. Figures show that Foreign Direct Investment (FDI) has almost tripled in the period 1981–96.[26] However, only 1 per cent of FDI goes to the forty-eight LDCs, which increasingly fall outside of the pathway of capital flows.[27] The LDCs also fail to derive benefits from the liberalisation of global trade. The linkage between trade and economic growth is much weaker in these states than in more advanced developing countries. In fact, export expansion tends to be associated with 'an exclusionary form' of economic growth, as well as with 'civil conflicts' in some of the poorest countries.[28] For this reason, it remains true what is often said about globalisation: it continues to leave considerable parts of the world comparatively unaffected.[29] And precisely for this reason, it is often predicted that 'a further polarisation is a more likely scenario, compared to a scenario where poor states are able to kick-start their economies and leapfrog the stages that developed states went through'.[30] The UN notes in its 2004 report on LDCs that judging by past trends, 'the LDCs are likely to become the major locus of extreme poverty in the world economy by 2015'.[31]

Rising income inequality within states is also strengthened by differences in education and access to information, even if recent trends show a slight decline in inequality of education.[32] Manuel Castells, for example, argues that polarisation and inequalities are at the very heart of informational capitalism; its logic leaves entire populations and regions out of the loop of economic growth, rendering them unproductive and irrelevant.[33] This is the pessimistic perspective on modernisation in the digital age where the growing importance of technology, knowledge and expertise means that skilled labour will be relatively more important and well-paid than unskilled, causing not only further growth in the wage gaps between rich and poor, but also increased 'brain drain' in developing countries.[34] The current level of brain drain is already quite high, with losses of highly skilled persons of up to 30 per cent or more in some countries. It contributes significantly to the economy in the North, but less so in the South.[35] Similarly, the trend towards more mechanised, digitalised and robotic production modes, which are far less reliant on cheap labour, is likely to further marginalise the poorest countries.[36] An important trend in the global labour market is that it is 'increasingly integrated for the highly skilled' who are highly mobile and enjoy generous wages. With regards to unskilled labour, however, the global market is still very restricted by national barriers.[37]

Income inequality is not only a North–South phenomenon, but is an acknowledged societal problem in Western societies, too. In 2002, the USA had an official poverty rate of 12.1 per cent, which meant that 34.6 million people lived in poverty. Among these, black and Hispanic minorities, were overrepresented, with 24 and 22 per cent respectively. Since the late 1960s, the official poverty rate has oscillated between 10 and 15 per cent.[38] Other developed countries such as Canada, Germany and the United Kingdom had similar or only slightly lower poverty rates, 10–11 per cent on average during the early 1990s.[39] In Europe, social exclusion also has a socio-ethnic dimension, as immigrants from non-OECD countries are heavily over-represented in the statistics on poverty.[40] Studies of distributive implications of economic integration in Europe, based on the Spanish and Portuguese experiences, suggest that inequality increased after accession to the EU, despite measures to eradicate poverty and reduce income inequality: 'For new members of the EU an increased future polarisation of society can be predicted'.[41]

Emerging trends in Western labour markets may also provide hints about future inequality patterns. Internationalisation has implications for the labour market in that workers must adjust to company mobility and the pace of change. Technological development reinforces the trend towards less emphasis on the production of physical goods and more on information, services and non-repetitive tasks.[42] As a result, there will be a rising demand for highly skilled and specialised labour, resulting in a growing socio-economic distinction between different groups in society.

Another trend in the labour market, *individualisation*, will also impact negatively on income inequality by undermining labour unions. (There is much evidence that the well-organised labour movements have played a critical role in maintaining the growth of the welfare state in the West.[43]) The labour market is increasingly moving towards more flexible contractual forms of employment: it offers more part-time positions, short-term contracts, etc. More and more people become self-employed, by leaving their employers and pursuing independent careers as freelancers, consultants, independent contractors, owners of home-based businesses, etc.[44] According to Daniel Pink, the number of wholly or primarily self-employed in the United States stands at an estimated 30 million.[45] As a result of these flexible and individual arrangements, the picture will no longer be black and white with respect to whether a person is in or out of the workforce.[46] This suits businesses, as they will not have to make long-term hiring decisions in an economy that fluctuates to a greater degree and will thereby be able to maximise efficiency.

A consequence of this is a weakening of labour unions, which is likely to have long-term negative effects on income equality. The decline of labour unions is a trend in many post-industrial societies. One of the most extreme examples in Europe is the UK. The changing structure of the British economy, especially the decline of the old manufacturing industries like steel, coal, printing, the docks and engineering, in combination with a tougher competitive environment, have severely affected the trade unions, even if new public-sector unions have grown stronger. Trade-union membership has been reduced by nearly 50 per cent from 1980 to 2000. According to Richard Hyman at the LSE, being a union member 'has ceased to be the social norm' in the UK.[47] The influx of cheap foreign labour to many Western countries has also put labour unions on the defensive, while the threat of relocation has strengthened the hand of transnational corporations. Their decline is also the outcome of increased migration as foreign labour replaces national labour in an increasing number of professions and adds an ethnic dimension to the struggle between labour and capital. It is unlikely that an internationalisation of labour unions will be able to reverse the decline and provide cohesion in an increasingly fragmented, multifaceted and 'individualised' labour force. Even if a withering away of labour unions is unlikely, their decline will imply a loss of a powerful channel for addressing socio-economic grievances, since labour unions have traditionally been a key mediating force between state and society.[48]

For the legitimacy of the state, individualisation of the labour market also has an ambiguous effect. The social safety net will be less important to a number of workers, as they have more complex and more self-reliant arrangements. However, the safety net will be even more important to those social strata that are less able to adapt to the new economy. A more globalised market-oriented economy will continue to make inroads into state capacities to provide public goods and welfare. The net result will probably be a trend towards increased income inequality within states, also in the developed world.

A final point for consideration is future trends in horizontal inequalities. As alluded to above, immigration to developed countries has already created new inequality patterns that are no longer simply vertical.[49] In the West, immigrant populations from non-OECD countries have until now been over-represented among the poor. Since unemployment is a major source of poverty, discriminatory employment practices have fuelled social tensions and have been an important source of social unrest in Western societies over the past decades. This new horizontal dimension in inequality patterns in the West will probably impact on the propensity for political violence, too. There is a possibility that these effects will be mitigated by the growth of a middle class with an immigrant background in the West. The combination of continued influx of highly skilled persons from developing countries and a continued shift towards highly educated labour in the fast-growing private service sector have the potential of eventually creating broader social strata of wealthy ethnic minorities in the West. If this development is not limited to a few selected ethnic groups, it might reinforce the 'criss-cross' dimension in the horizontal inequality patterns and reduce the potential for violent conflict.

Implications for terrorism

In the public debate on terrorism and its causes, one has perhaps been too quick to dismiss the relevance of poverty and socio-economic inequality, following a widely cited 2002 World Bank study where any direct causal relationship was outright dismissed.[50] A number of studies demonstrate that poverty and inequality strongly predispose society for civil wars and violent conflicts, especially if inequality patterns also are 'horizontal', i.e. inequality among culturally defined groups.[51] Studies of terrorism patterns in Western Europe also find that the socio-economic inequality is significant in accounting for variations in levels of ideological terrorism.[52] In developing countries where state capacities are weak, poverty and socio-economic inequality have a serious effect on violent conflict patterns, where both grievance and greed motivations pave the way for insurgencies.

As for the overall effect of continued or greater income inequality on the occurrence of terrorism, it is reasonable to assume that those regions most affected by increasing in-country inequality rates will experience higher levels of terrorism. This trend will be more pronounced wherever vertical income inequality coincides with sharp cleavages of horizontal inequality. In developing countries, the trend towards open markets and increased flow of labour across national borders has the potential of consolidating new horizontal inequalities and new market minorities, similar to the Lebanese in west Africa and the Chinese in south-east Asia. In traditional clientalist economies, the rise of such market minorities is fraught with risks, especially if it causes rapid shifts in redistributive patterns.

There is less evidence that between-country income inequality fosters transnational terrorism, however. Students of scarcity and conflicts have sometimes suggested that underdeveloped countries might 'launch a war or terrorise rich countries, demanding a greater sharing of world wealth and resources'.[53] This seems unlikely, as the rise of religious terrorism during the 1990s has surpassed leftist ideologies in importance in transnational terrorism. However, the Soviet Communist era is gradually becoming distant history, and the leftist anti-globalisation discourse gains steadily more ground. Against this background, there is a chance that a deepening of current global inequality patterns might galvanise a new generation of leftist radicalism with terrorist groups on its fringes. The very visibility of global inequality will also gradually become greater with the steady advances of communication technologies.

There are several ways in which inequality patterns in the developed world might generate more propitious conditions for terrorism. The emerging poverty trends in Europe, for example, are characterised by persistent or deepening inequality caused by the integration of many new economies. In addition, there are new horizontal patterns of inequality as the growing immigrant population is overrepresented among the poor. This suggests an

103

emerging socio-economic basis for radicalism and terrorism. Moreover, the waning of labour unions, the individualisation of labour and the influx of foreign workers will probably have a similar effect.

Labour unions have usually a mediating and moderating influence on radical politics and, probably for this reason, one has found a negative correlation between the level of unionisation in west European societies and the occurrence of ideological terrorism.[54] As Ronaldo Munck has noted, labour unions have historically used strikes, public rallies and violence to further their cause, but new forms of non-violent protest have emerged during recent decades, from Band Aid concerts to consumer boycotts.[55] Munck therefore finds that 'urban guerrilla warfare, and popular insurrections have far weaker ideological resonance than two decades ago'.[56] While this is still true, it might well be changing judging from the G8 summit in Genoa in July 2001, where violent clashes between anti-globalisation activists and security forces resulted in one demonstrator, Carlo Guiliani, being shot dead by the police and widespread allegations of police brutality. Subsequently, a number of terrorist incidents occurred in the name of Guiliani in Italy, Spain and Greece.[57] There is the potential that Guiliani's killing or similar incidents in the future may have a radicalising effect on leftist movements in Europe, creating a basis for new terrorist organisations. The reappearance of the Red Brigades in Italy over the past years may also be a hint of what the future holds.[58] The new inequality patterns may also generate terrorism of other ideological colours. A possible scenario is that the combination of deepening levels of poverty and unemployment on the one hand and the emergence of one or several high-profile wealthy social strata based in the immigration communities on the other may give a new lease of life to racist, right wing, anti-immigration violence.

Militancy and radical politics are already visible in the immigrant communities in the form of support networks for overseas insurgencies and in the Europe-wide expansion of pro-al-Qaida jihadist networks.[59] It is likely that the emerging pattern of horizontal inequality in Europe, especially with regard to the growing Muslim diaspora, may cause a trend towards a more home-grown jihadism. The discovery of explosives and half a ton of ammonium nitrate fertiliser in a warehouse and the arrest of eight British men of Pakistani origin across and near London in late March 2004 raised fears that new home-grown jihadist groups were being formed, connected only via ideological allegiances to the Afghan–Arab movement and the al-Qaida network.[60]

A final point for consideration is the related theme of poverty and terrorism, and the possible impact of poverty eradication on terrorism. Poverty is a powerful explanatory factor to civil wars. For this reason, poor countries also tend to have higher levels of domestic terrorism, occurring as part of the civil-war-related violence, than have wealthier countries. It is therefore likely that poverty reduction may have a long-term positive effect in reducing the level of terrorism in some regions.[61] The inhibiting effect of this trend has certain caveats, however. Even in the unlikely scenario of tremendous progress in poverty eradication over the next decades, hundreds of millions of people will still live in abject poverty. Moreover, other conflict-generating factors, such as relative deprivation and sharp socio-economic inequalities, tend to increase in rapidly modernising societies. Modernisation, poverty reduction and the emergence of stronger states tend to cause a conflict transformation, in which civil wars and guerrilla insurgencies are replaced by urban terrorist campaigns by remaining armed elements. This is especially so in regions where problems of political legitimacy and ethno-nationalist grievances are deeply entrenched. Unfortunately, terrorism often tends to linger on after civil-war cessation.

Powerless politicians? Powerful businesses?

Postulate: The norm of market-orientation and privatisation will remain dominant for the foreseeable future. As a result, transnational corporations (TNCs) will expand in size and scope of activities across the globe. In many countries, private companies will offer an increasing range of security, police and military services and technologies.

Possible implications for terrorism: As business corporations expand globally, the opportunities for transnational terrorism to strike at high-profile business targets will increase since such targets will multiply and be present in a growing number of countries. By expanding their security- and military-related portfolios and engaging more directly in policing and military interventions, TNCs are likely to attract increased attention from local insurgents as well as transnational terrorists. Furthermore, the commercialisation of military- and security-related hardware and technologies will allow insurgents and transnational terrorists to increase their operational effectiveness and sophistication.

Terrorism has by definition an 'upward direction' (see Chapter 1). Terrorist violence aims at coercing and intimidating governments in a public theatrical battle with many audiences. As the principal carrier of political authority, state authorities are the main target, even when the victims are random civilian bystanders. It has long been common wisdom that the international system is no longer dominated simply by national governments, but that a range of non-state actors are also making a bid for power and influence. In Manuel Castells' words: 'the new power system is characterised by the plurality of sources of authority and power, the nation state being just one of these sources'.[62] What happens if the state is no longer seen as the ultimate source of power? Are governments still attractive targets for terrorism if their power is perceived as circumscribed, or at least diluted, by other powerful actors? Is the future of terrorism then a privatised war, where new centres of power are assaulted rather than the state? To address this issue, I examine the role of one of its prime contenders for political and economic power: the TNC. I also look specifically at the rise of private police and private military companies.

There are arguably many signs of erosion of state authority. One is the national economy. Whereas governments still exercise some control over cross-border trade, the deregulation of financial markets has meant that governments are no longer in a position to strongly influence cash flows. As McRae has noted, the 'rise of power of the financial markets, together with their increasingly international nature, has inevitably reduced the power of individual national governments'.[63] Another example is the trend towards privatisation, marketisation and outsourcing within a number of core state functions such as the provision of welfare, health care and public transportation. This trend has also made inroads into the very heart of the state, by a privatisation process in the domain of public security and national defence. Although governments usually retain a relatively larger influence on these areas through regulation and legislation, the very act of privatisation weakens the ideational basis for the state as the main provider of security and welfare.

The rise of transnational corporations

We will return to the privatisation of public security and national defence in a moment. Let us first consider the impact of TNCs, arguably one of the most explicit symbols of globalisation. Not only are most of the largest TNCs based in the USA, they are widely seen as American enterprises and hence as extensions of US global economic hegemony. By their very size and global reach they also defy the image of the state as the key decision-maker in economics. Their role has also become important as the privatisation of military capability opens up the possibility for quickly transforming financial resources to military power (see pp. 112–15).

Over the past decades, TNCs have played a leading role in the process of economic globalisation. This has increased the influence of TNCs and other business enterprises on the economies of most countries as well as on international economic relations.[64] By some accounts, they have gained 'historically unprecedented power in the political world-economy'.[65] They have expanded massively since the 1960s, with many of the major industrial manufacturers establishing overseas subsidiaries and operating in almost every major economic sector. The number of major TNCs operating globally was estimated at 7,200 in 1968, compared to 35,000, with nearly 147,000 subsidiaries, in 1990. By the turn of the century, this figure has risen to 45,000. Of these nearly 85 per cent were located in developed countries.[66] The global expansion of TNCs, the scale of their activities and the complexities of their transactions are said to have 'a major political impact' on the world economy as well as on the national economies of individual countries.[67] For example, during the financial crisis in Asia in 1997–8, many local corporations merged with or were taken over by TNCs, mainly because local companies lacked other sources of capital.[68]

Recent studies have cautioned about exaggerating the economic weight of TNCs in the world economy, noting that widely cited reports about fifty-one of the 100 largest economies in the world being TNCs, not states, were based on conceptually flawed methods of calculation.[69] Still, even with improved methods of comparison, one finds that a substantial number of TNCs have economic assets comparable to states.[70] In fact, according to a 2002 UNCTAD study, ranking states and TNCs based on GDP and value-added data respectively, found that Exxon ranked forty-fifth on the list, just next to Chile and Pakistan; the oil-rich regional power Nigeria ended up between DaimlerChrysler and General Electric, and Philip Morris was on a par with Tunisia, Slovakia and Guatemala.[71] In fact, the UNCTAD study found that as many as twenty-nine of the world's 100 largest economic entities were TNCs in 2000, while the remaining seventy-one were states. It also showed that the 100 largest TNCs had a higher growth rate in comparison to that of national economies since 1990. In terms of value-added activities, the TNCs accounted for 4.3 per cent of the world GDP in 2000, which was a 0.8 per cent increase from 1990.[72] Not everyone agrees that the relative importance of TNCs in the global economy is on the rise, however. De Grauwe and Camerman found that the economic size of TNCs relative to states 'has tended to decline somewhat during the last 20 years'.[73] Whatever their exact economic influence in the world economy, there is little doubt that the *perception* that omnipotent TNCs govern the world behind the scene continues to be a very powerful one.

TNCs and terrorism

There are several ways in which TNCs are seen to contribute to motivating and facilitating transnational terrorism. Radical movements across the ideological spectrum invariably perceive TNCs as one of the most prominent symbols of a US-led global and predatory capitalism, which must be fought at all costs. Left wing terrorist and guerrilla movements have been known to target TNCs frequently. For example, Italian and German left wing terrorists put top business leaders on their list of preferred targets, while Latin American urban guerrillas tended to prefer foreign corporate figures. Even the ethno-nationalist group ETA has put corporate executives on its death list, alongside Spanish government leaders, police, army and guardia civil.[74] As for transnational terrorism against US interests, one finds that most of these attacks have been aimed at American businesses overseas.[75]

Such attacks are not limited to leftist groups, but also increasingly to radical Islamist organisations. In the wake of 9/11, the fear of new waves of attacks on US businesses abroad increased, following a spate of attacks on McDonald's restaurants and other prominent US business symbols in Asia and the Middle East, mostly by Islamist radicals.[76] The multiple al-Qaida suicide-bombings of British-owned banks in Istanbul, as well as the spate of bombings, assassinations and even massacres of Western employees in Saudi Arabia in 2003 and 2004 illustrate how business interests have become key terrorist targets for radical Islamists. Al-Qaida's explicit emphasis on breaking the US military power by undermining the US economy also highlights its relative ideological closeness to previous left wing terrorism, despite the vast differences in their modus operandi.

Given terrorism's ideological and tactical preference for soft business targets, the proliferation of Western-owned TNC facilities in the developing world in general and in conflict zones in particular, will obviously create new opportunities for transnational terrorism by increasing the number of such targets. The question remains, however, whether the global expansion of TNCs represents a new development in terms of increasing the ideological motivation for targeting business interests. The TNCs have arguably long been an object of hate among radical groups as a symbol of the unholy alliances of imperialist powers and local capitalist elites. The image of unbridled turbo-capitalism spearheaded by greedy TNCs has been a staple in radical anti-imperialist rhetorics for decades.

As for the TNCs effect on civil-violence-promoting factors such as increased socio-economic inequality, poverty and weak states, the trends are not unequivocal. Cross-country studies from the 1960s and 1970s found that the TNCs' impact on national economies, especially with regard to economic growth and socio-economic inequality, were rather negative, at least in developing countries. Deliberately or not, the TNCs perpetuated the status quo and reduced the growth potential of their host states, exacerbated inequality and underdevelopment, rather than being catalysts of development and worldwide economic convergence. This thesis no longer necessarily holds, however. Recent research published in the *Journal of World-System Research* has not found similarly negative effects of TNC presence on economic growth and inequality over the past two decades. On the contrary, this research suggests instead that 'adequate countervailing state actions' have been able to arrest and overcome the negative and retarding effects that TNCs previously had in developing countries.[77]

This does not mean that TNC activities today are never harmful. The role of foreign oil companies in Angola, Nigeria, Azerbaijan and elsewhere has arguably contributed to sustaining corrupt and cleptocratic elites and assisted directly in prolonging civil wars. TNCs have undoubtedly become more visible and are often involved in emerging markets where human-rights abuses and corruption are rampant. Still, it is increasingly understood that irresponsible behaviour by TNCs must be dealt with, and that this can be done if governments act collectively.[78] TNCs are under closer scrutiny by a growing community of NGO watchdogs.[79] Recent years have witnessed a rise of networking activists organising effective protest campaigns against corporations. Their campaigns have inflicted significant business losses on a number of TNCs, including Shell, Nike, De Beers, Nestle and PepsiCo due to negative publicity. This has made corporate business more aware of the need to be more sensitive and responsive to public criticism.[80] Moreover, a variety of multilateral initiatives have been launched to increase corporate responsibility and limit the detrimental effects of TNCs in the developing world. For example, the UN has drafted a Code of Norms on the responsibilities of TNCs with regards to human rights.[81] The role and responsibilities of business corporations with regards to preventing armed conflicts and contributing to peace-building have also been put more forcefully on the policy agenda.[82]

The image of TNCs has suffered by the financial scandals in the United States, in particular the Enron and the WorldCom cases, which prompted the US Congress to pass the Sarbanes–Oxley Act, the hitherto 'most sweeping regulation of public corporations since the Great Depression'.[83] Similarly, the controversies surrounding the Halliburton Corporation and its subsidiaries in Iraq have added to the concerns about Western and in particular, US corporate politics.[84] Still, Western-based corporations are subject to less accountability in their investments in the developing world than at home.[85] There is a chance that the dominant norm of privatisation and market-oriented economy may in the long term undermine the progress that has been made in bringing TNCs under greater accountability. For example, the UN Center on Transnational Corporations, which previously has done important investigative work on the TNC activities,[86] has recently been demoted in the UN system and has had its work stifled by the USA, apparently on behalf of US-based TNCs.[87] On balance, however, the trends seem to suggest that TNC capitalism is not likely to aggravate civil conflicts in the future beyond what is already the case.

The worldwide expansion of TNCs does, however, contribute to locking national and local economies more closely into the global economy, and will expose local communities to the vicissitudes of foreign-investment policies, corporate strategies and their relationships with local corrupt politicians.[88] Hence, corruption scandals, severe economic downturns or societal maladies that can be attributed to Western corporate involvement in one way or another are likely to sustain or possible aggravate local anti-Western sentiments in many developing countries. Coupled with the rise of the anti-globalisation movement and their anti-corporate rhetoric, there is a potential for a rise in various forms of violent militancy targeting corporate interests.

Weak states provide a more permissive environment for transnational terrorism than strong states do. A key question would then be whether the rise of TNCs contributes to weakening the territorial state. The answer is 'yes and no'. With regards to economic decision-making, it is not clear that

TNCs have weakened states dramatically. It has been argued that TNCs have grown increasingly powerful, due to their immense accumulation of capital and their ability to shift investment from restrictive countries to more compliant host nations. Following a period of growing restrictiveness in the 1970s and 1980s, states have moved from wanting to control TNCs to wanting to attract them – often by providing a less restrictive environment than other countries. TNCs are attractive to states, because they bring with them technology, investments, job opportunities and access to international markets for export industries.[89] According to critics, governments are becoming powerless in the face of a globally mobile capital. Large TNCs possess political power through their ability to put pressure on and lobby foreign governments while evading government attempts to control financial flows, impose trade sanctions or regulate production. Business lobby groups blame fierce global competition and demand that governments pass legislation that favours their business interests and pursues a hands-off approach or risk businesses and jobs moving abroad. Some observers go so far as to argue that in many regards, it is 'beyond the powers of national governments to regulate these companies' and as a result of the TNCs, 'the sovereignty of most governments is significantly reduced'.[90]

This criticism was quite common during the 1990s. It is increasingly acknowledged, however, that states continue to remain the central player in the international economic system; the expansion of multilateral institutions and global trade frameworks have served to put the interests of states rather than of corporations on the top of the agenda.[91] There is no such thing as a truly anational corporation. TNCs are usually very nationally embedded. Despite their expensive investments in dozens of countries or more, and despite an intricate web of transnational activities, TNCs are – in structure, finance and innovation techniques – products of their parent countries; they maintain distinctive national styles.[92] Businesses cannot escape their territorial affiliation. As Jones has pointed out, '[t]he persistent national influence on international business has been one of the most striking features of continuity'.[93] The state still forms the territorial basis for business, in that it is the place of business and provides the rules for business activity.[94]

There is one area in which TNCs are likely to become more important than they are today in terms of influencing future patterns of terrorism. This is the current privatisation of public security and national defence. A privatisation of these two core areas of state sovereignty is likely to have several important implications for the future of terrorism. As will be explained below, this process moves business interests into the actual exercise of coercion, whether it is on the streets of crime-prone cities or on physical front lines of armed conflicts. This contributes to blurring the civil–military divide, which in turn reduces the ideological dilemma for radical groups with regards to targeting corporate business interests involved in the private security and defence industries. Another important side effect is that the privatisation process commercialises military- and security-related technology and potentially makes it more easily available for terrorist and insurgent groups.

Privatising policing and warfare

The proliferation of private security services over the past decades has been tremendous. In several Western countries the number of private security companies and their budgets exceeds that of the public law-enforcement agencies. In the USA, more than twice as much money is spent on private security as on the public police, while the private security business employs three times as many people. In Germany the number of private security companies doubled between 1984 and 2000. In the UK, more than 250,000 people are employed in the private security industry as opposed to only 10,000 in 1950. The security industry expands steadily into new areas. For example in the USA, private companies run an increasing number of correctional facilities, and a private contractor, the Wackenhut Corporation, provides emergency response SWAT teams for a number of US nuclear-weapons facilities.[95]

The apparent success of private security firms in reducing crime has earned them strong advocates, but the objections to their increased role are numerous.[96] Private police are considered less reliable, less accountable and less exposed to judicial scrutiny and control. They serve their employer rather than justice.[97] Incidents of violent vigilante actions by private security guards have also tarnished the business's image.[98] More important are the broader societal implications of the expansion of privately policed communities. Sklansky has warned against this privatisation process, because it undermines the state's ability to guarantee all citizens, regardless of wealth, the equal protection provided by the law.[99] He has predicted that private police will ultimately replace the state's responsibility to provide security, resulting in a two-tiered society where only the affluent will be in a position to purchase their safety. Hence, the rise of private police reinforces the inequality trends discussed previously in this chapter.

The growth in private policing goes hand in hand with the spread of 'gated communities' where affluent people seek protection and privacy behind fences, walls, electronic surveillance devices and privately paid guards. Such communities have seen huge growth in the Americas, South Africa, the Middle East and south-east Asia while they are less widespread in Europe, Canada, Australia and New Zealand, although almost every country now has some examples.[100] Not all gated communities are luxurious and wealthy; the phenomenon has also spread to the middle classes.[101] Nevertheless, gated communities tend to reinforce patterns of inequality and segregation between the haves and the have-nots, as local communities are split up and divided in a physical sense and are deprived of shared public spaces where groups of different socio-economic strata interact. They are also criticised for hollowing out local government as gated community residents no longer see themselves as citizens, but 'shareholders of a private community'. Gated communities herald the rise of 'the city-states – or better, enclave states – of the future'.[102] Hence, the rise of private security appears to be part of a broader trend towards social stratification, and segregation, weakening the public space and the loyalty to the state.

While the growth of private policing in the northern hemisphere takes place within a relatively well-established legal framework, this is less the case in the developing world. In many transitional societies the rise of private policing has been both dramatic and socially disruptive, since private police forces are not brought under firm legislative and judicial control, and some of these forces are made available to organised crime networks and their collaborators in the political establishment.[103] Latin America has seen a real explosion in such companies, basically because state policing is ineffective, crime rates are rampant and wealth disparities are immense. In both post-Communist Russia and the new South Africa, the proliferation of private security agencies was overwhelming during the 1990s. Their rise has assumed additional significance by the recruitment of former (and current) military, intelligence and secret-police officers, which in certain cases may blur the distinctions between state and private policing.

The economic weakness of states undergoing major upheavals and societal transition may unwittingly force a degree of privatisation onto the police. This was the case in Russia in the 1990s where public-security functions became de-facto privatised ones to a significant degree, partly because the authorities failed to fully cover the operational budget of many state security services. For the rest, they had to rely on a share of any unpaid taxes they could retrieve, complemented by their own profit-making businesses.[104] Wealthy Russians also established something close to their own personal militias. In the mid-1990s, there were an estimated 6,500 private security firms in the Russian federation, and Russian officials estimated that approximately c.800,000 individuals were employed in various private security agencies.[105] By 2003 the number of companies had almost doubled. In 1999, there were over 3,000 private security agencies in Moscow alone, but only about fifty with a fully professional reputation.[106]

The expansion of the security industry is also driven by the growing number of large TNC investments in conflict-ridden Third World countries. The private security companies offer guards to protect assets like industrial sites, mines, pipelines and oil wells. It is reported that oil companies in Algeria spend as much as 9 per cent of their operational budgets on protection, while in Colombia the figure is about 6 per cent.[107] As for its future development, there is little reason to believe a sharp slowdown of the expanding security industry. In 2000, the US-based security industry was expected to double by 2010, assuming there was no major terrorist attack in the USA in the meantime.[108]

A second major challenger to the traditional role of the state is the trend towards privatisation in the military. Since the end of the Cold War the proliferation of private military companies (PMCs) has gained considerable ground, prompting scholars to predict a coming 'privatisation of warfare'.[109] Several factors have facilitated this trend. Around the world, the norm of marketisation and privatisation has made tremendous inroads over the past decades, especially after the collapse of the Communist bloc. It has become deeply entrenched in a growing number of sectors as the only viable route to economic efficiency. The expansion of private military companies is not simply a response to greater demands for a market-oriented approach. PMCs also find a receptive audience among those affected by the downsizing of militaries and of defence budgets as the world's armies shrank by an estimated 6 million people during the 1990s. The technological advances in military technology have also increased the demand for highly qualified civilian experts, provided by the private industry, while reducing the need for foot soldiers. In many Western countries, it has become a more attractive option to hire the relevant military expertise on a contract basis as the need arises rather than maintaining large standing forces.[110] The demand for, and hence profitability, of private security contractors has also grown tremendously due to increased international interventionism in armed conflicts over the past fifteen years.

PMCs are considered a necessary supplement, and in some cases even a viable alternative, to national military forces in foreign military engagements overseas. From 1994, the well-connected Virginia-based Military Professional Resources Inc. (MPRI), ran a controversial train-and-equip programme in Croatia and Bosnia-Herzegovina, which reportedly played a key role in turning the tide on the battlefield against the Serb forces. Indeed, Operation Storm in 1995 saw the Croatian army liberate the Krajina region, forcing up to 100,000 Serbs to flee from what became one of the most thoroughly ethnically cleansed area in the region.[111] The US also hired a private contractor to man the UN observer mission in Kosovo, UNMIK. During the US-led air campaign in Kosovo in 1999, American PMCs provided logistical services, conducted information-warfare operations and operated refugee camps. In the Middle East, private US contractors have been involved in anti-terrorism training programmes for Palestinian intelligence services on behalf of the CIA.[112] In Saudi Arabia, a host of Western firms are heavily involved in running most parts of the kingdom's armed forces.[113]

Several PMCs based in South Africa and the UK have offered not only military training and equipment services but also actual combat and combat-support units to Third World governments. The Jersey-based Gurkha Security Guards, Ltd (GSG), founded in 1989, offered British-trained Nepalese Gurkha officers to Angola, Sierra Leone, Mozambique and Somalia during the 1990s, mainly in the area of commercial security for mining and oil companies and landmine removal. It also provided combat-support units to the Sierra Leone government. The GSG pulled its contingent out of the country, however, after their American and British commanders were killed and reportedly cannibalised by rebels in Sierra Leone.[114] The Pretoria-based Executive Outcomes fought civil wars in a number of African countries during the 1990s and credited itself for having forced rebels in Sierra Leone and Angola to the negotiating table. A London-based company, Sandline International, signed a contract with the Papuan government in 1997 to 'provide personnel and related services and equipment' to 'conduct offensive operations' against an insurgent group, the Bougainville Revolutionary Army (BRA) to regain control over the lucrative copper mine in Panguna.[115] Serious disturbances erupted, however, when the contract's terms became known, and the government was forced to evacuate the Sandline team from Papua New Guinea.[116] While Executive Outcomes and Sandline International reportedly went out of business, Sandline's chief executives have reappeared in post-Saddam Iraq, which was literally swarming with PMC personnel in 2003–4.

More than any previous multinational intervention force, the US-led Coalition in Iraq depends on private contractors in nearly all fields of operations. In 2003, the ratio of private contractors compared to military personnel in Iraq was ten times higher than in the 1991 Gulf war. They are the second largest contributor of manpower in Iraq after the US army.[117] By mid–2004, the country hosted reportedly nearly 20,000 PMC personnel from a wide variety of nations, including an estimated 6,000 armed bodyguards. A number of these private forces have been engaged in direct military confrontations with Iraqi insurgent forces, and more than 100 private security personnel had been killed.[118] Their personnel often consists of former special-forces officers, mostly from the USA and the UK, but also Fijian paramilitaries, Indian special forces, Gurkha mercenaries and personnel who spent their military careers under less than reputable regimes, such as Apartheid South Africa, Pinochet's Chile, and Milošević's Serbia.[119]

Even if companies like Sandline and Executive Outcome have shaped the popular image of PMCs, their overall significance has been limited. The main long-term security-policy impact of PMCs is not individual mercenary firms operating on borders of legality, but the expansion of corporate multinational military businesses, or military TNCs. These are legal entities, offering a wide array of services from training, logistics, technical support and security guards to weapons procurement and even close combat support. Their annual revenues were estimated at 100–200 billion US dollars before the Iraqi war and have grown considerably since then.[120] Between 1994 and 2002, the Pentagon had reportedly more than 3,000 contracts worth more than 300 billion US dollars with US-based PMCs alone.[121] The industry is also witnessing a merger-and-consolidation process resulting in a number of military multi-billion-dollar TNCs. The dramatic expansion of PMCs is not just measured in numerical terms but also in the scope of tasks, variety of missions and diversity of their business clientele.

According to Harvard scholar Peter W. Singer this development is unprecedented in modern times: 'Not since the eighteenth century has there been such reliance on private soldiers to accomplish tasks directly affecting the tactical and strategic success of engagement'.[122] Judging by the driving forces behind the military privatisation trend, he sees no changes that might reverse or slow down this trend. The USA is spearheading this development. Reports published in 2002 suggest that as much as a third of the US defence budget was going to private contractors.[123] Other Western countries have also embarked on military privatisation, but not to the same extent. Some observers have argued that the PMCs have penetrated Western warfare so deeply that 'the phenomenon may have reached the point of no return'.[124] The US, and perhaps also the British, military would not be able to wage war effectively without the PMCs.[125]

The societal and political implications of the heavy reliance on PMCs are numerous. While many states are attempting to assert greater control over PMC activity, problems of accountability and transparency remain considerable. For example, many PMCs are multinational corporations and run activities in conflict zones with weak or absent state authorities, and have obtained immunity from prosecution from their clients. Outsourcing inevitably dilutes the responsibility of governments for actions taken in the theatre of war. States also become less dependent on public opinion for engaging in war and military interventions abroad since PMCs offer an opportunity to lower the number of soldiers who have to be deployed. Human losses in PMC operations in Iraq are rarely reported by the companies and do not expose governments to public pressure.[126] PMCs also offer a certain cover for 'plausible deniability' if a sensitive operation should go wrong.[127] PMC contracts are often secret and reduce the scope for accountability by legislators. For example, even if US soldiers are banned from aiding the Colombia government forces against left wing rebels and from training army units with links to right wing paramilitary groups, such restrictions are not extended to PMCs. Since the late 1990s, a number of private contractors have operated in Colombia, receiving an estimated 1.2 billion dollars from US budgets for anti-drug operations as well as assisting the Colombian army in subduing the drug-financed rebel armies.[128]

The bottom line is that the PMC expansion highlights the more fundamental political question of who has the right to legitimate use of violence. As O'Brien has noted, even in situations where PMCs provide security for economic activities and assist in reconstructing the state, 'they are also removing the state's right to control violence and war'.[129] If left unchecked, this development will necessarily have far-reaching implications for the ideational basis of the state. According to Singer, the PMCs continued growth and steady expansion into new fields basically means that we are witnessing 'the gradual breakdown of the Weberian monopoly over the forms of violence'.[130]

Implications for terrorists and insurgent groups

The spectrum of services offered by today's PMCs implies that actors other than governments can make use of a variety of military capabilities simply through a business contract. Even if many PMCs offer their services primarily to states, their clients also include non-state actors. As for the private security industry in general, private buyers are the rule, not the exception. Typically, Singer's list of recent examples of PMC customers include: 'a ragtag militia looking to reverse its battlefield losses, [. . .] a multinational corporation hoping to end constant rebel attacks against its facilities, a drug cartel pursuing high-technology military capabilities, a humanitarian aid group requiring protection within conflict zones'.[131] Western states have contracted PMCs to assist non-state entities and rebel armies in enhancing their military and security capabilities. I have already mentioned US contractors aiding the Palestinian National Authority in the field of intelligence and anti-terrorism (see p. 113). US and British contractors have also worked with the Kosovo Liberation Army (KLA), a relationship which started before Kosovo came under UN and NATO control. According to media reports, MPRI was tasked with aiding the KLA with military training and arms in their separatist struggle against the Serbian regime in 1998. Some of the training programme was reportedly subcontracted to two British security companies.[132]

In developing countries, private military contractors not only do business with governments but also with insurgents. Rebel armies in Sierra Leone, Angola and DRC all contracted military-provider firms to enhance their capabilities. Since mercenary companies are often frowned upon by the mainstream private military industry, they are more likely to nurture shadowy business contacts.[133] The history of the former Israeli officer Yair Klein is a case in point. A former lieutenant colonel in the Israeli Army, Klein founded a military and security training company based in Israel, named Hod Hyanit ('Spearhead') back in the 1980s. Through his company, he began sending arms and providing training to clients in Latin America. This occurred at a time of considerable Israeli and US involvement in covert military assistance to anti-Communist forces, both rebels and governments, throughout South America. Klein was particularly involved in Colombia, and in 1989 he was apprehended by the Colombian authorities together with a group of former Israeli officers and charged with having assisted the Medellín cocaine cartel with arms purchases and paramilitary training. Klein was widely believed to have trained Carlos Castãno's infamous right wing paramilitary squads as well as mafia operatives who later assassinated several Colombian politicians. He was indicted on these charges in Colombia in 1998 together with three former Israeli reserve officers and two Colombians. In the late 1990s Klein was reportedly organising arms transfers to the Revolutionary United Forces (RUF) rebels in Sierra Leone as well as recruiting mercenary forces on behalf of the insurgents.[134]

Klein's story is not unique. In and around Africa's diamond mines, various private contractors have swarmed in to get a piece of the pie, even if it implied assisting brutal rebel armies. The diamond link to terrorism was underscored in 2001, when it became known that al-Qaida operatives had forged important contacts in the diamond markets in Sierra Leone, buying diamonds from the rebels and managing thereby to convert millions of US dollars of cash into more easily hideable diamonds.[135] In the late 1990s the retired South African army intelligence officer Fred Rindle assisted the RUF in military training ahead of the offensive on Freetown in late 1998. His military company also supplied arms to the União Nacional para a Inde-pendêncis Total de Angola (UNITA) rebels in Angola.[136] In 2004, some seventy personnel from another of South Africa's numerous private security companies were apprehended at the airport in Zimbabwe as they picked up a cargo of arms. The men professed they were hired to provide security for mining operations in the DRC, but the governments of South Africa, Zimbabwe and Equatorial Guinea believe they were heading to Equatorial Guinea to be part of a planned *coup d'état*.[137]

Even if these examples seemingly involve 'rogue elements' on the margin of the private military industry, the PMCs are nevertheless independent actors and pursue profit, not state interests. Hence, in principle, both state and non-state actors can gain access to what were previously military capabilities exclusively reserved for states. Their ability to empower non-state actors cannot be ignored. Through PMCs, an increasing range of military relevant technology and hardware has been commercialised, spanning from unmanned aerial vehicles (UAVs), specialised armoured four-wheel-drive vehicles, night-vision goggles and long-range large-calibre sniper rifles to advanced wire-tap and surveillance equipment. There are several examples of illegal non-state actors reportedly benefiting from the services of the legal as well as the more shadowy elements of the security industry. Organised crime gangs have long benefited from commercialisation of military and security equipment. A multinational robbery gang purchased much of their protective gear and surveillance equipment from a private security company in Oslo, prior to their deadly military-style raid on Norway's central cash service in April 2004, where they outgunned the police with superior firepower.[138] The abundant inventory at US gun shops and the laxity of US gun-law enforcement have attracted foreign terrorist groups looking for new and effective hand weapons. There are examples of botched attempts at exporting weapons from the US to the Colombian leftist guerrilla group ELN, the Lebanese Hizbollah and the IRA in Northern Ireland.[139]

There are also examples of extremist organisations themselves establishing private security companies with a view to training members, accessing technology and expertise and providing security for their facilities. The radical Islamist Jamaat al-Fuqra (JF) organisation, founded by the Kashmiri Shaykh Mubarak Ali Gilani in the 1980s, was in 2002 reported to own two private security companies in Brooklyn, which provided armed protection for the groups' facilities and walled-in communities, or *jamaat*, in the USA, Canada and the Caribbean. JF has been described as 'an obscure Muslim sect with a history of violence in the United States'.[140] It is listed as a banned terrorist organisation by the US Department of State, and its Pakistani-based leader has been investigated for his alleged ties to al-Qaida as well as for complicity in the killing of US reporter Daniel Pearl.[141]

The London-based Sakina Security Services Ltd is another case in point. Founded by Sulayman Bilal Zain-ul Ibidin in the late 1990s, the company offered young Muslims the chance to train for holy wars abroad. The company's web site gave out Pretty Good Protection (PGP)-encryption programmes to users to enable them to conceal their identities. It offered a two-week American-based training course, costing 3,000 US dollars. Entitled the 'Ultimate Jihad Challenge', the course included training in hand-to-hand combat, how to 'improvise explosive devices' in live operations, 'the arts of bone-breaking', 'foreign firearm instruction', and gun-training sessions in the United States at a live firing range.[142] The web site also asked for donations for various jihadi causes, such as the liberation of the al-Aqsa mosque in Jerusalem and the Chechen war of liberation. It had more than 15,000 visitors until it was shut down in late 2001. After 9/11, Zain-ul Ibidin, Sakina Security Services' founder, was charged under the British Terrorism Act of 2000, but was later acquitted.[143]

There can be little doubt that the long-term impact of the growing private security industry is the commercialisation of an expanding range of military- and security-related technology, making it more easily available for terrorist and insurgent groups. PMCs and security firms pursue profit, not national security, and they make their hardware available to customers without necessarily checking their credentials too closely. While this is not the case regarding sensitive military technology, the variety of military hardware now being commercialised will eventually contribute to increasing the effectiveness and sophistication of transnational terrorists as well as rebel armies.

Returning to the question raised at the beginning of this section, Whether corporate businesses are the primary terrorist targets of the future?, there are several trends pointing to the increased relevance of big business as a target of terrorism. Economic globalisation has increased the size, visibility and global presence of business corporations in many vital sectors. Even if TNC capitalism is under scrutiny and is not necessarily growing out of control, and even if in terms of size and global weight, they are by no means overtaking the state, the presence of a forceful anti-globalisation movement has made them into key targets of leftist militancy in the West. Furthermore, their increased involvement in conflict areas will make their business interests potential targets for rebel armies. Wherever PMCs are decisive in winning wars, they are likely to be perceived as a primary enemy of the surviving rebel forces and their overseas sympathisers and an object for vengeance and retribution. These and other motivational links created by PMC involvement in conflict overseas will be increasingly important, simply because globalisation decreases the importance of geographical distance and brings civil-war zones closer to the developed world's metropolises and the Western world's backyard.

Already the TNCs are widely seen as the key source of power behind US and Western military strength, putting them high on the priority list for future attacks by radical Islamists. Their increased involvement at the physical front lines of armed conflicts in the developing world and abuses attributed to them, such as the Abu Ghrayb prison affair in Iraq, will undoubtedly enhance terrorist motivations for going after business targets, which after all are considered soft and easy to hit. Similarly, the proliferation of companies within the private policing industry and their consolidation into larger corporations might also stimulate a similar trend with regards to this industry, as their security guards, and not the public police, are engaged in guarding the corporate elite and eliminating security threats to their business interests.

The privatisation of police and military functions also serves to tear down the civil–military divide, which is so essential to the protection of civilians in war. This will undoubtedly reduce any ideological qualms that radical groups might have with regard to targeting corporate business interests. In this regard, it is interesting to read one of the recent communiqués of the *general command of The Islamic Army of Iraq*, an alliance of Iraqi resistance groups, in which it lists various commercial labels by which 'the mujahidin brigades' can identify vehicles and containers of companies transporting supplies to the US forces:

> They are therefore to be considered military targets to be treated in accordance with the military methods available to the mujahideen. God is the ultimate aim. Glory to Islam and the mujahideen! The commercial labels in question: APL, CAI, CMA, Tex, STALCO, Hangin, Maersk, FLORENSE, EVERGREEN, EXTRA International. Signed, The Islamic Army of Iraq General Command, 5 Jumada al-Ula 1425 Hijri, 23 June 2004 CE.[144]

In practice, many insurgent and terrorist groups are likely to be even less careful about investigating whether corporate employees, foreign or local, are actually involved in assisting the enemy regime and its military forces. A rebel insurgency can hardly occur without civilians being targeted. Still, the privatisation of warfare inevitably contributes to reducing barriers against terrorist attacks on civilians by insurgent armies.

A final side effect that should be mentioned is that the worldwide expansion of TNCs and the drive for marketisation, privatisation and globalisation of the economy result in the accumulation of tremendous wealth in private hands. While this is nothing new, the rise of broader strata of wealthy non-Western elites is a comparably recent phenomenon, as is the very size of private capital assets, which in many cases go beyond the annual GDP of several of the world's states. In this context, it is interesting to note the emergence of the phenomenon of private sponsors of terrorism, spearheaded by Osama bin Laden's example. Even if his own private fortune, an inheritance from his father's business empire, was of modest significance in financing the network of al-Qaida and like-minded Islamist groups, there were many wealthy private donors assisting his networks, and not only from Saudi Arabia. The new-found effectiveness of private sponsorship of terrorism is also illustrated by the growth of wealthy terrorist and rebel organisations, from the Colombian FARC guerrillas, the Pakistani Lashkar e-Tayba and the Lebanese Hizbollah. The latter has remained financially very viable even after Iran cut back its support. All these groups have in turn used their resources to train and finance other terrorist organisations. Private terrorism sponsorship will clearly be the trend of future terrorism-financing as overt state support for international terrorism has become too costly. In this respect, one may argue that terrorism is being 'privatised' in more than one sense: not only is there a trend towards increased terrorist targeting of corporate business interests, but terrorism is also increasingly relying on private sponsorship.

The globalisation of organised crime

Postulate: Transnational crime organisations (TCOs) will continue to grow in diversity and sophistication in many regions in the world, and their global reach will be more pronounced. New and profitable areas of organised crime will emerge. Developed countries will be more affected by TCOs than in the past.

Possible implications for terrorism: The increased global reach and sophistication of organised crime networks will provide a number of tactical advantages for transnational terrorists, in terms of increased across-the-globe availability of such services as false ID papers, illegal weapons, explosives, military equipment, etc. Indirectly, TCOs also facilitate the spread of terrorism by weaking state capacities and increasing the chances for new failed states and ungoverned territories. In developed countries, the spread and sophistication of TCOs will sap the resources of law-enforcement capacities and make it harder to sustain the current level of activities against terrorist cells and their support networks.

Transnational crime organisations (TCOs) have long been an important issue in terrorism research. Studying patterns of transnational organised crime is a key avenue to understanding future trends in terrorism. Even if crime syndicates rarely form long-lasting alliances with terrorist organisations, there is little doubt that their presence weakens state institutions and creates a more permissive environment for transnational terrorism, especially with regard to facilitating illegal fund-raising, the falsification of identity cards, illegal border-crossing, the procurement of weapons and explosives, etc. Where organised crime opportunities flourish, there is also a greater likelihood that insurgent groups may transform into profit-seeking entrepreneurs. This is especially the case when political changes have eroded the justifications for their existence.

After the end of the Cold War, TCOs have been an important focus in future security-threat assessments. Some analyses have even described the growth of TCOs 'as a major threat, perhaps the major threat to the world system in the 1990s and beyond'.[145] Many TCOs are seen as increasingly more sophisticated and more global in their orientation. Cross-regional co-operation between networks has become more common and new ethnically based mafia organisations are consolidating themselves in a number of Western countries. New forms of transnational organised crime, such as human-trafficking and various types of 'intellectual property crimes' and on-line financial fraud are proliferating.

Drug trade, human-trafficking, alien smuggling

The largest and most lucrative component of transnational organised crime today is drug trafficking. In fact, the size of the illegal-drug-trade economy was estimated at 400–500 billion US dollars in the mid-1990s, which is about 8–10 per cent of the world trade.[146] Since the 1970s drugs have emerged as the major source of income for organised crime, transforming local and regional mafias into global organisations. TCOs do not usually grow raw materials or sell the refined drugs on the street but monopolise the refining and transport sectors. The global supplies of opium-heroin have grown dramatically over the past decades, from an estimated worldwide production of 500 tons in 1950 to nearly 3,500 in 1990.[147] By 2003, it had reached more than 4,500 tons and was expected to increase still further due to a continuous surge in poppy production in post-Taleban Afghanistan, the source of nearly 75 per cent of global opium-heroin production.[148] Colombian heroin production has also rocketed from nearly zero to becoming, together with the Mexican output, the main supplier to the US market during the 1990s. The global production of coca-cocaine has also increased sharply, doubling its volume in the same period.[149]

There are no indisputable explanations for fluctuations in the drug trade, but it seems clear that both anti-drug action and political events, as well as economic liberalisation do have an impact. In 1970 Turkey produced 80 per cent of the world's opium. The USA exercised considerable pressure on Turkey to eradicate poppy production, and Turkey's role as the world's premier supplier soon ended. The Islamic Revolution in Iran in 1979 led to a crackdown on opium production and heroin use, which seriously curtailed opium supplies. The Soviet invasion of Afghanistan also reduced Afghan opium production somewhat, but it has since then risen sharply, only interrupted for a short period following Taleban's ban on poppy cultivation in July 2000. Reductions in one country have only had limited and short-lived effects on the global illegal-drug production. Following the crackdowns in Turkey, Iran and Afghanistan, opium cultivation shifted to other regions, primarily the Golden Triangle (Myanmar, Laos and Thailand), which explains the increase in production there in the 1980s.[150] In 2002, the Myanmar-based United Wa State Army (UWSA), one of several armed ethnic insurgent groups controlling remote mountainous border regions in the Golden Triangle, reportedly dominated the Asian heroin and amphetamine trade.[151] As for coca-cocaine and other drugs, production is spread across many countries, although most coca is grown in Peru, Bolivia and Colombia.

Despite recent progress in reducing cultivation in some regions, such as Colombia and the Golden Triangle, the profitability and the high level of annual demand, estimated at over 4,000 tonnes of opium, ensure that the illicit-drug industry prospers.[152] In recent years, the production and use of synthesised drugs, such as Ecstasy and methamphetamine, has grown exceedingly fast. A 2003 UN study shows that 'the ATS [Amphetamine-Type Stimulants] market is changing in depth, breadth and shape. Current production is estimated at 500 tonnes per year, and is growing in size and sophistication'.[153] In sum, there is no doubt that both drug use and drug supplies have increased over the past decades, sustaining a large-scale transnational illicit economy, the key mainstay of the powerful TCOs.

So far, attempts to curb the drug trade have only yielded limited or temporary results. One reason is that producer countries often lack the institutional and financial wherewithal to effectively fight poppy and coca cultivation. Local communities in many developing countries depend economically, at least indirectly, on revenues from the drugs trade. Since the flow of illicit drugs has a strong South–North economic undertone, governments in the developing world are often hesitant to act decisively against drug cultivation, even under foreign pressure.[154] Furthermore, even if it rarely receives much political attention, the process of economic liberalisation, the opening of markets and free movement of goods and services have greatly facilitated drugs-trafficking. Illegal drugs more often cross borders in ordinary commercial or personal goods, than through clandestine air-drops and night-time high-speed boat trips. Recent studies suggest that currently 'the countervailing pressures of economic liberalization' seriously hamper the legal regimes of international drug prohibition, and will increasingly do so in the future: 'Each step toward increased market access, deeper integration, greater trading volume, and a more efficient global division of labor will create collateral damage in the current international drug control regime.'[155]

A driving factor behind the surge in transnational organised crime is the continuous opening of new lucrative illegal business opportunities. The most important of these are human-smuggling (i.e. voluntary procurement of illegal entry into another country) and human-trafficking (i.e. transport of people for exploitation in the sex industry, forced labour, etc.).[156] Enormous disparities between countries in terms of job opportunities, social welfare and security drive millions of people to seek a better life elsewhere. As a result of the crackdown on illegal immigration, human-smuggling has become increasingly profitable, attracting the attention of sophisticated organised crime groups. For example, increased policing of the US–Mexican border, through measures such as the erection of fences across southern California and the tripling of the number of US border patrols between 1993 and 2002, has had the side effect of making the smuggling services of the Mexican coyote groups far more profitable than ever before.[157]

The profitability, scope and global dimensions of the human-smuggling and trafficking industry make it an ideal business for well-established transnational crime networks. Its expansion is also due to its low-risk high-profit nature as compared to drug trafficking.[158] At any given time there are 'hundreds of thousands of people in the smuggling pipeline', that is, being held in custody by smugglers, waiting for new travel documents, safer routes to open up, etc., according to US officials.[159] They estimate that some 600,000–800,000 men, women and children are trafficked across international borders each year.[160] According to the UN Office on Drugs and Crime (UNODC), human-trafficking is a highly lucrative global industry with annual illicit revenues at an estimated 7 billion US dollars. This makes it the third largest criminal enterprise in the world. US intelligence puts the figure as high as 9.5 billion US dollars.[161] It is mostly controlled by powerful criminal organisations, such as the Japanese yakuza, the Chinese triads, the Italian mafia, Mexican coyote groups, Albanian and Russian crime organisations, etc.[162] The destinations for trafficking in women include the USA and the European continent, especially countries with legalised prostitution, as well as the wealthy oil states in the Gulf. The largest trafficking routes are in Asia, however, where, for example, Thailand constitutes the centre of the sex trade and Japan has the largest number of 'entertainment establishments', while Taiwan, China and countries beyond the region are destinations for bride trafficking from Asia.[163]

Trafficking in explosives

While alien smuggling and trafficking in humans and drugs may provide transnational terrorist groups with ample opportunities for generating funds and transporting operatives across borders, the widespread trafficking in small arms and explosives presents an even more direct tactical advantage.

Global trafficking in small arms and explosives is partly driven by local armed conflicts and partly by profitability and availability. Although few reliable figures on illegal trafficking of light weapons exist, anecdotal evidence suggests that it still is a large-scale business. According to recent studies, illicit trade probably represents less than 1 billion US dollars, while the total legal international trade in small arms reportedly amounts to nearly 4 billion US dollars. Even if the total volume of this trade seems to have declined since the mid-1990s, the trafficking in small arms continues and 'the dangers of the illicit trade remain unabated'.[164]

While trafficking in small arms is a significant part of transnational organised crime, the illicit manufacturing and smuggling of explosives are often concentrated around conflict areas and figure far less prominently in surveys of organised crime.[165] Post-conflict countries also experience significant trade and trafficking in explosives left over after the war. In Vietnam and China there is widespread illicit manufacturing and trafficking in explosives and fireworks. Explosives are widely used in fishing in Vietnam.[166] China has a large illegal explosives and fireworks industry. A string of nearly simultaneous bombings in March 2001, killing 108 and injured thirty-eight people in north China, revealed the ease by which a terrorist campaign could be staged there, due to easy access of explosives. The bombings triggered China's biggest manhunt in eighteen years, but the perpetrator was neither a sophisticated crime syndicate nor a terrorist organisation. He was a forty-one-year old deaf man, with a long-term fascination for explosives, a rape conviction and a visceral hatred for his stepmother, his estranged wife and other family members who lived in the dormitories he blew up. The explosives had been bought for as little as 950 yuan (115 US dollars) from an illegal explosives workshop at a nearby village.[167] Clearly, this easy access to explosives in China, and the presence of numerous Chinese TCOs with a global infrastructure may prove an extremely deadly combination under the right circumstances.

There exists a significant black-market trade of explosives in Europe and the USA, too. According to a 2002 UN study, which surveyed the scope of illicit manufacturing of and trafficking in explosives, the USA reported nearly such 2,000 incidents (0.72 per 100,000) on average per year for the 1995–9 period. Countries with recent civil wars such as Peru and Lebanon reported more than twenty times higher numbers per capita. A number of the former Communist states in east and central Europe had also experienced significant numbers of incidents of transnational trafficking involving explosives.[168] Most of these incidents were explosives and munitions from remaining Soviet-era stocks, which were smuggled to other countries by organised criminal groups. The numbers for western Europe were also significant. Denmark reported nearly 150 incidents (2.85 per 100,000), while the Netherlands reported c.178 (1.12 per 100,000), and Germany only around thirty-five (0.04 per 100,000). Nearly half of the UN states questioned in the study responded that 'the illicit manufacturing of, or trafficking in, explosives, or their use for criminal purposes' represented a serious problem, and a third of the respondents also saw the problem as involving 'significant transnational elements'.[169] The UN report also referred to cases in which Semtex and other military munitions were smuggled by organised criminal groups, both for the purposes of use and resale.

The study highlighted that the issue of trafficking in explosives has clearly not received sufficient attention among UN member states. Many states were unable to participate in the survey since they lacked public records about illicit explosives incidents. Furthermore, the fact that countries with extensive record-keeping data reported relatively higher numbers than others suggested that the level of the problem was far greater than the figures reflected. For example, in the five-year period surveyed, the study found 171 separate incidents in which more than 100 kilograms of explosives were involved. Since 151 of these were in the USA alone and eight others occurred in Sweden, Germany and Switzerland, it was inferred that under-reporting from states with less extensive regulatory controls and record-keeping structures masked the true extent of the threat.[170]

Anecdotal evidence from press sources suggest that the black-market trade in explosives is considerable, providing mass-casualty terrorists with a potential source of large amounts of deadly weaponry. Shortly after the Madrid bombings, when it became known that the terrorist cell had obtained the explosives from a Spanish black-market trader, other stories of trafficking incidents were related. For example, Radio Praha reported that only weeks before the Madrid blast, 'a truck loaded with illegal explosives [had] passed through several European states without any problems at all', and that the Czech police had recently confiscated a shipment of 300 tons of explosives, reportedly from military stocks in a Scandinavian country.[171] A Norwegian government agency, responsible for civil protection and emergency planning reported that an average of nearly 50 kilograms of dynamite each month are reported as stolen from various stockpiles across the country and called for measures to tighten control.[172]

The threat from trafficking in dangerous weapons was one of the causes for NATO to launch its Operation Endeavor in the wake of 9/11, although the official mission was to protect vessels from maritime terrorism and to interdict terrorist operatives on their way to Europe. A prominent case during Operation Endeavor was the storming of a mostly Ukrainian-manned ship in June 2003, carrying some 680 tonnes of explosives. The ship was sailing from Tunisia inside Greek territorial waters under a Comoran flag, apparently destined for a firm in Khartoum, but the post-office box listed as the company's address apparently did not exist. The crew had also failed to provide the required 24-hour notice before entering Greek territorial waters of a vessel carrying dangerous cargo. The amount of explosives onboard the ship was said to be 'equivalent to the power of an atomic bomb'.[173]

Changing patterns, underlying causes

Over the past decade, organised crime has globalised. TCOs previously operating in specific routes or regions have expanded their geographical scope. Some TCOs have merged or formed co-operative relationships in order to explore new markets and exploit new opportunities in a globalising economy.[174] This has led to more collaboration between previously competitive crime groups, especially in the field of alien smuggling and human-trafficking. Different ethnic crime groups have recognised the need for closer co-operation to provide safe houses, local contracts and documentation. For example, Italian organised crime groups in New York and New Jersey have collaborated with Russian groups to supply women to nightclubs and peep shows, while Mexican smuggling rings have been subcontracted by Chinese groups to smuggle Chinese migrants over the US–Mexican border. The triads have also worked together as partners with the yakuza, as well as with the Italian mafia in the field of human-trafficking.[175] Crime syndicates, which are nearly impenetrable due to close family and tribal links as well as harsh internal discipline, are making themselves felt both in developing and developed countries. Chinese 'snakehead gangs' are, for example, said to operate 'in every corner' of the UK, causing a surge in kidnappings for ransom and violent burglaries. They were also involved in violence against illegal workers who could not pay their debts. In Dublin, Chinese crime syndicates have been involved in extortion and kidnapping attempts on Chinese students.[176]

The consolidation of global organised crime networks based on ethnic TCOs has been facilitated by the magnitude and global nature of migration and the rise of large diaspora communities in the developed world. As Friman and Andreas have observed, today's TCOs follow in the footsteps of immigration on a global scale:

> New immigrant communities, often ethnically isolated from the surrounding society and wary of state institutions in their new country, offer markets and bases for operations for ethnic crime groups. [. . .] Albanians, Chinese, Colombian Nigerian, Russian, Chechnyan, Ukrainian, Jamaican, Italian, Sicilian, and other ethnic crime groups can be found working within new immigrant communities across North America, Europe, and Asia. These communities also serve as potential intermediaries, providing personnel who can link members of transnational criminal organisations with counterparts in indigenous crime groups.[177]

As part of this 'ever-increasing internationalisation of crime' there is also a contagion process in which local crime gangs learn to adopt organisational structures, tactics and modus operandi from their foreign colleagues.[178] As for the nature of the relationship between the immigrant community and ethnic-based TCOs, it varies widely, depending on the size of the community and which function the host country serves for the TCOs, as each country offers different profit opportunities.[179] Organisation-wise, TCOs are very different, depending on their primary operational focus. Bruinsma and Bernasco find, for example, that TCOs operating in the large-scale heroin market tend to be 'close-knit, cohesive and ethnically homogenous', while groups trafficking in women or operating in the market for stolen cars, tend to adopt a less cohesive and more chain-structured organisation.[180] Large hierarchical crime syndicates, such the Cali and Medellín cartels in Colombia, are in some regions giving way to smaller, nimbler and less penetrable organisations.

Trends in organised crime vary greatly from one country to another, but they are characterised by a shift towards newer and more profitable businesses with human-smuggling and human-trafficking showing great profit potentials. In an analysis of organised crime statistics in Germany for the 1994–2001 period, von Lampe found that alien smuggling has increased tremendously since 1993, from c.1,500 cases to more than 9,000 cases in 2001. Drugs-trafficking cases almost doubled, while trafficking in humans increased sharply after the end of the Cold War but have, since 1996 remained on a high level without any further upward trend. Money-laundering also shows a steady and substantial increase, particularly since the early 1990s, while pimping shows a less consistent upward trend. Motor-car thefts, also classified as organised crime, exploded during the early and mid-1990s, reaching more than 200,000 cases a year, but have since then gone down to previous levels between 50,000 and 100,000 cases. Interestingly, the classic organised crime of illegal gambling has fallen significantly and consistently over the past fifteen years.[181]

As alluded to above, the underlying causes for the surge in transnational organised crime are rooted in global political and economic changes. According to Castells, global organised crime is 'a fundamental actor in the economy and society of the Information Age'.[182] New communcation technologies make TCOs more sophisticated in exploiting expanding global markets and their loopholes as states relinquish more and more control over transborder trade and transnational activities of non-state actors. Willetts has similarly observed, 'the operations of criminals and other non-legitimate groups have become more complex, spread over a wider geographical area and increased in scale, because improvements in communications have made it so much easier to transfer people, money and weapons and ideas on a transnational basis'.[183]

The emergence of new types of conflict in the post-Cold War era also encourages growth in transnational crime. Armed conflicts today are less characterised by ideology and increasingly dominated by warlords with local horizons and leaders aiming to accumulate wealth for redistribution to followers, loyalists and clients rather than seeking to implement a political programme for a state. This new war economy fuels the growing transnational parallel trade, grey economic activities and illegal trafficking; it represents in many ways an 'innovative adaptation' to globalisation.[184]

The post-Cold War surge in transnational organised crime is also a result of the hapless economic and political conditions in many of the former Communist countries. Transitional societies are particularly susceptible to surges in crime, which often undercut popular support for both democratic rule and economic marketisation. Many former Communist states have been largely unable to create sustainable economic growth at home. In an environment of contested transformation of ownership, low profitability of legal business and insufficient judicial mechanisms in place to protect legal investments, organised crime has thrived.

The situation in the Russian federation has long been a particular source of concern, in particular with regards to trafficking in nuclear and other WMD-related material. While Russian officials argue that they largely contain illegal trafficking in nuclear material, reports from other ex-Communist states still point to the availability of such sensitive material on the illegal market.[185] Judging by recent trends, drugs-trafficking is set to become an even more important part of Russian organised crime. Russia and east Europe have become targets for expansion by international drug traffickers. More than half of all narcotic substances seized in Russia in recent years have foreign origin.[186] Interviews with Russian officials in Interpol in Moscow also reveal that Russian crime-fighting organs primarily hope that they will be able to limit the growth rate of organised crime and prevent its expansion to new spheres, rather than bring about an actual reduction in organised crime.[187]

As for the situation in the Balkans, the post-war period from the mid- and late 1990s has seen a surge in organised crime, especially in drugs- and human-trafficking. Despite the crackdown on organised crime following the 12 March, 2003 assassination of Serbian Prime Minister Zoran Djindjic, there is a lingering belief that powerful criminal structures 'remain in place, with close links to the worlds of politics, business, and the security forces'.[188] The Kosovo–Albanian crime syndicates have gained a leading role in organised crime throughout Europe, first and foremost in the heroin trade. Weak governments, poorly equipped and underpaid border guards, widespread corruption and dysfunctional economies ensure the TCOs' continued existence in the region. The Balkans will most likely remain the leading area for the drugs trade and organised crime in Europe for the foreseeable future, even though the aspirations to join the EU and NATO appear to provide strong incentives for governments to act against crime syndicates operating in their territory.[189]

In the case of Mexico, drugs-trafficking has emerged as the single most serious threat to state and society over the past decade. As the Mexican political system appears less capable of managing corruption, the drug cartels have reportedly 'moved from a relationship of symbiosis with and subordination to the authorities to one of dominance and intimidation of them'.[190] There are fears that the growing militarisation of Mexican anti-drug efforts also will militarise the political system and lead to a civil war, similar to the situation in Colombia.[191]

Implications for transnational terrorism

Reduced state sponsorship and more stringent anti-terrorism laws have made transnational terrorist organisations more dependent on funds generated from 'in-house' organised crime activities. Drugs-trafficking, alien-smuggling and human-trafficking are all areas in which terrorist groups have been involved to a varying degree. Some fourteen of the thirty-six foreign terrorist organisations designated by the US Department of State are reportedly making money from drugs-trafficking. The most well-known cases are the Colombian FARC guerrillas and the Kosovo–Albanian KLA. The lucrative business of drugs-trafficking has funnelled enormous sums of money to FARC, enabling it to procure advanced weaponry and a standing army of thousands of well-equipped fighters. Al-Qaida and its central Asian affiliate groups, in particular the Islamic Movement of Uzbekistan (IMU), have also been involved in drugs-trafficking. Before the toppling of the Taleban regime, the IMU was said to control channels for opium-trafficking from Afghanistan to central Asian countries and to handle 70 per cent of that trade through central Asia.[192] There is also mounting evidence that the former al-Qaida associates in the Philippines, the MILF guerrillas and the Abu Sayyaf Group, are involved in drugs-trafficking by permitting clandestine *shabu* (or crystal methamphetamine) laboratories on territories under their control in central and western Mindanao and by acting as protectors for foreign trafficking syndicates.[193] Partiya Karkeren Kurdistan (PKK) (the Kurdistan Worker's Party) has benefited considerably from the drugs trade. It used to receive generous funding from large drugs-trafficking families who were supporters or sympathisers of the PKK. These drugs-related support networks extended to the large Kurdish diaspora in Europe.[194]

Transnational terrorists may eschew organised crime for many reasons, however. High-profile involvement in drugs-trafficking may easily alienate ideologically committed members and cause a 'degeneration' of the group into an organised criminal enterprise with no political or ideological appeal. Many transnational terrorist groups tend to engage in relatively small-scale crime and avoid risky high-profile organised trafficking, such as the heroin trade. Deep involvement in organised crime represents a serious security risk for transnational terrorists. Any long-term co-operation, not to speak of rivalry with crime syndicates are fraught with dangers. Instead, they diversify crime-related fund-raising activities in order to meld into the general stream of ordinary crime. The cell behind the Madrid bombings on 11 March, 2004 is a case in point. It raised money by dealing with hashish, pills, fencing luxury cars into Spain, ATM fraud and smuggling aliens.[195] Another similar example is Hizbollah's involvement in the widespread crime practices of running tobacco rackets in the USA and Canada.[196] The huge profits involved and the low penalties for arrest and conviction have made illicit cigarette-trafficking a very popular funding choice for terrorist groups, according to US law enforcement analysts.[197] The case study of the Algerian Groupe Islamique Armée (GIA) (Armed Islamic Group) (see Box 4.1) is also illustrative of the relatively small-scale and diversified nature of crime-related fund-raising of transnational terrorists.

Box 4.1 Fund-raising through crime: the case of the Algerian GIA in Europe

Since its establishment in Algeria in the early 1990s, the GIA devoted considerable efforts to fund-raising efforts in Europe.[1] One avenue for fund-raising was the numerous mosques throughout Europe where money was collected for charity. A portion of the funds from certain mosques was apparently channelled to the GIA and other radical Islamist groups, often without the knowledge of Muslim congregations. The GIA has also demanded 'war taxes' from Algerian businesspeople and ordinary workers. Some contributed voluntarily, while others were coerced. Several shopowners in immigrant suburbs of France brought charges against GIA activists for subjecting them to a strong 'moral pressure' by implying that they would lose clients and get in 'trouble' if they refused to pay. In addition, illegal immigrants have been black-mailed into giving away considerable portions of their wages and people with relatives or property, or both, in Algeria were told to pay for their 'protection'. The GIA also raised money from a variety of black-market activities. They received percentages from sales of pirated and black-market products throughout Europe and probably also from smuggling of consumer goods from Europe to Algeria. The GIA also appears to have dealt with stolen cars and was further involved in more serious crime, such as dealing in drugs, arms and forged documents. Reports indicated that Algerian Islamist activists in France, presumably from the GIA, attempted to take over the lucrative drug trade in some areas by setting up their own 'Islamist anti-drug vigilante squads' ostensibly to combat drug-dealing but in reality to eliminate competitors. Some GIA members committed armed robberies and thefts. For instance, Khaled Kelkal, widely believed to be a ringleader in the GIA bombing campaign in France in 1995, reportedly plundered shops and dealt in hashish and stolen cars in order to finance the purchase of weapons for Algerian guerrillas. In early 1996 an armed gang operated in the Roubaix area on the Franco-Belgian border, where it committed a series of armed robberies of bullion vans and convenience stores. The gang, which by all accounts must have been a GIA cell, was not exclusively Algerian, but included also Moroccans and a French convert. The guerrilla-style operational patterns of the cell inspired local newspapers to write alarmist articles about this new phenomenon of 'gangster-terrorism'. Wearing hoods over military fatigue and armed with grenade launchers and Kalashnikov assault rifles, the group would stop a van with a grenade and then 'pepper it with sustained automatic fire with no attempt to spare bystanders'. An Islamist preacher, who had toured the Roubaix area at the time, had reportedly bestowed the necessary Islamic legitimacy on such heavy-handed fund-raising methods. He had sanctioned armed robberies and crime as justifiable emergency means when it was part of the 'holy struggle'.

Note
[1] This account is taken from Brynjar Lia and Åshild Kjøk, 'Islamist Insurgencies, Diasporic Support Networks, and Their Host States: The Case of the Algerian GIA in Europe 1993–2000', *FFI Research Report* No. 2001/03789 (Kjeller: FFI, 2001), <http://www.mil.no/multimedia/archive/00002/Lia-R-2001-03789_2134a.pdf>. Accessed June 2004.

As for the future evolution of transnational organised crime, a continued growth in scope and diversity appears to be very likely, although regional differences will be very significant. A wide variety of ethnic TCOs are evolving into global networks with an infrastructure spanning many continents, embedding themselves in the growing diaspora communities in the developed world. Economic liberalisation, wealth disparities and improved communications in combination with weak governments, entrenched corruption and widespread unemployment in developing countries ensure that transnational crime will remain a systemic factor in the global economy. New and highly lucrative areas of transnational crime are rapidly evolving, undercutting the overall impact of law-enforcement successes in particular areas. It is likely that transnational organised crime will remain highly flexible and adaptable to changing global circumstances, especially the information technologies.[198]

Terrorist groups probably stand to gain from the future evolution of transnational organised crime. While the chances for long-term co-operation between TCOs and terrorist organisations are small, the increasingly more globally oriented TCOs will have more to offer their many clients in the underworld than before, for example transporting personnel across well-guarded borders and providing advanced technical equipment, weaponry, explosives, clean passports, etc. Transnational terrorists are usually adept at exploiting these services, often unbeknownst to the TCOs.

TCOs may also indirectly facilitate the operations of terrorist groups. By exacerbating fragile and failing states and undermining confidence in democratic governance in transitional states, TCOs contribute to creating more propitious circumstances for terrorism. In developing countries, one may witness enhanced co-operation between insurgent groups and TCOs in sustaining territorial control of significant geographic areas, similar to the FARC-controlled parts of Colombia, or the MILF-controlled enclaves in southern Mindanao. In developed countries, the increased threat from powerful TCOs may also aggravate the terrorist threat, since fighting serious organised crime saps the resources of law-enforcement agencies. Failure to continuously fight and monitor low-level crime has become more risky in a counter-terrorism perspective, since this area will remain a preferred area for terrorist fund-raising in Europe and the USA. This will probably continue to be the case since financing through state sponsorship and legal front organistions have become increasingly difficult.

Middle East petroleum and the future of the energy trade

Postulates: Most economies in the Middle East and North Africa (MENA) will remain heavily dependent on hydrocarbon exports. MENA's contribution to the world's energy supply will increase significantly over the next two to three decades. All industrial oil-importing regions, the USA, Europe and, in particular, Asia will directly or indirectly grow increasingly dependent on energy supplies from the MENA region. Global trade in fossil fuel will expand dramatically, especially in natural gas.

Possible implications for terrorism: First, the (semi-)authoritarian 'rentier' character of most Middle Eastern regimes will deepen, enabling the regimes in power to stave off demands for peaceful political change, while sustaining at the same time the incentives for terrorism and violent revolts. Growing energy dependence on Middle Eastern oil will promote Western interest in regime stability, not reform. In combination, this suggests that the region will remain a heavy contributor to future anti-US and anti-Western transnational terrorism.

Second, the growing strategic importance of MENA's energy supplies over the next decades will make petroleum-related targets more attractive to transnational terrorist groups. Greater use of natural gas in industrialised countries and the transportation infrastructure for this purpose such as new high-pressure pipelines, local storage sites, terminals, ships, trucks and trains transporting natural gas, will also create an expanded range of opportunities for mass-casualty terrorists.

An assessment of future trends with regard to Middle Eastern oil economies may reveal new insights into future patterns of transnational terrorism. There are several reasons for this. Dependency on Middle East oil has long been a major factor in US political, economic and military involvement in the region. In recent years, this has resulted in a more explicitly 'imperial' role for the USA in the Middle East than in other regions of the world. Securing global access to oil production in the Middle East has been the primary US policy aim in the Arab world, second only to protecting Israel's security and territorial interests and, during the Cold War, denying Soviet influence in the region. These partly conflicting policy goals are often seen as the main background for repeated US interventions in the Middle East and its close relationships with authoritarian regimes in the region. As discussed in several studies, the high degree of US interventionism in the Middle East, especially after the end of the Cold War, has been a key factor in generating anti-US transnational terrorism.[199] (The opposite is also true). Over the years, the Middle East has spawned perhaps more anti-US and anti-Western terrorist organisations than any other region. While the US role in the Arab–Israeli conflict undoubtedly is a key factor in explaining this, the above-mentioned geopolitical relationships built around the Middle East oil economy have also played a significant role.

The argument of Western 'theft' of Arab oil in collaboration with corrupt elites has been and continues to be a common staple in the ideologies of a number of Middle Eastern terrorist organisations, including al-Qaida.[200] This has not only motivated attacks on Western interests, but also a substantial number of terrorist and sabotage operations against petroleum-related targets. Nearly 2 per cent of all transnational terrorist incidents worldwide since 1968 have targeted the petroleum industry, a major share of them being related to the Middle East.[201] Such attacks have primarily been motivated by opposition to the national authorities as well as to foreign 'exploitation' of oil resources. The spate of terrorist attacks in mid-2004 against foreign employees in the Saudi Arabian oil industry and reported al-Qaida plans to sabotage the Saudi oil complex in Ras Tanura in 2002–3 highlight the relevance of oil in the calculus of al-Qaida's terrorism.[202] Following the suicide-bombing of the *Limbourg* oil tanker outside Yemen in October 2002, al-Qaida issued a communiqué describing the export of Middle East oil as 'the umbilical cord and lifeline of the Crusader community'.[203]

In addition to providing motivations and targets for transnational terrorism, the presence of an international oil industry may also have an indirect impact on terrorism. Heavy dependence on petroleum exports in developing countries is systematically associated with non-democratic rule, clientalist 'corrupt' economies and increased likelihood of violent conflict.[204] Hence, a development that sustains or increases the dominance of hydrocarbon exports in Middle Eastern economies will also increase the probability for further violence. The resort to terrorist violence is also more likely in the region than elsewhere since it has a recent history of such violence, both domestic and transnational.[205] (Terrorism as a region-wide phenomenon may be explained by the so-called contagion theory, suggesting that the level of terrorism in one country tends to affect the level of terrorism in neighbouring countries.

This effect is likely to increase as a result of improved communications and transnational contacts.)

The long-term propensity for new campaigns of terrorism will arguably be weaker if oil dependence is reduced and a more healthy economy emerges in which foreign-dominated government-controlled extraction of natural resources figures less prominently. Conversely, continued or increased oil dependence in Middle Eastern economies, especially in a situation with rising oil prices, reduces government incentives to embark on serious political reform. It will allow the elites to postpone democratisation through a mixture of redistribution of rent and coercion. This latter scenario is likely to sustain or possibly increase the present propitious conditions for terrorism in and from the Middle East.

Future trends in petroleum energy dependence

Unfortunately, a scenario of a continued 'petroleumification' of Middle Eastern economies seems very likely. In recent years, the MENA countries have made only limited efforts at reducing their dependence on hydrocarbon exports. While some countries have established build-up dedicated financial assets and stabilisation funds to reduce the economic impact of reduced petroleum revenues, efforts at diversifying their economies have not been very successful. There has been some development of the petrochemical industry in some countries, including Kuwait and Saudi Arabia, but on average, the non-hydrocarbon sector is weak. Economic indicators for eleven oil-producing MENA countries show that their non-oil GDP is fairly small. In fact, for nearly all of these states, it has remained below 7 per cent between 1995 and 2001 and has even declined for several states.[206] Hence, the MENA countries remain excessively dependent on petroleum revenues and are expected to do so in the foreseeable future, with the possible exception of countries with declining oil production such as Egypt. Also beyond the oil-rich countries, the national income of most of the MENA region is heavily dependent on sources directly controlled by the regime. For example, export of minerals (phosphate) is a major source of state revenues in Morocco. Similarly, the government-controlled Suez Canal revenue is an important economic pillar for the regime in Cairo, in addition to its hydrocarbon exports. Hence, the rentier nature of Arab states is deeply-entrenched. It has been a significant factor in discouraging regime accountability in the region and has created conditions favourable to political violence.[207]

In addition to the oil-dependence factor, a development towards increased strategic importance of Middle Eastern petroleum is likely to enhance its symbolic and political value for terrorist organisations. During and after the Arab oil embargo in 1973–4, Palestinian and Arab groups carried out a series of strikes on petroleum facilities in Europe. More recently, the Algerian GSPC has threatened attacks on Algerian and foreign petroleum facilities, including the trans-Mediterranean gas pipelines, carrying liquid gas from Algeria to Spain and Italy, as well as the giant refineries on the Mediterranean ports of Arzew and Skikda.[208] Al-Qaida attacks on 'soft targets' (i.e. foreign employees) in the Saudi oil industry in May and June 2004 led to considerable jitters in the oil markets, sustaining the 'fear factor' among analysts and pushing oil prices up to record high levels.[209] It is likely that the more dependent Western economies become on Middle Eastern oil supplies, the greater the political impact from high-profile terrorist strikes against such targets. If future trends point to increased foreign dependence on and involvement in the Middle East petroleum industry, petroleum targets will most likely grow in importance in the overall calculus of transnational terrorist groups, for ideological as well as for tactical reasons.

Regrettably, Western and Asian economies are expected to greatly increase their imports of hydrocarbon over the next two decades. Despite increased output from Russia and other suppliers, the MENA region is likely to become an increasingly more important source of global energy supplies. Saudi Arabia alone has nearly 25 per cent of the world's proven reserves of oil, and together with four of its neighbours it holds perhaps a 60 per cent share of the global oil reserves. Furthermore, they have yet to produce at maximum capability. Their share of the world oil market is likely to grow over the next two decades due to Saudi Arabia's huge reserves of cheap oil and lack of alternative large-scale sources of oil at similarly low prices.[210]

The authoritative International Energy Agency (IEA) in Paris predicts that global primary energy demand will increase some 1.7 per cent annually from 2000 to 2030, which is slower than the growth over the past three decades. More important, it also believes that fossil fuel will remain the primary source of energy and constitute more than 90 per cent of the increase in demand: 'oil will remain the fuel of choice in road, sea and air transportation'.[211] IEA also expects that increased production in the Middle East and the former Soviet Union will meet most of the growth in demand for hydrocarbon energy. Most of the 60 per cent increase in global oil demand over the next three decades will be covered by OPEC producers, in particular those in the Middle East, while oil production in other regions, such as North America and the North Sea will gradually decline.[212]

There is a chance that an accelerated shift to natural gas and improved extraction technologies may slow down the relative decline in importance of non-Middle Eastern energy sources. However, unless alternative-energy technology becomes profitable in the transport industry, dependence on hydrocarbon fuel is set to grow, which in practice means more oil imports from the Middle East. There has been much speculation about how quickly hydrogen fuel cells and other energy sources might replace the current oil-based transportation economy, but most assessments see this as a relatively distant future. According to *The Economist*, it will take 'a decade or two' before these alternatives make a significant dent in the oil economy.[213]

At present, it is Asia, and not Europe or the USA, which imports most of the Persian Gulf oil, and its share of Middle East oil imports is likely to grow considerably. Asia is predicted to replace the USA as the leading energy consumption region. The growth in consumption will be most pronounced in China, and to a lesser extent in India and Japan. IEA predicts that China's oil imports over the next thirty years will see a fivefold increase; by 2030, it will import almost 10 million barrels per day. China's dependence on imported energy is expected to rise from less than 40 per cent in 2003 to nearly 80 per cent by 2020.[214] This scenario, however, is predicated on a continued economic growth in China, which is by no means certain (see Chapter 3).

It has been predicted that by 2015, 'only one-tenth of Persian Gulf oil will be directed to Western markets; three-quarters will go to Asia'.[215] As for energy dependence, however, this regional shift of oil-trading may not be very significant after all. Oil markets are to a considerable extent global, and prices are determined by supply. Only Saudi Arabia has the capacity of managing prices and coping with disruptions in supply through its large excess-production capacity. Given their growing weight in the oil markets, OPEC and Saudi Arabia are likely to increase their influence on price level and availability. The strategic importance of Saudi and OPEC oil to the USA will not diminish, even if Saudi oil is sold to someone else. Rather, US dependence on Middle East oil is set to increase. In fact, the IEA expects a sharp increase in US and Canadian energy import dependence, from less than 5 per cent in 2000 to more than 30 per cent in 2030.[216] This will probably make the USA even more determined than it is today to maintain a presence and project power in the Persian Gulf region well beyond Iraq.

Natural-gas resources are more widely distributed around the globe as compared to oil resources. Supply routes tend to be more regional than those of oil, however, although the shipping of liquefied natural gas (LNG) has become much more competitive than previously and is expected to rise sharply in coming years. Europe is growing increasingly more dependent on gas supplies from north Africa. The interdependence in the energy economy between the two regions, and the possibility that political instability and armed conflicts in the South might disrupt the petroleum export has long been a key issue in the debate on Mediterranean security. In fact, it was a dominant feature of Euro-Arab relations since the Arab–Israeli war and the oil embargo in 1973.[217] During the 1980s and 1990s, the EU countries' gas consumption was mostly covered by European suppliers, such as the UK, the Netherlands, Norway and Russia, but this has changed.[218] North Africa, and Algeria in particular, has emerged as one of the leading suppliers of gas to the EU, primarily to southern Europe.

A substantial expansion of natural-gas pipelines from north Africa to Europe was completed in the 1990s. The expansion of the trans-Mediterranean (Transmed) natural-gas pipeline was completed in 1995, linking Algeria to Italy through Tunisia and Sicily. The Maghreb–Europe Gas

(MEG) pipeline from Algeria to Spain and Portugal through Morocco has operated since November 1996. A projected underwater pipeline from Libya's offshore natural-gas fields via south-eastern Sicily to the Italian mainland and France is to be operative by 2006. Other pipeline projects are underway as well. The effect of this is that future gas export to Europe from north Africa will increase substantially. North Africa has also a considerable oil export to Europe, and produces significant amounts of LNG for the Western market. By 1997, Algeria was already the second largest LNG exporter, with 22 per cent of the world's total LNG exports, mainly to western Europe and the United States.[219]

European dependence on north African energy supplies will most probably grow in the coming decade, especially for the southern European countries, which are already heavily dependent on Maghrebi gas imports. In the late 1990s, Algeria alone supplied some 70 per cent of Spain's gas supplies and 25 per cent of Italy's. Natural gas is increasing its share of the EU's energy balance, and it will reach some 26 per cent by the year 2010.[220] IEA predicts a 'rapid growth' in OECD gas demand over the coming years, amounting to more than a tripling between 2000 and 2020. (Nuclear energy and oil will shrink, coal and hydroenergy will increase slightly, and other renewables will remain peripheral, despite considerable growth.)[221] Increased demands for gas energy will be met exclusively by import as indigenous production is not projected to remain at 2000's level. Europe's growing dependence on north African gas supplies is somewhat tempered by expanding pipeline networks from eastern Europe as well as new LNG projects, which will increase export from oversea regions, including Latin America.

Growing energy demands and depletion of indigenous resources imply that cross-border and transcontinental energy transportation will surge. IEA predicts that international energy trade in fossil fuel, which will remain the overwhelmingly dominant form, will 'expand dramatically'.[222] It is expected to more than double between 2002 and 2030, and all oil-importing regions will import more oil, mostly from the Middle East. This increase is most pronounced in Asia. In absolute terms, Europe will see the biggest increase in gas imports. Its cross-border gas pipelines will multiply, and there will probably be a substantial expansion of LNG infrastructure.[223] LNG will also become far more important in the United States, even if popular opposition to LNG terminals is growing fast. The IEA foresees that the expected sharp increase in US and Canadian energy imports will be covered by LNG.[224] This means a rapid increase in the number of LNG ships arriving at US and Canadian harbours.

The steady increase in global energy demand and declining production rates at many older production facilities have prompted many warnings about an energy-supply crisis unless large-scale investments are made. According to the IEA, the funding requirements in order to sustain oil production 'will have to increase sharply' over the next years, but the mobilisation of such investments will be difficult since investments in the energy sector are considered risky.[225] This will cause a rising price level of energy, and increase its strategic importance to the major industrial powers.

Implications for terrorism

The impact on the future of terrorism of the trends discussed above is two-fold. The first part is related to opportunity structure and the second to structural factors, affecting terrorist motivations. As for the implications for terrorist opportunity structures, the evolving energy trends point to increased opportunities for terrorist exploitation in several regards. I have already mentioned the growing strategic importance of MENA petroleum supplies to the major industrial powers in Europe, the USA and Asia. As the future points to a concentration of critical energy sources in a region already heavily affected by terrorism, it is likely that those terrorist and insurgent groups who are capable of causing a degree of disruption in the flow of hydrocarbon energy will find their political leverage considerably enhanced. It may also increase their 'return of investment' in a more direct sense. Whenever a terrorist attack directly influences oil prices, which happened following al-Qaida's attacks in Saudi Arabia in May and June 2004, it may present a golden opportunity for those terrorist groups who are sufficiently knowledgeable to exploit their unique knowledge about the timing of the attack to earn quick money for their organisation on the financial markets. It is possible that al-Qaida applied this trick in September 2001. Just days before the attacks in New York and Washington there were reportedly an unusual number of 'put options' traded on American and United Airlines, as well as 'short-selling' of stock in European reinsurance companies, raising suspicions that someone with prior knowledge of the attacks was making profits from the tragedy.[226]

Another factor likely to make the future petroleum industry more exposed to terrorist targeting is the very fact that the international energy trade is set to grow quickly. There will be more pipelines, more terminals, refineries, oil and gas depots, oil tankers and LNG ships, as well as more trucks and trains transporting oil and gas. Furthermore, there will be more personnel involved in running these facilities. Judging by past patterns, all these are potentially attractive terrorist targets when political conditions are right.[227] Security measures might be sufficient to prevent attacks against key nodes in the global energy infrastructure, however. The inability of Algerian insurgents to strike effectively at Algerian petroleum-export facilities during the ten-year civil war suggests that the vulnerability problem should not be exaggerated. Similarly, al-Qaida's campaign against the Saudi regime and its targeting of the oil industry in the country have not yet caused any dramatic impact on supplies, although the market has become jittery at times.

Still, the growing scope of the industry and the shift towards natural gas and greater reliance on LNG will inevitably create new opportunities for transnational terrorist networks, as it is impossible to invest in heavy security measures all the way from production field to consumer. Only in the USA is there already an estimated 305,775 km of natural-gas pipelines, while rising gas prices and a decline in domestic have generated 'a surge of proposals to site LNG terminals'.[228] According to industrial reports, four existing terminals have been reopened, two are being expanded, and nine more terminals are likely to be built in the next decade.[229] As Oppenheimer has observed, the rise of al-Qaida 'has brought vulnerability of oil and gas complexes to the fore' and raised the spectre of a tanker ship blowing up in a vital harbour.[230] Especially for inventive mass-casualty terrorists, the increased presence of LNG ships will provide unprecedented opportunities. Even if LNG ships have perhaps unfairly been compared to floating Hiroshima bombs, it remains true that a fire in an LNG tanker might have catastrophic outcomes.[231] Similarly, high-pressure LNG pipelines, terminals and depots, as well as trucks and trains carrying natural gas, are all potentially attractive to inventive terrorists looking for ways to convert modern society's technological sophistication into deadly weaponry.

Terrorist groups have previously targeted natural-gas facilities, exploiting their explosive potential. In February 1993, the IRA attacked two huge natural-gas tanks in Warrington, 15 miles west of Manchester. Although no injuries were reported, 100 people had to be evacuated from their homes.[232] There are a number of reports that al-Qaida has considered using natural-gas and fuel supply as a terrorist weapon. A full-scale plan to use an LNG tanker as a floating super-firebomb has not yet been revealed despite lingering suspicion that the LNG terminal near Boston Harbour might have been a target.[233] Smaller-scale attacks have been contemplated and carried out, however. In 2002, a Tunisian al-Qaida member attacked a synagogue on the Tunisian island of Djerba, using a LNG vehicle, killing twenty-two people.[234]

A very simple and ingenious plot was that of José Padilla, a Muslim Puerto-Rican convert and a former Chicago gang member who joined al-Qaida in Afghanistan and returned to the USA for an al-Qaida operation. Together with an accomplice, Adnan Shukrijumah aka Jáfar the pilot, he was to rent apartments in New York in three high-rise apartment buildings, which had natural-gas heating supplied to the floors, seal all the openings, turn on the gas, and set timers to detonate the buildings simultaneously.[235] Another al-Qaida plan, where petroleum energy was to be exploited, involved tanker trucks, which the designated operatives would steal or hijack and subsequently crash into fuel pumps at filling stations.[236] Future terrorist organisations will be able to build on the experiences of their predecessors and develop more ingenious and effective attacks, exploiting the growing presence of natural gas infrastructure in developed societies.[237]

As for structural causes affecting terrorist motivations, future energy trends will arguably have a negative and corrupting effect on political regimes in the

MENA region. It deepens the Arab rentier state, prevents political and economic reform, and sustains illiberal, semi-authoritarian and clientalist forms of government. This negative effect is compounded by the growing strategic importance of hydrocarbon energy to the major oil-importing industrialised regions, the USA, Europe and Asia, since it reduces the incentives and the effectiveness of sustained external pressure for political reform. Despite recent US protestations of a new democratisation effort, the need for effective counter-terrorism co-operation will continue to override the democratisation agenda. The rapidly growing Asian energy dependence on the Middle East will also ensure that the MENA regimes will be able to draw upon their Asian allies in case Western powers should move more aggressively forward on a democratisation programme.

As for Europe, the deepening of economic interdependence between Europe and the southern Mediterranean, and increased European investments in the petroleum sector in north Africa, have also created additional interest in maintaining regime stability in the region, rather than promoting genuine democratisation.[238] Despite the lip service that is paid to human rights and democratisation in the Euro-Mediterranean Partnership,[239] European states have often proved to be more than willing to offer economic and military aid, intelligence co-operation and diplomatic support to the authoritarian regimes in the South in order to help them fend off the Islamist opposition movements who, should they manage to take power, may threaten foreign investments and vital energy supplies.[240] Altogether, this means that a genuine democratisation in the MENA region is unlikely in the near future. Instead, there will be regime types in the Middle East that increase the prospects for continued violence.

Domestic terrorism and political violence have long been a problem in many Middle East countries, and they have frequently transformed themselves into international terrorism. Previously, this also occurred frequently at the instigation of the regimes. In the future, it seems likely that evolving patterns of energy dependence will have the unintended effect of sustaining and in some cases increase the level of spillover of transnational terrorism from the Middle East.

5

THE DEMOGRAPHIC FACTOR

> In cities in six West African countries I saw [. . .] young men
> everywhere – hordes of them. They were like loose molecules in
> a very unstable social fluid, a fluid that was clearly on the verge
> of igniting.[1]
>
> (Robert D. Kaplan, 1994)

Is there a direct connection between demography and the occurrence of terrorism? The answer is no. There are, however, several important indirect links
which make it worthwhile, in a study on the future of terrorism, to examine
demographic trends and international migration patterns. For example, rapid
population growth usually skews the age pyramid in favour of young people,
and violence – both political and criminal – is overwhelmingly the work of
young males. Hence, societies that have a disproportionately high density of
youth turn out to be more predisposed to high levels of violent conflicts
than comparable societies with a much older population.[2] Similarly, high
'sex-ratio societies', where there are far more males than females, are also
likely to experience higher levels of violence than similar countries without a
skewed gender balance.[3] Furthermore, unlike guerrilla warfare, terrorism is
predominantly an urban phenomenon, and states undergoing rapid urbanisation are therefore likely to provide a more facilitating environment for
terrorist organisations compared to countries in which the society remains
largely premodern and rural. Finally, international migration, which will be
examined in the last part of this chapter, has the potential to rapidly change
the ethnic compositon of a country and thereby unleash violent responses.
Fleeing from repressive regimes and civil wars, international migrants also
tend to link their new host countries more closely to distant conflict zones
and the various terrorist and insurgent groups operating there.

Demographic trends

Postulates: A number of developing countries, including the MENA states
will continue to have significant population growth, although the growth rate
is gradually declining and the current 'youth bulges' are mostly decreasing.
In the developed world, population growth will be slow, and in some countries even negative. In general, the population across the globe, and especially

in the industrialised world, will grow older. Some Asian countries, China and India in particular, will have an extremely skewed gender balance, with far more male citizens than female. The process of urbanisation will continue unabated and by 2025 two thirds of the world's population will live in cities.

Possible implications for terrorism: The continued rapid urbanisastion will also 'urbanise' warfare, making terrorism a more widespread tactics in future wars. The growing mega-cities in the developing world, the skewed gender balance in some Asian countries, and the socio-economic problems associated with 'youth bulges' will continue to be a fertile ground for terrorist organisations. In the long term, however, declining population-growth rates and the rapid 'ageing' of most Third World societies, including those in the MENA region, will counter this trend.

During the twentieth century there has been a tremendous growth in the world's population, rising from less than 2 billion people during the first quarter of the century to 4 billion in 1976, and finally reaching 6 billion at the end of the century.[4] If current demographic trends continue, the world's population will almost double to about 11 billion in the latter part of the twenty-first century.[5] Population growth will take place almost exclusively in the developing world, shifting the geographic distribution of the world's population and decreasing the share of people living in developed countries. During the twenty-first century the demographic growth in the developing world will also slow down significantly, although the growth rate will remain relatively high for the next few decades.

Population growth has long been an object of much concern. Since the 1950s, one has feared that rapid population growth would create global problems of catastrophic dimensions. For example, in a booklet *The Population Bomb*, published in 1954, T. O. Greissimer wrote that 'the population bomb threatens to create an explosion as disruptive and dangerous as an explosion of the atom bomb, and with as much influence on prospects for progress or disaster, war, and peace'.[6] One argument was that 'the stork has passed the plow'.[7] Widespread hunger and starvation would be the result of continued population growth, causing the death of hundreds of millions of people. This Malthusian line of thinking on population growth also informed the debate in the security-policy community, but from another perspective. Many US government officials viewed 'social unrest, Communist insurgency, and guerrilla warfare in poor countries as the likely political product of "overpopulation"'.[8]

Today, scholars mostly agree that Greissimer's 'population bomb' has fizzled, largely because socio-technological revolutions have dramatically altered the relation between population growth and food supply.[9] First, the world's population is growing more slowly than demographers in the 1960s had expected.[10] Growth rates for the global population have declined steadily over the past two decades, from 2.2 per cent in 1980 to 1.7 per cent in 1992, and is predicted to go down to 1 per cent by 2015, and merely 0.5 per cent by 2050.[11] This reduction is most marked in the developed world, but a number of Third World countries have slowed their population growth significantly in a very short time. Second, food production rose more sharply than experts had foreseen in the 1960s. Contrary to what demographers and population controllers warned, food production has not only far outstripped population growth, it has also taken place in those regions in which they least expected it to happen, in the developing world. Food prices have also fallen.[12]

This is indeed good news for the future. Yet population growth is still a major concern. High population growth tends to occur in societies that can least afford it. Some scholars have warned that '[g]iven the existing strains in such societies, rapid population growth will lead to increased scarcity, violence and possible genocide'.[13] The social and political effects of rapid population growth and resource scarcity are quite complex, however. Many recent studies have pointed out that natural-resource abundancy, rather than scarcity, has often been an important source of violent conflicts, while population growth in many countries is also an engine for economic growth.

An important aspect of contemporary population growth is that it tends to be accompanied by even more rapid urbanisation, as traditional rural societies cannot employ the growing number of people, and city life proves more attractive. There has been an explosive urbanisation rate in the non-OECD world, and the growth of larger cities has been dramatic. The number of so-called 'mega-cities', cities with more than 10 million inhabitants, is likely to increase from fourteen in the mid-1990s to twenty-five or more by 2015, with a clear majority in the developing world. By 2015, more than half of the world's population will be urban. Ten years later, in 2025, two thirds of the world's population is predicted to live in cities as opposed to just over one third in 1975.[14] In most Third World cities social and economic problems are acute, and these developments have raised serious concern.[15] Back in the 1990s, the head of the Habitat II Conference Wally N'Dow warned against the 'explosive nature' of many of the world's cities in which hundreds of millions of people are officially homeless or living under life-threatening conditions: 'A low-grade civil war is fought every day in the world's urban centres. Many cities are collapsing. We risk a complete breakdown in cities'.[16] This is not simply rhetoric. Poverty and drugs have caused soaring violent crime rates in many Latin American cities, especially in Rio, where the state has been more or less absent from the teeming shanty towns (favelas) for years and where heavily armed narco-militias ('The Red Command', 'The Third Command', etc.) not only rule the favelas with relative impunity, but also extend their influence into wealthy neighbourhoods as well. These drug gangs have resorted to terrorist tactics on a number of occasions.[17]

While rapid urbanisation in the developing world poses serious challenges for the future, urbanisation in the developed world will probably be less problematic. The flexibility of the labour market and developments in information technology may also slow down the process of urbanisation as cities need not be the physical centres of business. Still, the developed world may not entirely escape negative consequences of urbanisation processes. It has long been common wisdom that violent crime rates tend to be higher in urban environments than in rural areas. Buvinić and Morrison have argued that 'population density' has an effect on the occurrence of violence, citing studies of crime in Latin America, where violent crime is strongly correlated with city size. Crowding apparently 'intensifies antisocial behaviour and facilitates anonymity and imitation of violent acts'.[18]

Another key effect of rapid population growth is the tendency to produce a relatively large segment of young people in the population or so-called 'youth bulges'. (A 'youth bulge' occurs when the ratio of the population aged fifteen to twenty-nine years to the population aged thirty to fifty-four years reaches 1.27 or above.)[19] This is significant because young people are generally far more violent than middle-aged and elderly people. Males between the age of eigtheen and twenty-four commit a large portion of violent crimes and comprise the largest share of the victims of violence.[20] These findings do not vary significantly across cultures. High population growth, then, tends to boost the segment of the population that is especially prone to violence. Indeed, global violence measured in homicide frequencies has been on the rise since the 1970s. According to Buvinić and Morrison, the phenomenon of rising global violence is 'best understood by examining key demographic realities that have set the stage for increased violence'.[21]

There are strong indications, however, that over the next decades, the age groups at risk will decline markedly in nearly all parts of the world.[22] Africa may still remain an exception as the share of the fifteen to twenty-four age group is expected to continue to rise. Population forecasts for Africa are highly uncertain, however, given the enormous magnitude of the AIDS/HIV epidemic, which has already significantly reduced the prospects for population growth in many African countries.[23] Whether the expected relative decline in youth population will reduce the level of violent crime is uncertain, at least in the short term. Since the 1980s the share of young people has decreased in the developed world after the peak in the early 1980s, but homicide rates have not followed suit, highlighting that a certain 'criminal inertia' is at work.[24]

The population growth in the Middle East and north Africa is of particular interest to our study because of the region's long history as a source of anti-Western transnational terrorism.

As can be seen from Table 5.1, the annual population growth in the MENA region is in the range of 1.5–2.5 per cent with Tunisia (1.09 per cent) and the Gaza Strip (3.89 per cent) representing the two extremes. In the five-year period from 1998 to 2003, the growth rate has declined significantly for nearly all countries. This has also reduced the 'youth bulge' considerably. In 1998, the share of the population below the age of fifteen varied from a

Table 5.1 Demographic statistics for Middle East and north Africa in 1998 and 2003[1]

Country	Annual population growth 1998/2003 (%)	Population below 15 years 1998/2003 (%)	Population July 1998 and July 2003 estimates (millions)	Life expectancy, years
Western Sahara	2.4 / no data	no data/ no data	0.23 / 0.26	48.4 / no data
Morocco	1.89 / 1.64	36 / 33.2	29 / 31.6	68.5 / 70.04
Algeria	2.14 / 1.65	38 / 32.8	30.5 / 32.8	68.9 / 70.54
Tunisia	1.43 / 1.09	32 / 27	9.4 / 9.9	73.1 / 74.4
Libya	3.68 / 2.39	48 / 34.5	5.7 / 5.5	65.4 / 76.07
Egypt	1.86 / 1.88	36 / 33.9	66 / 74.7	62.1 / 70.41
West Bank	3.71 / 3.3	45 / 44.1	$1.6 + 0.32^2$ / $2.2 + 0.36^3$	72.5 / 72.68
Gaza Strip	6.4 / 3.89	52 / 49.4	1.05 / 1.27	72.9 / 71.4
Jordan	2.54 / 2.78	43 / 35.9	4.4 / 5.4	72.9 / 77.88
Syria	3.23 / 2.45	46 / 38.67	16.7 / 17.6	67.8 / 69.39
Lebanon	1.62 / 1.34	30 / 27.1	3.5 / 3.72	70.6 / 72.07
Israel	1.91 / 1.39	28 / 26.9	5.6 / 6.11	78.4 / 79.02
Turkey	1.6 / 1.16	31 / 27.2	64.6 / 68.1	72.8 / 71.8

Notes
[1] CIA World Factbook 1998 and 2003 <http://www.odci.gov/cia/publications/factbook>.
[2] Number of Jewish settlers in the West Bank and East Jerusalem per July 1997.
[3] Number of Jewish settlers in the West Bank and East Jerusalem per July 2002.

moderate 30–2 per cent for the lower tier (Tunisia, Turkey and Lebanon) to a staggering 46–52 per cent for the top three (Libya, Syrian and the Gaza Strip). In 2003, these numbers were down to *c.*27 per cent for the first group and 35, 39 and 49 per cent for the second. Apparently, the youth bulge is declining at a significant rate. Over the long run one might expect that the age pyramids in these countries will come to resemble west European countries with far more elderly than young people. In fact, one study predicts that in the Arab world only Gaza, Saudi Arabia and Yemen will have youth bulges by 2015.[25] In the short term, however, the youth-bulge problems will persist and will continue to place significant strain on the education and health-care systems and state-sponsored social welfare programmes, as well as on the economy which is unable to absorb the swelling ranks of educated young people entering the labour market each year.

The large proportion of youth in the MENA populations, in combination with other ongoing painful social-transformation processes, is likely to continue to have a radicalising effect in the sense that it provides new recruits to militant groups in the region.[26] The significant expansion of education in the region in recent decades has coincided with an unprecedented urbanisation, and, together, these social-transformation processes have contributed to fostering a large class of educated and semi-educated youth. As a rule, they are less likely to be content with the low-paid manual jobs performed by their less educated parents. Structural unemployment tends to be very high, and there are glaring socio-economic inequalities. Adding to these grievances, the young generation has been profoundly influenced by the consumerism of Western societies, not the least through the information revolution, which has provided Internet access, satellite dishes and cable television to a growing number of people. The information revolution allows an increasing number of slum dwellers throughout the world to base their material aspirations on soap operas. In the Arab world, the image of Western consumerism conveyed to young people through the media, 'increases their frustration and stimulates their hostility towards state authorities that are accused of having confiscated the benefits of an independence derived from petroleum wealth.'[27] The young generation is also sufficiently educated and literate to form political opinions. The combination of rapid population growth and expanding education is thus making 'youth [. . .] the key group which forces states from the Nile valley to the Maghreb to modify the way they practise politics'.[28] Opportunities of raising sufficient money for marriage and family before the age of thirty-five are limited for men from the lower middle classes. Living in societies with enforced gender segregation and a ban on premarital sex, these frustrated bachelors are prone to recklessness and risks. Under the right circumstances, these young men are obviously a fertile recruitment ground for violent political movements.

In addition to the MENA region, Asia has been a growing source of concern with regard to transnational terrorism since the 1990s. While demographic patterns vary widely in that region, a characteristic feature in the two most populous Asian countries is the emergence of an extremely skewed gender balance in favour of males. According to Hudson and Den Boer, a vast demographic shift has been taking place in Asia over the past two decades, engendered by social preferences for sons rather than daughters.[29] Both China and India are approaching a young adult sex ratio of nearly 1.20, and are likely to surpass that level in the next twenty years. This massive demographic reconstruction will most probably have serious social ramifications as millions of 'surplus males' will be unable to marry and start families. Historical experience suggests that such high levels of 'bare branches' are a serious source of social instability and violence.

While low standards of living and high population-growth rates sustain a large youth segment in the developing world, very low population growth combined with high standards of living, which is increasingly the norm in the industrialised world, tends to produce an ageing population. If current demographic trends continue, the population of the developed world will grow significantly older in the future. The share of young people in the developed world has already begun to decrease after a peak in the early

1980s.[30] In some east European countries, very low birth rates (and in the case of Russia, low life expectancy) have actually produce negative population growth. In fact, many post-Communist countries as well as Japan, Italy and Spain, are expected to have declining populations by 2015.[31] By mid-century, the population growth is predicted to be −0.2 per cent on average in 'more developed nations', and as much as −0.4 for Europe.[32] A shrinking population in complex industrial societies is a totally new experience, and its socio-economic effects are hard to predict. Some scholars warn that population contraction will cause economic recession. Others, like McRae, suggest that an older society will be characterised by low tolerance for disorder and a correspondingly high tolerance for government intervention.[33]

Summing up, current demographic trends clearly point to a reduced population growth in the future in the developing world, albeit with a continued rapid urbanisation rate, and a persistent youth-bulge problem, at least over the short run. The developed world will have an ageing and, in some countries, shrinking population.

Implications for terrorism

Are we witnessing two opposing trends in which the South will have swelling volatile mega-cities with a large number of violence-prone young males, while the North will have an ageing docile population, vigorously supportive of more law and order? If so, what does this mean for the future of terrorism?

Theories on political violence are not fully developed when it comes to explaining the effects of demography, urbanisation and violent crime rates. We have seen, however, that rapid modernisation and urbanisation tend to be associated with increased levels of terrorism. With steadily more people living in cities, it is likely that a greater part of future violent conflicts will take place in urban areas where it often assume the form of terrorism. Guerrilla warfare tactics are much more difficult to practise in an urban environment. If the urban environment becomes the prime scene of future warfare, terrorism will inevitably become an increasingly more important part of insurgent warfare.[34]

We have also seen that demographic realities in the MENA region, in combination with other social changes, have created an environment conducive to continued radicalisation in the short term. Demographic changes in the developing world will contribute to sustain or possibly increase the levels of terrorism. The driving factors behind this trend are the combined effect of the growth of mega-cities, the persistence of national age pyramids highly skewed in favour of (violent-prone) youth, as well as rising levels of education, the information revolution and growing social inequality, providing incentives for radical mobilisation. This is particularly true for countries where the demographic crisis is exacerbated by autocratic and patriarchial forms of government where younger generations from the lower middle classes have few opportunities for upward social mobility. Hence, radicalised youth, particularly in the MENA region, will continue to be a key source of political unrest and political violence, directed primarily against the regimes and its supporters. This is arguably already the case, and the potential for continued spillover of transnational terrorism as a result of internal conflicts in the South will not be reduced in the short term.

In a long-term perspective, however, the demographic prospects are better. Over the long run, the current youth bulges are likely to shrink significantly and mitigate the problems associated with them. In conjunction with other terrorism-inhibiting factors this might contribute to reduce the levels of terrorism in developing countries. In the developed world, the long-term effect of demographic changes may also be reduced levels of terrorism. As the population is set to become older, society may become less tolerant for disorder and violent crime and have a correspondingly high tolerance for government intervention. It is probably safe to assume that an ageing population will be more docile, less violent-prone and more supportive of measures to uphold law and order than a predominantly young population. Radical groups will find fewer potential sympathisers and be more vulnerable to government repression.

The immigration dilemma

Postulate: Migration in and between regions will increase and will make countries more ethnically heterogeneous. The influx of asylum-seekers and immigrants – both legal and illegal – into Europe and North America will continue in the future and significantly increase the size of their respective non-Western diasporas. An increasing number of people in the West will have ethnic and political ties to overseas conflict areas.

Possible implications for terrorism: Diaspora communities in the West will remain prominent in the financing, recruitment and political support for overseas insurgent groups and, to a lesser extent, for transnational terrorist organisations, operating against targets located in the West. The growing human-smuggling business will further facilitate the activities of transnational terrorist organisations in more than one way. Conflicts over immigration issues and ethnic minorities will persist, leading periodically to incidents of hate crimes and low-level political terrorism and, more rarely, serious campaigns of inter-communal violence. In the long run, there is also a distinct possibility that new forms of 'home-grown' ethnic terrorism may arise, linked to the new ethnic diaspora communities or in violent opposition to these.

Is terrorism in some way linked to migration and changes in the ethnic composition of countries? While I am aware of no studies explicitly examining the relationship between immigration as such and the occurrence of terrorism, ethnicity has clearly been a key factor in violent internal conflicts, including conflicts involving terroristic violence. Even if many ethnically hetero-geneous societies do not suffer from ethnic violence, such societies are by definition more predisposed to violent conflicts over ethnicity issues than homogenous societies. Furthermore, studies show that unsolved ethnic demands have been a main factor in explaining terrorism. Political conflicts over immigration issues have been accompanied by violence in a number of countries. Finally, diaspora communities in many parts of the world, and in particularly in the West, have been important sources of financing, recruit-ment and political support for overseas insurgencies and, in many cases, transnational terrorist organisations.[35] While none of this proves direct link-ages between immigration and terrorism, it suggests that future migration patterns may tell us something about the future evolution of terrorism.

Migration and ethno-demographic changes

Historically, migration has been a major force of demographic change in a number of countries and regions. During the nineteenth century and in the early decades of the twentieth century, emigration from Europe profoundly shifted the demographic set-up in other parts of the world. Patterns of migration have changed dramatically since the Second World War, however, and the developed world has since then become the primary destination for millions of immigrants seeking a better life abroad. Today's migration pat-terns are admittedly complex and rapidly changing. Predictions about future migration patterns are therefore highly uncertain.

Since the end of the Cold War, the rate of migration appears to have accelerated, and more countries are being more affected by global migration patterns than before.[36] Even if the number of refugees and asylum-seekers has declined from 16.3 million in 1994 down to 11.9 million in 2003, patterns of migration have not followed suit.[37] On the contrary, a recent OECD report on trends in international migration found that 'record numbers of people are moving to many OECD countries' which reinforces 'the upward trend in international migration which began in the mid-1990s'.[38] Most forecasts point to increased, rather than decreased, migration to the developed world. *Global Trends 2015* talks about 'a dramatic increase in the global movement of people through 2015'.[39] Furthermore, immigration has caused major ethno-demographic changes in the West, especially in major cities, and this trend is likely to continue or possibly accelerate. Even if there has been a rapid growth in the number of migrants living in developing countries over the past dec-ades, international migrants constitute a far greater proportion of the popula-tion in the developed countries than is the case in Third World states.[40]

Targets for future migrating populations are most likely to be the trad-itional immigrant countries, such as the USA, Canada and Australia, even if the EU has also become a much sought-after destination, having received several million immigrants and asylum-seekers over the past decade. Still, in much of the newly developed world, much of the migration will take place within rather than between countries or regions.[41] The North–South division is less clear-cut now than during the 1970s. The economic expansion of the Asian economies and the internationalisation of the world economy have contributed to diluting the traditional distinction between developed and developing countries. Still, there are a number of fault-lines, which have only become sharper over the years. The US–Mexican border is one example; another and perhaps sharper fault-line runs along the Mediterranean. George Joffé noted back in 1996 that 'hardly any economic power relationship between two regions [...] is so "essentially asymmetric" as the one between Europe and the Middle East/North Africa'.[42] Since then, the economic disparities have deepened further, increasing the incentives to emigrate to the North.

The scope of the demographic shifts caused by immigration is in many cases quite dramatic. The USA is expected to grow by as many as 130 million during the first half of this century, most of this growth owing to the newcomers. Immigration to western Europe is expected to be lower, only half of that to the USA, but the total population is not expected to rise significantly.[43] Hence, also in Europe, the ethno-demographic face of the continent is going to change considerably. Between 1996 and 2001, the USA received 27 per cent of the world's international migrants while western Europe as a whole took in 21 per cent, Germany being the major destination with 9 per cent alone. Most international migrants come from developing countries such as China and Mexico.[44] In Europe, historical relations between countries of departure and arrival have been important in determining patterns of immigration: France has received the majority of North Africans, Germany has been the destination of the greater majority of Turkish immigrants, and the UK has received large populations of Indian, West Indian and Pakistani origin.[45]

There are many reasons why transnational migration to the North will continue and possibly increase in the coming decades. True, there will certainly be ebbs and flows, the exact set-up of the South–North migration axis will change from time to time and, in recent years, tighter immigration control has been applied in both Europe and the USA. Still, the pull and push factors that drive the immigration to the Western world will not go away. Most developing countries have a flow of both legal and illegal immigrants seeking to escape from poverty or repression or to obtain greater freedom and economic opportunities elsewhere. In other cases, war, ethnic-cleansing, environmental degradation or political persecution are the driving factors for the exodus.[46] The 'pull factors' in the Third World have undoubtedly increased through the development of modern mass media and information technology as well as cheaper and more widely available international transportation.[47]

In his book on the economic sociology of immigration, Alejandro Porte writes that 'the fulfilment of normative consumption expectations imported from advanced countries becomes increasingly difficult under conditions of economic scarcity, while growing cross-national ties make it easier to seek solution through migration'.[48] Beare has also observed that '[i]ncreasingly, as all forms of commodities cross-borders [. . .] people will also move – pulled by the hope of better opportunities or pushed by violence and deprivations'.[49] It is a paradox, then, that while legal barriers to trade and investment abroad are falling and corporations relocate around the world and seek out or abandon adverse labour and environmental conditions almost at their will, migration control has been tightened. From the migrants' point of view, it may seem as though everything and everyone can move except non-specialised labour.[50]

Sociologists who study migration have noted that international labour migration largely originates at an intermediate level of development, not at the lowest level. The very poor and the unemployed are not the first to migrate.[51] This implies that future economic growth in the developing world will not necessarily reduce the push factors for emigration. On the contrary, it may well increase the motivation for and the ability to migrate to a country with better economic prospects and more political freedom. As I have shown in the previous chapter, economic inequalities between rich and poor states (as well as the visibility of this inequality), have generally widened over the past decades and are likely to continue to do so in the foreseeable future, presenting an additional incentive for increased migration.

In Europe a number of new circumstances also appear to set the stage for increased migration. The historic changes in eastern Europe and the former Soviet Union involved not only unprecedented changes to borders and systems of sovereignty, but dramatically reduced some of the main obstacles to emigration from or via these countries to western Europe. The introduction of the Schengen Agreement and the removal of internal border controls in the EU have also unwittingly facilitated increased immigration rates. Furthermore, the formation of sizeable European-based diaspora communities has created new cross-national ties and bonds of kinship, which in turn facilitates further immigration. Finally, depending on the scale of refugee flows from repressive regimes and armed conflicts, especially in Europe's periphery, European governments will be forced to keep their borders relatively open to refugees and asylum-seekers from the South.

There are a host of political and socio-economic implications arising with the immigration from the developing world to the West, and they cannot be dealt with in full scope here. We will focus on three possible long-term effects that are relevant to this study. First, the most obvious effect of current migration patterns is a slow but gradual change in the ethnic composition of recipient countries. By the end of the 1990s, legal and illegal migrants already accounted for more than 15 per cent of the population in more than fifty countries, and this ratio was expected to rise considerably.[52] Due to growing transnational migration and divergent birth rates between migrants and natives, most countries in the world, and particularly developed countries, are likely to experience increased ethnic heterogeneity over the next decades.[53]

In Europe, migration patterns have long been characterised by substantial immigration of non-Europeans, making the continent rapidly more multicultural and multi-ethnic. The situation in the USA and Canada with regards to non-Western immigration is somewhat different as both nations are built around immigration populations and have a much longer tradition of integrating immigrants into their societies. Still, high levels of immigration are also about to change the ethnic face of these countries. In the USA, the rapid growth of the Spanish-speaking population and the possible rise of 'an Hispanic majority' in many states, especially in the South, has become a very controversial issue. By 2050, US census experts have predicted that 'whites' will for the first time represent less than half of the US population, while Hispanics will be the majority in Texas. As late as 1980, two of every three Texans were white.[54] There is undoubtedly a separatist undercurrent among Mexican Americans in south-west, particularly in New Mexico, which has a history of separatist movements. Still, the predictions that 'it is an "inevitability" that the South-west will secede into a sovereign Hispanic nation' are very unlikely to hold.[55]

In the USA, assimilation, intermarriage, transformed identities and acculturation will greatly dampen ethnic differences, as they have done in the past. According to Harvard scholar Stephan Thernstrom, assimilation via the 'marital melting pot' has occurred at a rapid pace among the immigrants since 1945 and will continue to do so in the future. He predicts that by 2050 a very large proportion of all Americans will have some Hispanic, Asian or African 'blood'.[56] An assimilation process via intermarriage is slower in Europe, especially with regards to Islamic-origin immigrants, but even here 'the overall pattern is one of integration and incorporation'.[57] The rapid growth of non-Western immigration communities contributes to sustaining their ethnic separateness. Over the pasty thirty years, ethnic diaspora communities have increased in size, visibility and impact on the European continent and are likely to play more prominent roles in years to come.[58]

As for the implications of international migration patterns for the future of terrorism, these can be divided into three main themes: terrorism linked to hate crimes and ethnic issues, transnational terrorist support networks in the immigrant communities and, finally, terrorist links to illegal immigration and alien smuggling.

Hate crimes, racial riots and ethnic terrorism

One possible implication of this for terrorism is that more countries will experience violent conflicts over immigration and ethnic-minorities issues, or more intercommunal conflicts. Such conflicts may manifest themselves in terms of hate crimes and low-level political terrorism and may, under certain circumstances, escalate into serious campaigns of intercommunal violence. Growing ethnic diversity tends to foster intercommunal conflict and violence, but usually only in conjunction with other aggravating factors. In some countries waves of refugees from neighbouring countries have upset a sensitive ethnic balance and have caused the outbreak of violence. The growing ethnic heterogeneity of societies around the world has prompted some to predict that 'communal tensions, sometimes culminating in conflict, probably will increase' over the next decades.[59] This is less likely to occur on a wider scale in Europe or North America. Immigration to the West has certainly altered the face of most cities, and has also led to social unrest and serious incidents of hate crimes, but it has never come close to the kind of organised ethnic warfare that other parts of the world have seen.[60] Still, the rapidly changing ethnic composition of Western societies obviously presents very serious identity challenges for many people, resulting *inter alia* in increased support for radical right wing parties. Gang violence and hate crime emanating from violent right wing extremist and racist groups have also flourished in many Western countries. There have also been many occurrences of severe public disorder in western European cities involving immigrant youth. In August 1997, the Danish town of Nørrebrox erupted in severe riots, and four years later, in summer 2001, the UK had three days of race riots in Burnley, Oldham, Leeds and Bradford.[61] Furthermore, there have also been many cases where diaspora communities have attacked rival ethnic groups in their host countries in order to advance the causes of their respective home states or communities. In the mid-1990s, for example, there was a wave of political violence in Germany where Kurdish PKK-supporters launched a campaign of attacks against Turkish targets and Kurdish interests were also targeted by Turkish militants.

In a number of instances, hate-crime violence has escalated dangerously close to terroristic violence. One example of this was the series of explosions that rocked London in April 1999. One nail bomb hidden in a car exploded without any forewarning in a Bangladeshi quarter of London's East End on the Bengali New Year. Seven people were injured. Another blew up in Electric Avenue in Brixton in a predominantly black neighbourhood, injuring some forty people. A third bomb exploded inside Admiral Duncan pub in Soho, a central London district where the city's gay and lesbian community often hangs out, killing three and injuring more than eighty. The White Wolves, a breakaway group of Combat 18, one of the UK's most notorious extremist groups, claimed responsibility for the attacks, but the convicted perpetrator alleged he had acted alone.[62]

In the long run, there is a distinct possibility that new forms of 'homegrown' ethnically based terrorism may arise as a response to hate crimes, discrimination, alienation and the erosion of legal rights for immigrants in the Western democracies. Even if one has seen little of this so far, Castles and Miller warn against underestimating 'the potential for racism and anti-immigrant violence begetting terrorism in response'.[63] Such immigrant-linked terrorism may also arise in relation to specific conflict overseas or by drawing support from future separatist tendencies in the new ethnic diaspora communities in the West. The latter may occur if significant immigrant populations are not economically and politically integrated into their host societies, remain marginalised and alienated, and are territorially concentrated. Socio-economic disparities tend to be accompanied by a higher level of violence, including violence of a political character, especially when these disparities coincide with ethnic cleavages. Thus, much depends upon whether the growing immigrant communities become economically and socially integrated in Western societies or whether many of them remain a socially and politically excluded underclass. Current trends strongly indicate that many recent non-Western immigrants, including also second-generation immigrants, have higher unemployment rates and figure more prominently below the poverty lines than the general population. This is true both for Europe and the USA.

Diasporas, overseas insurgencies and transnational terrorism

While new forms of ethnically motivated terrorism in the West remain a real possibility, it appears more likely that the growing immigrant communities in the West will become more involved in armed conflict overseas through financing and support activities and, via these conflicts, become involved in transnational terrorism. In recent years, one has witnessed the rise of new transnational and cross-national allegiances in a process that may be described as deterritorialisation of social identity.[64] In many ways, this challenges the nation state's claim that exclusive citizenship is a defining focus of allegiance and fidelity. It is likely that the current models of integration–assimilation are one the wane and are de-facto being replaced by a new pluralism where transnational and communal diasporic allegiances compete with loyalty to the state. This development is likely to continue, and it is estimated that 'the very concept of "belonging" to a particular state probably will erode among a growing number of people' over the coming decades.[65] Instead, transnational ties to more than one state, through citizenship, residence, familial ties or other associations will grow stronger. Drawing upon the new opportunities for maintaining transborder contacts and ties, ethnic communal groups around the world will increasingly mobilise their co-religionists or ethnic kin to fight for their interests. Furthermore, many ethnic diaspora groups provide political, economic and other support for their brethen at home, and as long as the latter are at war, suffer under occupation or undergo times of great crisis, the former will continue to do so in the future. Immigrant communities will probably emerge even more prominently than today as 'ethnic lobbies' for their countries of origin, not only for government interests, but also for opposition movements, including insurgent and terrorist groups, operating in their home regions.[66] As Nichiporuk has noted, the growing web of information, communication and mass-media links as well as the expansion of global banking networks increase opportunities for globally dispersed ethnic diasporas to play a key role in military campaigns involving their home countries or territory.[67] Moreover, their ethnic kinship or co-religionists back 'home' are likely to expect more financial and political support from the diaspora communities in the wealthy privileged West than from diaspora communities elsewhere.

A good example of the linkages between immigration and the rise of terrorist support networks is the situation in Canada. In 2002 the Canadian Security Intelligence Service (CSIS) reported that

> with the possible exception of the United States, there are more international terrorist organisations active in Canada than anywhere in the world. [. . .] Canada, a country built upon immigration, represents a microcosm of the world. It is therefore not surprising that the world's extremist elements are represented here, along with peace-loving citizens. Terrorist groups are present here whose origins lie in regional, ethnic and nationalist conflicts, including the Israeli Palestinian one, as well as those in Egypt, Algeria, Sudan, Afghanistan, Lebanon, Northern Ireland, the Punjab, Sri Lanka, Turkey and the former Yugoslavia.[68]

Hence, increased immigration will probably make diaspora communities in the West even more prominent than they are today in the financing, recruitment and political support for overseas insurgent groups and, to a lesser extent, for transnational terrorist organisations operating against targets located in the West. If immigration should continue unabated, the opportunities for recruiting support networks as well as operative cells will inevitably increase. The more multi-ethnic and multicultural the Western world becomes, the easier it would be for foreign terrorist operatives to 'blend in'.

A continued high level of immigration to the Europe and North America will continue to provide a key link between the 'zones of turmoil' and the 'zones of peace', to borrow Singer and Wildavsky's well-known phraseology.[69] Even before the rise of al-Qaida, there were numerous incidents of international terrorism in the West, rooted in the conflicts in the MENA region, in particular the civil war in Algeria, the conflict in Lebanon, the Palestinian–Israeli peace process, the upheaval in Iran and the Kurdish conflict.[70] Immigration to the West, and in particular to Europe, has moved from being based on receiving countries's needs for labour, to becoming a safe haven for people fleeing from civil wars, insurgencies and repressive regimes. Paradoxically, this very selection mechanism makes it much more likely that today's migrants are politically affiliated with or sympathetic to violent opposition movements, rebel groups and terrorist organisations than was the case in the past when purely economic immigrants dominated, arriving through legal channels. As the diaspora communities in Europe will absorb thousands of new immigrants from conflict-ridden regions in the future, the links between the diaspora communities and overseas insurgencies will persist.

Judging by previous trends, support activities for overseas insurgencies will remain the dominant activity. To most insurgent groups, a large base of sympathisers and supporters in the diaspora community in the West is a most valuable asset, since they provide crucial political and material assistance. Terrorist acts in Europe or in North America would only put this essential support in jeopardy. This continues to be true today, even if Western governments are clamping down harder on terrorism-financing than a decade ago, and thereby reducing the value of their 'sanctuaries' in the West.

Recent developments suggest that support networks sometimes tend to mutate into operational networks. This is particularly the case for pro-al-Qaida terrorist groups. According to Canadian intelligence reports, many terrorist-support networks have moved 'from significant support roles, such as fund-raising and procurement, to actually planning and preparing terrorist acts from Canadian territory'.[71] This also seems to be the case in Europe. While Islamist terrorism in the West mostly has been a product of overseas conflicts, recent trends suggest an emerging domestic or 'home-grown' Islamist terrorism trend, where European Muslims are recruited into more distinctly European networks. For example, the terrorist suspects arrested in March 2004 in the UK were young men, all of them born and brought up in that country. Scotland Yard officials have referred to this and other networks in the UK as 'young radicalised Muslims' who defy the traditional profile of al-Qaida-affiliated terrorists.[72] The suspected cell apparently planned their attacks independently and was not dictated to by anyone in the al-Qaida hierarchy.[73] Neither were there indications that any Afghan-Arab veterans – a common staple in all other Islamist terrorist plots in Europe in recent years – were involved.

Over the past decade there have also been quite a number of examples of European and American Muslims participating in insurgencies and transnational terrorist attacks overseas. From being an arena for attacks carried out by foreign terrorist groups, the West is now emerging as an 'exporter of terrorism' to overseas conflict areas. The following examples will suffice to illustrate the point: in the mid-1990s several French Muslims planned an attack on a tourist hotel in Morocco and many others travelled to Algeria to fight with the rebels. British Muslims were implicated in a hostage operation in Yemen in 1998. British-born Pakistani Muslims have volunteered for suicide-bombings in Srinagar in the late 1990s and in Israel in 2003. A substantial number of citizens or residents from a variety of European countries were detained in Afghanistan in 2001 as they fought alongside the Taleban and al-Qaida.

Human-smuggling and transnational terrorism

A final terrorism-related implication of today's immigration pattern comes as a result of tightened immigration control in the West, causing a considerable rise in illegal immigration. This unregulated movement of people into Europe and North America has assumed significant proportions.[74] Expert commentaries put the number of illegal immigrants in the USA at 8 to 9 million, of which 4.81 million are 'undocumented Mexicans'.[75] The number of illegal migrants smuggled into the EU each year is estimated at around 400,000.[76] In the mid-1990s, France, for instance, already hosted some 200,000–350,000 illegal immigrants.[77] (In 2001, a NATO fleet assumed policing functions in the Mediterranean waters to ward off terrorist threats. A major impact of this operation was reportedly a considerable decline in illegal immigration to countries in southern Europe.[78])

Tighter immigration control paves the way for sophisticated TCOs, which profit greatly from the smuggling of humans. The broad range of illegal businesses arising in connection with human-smuggling and the presence of a huge number of illegal residents in the West have already become a major source of income for a number of TCOs.[79] Illegal immigration is already regarded as 'one of the most direct security challenges to Europe'.[80] The dilemma is that more restriction on immigration will only raise the stakes and hence the profits for criminal enterprises specialising in human-trafficking.

Since transnational organised crime and terrorism tend to be associated with, and mutually reinforce, one another, illegal immigration and the human-smuggling trade indirectly broaden the opportunities for transnational terrorists. The presence of an underground industry for forging ID papers and other travel documents is invaluable for transnational terrorists. Furthermore, even if other illegal fund-raising methods are more common for terrorist groups, there are many examples of terrorist-financing emanating from the lucrative human-smuggling business. Examples include the sprawling LTTE support infrastructure in Canada, a network of Kurdish Islamists in several Italian cities and the estimated 100 or so 'al-Qaida cells' operating out of Morocco.[81]

The case of the Kurdish Islamist Ansar al-Islam network in Italy is particularly telling, illustrating the importance of the human-smuggling trade for these networks. According to Italian police sources, a key terrorist suspect in Parma had reportedly received a number of forged travel documents. He used these to assist potential recruits in reaching military camps, mainly in Iraq, to move throughout Europe and to keep up contacts with other cells. He also provided false ID cards to help illegal immigrants to enter Italy. This case is not unique. In fact, most members in a suspected terrorist cell arrested in Milan were reportedly involved in human-smuggling, either for fund-raising purposes or for possible recruitment for terrorism activities. According to an Italian police report there is 'wide evidence that these structures have been used to recruit volunteers for military camps in Iraq, organised by "Ansar Al Islam" group, to help illegal immigration towards Italy via Greece and Turkey to provide financial and material means for terrorist activities'.[82]

In sum, there can be little doubt that under the broader umbrella of smuggling of illegal aliens, terrorist groups are able to find their niche, exploiting this business for financial, logistical and operational purposes. As immigration control is set to tighten and the push factors for migrating north are not diminishing, the human-smuggling business will remain a key feature of organised crime in the West and will probably have important linkages with transnational terrorism.

6

IDEOLOGICAL SHIFTS

> This is the century of the Islamic resistance after the govern-
> ments have weakened and kneeled down before the invading
> Crusader. Let's learn a lesson from Chechnya, Afghanistan,
> Iraq, Palestine where the authority has vanished or was
> removed from power but the resistance remained.[1]
>
> (Ayman al-Zawahiri, 1 October, 2004)

Extremist violent ideologies do not cause terrorism by themselves, even if
they are powerful instruments in the hands of eloquent leaders in propelling
people towards terrorist actions. The popularity of violent ideologies in some
countries and their near absence in others is mostly rooted in structural societal factors. On a psycho-sociological level, however, extremist ideologies
nevertheless play an important role in *shaping* terrorist actions, in addition to
motivating members and making violence intelligible and imperative for
them.[2] The decline of some strands of ideological extremism, and the persistence or growth of others, will therefore be indicators of future trends in
terrorism, primarily with regards to modus operandi.

This chapter is shorter than the others. The reason is that it is very hard to
make reliable predictions about something as intangible and fluid as extremist ideologies. Furthermore, the overwhelming diversity of extremist ideologies makes any attempt at providing a full-blown survey futile. We therefore
confine the discussion to a few suggestions about which ideological trends
appear to hold best prospects for being dominant among future terrorist
organisations.

The future landscape of extremist ideologies

Postulate: The future landscape of extremist ideologies will become even less
uniform and more multifaceted than it is today and it will also change more
rapidly. Still, the traditional ideological basis for terrorist action, in particular
separatist ethno-nationalism, and various versions of extreme leftist Maoist-
Marxism will remain dominant, especially in domestic terrorism. On a global
level, internationalist leftist militancy with terrorist fringes may experience a
renaissance. Religious extremism will also continue to flourish, especially
in conjunction with extreme nationalism. The internationalist versions of

jihadism will probably retain their dominant position among the global extremist ideologies for many years to come. In addition, fundamentalist movements and cults, emanating from other religions, may also proliferate and occasionally translate into terrorist actions. Right wing racist extremism, though clearly a very important source of hate crime, is unlikely to become a leading ideology in transnational terrorism. Violent single-issue extremism may, however, become more influential, especially in merged versions with other extreme leftist or religious ideologies.

Possible implications for terrorism: The future of terrorism will continue to be dominated by many incidents of mass-casualty terrorism, due to the continued strength of internationalist jihadism. At the same time, a resurgence of international leftist militancy may generate a more pronounced level of 'classical' international terrorism with highly restrained use of violence. An increased, but still marginal number of extremist cults will probably cause new forms of apocalyptic mass-casualty attacks. The fluidity and rapid changes of extremist ideologies may give rise to unexpected marriages of ideologies, which in turn may alter the terrorist modus operandi associated with the various ideologies. The contagious effect of terrorism also makes the spread of new tactics across ideological boundaries more likely.

Recent decades have witnessed significant ideological changes, some of which started before the collapse of the Soviet Union. The era of dominant ideologies and a clear-cut left–right axis in politics have been gradually overtaken by the rise of new political movements that defy traditional categorisation. Ideologies based on the traditional division of labour and capital no longer command the same respect. On the ruins of communism, Fukuyama proclaimed *'the end of history'* in 1992, pointing to the victory of the Western liberal capitalist model as the only viable way to development.[3] One year later Huntington proposed instead a world of clashing civilisations, seeing religion and culture on a supranational civilisational level as the coming foci of allegiance and identity for a growing number of people.[4] Others predicted a possible return to tribalism, disorder and anarchy with little place for global overarching ideologies.[5] The apparent spread of violent ethnic conflicts in the immediate post-Cold War era seemed to confirm the latter. In reality, however, this was no more than a reminder of the fact that militant ethno-nationalism has always been among the most powerful ideologies behind terrorist violence (see Figure 6.1). This will probably continue to be so in the foreseeable future, at least for domestic terrorism.

The highly diverging views in the early and mid-1990s about ideologies and powers that would determine the future world are indicative of the problems of forecasting extremist ideologies. It does not have to be pure guesswork, however. One obvious indicator lies in the relative unipolarity of the post-Cold War world order. As discussed in Chapter 3, it is highly unlikely that

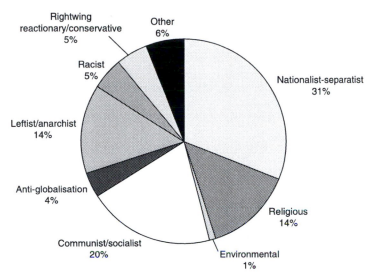

Figure 6.1 Terrorist incidents and ideologies, 1968–2004.
Source: Data from the RAND MIPT terrorism incident database, see <http://db.mipt.
org/mipt_rand.cfm>.

one will see the rise of a new state-based global challenger or 'counter-core' to the USA and the capitalist Western world, similar to the Communist bloc.[6] This probably implies that the kind of overarching global ideologies, which drew their influences from the clash between Western democratic liberalism and eastern Communism, will not re-emerge, at least not with the same strength. The collapse of the Soviet Union led to a drying-up of financial support for Communist or leftist insurgencies. Many leftist revolutionaries were bereaved of their sense of mission and lost their belief in the historical inevitability of victory in their struggle. The waning of Maoist–Marxist revolutionary thinking undermined the urban guerrilla-warfare model, which inspired a generation of leftist terrorist groups.

A resurgent left?

While these geopolitical changes may have demotivated socio-revolutionary terrorists and their potential sympathisers on the extreme Left, they have had less effect upon ethnic separatist groups with strong leftist orientations, since their very *raison d'être* was not affected by the collapse of Communism. A number of leftist guerrilla groups in the Third World have also managed the post-Cold War transition from state-sponsorship to economic self-sufficiency through drugs-trafficking, extortion, hostage-takings for ransom, etc., but without entirely losing sight of the revolution. In fact, the resilience of Marxist–Maoist rebel insurgencies in Colombia, Mexico, Nepal, the Philippines and India strongly suggest that the era of leftist insurgencies is not over. Fifteen years after the Berlin Wall collapsed, violent leftist ideologies still cast a spell in Europe too. The continued existence of active leftist terrorist groups in several countries including Italy, Greece and Turkey suggests that the impact of the Soviet collapse may only have a short-term effect on delegitimising extremist leftist ideologies. Italy is a case in point. After nearly a decade with very little domestic terrorism, Italy's tranquillity was shaken by several high-profile killings, first and foremost the New Red Brigades's assassinations of two government advisers on labour affairs in 1999 and 2002.[7] In 2004, the Brigades were also revealed to have computer records of addresses and daily routines of top Italian politicians, including Prime Minister Silvio Berlusconi, union leaders, economists and magistrates.[8]

The widespread popular rally around the multifaceted anti-globalisation and anti-war movement in many countries, and the spread of populist leftist governments in Latin America further indicate that mainstream leftist activism is alive and well and is capable of fostering militant fringes. New controversial US-led military interventions are also likely to boost and possibly radicalise the anti-war movement. Anti-capitalist ideologies may experience a resurgence as the Cold War and the excesses of the Communist era fade into the history books. Political instability and popular revolts against the economic disadvantages of globalisation are likely to give rise to new regimes built on ideologies that challenge the current doctrine of market economy.[9] Still, even if internationalist leftist ideologies are by no means dead, they cannot aspire to the kind of utopian universalism that characterised the heyday of Communism.

The challenge of Islamism and al-Qaidaism

Islamism, or 'Islamic fundamentalism', has frequently been touted as the most likely candidate for assuming the vacant throne of Communism. It has undoubtedly become the most powerful anti-imperialist anti-Western ideology in Muslim communities all around the world. The persistent popularity of Islamism has both political and cultural explanations. It cannot be reduced to a socio-revolutionary ideology in religious disguise, however. It is also partly a response to a Western-dominated paradigm that represented imported, not indigenous values.[10] Similarly, the rise of extremist nationalist parties and religious fundamentalist ideologies in various parts of the world is not simply a result of material and political disaffection by identifiable socio-economic and political issues. It represents, to varying degrees, broad responses to what is seen as 'Western imposition' of a cosmopolitan and alien culture, a vulgar McDonaldism, out of touch with local identities and idiosyncrasies.

Radical Islamism is not a new phenomenon. It has long been observed that militant groups in the Islamic world tend to adopt the ideological mantle of political Islam rather than secular ideologies. Secular nationalism and varieties of leftist Marxist ideologies were the preferred ideological battle cries for militant revolutionaries in the Middle East in the 1970s, but had gradually been replaced by militant Islam by the 1980s and 1990s.

At the same time, radical Islamism has not remained unchanged. Its transformation has at least two important aspects. First, militant groups in the Arab world used to be very inspired by the Iranian revolution in 1979 and tended to see the Sunni–Shiite divide as one of diminishing importance.[11] By the end of the 1990s, however, radical Islamism had become much more dominated by Saudi-inspired groups that were fiercely puritanical and doctrinally more rigid than mainstream political Islamism, which emanated from the Egyptian Muslim Brotherhood.[12] These new groups are often labelled Sunni-fundamentalists, Wahhabis, or salafi-jihadi groups.[13] Their leading activists often got their military and ideological training during the Afghan war of liberation in the 1980s. They no longer look to the Islamic Republic of Iran for inspiration. On the contrary, they view the Shiites, including the Iranians, as heretics and infidels. To these militants, the only true Islamic state that has existed in modern times was the Islamic Emirate of Afghanistan under Taleban rule. By the late 1990s, Afghanistan had also replaced Iran and Sudan as the most important sanctuary for militant Islamist groups. Their most prominent ideologues are Saudi clerics, who often provide detailed guidance and even sanctioning for Muslim militants across the globe.[14] The term 'salafi' appears in the names of several al-Qaida affiliated insurgent/terrorist organisations, such as the Salafi Group for Preaching and Combat (GSPC) in Algeria, the Salafiya Jihadiya Group in Morocco and the Salafi Fighting Group and the Salafi Islamic Army, both in Iraq.

We may speak of an ideological shift towards salafi-jihadism. This new subcurrent of political Islamism represents a combination of an uncompromising violent militancy and doctrinal and theological purity. A well-known Islamist web site thus described salafi-jihadism as 'Salafi in doctrine and Jihadi in method' (*salafi al-aqidah wa jihadi al-manhaj*).[15] The result of this merger of jihadi doctrine and salafi puritanism is an almost total loss of the political sophistication and flexibility that to some degree has characterised political Islamism since the emergence of the Muslim Brotherhood.[16] The salafi-jihadi attitude to politics can best be illustrated by their constant repetition of the slogan: 'Jihad and the rifle alone: no negotiations, no conferences and no dialogues', and by their vehement denunciation of democracy and elections as an un-Islamic 'innovation' (*bid'ah*).[17] The turn towards doctrinal purity hence implies a concomitant weakening of the political dimension of the radical Islamist agenda.

An important second aspect is that there has been a shift from the local revolutionary struggle to what one may term 'global jihad'. With the rise of al-Qaida as an instigator, financier, innovator and elite vanguard of Islamic militants, radical Islamism has witnessed a dramatic transformation. The Afghan war in the 1980s and al-Qaida's training camps in Afghanistan were crucial factors in this transformation, as they paved the way for contacts and co-operative arrangements and served as a melting pot of a multitude of Islamic militant trends. Insurgent groups struggling to topple their domestic regimes, which were previously relatively isolated, began to form a global network of like-minded militants.[18]

An important facilitating factor was the outbreak of a number of civil wars during the 1990s in which Muslims were often the weaker party. Their sufferings received worldwide media attention. These wars not only proved in the eyes of radical clerics that Islam was under military attack, but they also served as training bases and battlefields for thousands of Muslim volunteers from around the world who believed they were fulfilling the individual duty (*fard 'ayn*) for every Muslim to fight a defensive jihad. Parallel to the increased involvement of foreign volunteer fighters (*mujahidin*) in local conflicts, there was an ideological shift towards emphasising the need to fight the 'distant enemy' first, the 'Alliance of Christian Crusaders and Jews', represented primarily by the USA and Israel. Hence, the mujahidin should postpone the local struggle against the 'near enemy', that is Muslim governments supported by the West, until the distant enemy has been defeated. The shift has been visible on several levels. Local groups have become more internationalised by recruiting foreign volunteers into their ranks and have increasingly established working relationships with militant groups in other countries. Furthermore, they have also increasingly adopted the global-jihad model of al-Qaida by targeting US, Israeli and Western interests and by adopting al-Qaida's tactics such as simultaneous mass-casualty attacks using suicide-bombers.

The 9/11 attacks and the US declaration of war against al-Qaida have undoubtedly elevated *radical* Islamism, and especially its various salafi-jihadist versions, to one of the most powerful and attractive extremist ideologies on the marketplace of ideas. Still, the global appeal of this 'al-Qaidaism' is nevertheless hampered by its strictly Sunni-Muslim and salafi-jihadi orientation, its mass-casualty modus operandi and other ideological weaknesses. This ensures that the future growth potential of al-Qaidaism should not be exaggerated, even if pro-al-Qaida groups should be able to capture control over a state. Hence, despite its current predominance, al-Qaidaism will remain just one of several extremist ideologies opposing globalisation and Western hegemony in world politics.

In the coming decades, new Islamist revolutions in the Middle East are a real possibility. Even if regimes founded on the principles of political Islam, in particular Iran, Sudan and Taleban Afghanistan have suffered tremendous failures, Islamist myths and symbols 'will remain a potent tool for mobilising public support throughout the Muslim world for decades to come'.[19] Islamist movements will continue to mobilise popular support, exploiting the widespread hostilities towards US interventionism in the region, especially its high level of military, diplomatic and financial support for Israel and its alliances with authoritarian Arab leaders.

The remarkable transformation of radical Islamism over the past decade has had very important implications for terrorism. Due to its tremendous success in establishing itself as the only real enemy of the USA and its allies, radical Islamism in its internationalist jihadist form is likely to remain a formidable inspirational source of anti-Western mass-casualty terrorism over the next decade.

The new religious extremism

Among religious extremist groups, millenarian religious movements and apocalyptic sects stand out as particularly unpredictable actors. Doomsday cults are nothing new, however, and they are relatively few. For the foreseeable future the majority of the world's population are most likely to continue 'as almost exclusive adherents and practitioners of the traditional systemic forms [of religion]'.[20] Still, during the past decades one has witnessed a number of increasingly violent doomsday sects, inflicting mass violence on their members and, in rare cases, also on outsiders. The American Jonestown/People's Temple cult in Guyana, Latin America and the Movement for the Restoration of the Ten Commandments (MRTC) in Uganda perpetrated large-scale massacres, killing 900 and 780 of their followers respectively. Aum Shinrikyo in Japan was the first doomsday cult to use sarin gas in attacks against outsiders, killing twelve and injuring several thousands in their attack on the Tokyo subway in 1995. Eleven years earlier, the Bgwan Shree Rajneesh cult in Oregon, California, developed various poisons, including salmonella, and used these in several attacks against outsiders. In 1985 members of an American racist right wing cult, The Covenant, Sword, Arm of the Lord ran a cyanide-producing laboratory and stockpiled massive quantities of cyanide for the purpose of poisoning the water supply of a city in the USA.[21]

During recent years, the number of millennium sects appears to have increased. Michael Barkun observed that 'millenarian movements have grown in contemporary America as a hotbed'.[22] While most such collectives have not uniformly adopted violent strategies against outsiders, the potential for violent activism is clearly there, especially during periods when the group is experiencing external pressure and episodes of stress.[23]

At first glance, the current proliferation of new religious movements and sects seems counter-intuitive. How come modernity, prosperity and scientific progress do not only lead to the survival of religiosity but even cause a resurgence in extremist and cultist forms of religion? Hall and Schuyler in their study of the Solar Temple Order in Switzerland pointed to the anomaly that 'today's affluent mostly post-Catholic society of francophone Europe hardly seems to be a place where religious anxieties could take hold'.[24]

In his book *Religion and Globalisation*, Peter Beyer argues that 'modernity and globality do not result in the disappearance of religion either in terms of importance for the conduct of social life or in terms of visibility on the social landscape'.[25] Instead, the question is whether 'the globalised context means the gradual erosion of the religious system as a system to be replaced by a highly diverse ecology of religious culture'.[26] According to Beyer we are moving towards 'the market economy model of religion' in which 'people "consume" what they want from various religious producers'.[27]

Manuel Castells considers the paradox that the extraordinary rise of the Japanese Aum Shinrikyo, the popularity of the US anti-federal militias and the remarkable growth of radical Islamism over the past decades have occurred at a time when modernisation has spread further and deeper than ever before in history. The emergence of religious countercultures cannot be understood within a traditional development paradigm that presupposes the disappearance of primordial social formations and the gradual displacement of religion. Even if traditional religious practices may have receded on a global scale, other reformulated forms of religious practices have supplanted traditional religion.

In an attempt to predict the future evolution of religious practices, Felipe Fernández-Armesto argues that 'we can expect millenarianism to continue after 2000'.[28] One reason for this is that few millenarian groups have in fact attached special significance to the date 2000. Furthermore, Fernández-Armesto observes that in the West the number of adherents to religions was at a low point in the 1960s and the number of respondents to surveys who identify themselves as religious has 'been increasing ever since'.[29] At the same time, religious revival has been much stronger outside the mainstream churches than within them. According to Fernández-Armesto, there has been 'an explosion of new religions' all over the world since 1960, and 'the multiplication of numbers of faithful in traditional communions in Asia and Africa has been too swift to monitor accurately'.[30] Also *Global Trends 2015* predicts that religious revivalist movements will be important in the coming decades, possibly linked to environmental values.[31]

The example of Aum Shinrikyo is telling. The movement came into being as part of the second wave of new religions, the so-called 'new new religions', challenging established forms of religious practices in Japan. Participation in organised religion since Second World War in Japan had declined, while the needs for religiosity and spirituality evidently increased. The new new religions often appealed to the newly educated and more well-to-do classes and 'to the more spiritual and mystical desires of financially secure people'.[32] Sociological explanations of how a movement like Aum could attract so many followers focus on factors like the control-oriented and socially conformist society. Daniel Metraux has argued that Aum was able to attract young Japanese who sought meaning in their lives beyond a successful career: 'the restrictive education and the prospect of an equally boring and restrictive career in industry makes Aum's leader Asahara's false promises of scientific freedom sound appealing'.[33]

Towards a diffuse and rapidly changing ideological landscape

Globalisation accelerates the speed of change, it alters the media of discourse, and it connects peoples and ideas across great geographical distances. This suggests that in the age of globalisation, fluidity and rapid changes will characterise the future landscape of extremist ideologies. Violence-seeking belief systems will most likely proliferate in various mutations even more widely than before, aided by the new media of communication. No single ideology will be able to capture an entire generation like Marxism in its Maoist version was able to do. Instead, one will continue to see the mushrooming of extremist ideas and 'para-ideologies', borrowing ideas and ideological substance from a wide variety of sources, including the growing range of new religions.

This development also arises out of the process of 'individualisation of security', in Ulrich Beck's parlance.[34] Despite the rise of al-Qaida, inhabitants of Western societies no longer have a common external threat after the fall of Soviet Union. Furthermore, the modern welfare state has accelerated the dissolution of traditional loyalties and allegiances, such as extended family bonds. Even the 'two plus two' family is threatened as the nucleus of society. The rise of informational-capitalist societies has also undermined class consciousness and labour unions. The atomisation of Western societies has then taken a step further as even the common-enemy image disappeared. In this hyperindividualised postmodern world, everybody has their own enemy but no longer the same unifying external enemy.

The information revolution itself will certainly provide further impetus to the mushrooming of new and new-old ideological substance. Arquilla, Ronfeldt and Zanini, writing on information-age activism and organisational patterns of non-state groups, believe that there is a new generation of radicals and activists who are just beginning to create 'information-age-ideologies.'[35] These forms of ideologies come in conjunction with a shift of identities and loyalties from the nation-state to the transnational level of global civil society or other real or imagined supranational entities. New ideologies may provide a framework for the rise of for example 'anarchistic and nihilistic leagues of computer-hacking "cyboteurs" '.[36] In general, future ideologies and organisational patterns of radicals in a network society are likely to be diffuse and rapidly changing and 'odd hybrids and symbioses are likely'.[37]

Processes of fragmentation and syncretism will be the rule in the landscape of extremist thinking. It will be harder to distinguish theology from politics and ideological terrorism from economic crime and warlordism. Ideologies will not only be harder to use as a predictive model for terrorist actions. They may also become harder to identify in the first place as they rise out of a flood of syncretism for whatever is available on the ideological Internet bazaar. And they will mutate and reconfigure more quickly than before.

In the fluid landscape of ideological syncretism and fragmentation of established beliefs, countercultures appear to have found a particular fertile ground.[38] For countercultures the increasingly evident social side effects of informational capitalism – 'inequality, poverty, misery and social exclusion' serve as the major object of protest.[39] More often, however, countercultural religious movements rise in response to a rapidly changing socio-cultural environment in order to recreate social cohesion and moral authority at a time when established norms and traditions are being challenged and displaced.

The proliferation of countercultures is also partly a product of the globalisation process itself. The rise of countercultures is perhaps one of the most manifest examples of the dialectic interaction between people and technology, producing social and cultural responses to change. Ideas and ideologies are constantly being produced and reproduced in the informational society in which the very speed of transnational communication and diffusion of knowledge creates a wholly new situation of fluidity and uncertainty.[40] The rapidity of change produces social anomie and alienation. New breakthroughs in informational technologies will reinforce a progressive virtualisation of society, blurring established perceptions of reality and fiction and widening the scope for extremist conspiracy-driven ideologies. Further 'informationalisation' of society will most probably produce dramatic and unforeseen socio-cultural responses.

Such social and cultural counter-responses to globalisation will most likely find its most manifest expressions in the rise of transnational countercultures with a global outreach, but focused around specific causes and grievances. None of these will be hegemonic ideologies, however. There will hardly be any basis for *one* dominant global counter-ideology opposing the Western liberal paradigm.

Possible implications for terrorism

A significant theoretical school in the study of terrorism points to the role of ideas and ideology in motivating and shaping terrorist actions. The basic argument is that 'ideas have consequences' and that terrorists' attitudes and convictions are key to understanding the origin of their organisation and modus operandi.[41] Terrorists are not all equal. Ideologies do matter when it comes to target selection and the use of violence. For example, while leftist terrorists have traditionally been averse to indiscriminate killings, some right wing groups and many religious groups, including radical Islamist groups condone mass-casualty attacks. Ethnic terrorist groups vary widely in terms of tolerating mass killings of civilians. On the other hand, they generally seem less willing to export their conflict to other countries, compared to the internationalist terrorist groups among radical Islamists and on the extreme Left.

Due to the continued strength of internationalist jihadism and al-Qaidaism, the future of terrorism will continue to be dominated by many incidents of coordinated mass-casualty attacks against international targets. The contagious effect of terrorism may also contribute to spreading al-Qaida's tactics to other groups. The greatest potential for contagion is of course to the numerous locally oriented Islamist militant groups with a national-separatist orientation. A full-scale internationalisation of the Chechen, Palestinian and Iraqi insurgency campaigns will be a dramatic development in international terrorism. At present, there are already worrisome signs that some of the insurgent movements involved contemplate transferring their war beyond the territories of their enemy regimes in Russia, Israel and Iraq.[42]

As discussed above, various indicators point to a possible resurgence of international leftist militancy. A number of Third World leftist insurgencies are still ongoing, and leftist terrorist groups in the West have not entirely disappeared. The militant anarchist anti-globalisation groups and radicalised anti-war movements may foster a renewal of leftist terrorism, generating a more pronounced level of 'classical' international terrorism with discriminate use of violence.

The fluidity and rapid changes of extremist ideologies may give rise to unexpected marriages of ideologies, which in turn may alter the terrorist modus operandi associated with the various ideologies. Alliances and patterns of co-operation between extremist groups may become more unpredictable and surprising. Reports that for example right wing extremists have occasionally found a common cause with animal-rights defenders and that Islamist militant groups have nurtured contacts with avowedly racist groups in Europe point to an ideological landscape with unpredictable alliances and rapid change.[43]

An important part of this unpredictability of ideological orientation lies in the proliferation of extremist cults, sometimes married to other extremist ideologies. Religious terrorism appears to be more lethal and less casualty averse than any other form of terrorism. It tends to occur in the absence of clear-cut political motivations, while a more intangible desire for revenge or apocalyptic visions of triggering the long-awaited doomsday are the main forces driving these groups.[44] Such motivations, in turn, contribute to lowering the threshold for inflicting mass casualties. We will probably see new doomsday cults giving birth to mass-casualty attacks, although their violence will overwhelmingly be directed inwards and such incidents will remain relatively rare occurrences.

7

OUR TECHNOLOGICAL FUTURE

> Technology twists the shape of global space, initiating an age of
> international upheaval with warlike slaughters of unsuspecting
> foreigners at home and abroad. Witness the new architecture of
> death, unwittingly designed by engineers of modern efficiency –
> shopping malls, hotels, buses, and airplanes that collect and
> confine swarms of civilians unable to defend themselves against
> invisible enemies blending into the crowd.[1]
>
> (Donald Black, 2004)

Judging from past trends, technological advances in the civilian and military
domain are likely to have an effect on patterns of terrorism. Generally speak-
ing, modernisation and technological breakthroughs are part of the 'ecology
of terrorism', in the sense that they inadvertently provide new opportunities
for terrorists in terms of weaponry, targets, audiences and anonymity. Citing
terrorist use of TNT after it appeared in the First World War, RDX after the
Second World War and, more recently, plastic explosives, one scholar argues
that we face a dangerous evolution 'in which the terrorist seems to hold all
the cards'.[2] This seems inaccurate for several reasons. Technology helps governments to significantly increase their counter-terrorist capabilities. The
development of such technologies has become a mainstay in the ongoing 'war
on terror'.[3] By contrast, terrorist groups are ill-suited to reap much benefit of
new and sophisticated technologies. The acquisition of new and unfamiliar
technology is a very complex process for any organisation, let alone clandestine cell-structured illegal movements. Most terrorist groups have usually
only a few of the characteristics that are needed in an organisation in order
to acquire sophisticated technology.[4]

Studies of the relationship between terrorism and the evolution of technology usually paint a picture of terrorists as pragmatic or even conservative
in their choice of weaponry and technology. Terrorists are seldom 'techno-
enthusiasts'; they are clearly very capable of innovation, but not driven by it.[5]
Although technological developments in the military field may inadvertently
provide terrorist groups with new and more efficient weapons, terrorists dif-
fer fundamentally from the military by their heavy reliance on commercial or
black-market technologies. They use standard or even home-made hand
weapons, improvised explosives devices, off-the-shelf communication and
reconnaissance equipment, etc. Furthermore, terrorist tactics also involve

exploitation of emerging vulnerabilities of modern societies and harnessing their built-in energies for destruction. Hence, dual-use potentials in a broad sense are central to terrorist technologies.

In previous chapters I have alluded to several technological advances with a potential for altering the terrorist threat, such as the widening range of mid-level CB-risk agents emerging from the pharmaceutical industries, the proliferation of LNG industries and the commercialisation of sophisticated military and security hardware. Any attempt at surveying the full range of new technologies, potentially affecting terrorist modus operandi or, conversely, enhancing effectiveness of states' anti-terrorism efforts, is impossible within the scope of this book. In this chapter I will therefore confine the discussion to the impact of only a small sample of emerging technologies, with a focus on information technologies (IT), while the latter part of the chapter discusses emerging counter-terrorism technologies. While this is not sufficient to allow for any general conclusions, the discussion nevertheless points to important future trends.

Terrorism and technology

Postulates: There will be staggering advances over the next decades in IT, bioengineering, nanotechnology and a host of other fields. A rapid commercialisation of new technologies must be expected in most industries. IT and operative computers will support an increasing range of activities in all spheres of life, including critical infrastructure. New interconnecting technologies will enable more and more people to exchange larger and larger amounts of information at steadily declining costs and from an expanding range of devices.

Possible implications for terrorism:

1. Terrorist groups will become increasingly adept at exploiting IT in a growing number of fields. Multiple co-ordinated attacks on many targets at many different locations will be easier to carry out. Similarly, one will see more sophisticated reconnaissance and intelligence operations by terrorist groups. Critical infrastructure targets, operated by IT systems are likely to be targeted more frequently and more seriously than we have seen in the past. Proselytising, recruitment, training and planning will increasingly take place via virtual extremist communities, where various terrorist skills and expertise are shared and developed. 'Leaderless resistance' principles will become more widely used in terrorist networks, heralding a possible rise in individualised or 'loner' terrorism.
2. The range of 'dual-use' products will expand due to the rapid commercialisation of new technologies in most industries, such as biochemical and pharmaceutical products, aerosolisation techniques, robotics and

remote-controlled vehicles, etc. This may allow terrorist groups to increase the number and sophistication of their weapons.

The evolution of IT is staggering and its societal ramifications are immense. The information revolution undoubtedly represents the most significant global transformation since the industrial revolution. Already, most of the states in the developed world can be characterised as interconnected network societies dependent on IT for communication, production and services.[6] They are increasingly reliant on a wide range of information systems. Their infrastructure facilities, such as telecommunications, energy production and supply systems, air, rail and road transportation, banking and financial services, water supply, etc., are already heavily interconnected and based on interdependent information systems which are, in many cases, linked directly or indirectly to the Internet.

Advanced IT is used on the battlefield, in military operations and in sustaining critical military infrastructure. Increasingly, due to the expansion of electronic interconnectedness, even highly sensitive military information systems and networks of communication are becoming dependent upon civilian infrastructure. The cost-effectiveness of interconnected information systems makes it highly unlikely that the current trend towards more and more reliance on information systems to run critical infrastructure will be reversed.

Also on the level of everyday life, IT will continue to have a profound impact. New interconnecting systems will enable more and more people to exchange larger and larger amounts of information at steadily declining costs and from an expanding range of IT-enabled devices. According to *Global Trends 2015*, there will be 'a rapid diffusion of universal wireless connectivity' via handheld appliances and perhaps also 'a large number of low-cost low-altitude satellites'.[7] The future IT will combine increasing computing power, ubiquitous sensing, wireless communication networks and all-level integration to produce an 'Internet of things', which greatly enhances the utility of multipurpose IT devices for everyday life.[8]

The societal consequences of the introduction of IT are complex and can hardly be dealt with in depth here. Suffice to say that a key aspect of this evolution is network complexity. Since vital information systems are increasingly becoming interconnected, the complexities of the entire web of information systems are growing so fast that control and security agencies are increasingly unable to assess the consequences of possible system failures. The possible ramifications of a breakdown in one part of the system have become much harder to predict and assess. There is accumulating evidence that the growing reliance on IT and the interconnectedness and complexities of modern information systems make modern societies extremely vulnerable. The vulnerability of these systems is further increased by the growing concentration of support systems. The logic of the market dictates increased interconnectedness of vital support systems and resources, including a heavier reliance on the Internet. In many sectors, such as telecommunication and energy supplies, commercial demands for access and profitability are often given priority over security.[9]

There is a growing awareness of the inherent vulnerabilities, stemming from the introduction of IT in all spheres of life. These fears have been exacerbated by reports of high-profile cybercrime incidents and the hacking into sensitive information systems, as well as the spread of very damaging computer viruses. In 2000 the computer viruses Melissa, Chernobyl and ILOVEYOU incapacitated millions of computers and caused immense economic damage. Three years later, malicious codes such as the Slammer, MSBlaster and Sobig-F caused even more devastating attacks; the latter caused an estimated 36.1 billion US dollars in damage. At the end of 2003, computer experts stated the year had been 'the worst ever'.[10] This trend towards steadily more disruptive and economically damaging attacks continued throughout the first half of 2004.[11] Large-scale denial of service attacks on its thirteen root servers have shaken the very backbone of the Internet on at least one occasion. The impact of the stream of malicious codes has also been felt at critical infrastructural facilities. Emergency calls have been disrupted, ATM machines have been knocked out and airline travel has been delayed. Evidently, the growing interdependence of both commercial and, to a lesser extent, government information systems, suggests that sophisticated co-ordinated attacks may have unforeseen and large-scale cascading effects, with a paralysing effect on society.

Since the mid–1990s there has been a growing body of literature on emerging threats to national security emanating from the revolution in IT. Some of this literature presented a rather alarmist vision of the future information threat, warning against an imminent 'electronic Pearl Harbor' or 'a digital 9/11'.[12] While the overall threat has probably been exaggerated in this literature, there can be little doubt that the digital revolution opens up new multidimensional threats of digital sabotage, disruption, espionage, organised crime, etc. As the examples of malicious code above indicate, these challenges are very real indeed.

The future potentials of cyberterrorism: computers as weapons

There are far fewer indications of a direct cyber*terrorist* threat, however, in the sense that computers may become the actual weapons in inflicting deadly attacks on civilians.[13] Nor have terrorist groups been at the forefront in producing malicious codes to disrupt Internet services. A General Accounting Office (GAO) report noted for example that 'to date none of the traditional terrorist groups [. . .] have used the Internet to launch a known assault on the U.S.'s critical infrastructure'.[14] Using the definition of cyberterrorism as 'the use of hacking tools and techniques to inflict grave harms such as loss of life', Dorothy Denning also finds that 'there has been no reported incidents

173

that meet the criteria'.[15] Reports of alleged 'cyberterrorist' attacks have mostly been penetration of computer files, spreading of malicious codes, defacement of web sites and so on. One oft-quoted example is the Tamil Tigers' information attack on the Embassy of Sri Lanka in the late 1990s, inundating it with thousands of e-mails in a denial of service attack, as well as hacking into the government's web site and changing it. This attack was then termed 'the first known terrorist attack towards a country's computer systems', but this hardly qualifies as cyberterrorism.[16] More recently, various pro-Islamist hacker groups have emerged, some of them reportedly responsible for hundreds of electronic attacks each month.[17] In late 2004, a 259-page Arabic hackers' manual, *Sites UnDeR atTaCk*, circulated on a number of pro-al-Qaida web sites, providing detailed instructions for a variety of information operations.[18] This and similar reports have reinforced concerns that al-Qaida-linked hackers will eventually develop the capability to launch far more disruptive cyber attacks.

Back in 1998 Hirst raised the issue of whether 'the historical interfaces between technology and terrorism may be set to change as society itself becomes increasingly reliant on technology in every sector', thus 'technology will itself become a target for terrorism'.[19] In the short run, however, terrorist groups seem unlikely to launch a war on infrastructural targets in cyberspace. Not only are their cyberwarfare capabilities still quite limited, but also sabotage and disruption attacks rarely get much attention compared to savage hostage executions or deadly car bombs. Not surprisingly, sabotage attacks against civil infrastructure have seldom been a preferred modus operandi for transnational terrorists.[20] For these reasons, other actors than political terrorists are more likely to take advantage of the new opportunities for information disruption, in particular activists of different ideological colours. (Large-scale digital 'civil-disobedience campaigns' and 'sit-ins' have already been launched against government sites in support of various causes.[21]) Other real and prospective cyberspace-disrupters include insiders or disgruntled employees, leisure-time hackers, criminal networks and the intelligence services of enemy states. A number of states are known to be developing 'robust cyberwarfare arsenals', including the USA, Russia, Israel, China and France.[22]

Based on past experience, it is hard to see why information threats should be placed on a par with WMD as has been the case in much recent literature, or on a par with today's conventional mass-casualty terrorism. The threat of cyberterrorism has hence been constructed mainly on perceived vulnerabilities, rather than past experiences, but the hyping of the threat clearly served its purpose by inducing policy-makers to take the new vulnerabilities seriously. The alarmist vision – while useful in order to mobilise opinion and political will to face the new information threats – may thus serve to invalidate itself through the development it has already set in motion.

There is admittedly much uncertainty regarding the consequences of new

IT. The high level of IT competence among emerging generations of terrorist groups and their sympathisers, and the introduction of new IT devices in a growing number of areas is likely to increase the prospects that computers may be converted into weapons. Furthermore, future technologies will endow tiny handheld and easily hidden devices with unprecedented capabilities, which in turn empower non-state actors in the field of espionage and intelligence gathering. The very combination of greater technological insight and a widely expanded range of IT-dependent targets will increase the chances for cyberterrorism in the true meaning of the word.

Information technologies in conventional terrorism

While computers and networks may not necessarily be utilised as physical weapons, the new IT does contribute immensely, in terms of its numerous and very important auxiliary function in conventional terrorism. Since the 1990s, terrorist and extremist groups of most ideological colours have made use of computers and the Internet, harnessing the new information tools for an increasingly broader range of activities.[23] In the case of the salafi-jihadi movements, the ideological indoctrination of new recruits has been facilitated by the ready access to literally thousands of books, articles, communiqués, fatwas, etc., on the Internet. There are, for example, several on-line e-libraries, where thousands of volumes, tracts, articles, communiqués, video and audio tapes, poems, recitations and other material are accessible in full text on-line, usually compressed in zip files. The <http://www.almaqdese. com> web site is a case in point. Most radical jihadist groups, from the Algerian Salafist Group for Call and Combat (GSPC), the plethora of Iraqi groups such as Ansar al-Sunna Army, the Islamic Army of Iraq and the Tawhid wa'l-Jihad Group, the Palestinian Hamas, and the Lebanese Hizbollah all have one or more web sites where communiqués, ideological tracts and video clips from recent operations are posted. Audio-filed speeches of their leaders serve to keep up the spirit, while gory pictures of their victims are displayed in order to demoralise their enemies.

The existence of popular terrorist manuals such as the *Anarchist's Cookbook* and the *Terrorist's Handbook* in print and on the Internet have been well known for many years. These appear to have enabled less organised amateur domestic terrorists to manufacture weapons.[24] Al-Qaida and its sympathising groups have greatly exploited the new IT to facilitate training. Various electronic journals and on-line manuals offer instructions in everything from bomb-making and sniper-training to guidelines for establishing secret training camps and safe houses. One of al-Qaida's military-instruction publications is the electronic periodical *Mu'askar al-Battar* (The Camp of the Sabre) published on-line since late 2003 and still available on the Internet in at least twenty editions. Instruction videos in bomb-making and the construction of crude chemical weapons have also circulated on-line. In April 2004 the pro-al-Qaida Arabic web site <http://al3dad.jeeran.com> offered to its viewers courses in 'How to prepare RDX-explosives' and 'Remote-control explosion' and a 'Comprehensive course in explosives'. The bomb-making instructions on this and other web sites mostly originate from the comprehensive al-Qaida training manual *Encyclopedia of Preparation for Jihad* (*mawsu'at al-i'dad*), which appeared in its fourth and revised edition in late September 2004, and quickly spread to numerous web sites. The 700 MB-size collection contains training in every aspect of jihad, from physical training, intelligence, reconnaissance, counter-surveillance and counter-interrogation techniques, security, organisational work, training in all kinds of small arms, bomb-making, home-made chemical weapons instructions (see Figure 7.1) as well as biological weapons instructions.[25]

The Internet has also introduced a whole new arena for jihad. The term of 'electronic jihad' (e-jihad) has figured prominently on a large number of jihadist web sites, even if its meaning is still undefined. One key aspect of e-jihad is disruption of enemy web sites, whether by defacement, by stealing and publicising confidential information or by blocking access through denial-of-service attacks.[26] High-profile digital intrusions, such as the web-site defacement and stealing of sensitive credit-card data from the powerful American–Israeli Public Affairs Committee (AIPAC) in November 2000 bring considerable media attention to the 'hactivists'.[27]

The real value of the Internet to terrorists, however, lies in the realm of propaganda and secure long-distance communication. There is little doubt that al-Qaida has used the Internet for operative communications, illustrated by the Richard Reid 'shoebomber' case, the 9/11 Hamburg cell, and a number of other cases where instructions related to the attacks were sent via e-mail.

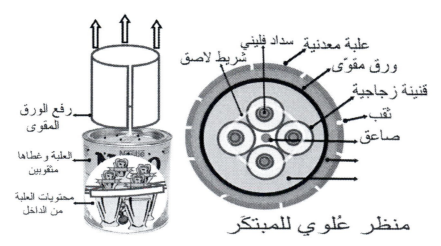

Figure 7.1 Document on chemicals, from the *Encyclopedia of Preparation for Jihad*, 4th edn.

The globalisation of empowering technologies

The Internet is not only the marketplace for ideas, extremist ideologies, training manuals and communication of operative orders. It is also a forum for procuring, in a discreet manner, products and material that enhance the effectiveness of terrorist organisations. The off-the-shelf availability of a host of advanced surveillance and eavesdropping equipment is a good example. Recent studies find that there is a virtually 'unchecked proliferation of surveillance devices and capacity amongst both private and public sectors'.[28] Commercially available technologies allow bugging, telephone-monitoring and visual surveillance during night or day over large distances. New forms of local, national and international communication interception networks and new human recognition and tracking devices are also for sale. Consider the following items that were on offer for sale in April 2004 at the web site of the Norwegian affiliate of Spyshop, a private security company:

- Parabole-microphone, range up to 200 m.
- Professional wall microphone. Eavesdrops through all kinds of walls, amplifies the sound up to 20,000 times.
- Keycatcher. Automatically logs all keystrokes on a PC, useful to snoop passwords.
- Nokia 3210 double function. Very capable for long-distance eavesdropping. Picks up conversations in a room even if it looks turned off.
- 220-volt plug with built-in microphone and transmitter, *c.*100–200 m range. Need no batteries. Will last 'forever'.
- KGB remote-controlled eavesdropping equipment. Extremely small semi-professional microphone. Crystal-clear audio at a range of up to 1,000 meters. Very hard to detect with anti-eavesdropping equipment.
- Micro-videocameras hidden in a tie, in a shirt button, or in a loose-leaf file.
- GPS tracking system with GSM transmission to PC. The tracking device is the size of a matchbox and can be hidden easily.[29]

The commercial availability of such equipment, in addition to the black-market availability of even more advanced and expensive devices, has important implications for terrorism. While electronic intelligence-gathering used to be the sole preserve of national security agencies, private actors now have access to surveillance, wire-tapping and listening devices which police authorities in many countries are prohibited from using, either by law or for budgetary reasons. Some of this equipment is already in use by private actors, such as infidelity detectives and insurance companies. There can be little doubt that terrorist and criminal groups are increasingly becoming more adept at utilising advanced equipment for reconnaissance and intelligence purposes. As such equipment becomes increasingly available, one must expect that terrorist operations may become far more operationally sophisticated and more difficult to disrupt than they are today. With the proliferation of easily hideable high-resolution cameras, reconnaissance by terrorists will be much harder to detect. The new communication devices will also make terrorists more skilled at launching simultaneous co-ordinated attacks.

The proliferation of interactive technologies will allow for greater use of 'leaderless resistance' principles in terrorism. Planning, reconnaissance and intelligence gathering for a wide range of targets can take place in extremist virtual communities where anonymous visitors share information which is combined into a terrorist 'project' and the final physical preparation, including the execution of an attack, is left to whoever responds to the call. These principles have already been applied in Islamist web forums. In one such forum, intelligence on targets in Saudi Arabia was provided by one anonymous member, accompanied by an appeal to anyone who sought jihad to 'strike' on the opportunity. Another pro-al-Qaida web-site appealed to sympathising participants to post information about 'important economic and military targets [. . .] of the American infidel Crusaders', including names and addresses of US military and intelligence officers in Saudi Arabia.[30] The proliferation of such virtual extremist communities may herald a possible rise in individualised or 'loner' terrorism.

Dual-use technology and improvised weapons

The example of surveillance technology highlights a key aspect of globalisation in the sense that it permits a commercialisation and proliferation of technologies, resources and possibilities that previously were available only to governments. As a consequence one has, for example, observed that 'the telecommunications and logistics infrastructure of drug traffickers, counterfeiters, or smugglers of people is often superior to that of the regulatory and law enforcement agencies of most countries'.[31] While this is mostly true, it is nevertheless striking how limited the terrorist repertoire has been, at least in terms of weapon technology. Compared to today's military industries, terrorist groups are very 'low-tech'. Bombs and explosives are still the weapon of choice for most groups. Costs and availability are paramount considerations. Hence, terrorists rely primarily on home-made weapons and explosives, synthesised from readily available and relatively inexpensive ingredients, rather than embarking on risky attempts at acquiring militarily advanced weapons.

While the technological dimension of terrorism should not be exaggerated, insurgent and terrorist groups are clearly benefiting from *a growing availability of dual-use products*, from which new kinds of improvised weapons can be made. We have already mentioned the expanding range of mid-level CB-threat agents emerging from the biochemical and pharmaceutical industries, especially in view of the completion in 2000 of the human genome sequence. Studies predict a rapid spread of advanced biotechnology, partly due to the massive governmental and corporate investments in these fields, and this will inevitably cause a considerable widening scope of dual-use threats.[32]

New aerosolisation technologies in various paint and pharmeceutical industries represent another dual-use non-conventional threat. When it comes to weaponisation of biological and chemical-risk agents, aerosolisation is one of the most critical technical hurdles for substate actors. The proliferation of new technologies in this area represents therefore a potentially new dual-use threat, which is yet to be addressed.[33]

Another example of the widening spectrum of dual-use challenges is the proliferation of commercial UAVs.[34] Such improvised delivery systems for explosives (or possibly CBW agents) involve a number of tactical advantages, especially with regards to targets, which are accessible only from air. Other remote-controlled vehicles are also potential delivery mechanisms for terrorist weapons, and the idea is not new. According to one study, there have been as many as forty-three cases involving fourteen terrorist groups in which remote-control delivery systems were 'either threatened, developed, or actually utilised'.[35] For example, experiments conducted by the Aum Shinrikyo involved the use of remote-control helicopters to spray dangerous chemicals from the air. Back in the 1980s the Spanish ETA also attempted to run an explosive-laden four-foot remote-control bomb into a Spanish patrol ship. With the evolution of more sophisticated robotic systems on the commercial market, the dual-use threat of these technologies may increase significantly.

Innovative improvisation of new and old technologies also lies behind the proliferation of terrorist missiles and mortars. Terrorist groups have become far more skilled in producing these weapons. All of ETA, PIRA, FARC, Hizbollah, LTTE, the Jaysh e-Muhammad group in Kashmir, the al-Aqsa Martyrs Brigades and the Islamic Resistance movement Hamas have proved adept at using home-made or military mortars.[36] In the 1990s, PIRA launched mortar attacks on a number of occasions against high-profile targets such as Downing Street in London, Heathrow airport and a British army barracks in Germany. The Iranian Mujaheedin al-Khalq also used mortars during their attacks on the Presidential Palace in Tehran in 2000.[37]

A number of groups have also managed to develop their own improvised missiles. Already, the previously mentioned *Encyclopedia of Preparation for Jihad* contains several files dedicated to the construction of Qassam missiles, the famous home-made missile of Hamas.[38] Qassam has appeared in several 'generations' with improved range. Despite its relatively small payload, the Qassam missile's psychological effect on the heavily fortified Jewish colonies cannot be underestimated. Expertise in constructing weapons from commercially available materials is not easily transmitted via web sites, however. An expert assessment on the value of such web sites for the Iraqi insurgents for whom improvised explosive devices (IEDs) are the major weapon, is that such expertise must be taught by trained weapons experts, not through web sites.[39] In the future, however, when greater Internet bandwith allows for much better real-time video transmission via handheld devices, it is likely that such skills will also be transmitted relatively anonymously via interactive teaching on the Internet.

As 9/11 demonstrated, aeroplanes may be extremely deadly weapons in the hands of terrorists. The idea is not new. In fact, as far back as in 1907 the combat organisation of the Socialist-Revolutionary Party in Russia invested much money in an inventor who was working on an aircraft hoping that they might be able to use it to bomb the tsarist palaces from the air. Before September 2001, the threat stemming from the possible proliferation of ballistic and cruise missiles to terrorist groups was addressed in several studies. (One maverick scientist in New Zealand has even started assembling his own low-cost cruise missile on a budget of no more than 5,000 US dollars, and he put the project details out on the Internet in order to prove the ease with which terrorists could produce such weapons.[40]) Terrorists prefer simple weapons, however, and military cruise missiles are clearly far too sophisticated to become a frequent terrorist weapon. Instead, innovative use of small private jets or model aircraft would enable terrorist groups to construct a crude cruise missile. Hirst noted almost prophetically back in 1998 that 'any kind of aircraft packed with explosives (or worse, armed with WMD) would be a cruise missile'.[41] While the 9/11 attacks relied on surprise, future airborne terrorist attacks are likely to exploit other vulnerabilities, in particular the extensive and poorly regulated private and helicopter jet industry. Another vulnerability is the range of new personal flying machines, enabling, for example, suicide bombers to attack well-protected targets from the air. Future technologies in the area of airborne vehicles may also present additional dual-use challenges.

New interactive mass-media technologies

With regards to the future impact of new forms of interactive mass media, one possible predictive factor is the historical observation that paradigmatic shifts in mass media tend to be accompanied with new and often more deadly forms of terrorism. Futuristic studies have suggested that news will become more and more a commodity that is searched for and purchased alongside other commodities and services, rather than something that is controlled by national news agencies and transmitted more or less uniformly to the masses. Even the technology to produce 'digitalised paper' may soon be available on the market, further undermining the notion of a newspaper as a standardised and mass-produced item.[42] The trend towards more diverse and interactive media is arguably having an effect, similar to that of the introduction of 'live' TV broadcast at the end of the 1960s, which precipitated more spectacular forms of terrorism designated for a international audience.[43] Not only is the terrorists' struggle for the global media world's attention intensifying, prompting the evolution of more dramatic media-savvy forms of terrorism, but new forms of interactive mass media are also permitting terrorist groups to bypass censorship and communicate directly with external audiences to a larger extent than before. The numerous televised beheadings of foreign hostages by salafi-jihadi groups in Iraq mid- and late 2004 is a case in point.

Counter-terrorist technologies

Postulate: Huge investments will be made in technologies specifically designed to serve counter-terrorism purposes.

Possible implications for terrorism: Emerging technologies, especially in the field of sensors, will improve governments' technological tool kits for combating terrorism. Protective technologies will also improve considerably. A host of political, economic and civil-liberty constraints will nevertheless limit the utility of some of these technologies. Terrorist groups also learn to adapt to new counter-terrorist technologies. The application of new counter-terrorist technologies in certain cases may also have a long-term adverse effect on terrorism.

One of the most basic issues in history is the way technological innovations have shaped the relationship between rulers and subjects. If generalisations on the history of man are at all possible, it must be that technology has allowed the rulers access to more and more powerful instruments of coercion and control, while it has more rarely enhanced the power of the individual or substate groups vis-à-vis the state. Technological innovations have played a fundamental role in paving the way for the centralised state by enhancing its control of violence and by improving its ability to extract resources from the subject population.

Throughout most of the twentieth century, technological progress tended to tilt the balance of power decisively in favour of states rather than non-state groups and organisations. Industrialisation revolutionised the state's coercive instruments and its power to control the population. During the twentieth century, then, political elites in the developed world for the most part learnt to tame the Leviathan by institutionalising checks and constraints on the use of violence and by nourishing political norms on accountability. Wherever these checks were absent, however, technologically potent states of the twentieth century emerged as the worst mass-murderers in the history of mankind, capable of terrorising and killing millions of people. The almighty omnipotent and ubiquitous state, portrayed in George Orwell's famous novel *1984* represented the culmination of a historical process towards an increased capability for state coercion. Terrorist and insurgent groups in the modern age have come to terms with the power of the modern industrialised state, and have more often tried to provoke the state's coercive apparatus into overreaction, rather than to defeat it.

In the future, technological advances are likely to yield far more sophisticated instruments for physical coercion, surveillance and control than previously seen. A working document on advances in the technology of political control submitted to the European Parliament gives us some hints of what the future holds in this particular field. A wide range of new technologies are emerging in the fields of identity recognition, area denial, surveillance systems based on neural networks, discreet-order vehicles, new arrest and restraint methods and non-lethal weapons, in addition to new restraint, torture, killing and execution technologies. The report identifies a worrisome 'trend towards militarisation of police technologies and the paramilitarisation of military technologies'.[44] Without democratic accountability and strict control, the implications for human rights of the proliferation of these technologies 'are literally awesome', the report concludes.[45] The need for safeguards and democratic accountability is also a common theme in much of the literature on counter-terrorism technology.[46]

As alluded to above, emerging IT is less intelligence friendly than it used to be. A good example is the so-called Echelon affair, the reported discovery of a worldwide telecommunication-interception network, targeting telephone, fax, and e-mail messages of private citizens, politicians, trade unionists, companies, etc. and run by the USA in co-operation with a few close allies. A 1999 EU report found that the available technology had the capability, as tasked, to 'intercept, process, and analyse every modern type of high capacity communication system to which access is obtained'.[47] It concluded, nevertheless, that the Echelon network is based on the 'technology of the past', as telecommunications were shifting to high-capacity optical-fibre networks, which made interception far more difficult. Furthermore, the report also found that 'the long war against civil and commercial cryptography has been lost'.[48] These and other critical aspects of the IT revolution (see previous section) suggest that certain emerging technologies appear to empower non-state actors more than governments.

For the most part, however, new technologies will allow governments to improve their counter-terrorism capabilities and protective measures against terrorism, while at the same time minimising their intrusive effects. In many Western countries and in the USA in particular, huge investments are being made in technologies specifically designed to serve counter-terrorism purposes.[49] Measures to reduce dual-use risks of new technologies are also being taken. While a complete review of new counter-terrorist technologies is beyond the scope of this book, a few examples of these efforts are listed in Box 7.1.

While a wide range of new counter-terrorist technologies are being developed, their utility inevitably depends on their integration into a wider anti-terrorism strategy. In nearly every country, anti-terrorism measures are

Box 7.1 Counter-terrorism technologies

Explosive detection, 'taggants', 'defusers'
In the field of explosive detection, new technologies are underway, superceding X-ray for scanning luggage and packages.[1] A thermal neutron analysis system has been developed, capable of analysing the chemical composition of a target and thus directly detecting the presence of an explosive. Other new and more powerful detection techniques include for example different versions of nuclear magnetic resonance imaging (MRI) and acoustic resonance techniques (which can also be used to detect CW agents). New technology may also make it much more difficult to use ammonium nitrate fertiliser as an ingredient in improvised terrorist bombs.[2]

CBW detection/protection
Technologies to counter the use of CBW agents by terrorist groups are making advances. In the burgeoning field of nanotechnology, one foresees a range of new technologies, such as 'miniaturised intelligent sensor systems' for detection of CBW agents, nanofibers for protective clothing and new ways to disrupt BW-agent viability.[3] New vaccines against bioterrorism are also being developed based on gene-transfer technology.[4]

Surveillance technology
More effective and smaller (invisible) digital video-camera surveillance systems will be available for the monitoring of public space in urban areas. New technologies enhance the effectiveness of border and costal surveillance as well as perimeter surveillance, where intelligent software reduces the number of false alarms.[5] New software allows security agencies to track individual's 'digital persona' through their use of telecommunication services, transactions, etc. 'Data-matching' systems which compare an individual's details between different computer databases are being used to great effect in many countries to combat crime. The latest intelligence-analysis software can trace logical threads through vast sets of free-form data.

Biometrics
New biometric technologies for identifying and detecting impersonation are developing fast. These include six different areas: fingerprint, hand/palm geometry, iris, retinal, facial and voice recognition. Iris recognition is seen as having the highest accuracy of all the biometric technologies. DNA analysis may also become applicable to instant identity checks some time in the future.[6] Biometric technologies

have already been put to use for certain passenger groups at airports, and they are likely to become a standard part of travel for foreign visitors to many countries.[7] By integrating biometric features in ID cards, passports, etc., the detection of false travel documents, which many terrorists depend upon for crossing borders, will become easier.[8]

New protective technologies

Technologies, which provide an additional layer of protection against terrorist attacks, are being developed. These include new bullet- and blast-proof composite materials for personal protection, design features and strengthening materials for protecting physical infrastructure and buildings and special techniques for minimising the consequences of explosions on aircrafts. Nanotechnology advances hold great promise for the development of new materials in these diverse fields.

Sensor technologies

Various sensory-enhancing technologies ranging from ambient light magnification, audio amplification and infrared light to more sensitive radars allow operators to 'integrate these impulses into a virtual reality depiction of, for example, the activities inside the perimeter of a hostage crisis.'[9] New sensor technologies are making control and screening of cargo and goods far more efficient than before. Sensor technology, including special naval electro-optical systems, also plays a key role in emerging maritime force protection technologies.[10] Technological advances in sensor technologies, combined with satellite communication, precision-guided missiles or UAVs with improved sensor suites and deployable weapons permit a more widespread use of assassinations against suspected guerrillas and terrorists without the use of ground forces. (In the long-term perspectives, however, this and other controversial counter-terrorist tactics may well be counterproductive.)

Notes
[1] This section draws partly upon Hirst, 'New and Old Technologies: Choice of Strategy and Targets'. Paul Hirst was Science and Technology Adviser to the UK Parliament.
[2] Anil Ananthaswamy, 'Defusing Fertiliser May Make Bomb-Building Harder', *New Scientist* 19 March 2004.
[3] Fernando de Souza-Barros, 'Role of Scientists in Disarmament', *International Network of Engineers and Scientists Against Proliferation Bulletin* No. 22, <http://www.inesap.org/bulletin22/bul22art12. htm#t15>. Accessed October 2004. See also Andy Oppenheimer, 'Nuclear, Biological and Chemical Detection: To Detect and Protect', *Jane's Defence Weekly* 14 April 2004.

4 'DNA-Based Vaccines Being Developed to Battle Bioterrorism', *Bioterrorism Week* 23 February 2004.
5 'Ears and Eyes on the Ground', *Jane's International Defense Review* 1 August 2003.
6 Clutterbuck, *Keeping Track of Terrorists after 1992*, pp. 303–4; and 'Biometrics: The Future of Security', *CBC News Online* 23 January 2004.
7 'Passports and Visas to Add High-Tech Identity Features', *New York Times* 24 August 2003.
8 Eric Chabrow, 'U.S. Urged to Take Lead in Issuing Biometric Passports', *InformationWeek* 5 March 2004.
9 David B. Perkins and Tomas C. Mijares, 'Domestic Law Enforcement's Use of Sensory-Enhancing Technology in Terrorist Situations', in Harvey W. Kushner (ed.) *The Future of Terrorism: Violence in the New Millenium* (London: Sage, 1998), p. 182.
10 Daniel Terdiman, 'Battening Cargo Against Terrorism', *Wired News* 8 March 2004; Mark Hewish, 'Small, But Well Equipped', *Jane's International Defense Review* 1 October 2002; Mark Hewish, 'On the Waterfront – and Beyond', *Jane's International Defense Review* 1 February 2003; T. Ország-Land, 'The UN's Seaport Safety Regime', *Jane's Terrorism and Security Monitor* 1 May 2003; and Joris Janssen Lok, 'Countering Threats with Naval Electro-Optical Systems', *Jane's International Defense Review* 1 June 2003.

subordinated to a host of other political and economic priorities, which reduce their effectiveness. The Bush administration, for example, has focused primarily on aviation security and bioterrorism, while measures to counter favourite terrorist weapons, such as truck bombs, 'have been very far down the list'.[50] Detection of suspicious sales of ammonium nitrate fertiliser, a key component in deadly truck bombs, is very difficult, since American farm and chemical lobbies resist government controls. Hence, nearly 5 million tons are sold each year without any regulations. US law also permits farmers to mix ammonium nitrate fertiliser with fuel oil 'for personal demolition uses'.[51]

Possible impact on terrorism patterns

Emerging counter-terrorist technologies will undoubtedly increase governments' ability to disrupt terrorist operations and provide better protection for high-value targets. These technologies will in principle help some governments to gain an upper hand in fighting terrorists and rebels. Still, as is evident from the above-mentioned examples, socio-economic and political factors will in many cases prevent these technologies from being effectively integrated into a wider anti-terrorism strategy. In many countries, concerns about civil liberties will greatly limit the use of intrusive or life-threatening technologies, while economic considerations and the shortage of local scientific expertise will play an additional inhibitive role in their use in the developing world. In certain countries, increased access to advanced counter-terrorist technologies will also assist elite groups in monopolising power, which in turn may generate increased motivations for anti-regime violence in the population.

Democratic governments will always be at odds against clandestine trans-national adversaries who fight with little consideration for civilian–military distinctions, territorial control and the sanctity of individual lives. Against such enemies, counter-terrorist technologies can only serve crisis-management purposes. They will never be a substitute for political solutions and socio-economic measures, which undermine recruitment, sympathy and popular support for terrorist organisations. Since counter-terrorist measures cannot be applied equally to all potential targets in every country, there will always be an almost infinite number of soft targets for transnational terrorists. They tend to adapt to new protective measures by shifting to less protected targets, either in the same country or in countries where similar targets can be found. Or, terrorists change their tactics to elude new countermeasures. During the 1980s one observed that greater fortification measures around foreign embassies, for example, tended to be followed by greater terrorist use of large truck bombs, while new protective measures at airports to prevent sky-jackings seemed to encourage the use of sky-bombings instead. In the future, terrorist groups and their sympathisers will also learn to evade or adapt to the new and sophisticated counter-terrorism technologies. In some cases, terrorist tactics may inadvertently become more instead of less deadly, and their organisational structures will have to become even more diffuse, more horizontal and more individualised in order to survive.

8

CONCLUSION

The only thing that is certain about the future of terrorism is that patterns of terrorism are going to change. Our guesses about the future do not have to be pure speculations, however. This book examines those societal conditions that cause terrorism to occur. Using these as analytical tools, I have explored more than a dozen different trends with a view to identifying how these are likely to impact on future patterns of terrorism. Through these analyses, I have provided empirical underpinnings for my initial proposition that the occurrence of terrorism is rooted in structural societal factors and that these factors are changing in ways, which makes transnational terrorism more likely to occur.

My selection of postulates can obviously be challenged, and for this reason I have considered the implications of several other propositions about the future. I have found no compelling evidence, however, that invalidate the basic theme of this book, namely that there are *important structural factors in today's world creating more propitious conditions for terrorism*. The inhibiting factors I have identified are fewer, and do not seem to carry the same probability and weight, at least not in the short run, as those factors facilitating sustained or higher levels of terrorism. In addition, there are important driving factors behind the mass-casualty trend in contemporary terrorism. In other words, this book shows that transnational terrorism today cannot be reduced to a single source or actor. The threat of al-Qaida and its global network of militant jihadis are undoubtedly key factors in today's international terrorism. The very resilience and longevity of the internationalist jihadist networks point to deeply rooted structural causes, however. Clearly, transnational terrorism will not go away if (or when) bin Laden and his leading lieutenants are captured or killed. The current wave of deadly terrorist attacks is rooted in global *structural* factors on more than one level. They include the unipolar exclusionist and interventionist world order, weak transitional states, non-state actors in global politics, globalisation of organised crime, privatisation of policing and warfare, Middle East oil dependence, migration and ethnic heterogenisation of Western societies, growing information interconnectedness and proliferation of deadly technologies. These systemic causes will continue to mould the future terrorist landscape and will increase the chances for a high level of transnational terrorism in the foreseeable future.

Let me recapitulate the basic findings from the discussions of various postulates. I argue that globalisation in the sense of increased intercon-nectedness, interdependence and deterritorialisation is set to continue. The implications of this for terrorism are likely to be a sustained, if not higher, level of transnational terrorism. Globalisation has disruptive effects, which motivate anti-Western, anti-US terrorism in the developing world. Quantita-tive research has lent at least partial support to this interlinkage. By reducing the importance of geographical distance, globalisation also tends to increase the potential of geographically distant conflicts to manifest themselves in transnational terrorism. Globalisation steadily reduces the physical distance between 'socially very distant' groups, which in turns lay the foundation for more mass-casualty terrorism.[1]

Armed conflicts are another powerful source of transnational terrorism. Even if the total number of conflicts remains the same, their potential for becoming internationalised and global in scope will increase in a more glob-alised world. An examination of trends in armed conflicts strongly suggests that illegal non-state actors are going to play a greater role in future armed conflicts than today. Their ability to raise funds from illegal or parallel trans-national economies will probably increase. I also find that future rebel and terrorist groups will have greater opportunities to engage in 'deter-ritorialised' modes of conflict in which they command authority and wield power without direct territorial control. The rise of al-Qaida has also intro-duced the 'global civil war' model as a new form of armed conflict, which is likely to be emulated by others in the future. Altogether, these trends point to sustained, or perhaps higher, levels of transnational terrorism in the future.

In the broad area of politics and international relations, I postulate that the world system will remain fairly unipolar over the next two decades. There is a possibility that regional power centres for example, China, India or the EU will grow stronger and more assertive and will contribute to a relative decline in the US global hegemony. I find no reason to predict a return to a Cold War-type bipolar military and ideological rivalry, however. Since state-sponsored terrorism is much more costly in a unipolar state system, I expect no rise in this type of terrorism, which declined significantly at the end of the Cold War. Non-state transnational terrorism directed against the imperial power, the USA and its closest allies is likely to continue and possibly increase.

The post-9/11 world will probably see more nuclear powers in the world. WMD-programmes will not go away but will continue in countries where the fear of foreign interventions is high such as in the Middle East and North Korea. Such programmes contribute greatly to the threat of WMDs becom-ing available to terrorist groups, especially in states, which are candidates for state failure and state collapse. The proliferation threat is compounded by technological advances in biotechnology, medicine and in the pharmaceutical industries, which inadvertently broaden the spectrum of risk agents. Although counter- and non-proliferation measures are likely to become even more intrusive in years to come, the likelihood of WMDs becoming available to terrorist groups will remain considerable and possibly increase, due simply to the growing spectrum of threats.

As for trends in democratisation, state formations and state strength, I also find trends pointing to sustained and even increased levels of terrorism. For example, I find that a growing number of states are likely to be neither autocracies nor fully fledged democracies. Transitional semi-democratic states are more vulnerable to state collapse and internal violent conflicts than are other regime types. They tend to experience higher levels of both domestic terrorism and transnational terrorism. I also identify a trend towards new state formations. As opposed to old, consolidated states, young states are often weak states and struggle with a host of deep-seated legitimacy problems, which by themselves often cause domestic terrorism. Weak states are also less capable of suppressing insurgents and terrorists present on their territories and denying them sanctuaries or transition. In a steadily more globalised world, the continued existence of a relatively small number of weak and collapsed states will ultimately cause higher levels of transnational terrorism.

What may counter this trend is a growing willingness and capability on part of the international community, represented by the UN, to engage in conflict prevention and peacekeeping. I postulate that peacekeeping activities will remain on a high level. While peacekeeping operations in armed conflicts will lead to many incidents of transnational terrorism, it is likely that the long-term effect will be a reduced scope for terrorism. This is because the outbreak of new conflicts are prevented, collapsed state situations are averted and internationalised armed conflicts are brought to a close. This outcome depends on the success of these interventions, however. Protracted and faltering peace processes, for example, are likely to precipitate more terrorism, at least on a local level.

Another caveat is the new trend towards an increased number of international US-led military interventions in ongoing armed conflicts in the Islamic world. These will most certainly fuel the ongoing campaign of anti-Western Islamist terrorism. The current world order is dominated by non-Muslim great powers. Hence, since military interventions are largely determined by power politics, the nature of the current world order reinforces the tendency that Muslim nations are more likely to be pressured to accept peacekeeping interventions than non-Muslim powers with large Muslim minorities. This regrettable fact strengthens the voice of jihadist ideologues who propagate that the Islamic nation is under a vicious military assault by an aggressive 'Jewish–Crusader alliance'. Peacekeeping interventions, while potentially an important vehicle for reducing transnational terrorism, may instead become a powerful motivating source for Islamist militancy.

Another important dimension of the international system is the growing web of multilateral institutions, international treaties and regimes. These are expected to play an increasingly important role in regulating relations between states as well as in internal politics inside states. A possible implication of this trend is that international terrorism, as a foreign policy tool, will become less attractive. International institutions foster interdependence, which in turn lays the groundwork for more peaceful inter-state relations. Further- more, the opportunity structure for transnational terrorism will diminish, as states and multilateral institutions move towards closer counter-terrorism co- operation. One may dispute this, however, by pointing to the fact that greater economic and political integration has unintended consequences in terms of, for example, reduced border control. This may decrease multilateralism's potential for lowering the level of terrorism. Furthermore, critical aspects of counter-terrorism co-operation, such as intelligence-sharing, are very hard to develop in a multilateral setting.

A final trend in future international politics is the continued growth of INGOs and other transnational non-state interest groups. They fill important functions in international politics and their prominence is likely to increase. Similar to the two latter trends, the implications of a future INGO expansion are ambiguous. The overwhelming number of INGOs are strongly support- ive of non-violence, and they have undoubtedly had a pacifying effect on certain insurgent groups, for example the Zapatistas in Mexico. By providing a powerful alternative channel for advocating rights and voicing peaceful protest, the growing number of INGOs may diminish the prospects for revo- lutionary terrorism in areas where they engage. As with most other aspects of globalisation, however, the INGO institution is being exploited by rebels and terrorists, and this is likely to continue despite recent crackdowns on al-Qaida-linked Islamic INGOs. I find that the existence of a large number of poorly regulated INGOs in many countries, particularly in conflict zones, tends to facilitate insurgencies and transnational terrorism in such areas as financing, logistics and propaganda efforts. A number of INGOs have even served as de-facto front organisations for insurgent and terrorist groups. To some degree, the INGOs also contribute more broadly as a diffuser of trans- national expressions of protest and resistance. The net effect of these coun- tervailing trends is impossible to determine, although the pacifying effect seems more indirect and more long-term than the front-organisation effect. Terrorist and insurgent campaigns, which enjoy high international atten- tion and relatively broad legitimacy, such as the Palestinian Intifada and the Kashmiri insurgency, are better placed to derive maximum benefit from INGO involvement without having to accept any evolution towards non-violence.

I have analysed four distinct trends falling under the broad label 'the global market economy'. The first of these relates to socio-economic inequalities. I find that they are likely to remain or become larger, especially between-country inequality, and that disparities in wealth are likely to become more visible. In the Western world, inequality patterns will also assume a more pronounced ethnic dimension, as non-Western immigrants are systematically overrepresented among the poor and unemployed. The possible implications of this for future terrorism patterns are manifold. Persisting socio-economic inequalities on a global level are likely to provide a basis for a possible resurgence of militant leftist anti-globalisation ideologies. These may manifest themselves in transnational terrorism. On a domestic level in Western countries, increased inequalities are likely to generate more civil violence, especially where they coincide with ethnic discrimination. This may well become a more serious source of domestic as well as transnational terrorism in the future.

A second important economy-related trend is the evolution of transnational corporations (TNCs) and privatisation processes. It seems clear that the norm of market orientation and privatisation will remain dominant for the foreseeable future. For this reason, TNCs are likely to expand in size and in scope of activities across the globe. Since most of the largest TNCs are headquartered in Western countries and controlled by Western capital, their increased presence throughout the world will present new opportunities for transnational terrorists, who often perceive Big Business as a legitimate target. Globalisation contributes to the proliferation of high-profile business targets, which inevitably increase the number of potential targets in a growing number of countries. What is equally, if not more, important is the growing prominence of private companies in the military and security industry. Commercial private companies are already offering a wide range of security, police and military services and technologies, and this privatisation of policing and warfare trend is likely to continue. By expanding their security and military-related portfolios and by engaging more directly in policing and military interventions, the TNCs are likely to attract increased attention from local insurgents as well as transnational terrorists. The commercialisation of military and security-related hardware and technologies will also have other negative repercussions. It allows insurgents and transnational terrorists to access more advanced military and security equipment, which in turn will increase their operational effectiveness and sophistication. We have seen many examples of how insurgents and terrorists benefit from commercially available military hardware, and the paramountcy of market liberalism will make it very hard to reverse this trend.

A third trend in the global economy is the multi-billion-dollar-sized illegal business of transnational crime organisations (TCOs). Previous trend patterns suggest that TCOs will continue to grow in diversity and sophistication in many regions in the world. Their global reach will be more pronounced, and new and profitable areas of organised crime will emerge. This means that developed countries will be more affected by TCOs than in the past. The possible implications of this for terrorism lie in the realm of opportunities rather than motivations. Sophisticated TCOs with a global reach will be capable of providing their customers with new services and products. Hence, transnational terrorists stand to gain tactical advantages from this development in terms of increased across-the-globe access of such products as false ID papers, illegal weapons, explosives, military equipment, etc. The many TCOs specialising in the very lucrative alien-smuggling business will ship well-funded terrorist operatives to their destinations, defying whatever border-control measures national governments are implementing. In part, TCOs are by themselves a product of weak state capacities, and in part, they are also an agent in the production of new failed states and new territories falling outside government control. In many developed countries, wherever sophisticated TCOs gain a strong foothold, they sap the resources of law-enforcement capacities and make it harder to sustain the current level of activities against terrorist cells and their support networks.

The last global economy-related postulate is regionally oriented around the Middle East and North Africa (MENA) region, which has been a major, if not *the* major source of international terrorism since the 1970s. Petroleum-export dependence characterises these societies, and economic trend analyses reviewed in this study predict that the MENA region will remain heavily dependent on hydrocarbon exports in the foreseeable future. Furthermore, its contribution to world energy supply will grow significantly over the next two-three decades. All industrial oil-importing regions, the USA, Europe and Asia, will directly or indirectly grow more dependent on energy supplies from the MENA region. Global trade in fossil fuel will expand dramatically, especially in natural gas.

The implications of this for terrorism are threefold. First, oil wealth is bad for government. It reinforces the (semi-)authoritarian 'rentier' character of Middle Eastern regimes. Their governments will remain capable of staving off demands for peaceful political change, while the existing incentives for terrorism and violent revolts will remain in place. Moreover, the increasing energy dependence on Middle East oil will promote Western interest in regime stability, not reform. The combination of these factors is disconcerting and reinforces the suggestion that the region will remain a heavy contributor to future anti-US and anti-Western terrorism. The second implication is related to the growing strategic importance of MENA's energy supplies over the next decades. The more critical Middle East oil supplies become to Western economies, the more resources terrorist groups will devote to disrupting the flow of oil. Unless affordable alternative-energy sources emerge, petroleum-related targets are set to become more and more attractive targets to anti-Western terrorist groups. The third implication is more specifically related to opportunity, rather than motivation. The exploitation of modern society's built-in energy concentrations for terrorist purposes has been a hallmark of al-Qaida's terrorism and is likely to remain one of its most important legacies in terms of terrorist innovations. In this regard, the trend towards greater use of natural gas in industrialised countries is worrisome because it inevitably creates new vulnerabilities to terrorism. The transportation infrastructure for natural gas, such as new high-pressure pipelines, local storage sites and terminals and ships, trucks and trains transporting natural gas, present an expanded range of opportunities for mass-casualty terrorists.

I have devoted a chapter to demography, even though there are admittedly only indirect linkages between demographic developments and the occurrence of terrorism. They include the observation that violence – both political and criminal – is overwhelmingly the work of young unmarried males. Hence, countries with a high density of such individuals tend to be more predisposed to high levels of terrorism than comparable societies. Another probable linkage is the fact that unlike guerrilla warfare terrorism is predominantly an urban phenomenon; states undergoing rapid urbanisation are therefore likely to provide a more facilitating environment for terrorism than rural societies. Judging by demographic-trend studies, I find that many developing countries, including most MENA states, will continue to have a high density of youth over the next decade, even if the so-called 'youth bulges' are mostly decreasing. In addition, some Asian countries, China and India in particular, will have an extremely skewed gender balance with far more male citizens than female. These demographic realities come in addition to a process of rapid urbanisation, which will continue unabated in the foreseeable future. By 2025 two thirds of the world's population will live in cities. These developments are likely to be important drivers in future terrorism patterns, particularly in the developing world, where the growing mega-cities, the skewed gender-balance in some Asian countries and the socio-economic problems associated with 'youth bulges' provide a fertile ground for terrorist recruitment. Similarly, the continued rapid urbanisation will also 'urbanise' warfare, making terrorism a more widespread tactic in future wars. There are some long-term countervailing forces, however. The trend towards slower population growth is not confined to the developed world. Across the globe the population is growing older and youth bulges are shrinking in most countries. Violence is closely linked to age and the rapid 'ageing' of most Third World societies, including those in the MENA region, is likely to have a certain mitigating effect on violence.

Another demographic trend with perhaps more far-reaching future implications for terrorism is migration. I find that movement of people in and between regions is likely to increase in the future, making societies more ethnically heterogeneous than they are today. The influx of asylum-seekers and immigrants, both legal and illegal, into Europe and North America will continue in the future and significantly increase the number of people in the West with ethnic and political ties to overseas conflict areas. As assimilation trends appear to be slowing down in favour of transnational identities and allegiances, diaspora communities are likely to grow as a result of continued immigration. The possible ramifications of these trends for future terrorism patterns are manifold. Diaspora communities in the West are already being targeted for financing, recruitment and political support by overseas insurgent groups as well as by transnational terrorist organisations, operating against targets located in the West. A growth in the number and size of ethnic diaspora communities may facilitate such efforts. Furthermore, I find that the expanding illegal business of human-smuggling, which is a product of new immigration control measures, facilitates the activities of transnational terrorist organisations in terms of fund-raising and smuggling of operatives. Also on the level of motivational factors, future migration trends will probably have an impact. Conflicts over immigration issues and ethnic minorities are likely to persist, leading periodically to incidents of hate crimes and low-level political terrorism and, more rarely, serious campaigns of intercommunal violence. I also hypothesise that new forms of 'home-grown' ethnic terrorism may arise, linked to the new ethnic diaspora communities or in violent opposition to these.

Extremist ideologies are very powerful in shaping terrorism. A chapter on extremist ideologies is therefore very much needed, but it is also admittedly the most speculative and weakest in terms of predictive powers. World opinion surveys and other research have found clear linkages between societal developments on the one hand and the prevalence of broad mainstream attitudes on the other. As for the driving forces behind the emergence of extremist ideological currents, however, one has to rely on extrapolation of previous trends and imagination. Inspired by the idea that globalisation accelerates the speed of change, and spreads ideas more quickly and widely than before, I argue that the future landscape of extremist ideologies will become even less uniform and more multifaceted than it is today. It will also change more rapidly, even if traditional ideologies for terrorist action, in particular separatist ethno-nationalism, will probably remain dominant in domestic terrorism. I hypothesise that religious extremism will continue to flourish, especially in conjunction with extreme nationalism. There are no indications that the internationalist versions of jihadism will lose their dominant position among the global extremist ideologies in the foreseeable future. Still, fundamentalist movements and cults, emanating from other religions than Islam, are likely to proliferate and occasionally translate into terrorist actions. Violent single-issue extremism may also become more influential, especially in merged versions with other extreme leftist or religious ideologies. I also find reasons to suggest that internationalist leftist militancy with terrorist fringes may experience a renaissance. Right wing racist extremism, though clearly a very important source of hate crime, and less often domestic terrorism, is unlikely to become a leading internationalist ideology in transnational terrorism.

If these trends are correct, the future of terrorism will continue to be dominated by many incidents of mass-casualty terrorism, due to the continued strength of internationalist jihadism. At the same time, one may also see more incidents of international low-casualty terrorism against symbolic targets, if internationalist leftist militancy becomes more radicalised. An increased, but still relatively small, number of extremist cults will probably cause new forms of apocalyptic mass-casualty attacks. If globalisation indeed produces more fluidity, rapidity and sudden changes in the landscape of extremist ideologies, many surprises will lie ahead in terms of unexpected marriages of extremisms. These will in turn alter the terrorist modus operandi associated with the various ideologies.

The final chapter about technology has also been very difficult to write, since the field is extremely broad and linkages to terrorism patterns are tenuous. As with ideologies, technological developments have had such an important impact on terrorist modus operandi that they cannot be ignored. I postulate that the future holds staggering advances in a range of technologies, in particular information technology, bioengineering and nanotechnology. I also expect that most new technologies will rarely remain government and military secrets for very long, but instead undergo rapid commercialisation if they are not privately owned and commercially available from the very beginning. The importance of information technologies will be a very characteristic feature of future societies. Operative computers will support an increasing range of activities in all spheres of life, including critical infrastructure. New interconnecting technologies will enable more and more people to exchange larger and larger amounts of information at steadily declining costs and from an expanding range of devices.

The consequences for future terrorism of these technologies lie primarily in the field of new opportunities. Terrorist groups are already becoming increasingly adept at exploiting information technologies in a growing number of fields. Their use of the Internet is a primary example. In the future, they will learn to derive even more benefits from cyberspace, while the nature of information technologies is such that it does not allow for effective censorship against 'terrorism on the Internet'. As the World Wide Web is set to become ubiquitous, I foresee that terrorist proselytising, recruitment, training and planning will increasingly take place via virtual extremist communities, where various terrorist skills and expertise are shared and developed. This may make 'leaderless resistance' principles more widely used in terrorist networks than is the case today. We may be on the verge of a rise in individualised, 'loner' or 'tiny group' terrorism, which is unconnected to known organisations and which will be extremely hard to foresee and prevent. Another possible trend in terrorist modus operandi is that multiple co-ordinated attacks on many targets at many different locations will become more widespread. For some groups, this is already a reality, but this trend may be reinforced by steadily better technology to synchronise and communicate anonymously in real time across the globe. Finally, the evolution of cyberspace also suggests that critical infrastructure systems, operated by IT systems are likely to be targeted more frequently and more seriously than has been the case so far.

As for other technologies, I take particular notice of the proliferation of relatively advanced surveillance technology to private actors. This is likely to make terrorist groups far more capable than they are today of undertaking sophisticated reconnaissance and intelligence operations and attacking well-protected high-profile targets. This 'micro-proliferation' problem is discernible in a number of industries. The rapid commercialisation of new biochemical and pharmaceutical products as well as new aerosolisation techniques in paint industries clearly creates a host of new CBW vulnerabilities that may be exploited by new generations of innovative terrorists. Similarly, future technologies in robotics and remote-controlled vehicles will create new opportunities for airborne and maritime terrorism and new vulnerabilities for well-protected targets. The combination of rising levels of education around the world and the proven adeptness of terrorist groups to convert civilian technology into weapons is likely to increase the number and sophistication of improvised terrorist weapons.

Research and development of new counter-terrorism technologies have been touted as the USA's main advantage in the war on terrorism. Huge investments are already being made in such technologies. While my discussion of this trend is admittedly cursory, I see a number of promising emerging technologies, especially in the field of sensors, that undoubtedly will improve governments' technological tool kits for combating terrorism. The development of new protective technologies is also making significant progress and may reduce the overall damage of many future terrorist attacks. I do see several countervailing forces, however, which will weaken the overall impact of these technologies. A host of political, economic and civil-liberty constraints will clearly limit the utility of some of these technologies. More important, terrorist groups quickly learn to adapt to new counter-terrorist technologies, and past patterns indicate that the application of new protective measures against certain targets prompts terrorists to shift to other softer targets or loopholes that have yet to be addressed.

Unless the socio-economic and political causes of terrorism are addressed in a multidimensional manner, technology will simply remain a mitigating tool rather than a long-term solution. At the same time, one should be under no illusion that there exist any ready-made solutions to the problems of terrorism. The current international political system with its global market-economy principles, its unipolar hegemony power structure and its interconnecting technologies and transborder movements, is by its very nature a very fertile ground for the rise of transnational terrorist movements. Imperial powers always had to fight insurgencies in their peripheries. In a globalised world, these insurgencies manifest themselves less in territorialised rebel armies and more in shadowy networks of individualised cells, which are interconnected, but still individualised, powerful, but still decentralised. It is obviously too simplistic to blame Western leaders for having 'created' transnational terrorism by their stationing of military troops in Saudi Arabia, the unjustified war on Iraq and their quiet acquiescence of Israel's settler-colonial project, even if these factors undoubtedly have been very important in mobilising supporters around the internationalist jihadist movements. This book has demonstrated that transnational terrorism has emerged as an immanent quality in the global system. It is a structural out-come of intended and non-intended processes in which vulnerabilities are created, terrorist motivations are generated, and the countervailing forces of the past are disappearing. Regrettably, high levels of terrorism are going to be with us for a very long time.

NOTES

1 INTRODUCTION

1 Stanley Hoffmann, 'Clash of Globalisations', *Foreign Affairs* 81 (4) (July–August 2002), p. 104.
2 For an early review of this debate, see Asta Maskaliunaite, 'Terrorism and Globalisation: Recent Debates', *Rubikon E-journal* (October 2002).
3 See, for example, Hoffmann, 'Clash of Globalisations', pp. 104–15; and Benjamin R. Barber, *Jihad vs. McWorld: Terrorism's Challenge to Democracy* (London: Corgi Books, 2003).
4 See, for example, Albert J. Bergesen and Omar Lizardo, 'International Terrorism and the World System', *Sociological Theory* 22 (1) (March 2004), p. 43.
5 Two different arguments have been advanced: the events of 9/11 and subsequent attacks may slow down certain aspects of the globalisation process, such as transborder trade, transportation, migration, etc. as states become more wary of opening up their borders. This sounds plausible since there is much evidence of the significant impact of terrorism in reducing the volume of trade. Volker and Schumacher find 'compelling evidence' for this impact. They also calculate that on average, 'a doubling in the number of terrorist incidents in a year is associated with a decrease in bilateral trade by about 4 per cent already in the same year'. Conversely, others argue that after the 9/11 attacks, the international economy has adapted to the new security situation. Moreover, the political consensus on fighting al-Qaida has forged new patterns of co-operation among states, and has underlined the need for international co-operation to fight terrorism, just as global co-operation is needed to tackle other global maladies from poverty and HIV/AIDS to environmental degradation and transnational organised crime. See Nitscha Volker and Dieter Schumacher, 'Terrorism and International Trade: An Empirical Investigation', *European Journal Political Economy* 20 (2) (June 2004), p. 432; and Hoffmann, 'Clash of Globalisations', p. 112.
6 Since 9/11, a number of studies have appeared examining certain aspects of the relationship between globalisation and terrorism, see for example Audrey Kurth Cronin, 'Behind the Curve: Globalisation and International Terrorism', *International Security* 27 (3) (winter 2002–3), pp. 30–58; John Mackinlay, *Globalisation and Insurgency* (Oxford: Oxford University Press, 2002, Adelphi paper No. 352); Quan Li and Drew Schaub, 'Economic Globalisation and Transnational Terrorism: A Pooled Time-Series Analysis', *Journal of Conflict Resolution* 48 (2) (April 2004), pp. 230–58; and Omar A. Lizardo, 'The Effect of Economic and Cultural Globalisation on Anti-U.S. Transnational Terrorism 1971–2000', research paper, Univeristy of Arizona, 16 June 2004, <http://www.members.cox.net/~olizardo/terror_glob.pdf>. Accessed June 2004.

7 One good exception is David C. Rapoport, 'The Four Waves of Rebel Terror and 9/11', *Anthropoetics* 8 (1) (spring–summer 2002).

8 See, for example, Walter Laqueur, *The New Terrorism* (Oxford: Oxford University Press, 1999); Nadine Gurr and Benjamin Cole, *The New Face of Terrorism: Threats from Weapons of Mass Destruction* (London: I. B. Tauris, 2000); Ian O. Lesser, Bruce Hoffman, John Arquilla, David F. Ronfeldt, Michele Zanini and Brian Michael Jenkins (eds) *Countering the New Terrorism* (Washington, DC: Rand, 1999); Jessica Stern, *The Ultimate Terrorists* (Cambridge, Mass.: Harvard University Press, 1999); Richard A. Falkenrath, Robert D. Newman and Bradley A. Thayer, *America's Achilles' Heel: Nuclear, Biological, and Chemical Terrorism and Covert Attack* (Cambridge, Mass.: MIT Press, 1998); and Bruce Hoffman, *Inside Terrorism* (New York: Columbia University Press, 1998).

9 Bruce Hoffman is an exception. He consistently warned against terrorist threats along the whole technological spectrum, and warned against the narrow focus on worst-case scenarios. See, for example, Bruce Hoffman, 'Responding to Terrorism across The Technological Spectrum', *Terrorism and Political Violence* 6 (3) (autumn 1994), pp. 366–90; and Bruce Hoffman, 'New and Continuing Forms of Terrorism', Proceedings from an international seminar in Oslo, organised by the Norwegian Defence Research Establishment, September 2000, <http://www.mil. no/multimedia/archive/00005/Lia-R-2000-06444_5620a.pdf>. Accessed June 2004.

10 See, for example, Cindy Combs, *Terrorism in the Twenty-First Century* (Upper Saddle River, NJ: Prentice Hall, 1997); and Moorhead Kennedy, 'The twenty-first Century Conditions Likely to Inspire Terrorism', in Harvey W. Kushner (ed.) *The Future of Terrorism: Violence in the New Millenium* (London: Sage, 1998), pp. 185–94.

11 Yehezkel Dror, 'Terrorism as a Challenge to the Democratic Capacity to Govern', in Martha Crenshaw (ed.) *Terrorism, Legitimacy, and Power* (Middletown, Conn.: Wesleyan University Press, 1983), pp. 76–7.

12 A highly controversial terrorism-prediction programme was the so-called Policy Analysis Market (PAM), set up by Pentagon's Defense Advanced Research Projects Unit (Darpa) in 2003, but terminated shortly afterwards. It planned to establish an on-line trading market to help predict terrorist attacks, on the grounds that markets are believed to be 'extremely efficient, effective and timely aggregators of dispersed and even hidden information'. In the proposed PAM mechanism, traders would have deposited money in an account and used that to trade in contracts, earning money if their predictions came true. The project was terminated on the grounds that it would 'trade in deaths' and 'could provide an incentive actually to commit acts of terrorism'. See 'Pentagon Axes Online Terror Bets', *BBC News* 29 July 2003; and Rowan Wolf, 'DARPA's FutureMAP – Trading In Terrorism', *Uncommon Thought Journal* Web site 29 July 2003, <http:// www. uncommonthought.com/mtblog/archives/001298.html>. Accessed June 2004.

13 Walter Laqueur, *The New Terrorism* (Oxford: Oxford University Press, 1999).

14 Martha Crenshaw, 'The Causes of Terrorism', Charles W. Kegley, Jr. (ed.) *International Terrorism: Characteristics, Causes, Controls* (London and New York: St Martin's Press, 1990), pp. 113–26.

15 Nils Petter Gleditsch, 'The Future of Armed Conflict', The Madame Madeleine Feher European Scholar-in-Residence Lecture, Bar-Ilan University, Israel, December 2002, <http://www.biu.ac.il/SOC/besa/feher6.pdf>. Accessed April 2004, p. 12.

16 National Intelligence Council, *Global Trends 2015: A Dialogue about the Future*

with Nongovernment Experts, NIC 2000–02, December 2000, <http://www.cia.gov/cia/reports/globaltrends2015/globaltrends2015.pdf>. Accessed April 2004, p. 5.

17 In principle, the causal linkages also go the opposite direction as the course of globalisation is influenced by, for example, power shifts in the international system as well as technological advances.

18 We have deliberately not chosen scenarios that are less likely, but ones that have a more dramatic effect on the occurrence of terrorism. Hence, our postulates are not designed in order to test the limits and robustness of, for example, a state's counter-terrorism capabilities.

19 Brynjar Lia and Katja H.-W. Skjølberg, 'Warum es zu Terrorismus kommt: ein überblick über theorien und hypothese zu den ursacken des terrorismus', *Journal für Konflikt und Gewaltforschung* 6 (1) (spring 2004), pp. 121–63.

20 Hoffman, *Inside Terrorism*, pp. 28–9.

21 Carlos Marighella, 'Minimanual of the Urban Guerrilla', Brazil, 1969, <http://www.military-media.com/download/mini.pdf>. Accessed April 2004.

22 Shaykh Hamud bin Uqla al-Shuaybi, 'The Meaning and Truth of Terrorism [in Arabic]', *Minbar al-Tawhid wal-Jihad* 5/9/1422h or 21 November 2001, <http://www.almaqdese.com>. Accessed September 2004.

23 Charles Tilly, 'Terror, Terrorism, Terrorists', *Sociological Theory* 22 (1) (March 2004), abstract.

24 See, for example, criticism of the widely used ITERATE dataset in Alex P. Schmid and Albert J. Jongman et al. *Political Terrorism: A New Guide to Actors, Authors, Concepts, Data Bases, Theories and Literature* (Amsterdam: SWIDOC, 1988), p. 145. A Ph.D. student at FFI, Katja H.-W. Skjølberg, has expanded the *Terrorism in Western Europe – Event Dataset* (TWEED) to include all democratic countries without civil wars for the past ten years. This is probably one of the most scientifically sound datasets on domestic terrorism, but is not yet publicly available. See Jan Oskar Engene with Katja H-W Skjølberg, 'Data on Intrastate Terrorism: The TWEED Project', paper for Uppsala Conference on Conflict Data, 8–9 June 2001, <http://www.pcr.uu.se/conferenses/Euroconference/tweed-uu.pdf>. Accessed May 2004.

25 Bergesen and Lizardo, 'International Terrorism and the World System', p. 40.

26 Ted Robert Gurr, 'Empirical Research on Political Terrorism: The State of the Art and How it Might Be Improved', in Robert Slater and Michael Stohl (eds) *Current Perspectives on International Terrorism* (Basingstoke: Macmillan, 1988), p. 115.

27 Schmid and Jongman et al., *Political Terrorism*, p. 179.

28 Roberta Senechal de la Roche, 'Towards a Scientific Theory of Terrorism', *Sociological Theory* 22 (1) (March 2004), p. 1. See also Bergesen and Lizardo, 'International Terrorism and the World System'.

29 Adrian Guelke, *The Age of Terrorism and the International Political System* (London: I. B. Tauris, 1997), p. 31.

30 US Department of State, *Patterns of Global Terrorism 2003*, p. xii.

31 ibid.

32 See, for example, Jan Oskar Engene, *Patterns of Terrorism in Western Europe, 1950–95* (Bergen: University of Bergen, 1998), Ph.D. thesis; and Peter Waldman, 'Terrorismus im internationalen Umfeld', *Internationale Politik*, 54 (2–3) (1999), pp. 21–8.

33 Guelke, *The Age of Terrorism and the International Political System*, p. 31.

34 Schmid and Jongman et al. *Political Terrorism*, p. 48.

35 Senechal de la Roche, 'Towards a Scientific Theory of Terrorism'; Roberta Senechal de la Roche, 'Collective Violence as Social Control', *Sociological Forum*

11 (1) (March 1996), pp. 97–128; and Donald Black, 'The Geometry of Terrorism', *Sociological Theory* 22 (1) (March 2004), pp. 14–25.

36 The term 'collective liability' refers to a form of accountability by which most members of a social group (nation, religion, ethnicity, etc.) are punished for the alleged crimes or sins of their fellow members. Senechal de la Roche, 'Towards a Scientific Theory of Terrorism', p. 2.

37 Senechal de la Roche, 'Collective Violence as Social Control'.

38 Black, 'The Geometry of Terrorism', p. 17.

39 ibid., p. 16.

40 ibid., pp. 18–19.

41 Schmid and Jongman et al. *Political Terrorism*, p. 28.

42 Alex Schmid and Janny de Graaf, *Violence as Communication: Insurgent Terrorism and the Western News Media* (Beverly Hills, Calif.: Sage, 1982); R. D. Crelinsten, 'Terrorism as Political Communication: The Relationship between the Controller and the Controlled', in Paul Wilkinson and Alasdair M. Stewart (eds) *Contemporary Research on Terrorism* (Aberdeen: Aberdeen University Press, 1987), pp. 3–23; and Gabriel Weimann and Hans-Bernd Brosius, 'The Predictability of International Terrorism: A Time-Series Analysis', *Terrorism* 11 (6) (1988), pp. 491–502.

43 See, in particular, Philip Kraber, 'Urban Terrorism: Baseline Data and a Conceptual Framework', *Social Science Quarterly* 52 (3) (1971), pp. 527–33.

44 Brian Jenkins, 'Will Terrorists Go Nuclear?' *Orbis* 29 (3) (fall 1985), p. 511.

45 See, for example, Engene, *Patterns of Terrorism in Western Europe, 1950–95*.

46 R. James Woolsey quoted in 'Countering the Changing Threat of International Terrorism', *Report from the National Commission on Terrorism*, June 2000.

47 For an analysis of Russian organised crime, see Rolf-Inge Vogt Andrésen, 'Terrorism and Organised Crime in Post-Soviet Russia', *FFI Research Report* No. 2001/03417 (Kjeller: FFI, 2001), <http://www.mil.no/multimedia/archive/00002/Andresen-R-2001-03417_2131a.pdf>; and J. Granville, 'The rise of Russian organised crime and Russian kleptocracy', *Global Society* 17 (3) July 2003, pp. 323–30. Accessed June 2004.

48 Quantitative armed conflicts and civil-war studies have progressed much further in the theoretical field than terrorism research. New research on the causes of terrorism has demonstrated that causal relationships between economic and political conditions and terrorism are in several areas quite similar to what has previously been found in civil-war studies. This makes us more confident in drawing more upon this literature than previous authors have done. See for example Li and Schaub, 'Economic Globalisation and Transnational Terrorism'; Brian Lai, 'Explaining Terrorism Using the Framework of Opportunity and Willingness: An Empirical Examination of International Terrorism', research paper, Department of Political Science, University of Iowa, April 2004, <http://rubagalo.polisci.uiowa.edu/~fredb/workshop/lai2004-04-18.pdf>. Accessed July 2004; and Engene, *Patterns of Terrorism in Western Europe, 1950–95*. See also Crenshaw's remarks on the lack of applicability of this literature in terrorism studies in Crenshaw, 'The Causes of Terrorism', p. 114. See also Brian Jenkins, *Future Trends in International Terrorism* (Santa Monica, Calif.: Rand Corporation, 1985, Rand Report No. P-7176), p. 6.

49 In explaining the occurrence of terrorism, one may distinguish between four different levels of explanations: the psycho-pathological (individual) and psycho-sociological levels (group), the societal (state, nation) and the international/world-system levels. See our analysis in Lia and Skjølberg, 'Warum es zu terrorismus kommt: ein überblick über theorien und hypothese zu den ursacken des terrorismus'.

50 Brynjar Lia, 'Causes of Terrorism: An Updated and Expanded Review of the Literature', *FFI Research Report* No. 2004/004307 (Kjeller: FFI, 2005).

2 GLOBALISATION AND ARMED CONFLICTS

1 Tony Blair, Speech to the Lord Mayor's Banquet during November 2001 at the Guildhall in London.
2 Anthony Giddens, 'Globalisation: An Irresistible Force', *Daily Yomiuri* June 7, 1999, <http://www.globalpolicy.org/globaliz/define/irresfrc.htm>. Accessed March 2004.
3 Geoffrey Garrett, 'Global Markets and National Politics: Collision Course or Virtuous Circle?' *International Organisation* 52 (4) (autumn 1998), p. 788.
4 Caroline Thomas, 'Poverty, Development and Hunger', in John Baylis and Steve Smith (eds) *The Globalisation of World Politics: An Introduction to International Relations* (Oxford: Oxford University Press, 1999), p. 464.
5 For example, Katzenstein, Keohane and Krasner define globalisation as '[i]ncreasing levels of transboundary movements and their associated effects'. See Peter J. Katzenstein, Robert O. Keohane and Stephen D. Krasner, 'International Organisation and the Study of World Politics', *International Organisation* 52 (4) (fall 1998), p. 669.
6 Hans-Henrik Holm and Georg Sørensen, *Whose World Order? Uneven Globalisation and the End of the Cold War* (Boulder, Col.: Westview, 1995), p. 4.
7 Erik Oddvar Eriksen, *Globalisation and Democracy* (Oslo: University of Oslo Press, 1999), ARENA Working Paper No. 23, p. 1.
8 Jan Aart Scholte, *Globalisation: A Critical Introduction* (London: Palgrave Macmillan, 2000), p. 46.
9 Anthony G. McGrew, 'Globalisation: Conceptualising a Moving Target', in John Eatwell, Elizabeth Jelin, Anthony McGrew and James Rosenau (eds) *Understanding Globalisation: The Nation-State, Democracy, and Economic Policies in the New Epoch* (Stockholm: Almquist & Wiksell International, 1998), p. 21.
10 Richard Devetak and Richard Higgott, 'Justice Unbound? Globalisation, States and the Transformation of the Social Bond', *International Affairs* 75 (3) (July 1999), p. 491.
11 Benjamin R. Barber, *Jihad vs. McWorld: How Globalism and Tribalism are Reshaping the World* (New York: Ballantine Books, 1996).
12 Rainer Bauböck, 'Towards a Political Theory of Migrant Transnationalism' (Wien: Österreichische Akademie der Wissenschaften Forschungsstelle für Institutionellen Wandel und Europäische Integration, October 2002), IWE Working Paper Series No. 34.
13 For two critical accounts, see Michel Chossudovsky, *The Globalisation of Poverty: Impact of IMF and World Bank Reforms* (London: Zed Books, 1997); and Manuel Castells, *End of Millennium: The Information Age: Economy, Society and Culture* (Oxford: Blackwell, 1998).
14 Louise Richardson, 'Terrorists as Transnational Actors', *Terrorism and Political Violence* 11 (4) (winter 1999), p. 210.
15 NIC, *Global Trends 2015*, p. 6.
16 Bill Clinton, lecture at London School of Economics, 13 December 2001.
17 Author interview in Gaza City, December 1996.
18 Devetak and Higgott, 'Justice Unbound?'; and UNDP, *Human Development Report 1999* (New York: Oxford University Press, 1999), pp. 7–8.
19 A proponent of this view is John Gray. See his 'Geopolitics and the Limits of Growth', *The Globalist* 17 March 2004.

20 Hoffmann, 'Clash of Globalisations', p. 108.
21 Castells, *End of Millennium*, pp. 161–5.
22 ibid., p. 164.
23 ibid., p. 165.
24 See Li and Schaub, 'Economic Globalisation and Transnational Terrorism'; and Lizardo, 'The Effect of Economic and Cultural Globalisation on Anti-U.S. Transnational Terrorism 1971–2000'.
25 Social distance refers to difference between social locations, involving categories such as wealth, authority, integration, culture, intimacy, organisation, activities, etc.
26 Black, 'The Geometry of Terrorism', pp. 14–25; and Senechal de la Roche, 'Collective Violence as Social Control'.
27 There are important exceptions such as colonial societies, multi-ethnic states (India, Indonesia) and ethnic enclaves in mainly homogeneous societies such as the Gypsies and Jewish ghettos in pre-modern Europe.
28 Black, 'The Geometry of Terrorism', pp. 20–1.
29 National Intelligence Council, *Global Trends 2015*.
30 Black, 'The Geometry of Terrorism', p. 22.
31 ibid., p. 24.
32 Ronald Inglehart and Wayne E. Baker, 'Modernisation's Challenge to Traditional Values: Who's Afraid of Ronald McDonald?' *The Futurist* 35 (2) (March/April 2001), p. 20.
33 Quoted from a book review of John C. Condon, *Good Neighbors: Communicating With the Mexicans* (Yarmouth, Maine: Intercultural Press, Interact Series, 1997), <http://www.amazon.com/exec/obidos/tg/detail/-/0933662602/102–3128979–5314547?v=glance>. Accessed July 2004.
34 Michael Doran, 'Somebody Else's Civil War', *Foreign Affairs* 81 (1) (January–February 2002), pp. 22–42. See also Tony Addison and S. Mansoob Murshed, 'Transnational Terrorism and a Spillover of Domestic Dispute in Other Countries', Helsinki, United Nations University, World Institute of Development Economics Research, December 2002, Discussion Paper No. 2002/120.
35 See discussion in Lia, 'Causes of Terrorism', Chapter 4.
36 For a poignant criticism of that view, see Yahya Sadowski, 'Ethnic Conflict', *Foreign Policy* No. 111 (summer 1998).
37 See <http://www.prio.no/cwp/ArmedConflict>. See also Mikael Eriksson, Peter Wallensteen and Margareta Sollenberg, 'Armed Conflict, 1989–2002', *Journal of Peace Research* 40 (5) (September 2003), pp. 593–607; and Gleditsch, 'The Future of Armed Conflict'. Accessed May 2004.
38 For the debate over the future probability of 'major war' see also Michael Mandelbaum, 'Is Major War Obsolete?' *Survival* 40 (4) (winter 1998–9), pp. 20–38; and Donald Kagan, et al., 'Is Major War Obsolete? An Exchange', *Survival* 41 (2) (summer 1999), pp. 139–52.
39 Gleditsch, 'The Future of Armed Conflict', pp. 7, 10.
40 Dan Smith, 'Interventionist Dilemmas and Justice', in Anthony McDermott (ed.) *Humanitarian Force* (Oslo: PRIO, 1997), PRIO-Report No. 4/97, p. 20.
41 Peter Wallensteen and Margareta Sollenberg, 'Armed Conflict 1989–98', *Journal of Peace Research* 36 (5) (September 1999), p. 597.
42 Max Singer and Aaron B. Wildavsky, *The Real World Order: Zones of Peace, Zones of Turmoil* (London: Chatham House Publishers, 1993).
43 Gleditsch, 'The Future of Armed Conflict', p. 11.
44 David A. Lake and Donald Rothchild, 'Containing Fear: The Origins and Management of Ethnic Conflict', *International Security* 21 (2) (fall 1996), pp. 44–5.

Wallensteen and Sollenberg reflect this thinking and divide the structural causes into two main categories, referring to incompatibility concerning government and incompatibility concerning territory. Wallensteen and Sollenberg, 'Armed Conflict 1989–98'.

45 Lake and Rothchild, 'Containing Fear', pp. 43–4, 47–9; and Bronson, 'Cycles of Conflict in the Middle East and North Africa', p. 205.
46 Wallensteen and Sollenberg, 'Armed Conflict 1989–98', pp. 596–7.
47 James D. Fearon and David D. Laitin, 'Ethnicity, Insurgency, and Civil War', *American Political Science Review* 97 (1) (February 2003), p. 88.
48 Lake and Rothchild, 'Containing Fear', pp. 41–2. See also Jonathan Goodhand, David Hulme and Nick Lewer, 'Social Capital and the Political Economy of Violence: A Case Study of Sri Lanka' *Disasters: The Journal of Disaster Studies, Policy and Management* 24 (4) (December 2000), pp. 390–406; and Mary Kaldor, *New and Old Wars: Organised Violence in a Global Era* (Stanford, Calif.: Stanford University Press, 1999).
49 'Sharon, Ariel', *Microsoft Encarta Online Encyclopedia 2004*, <http://encarta.msn.com>; and 'Kosovo', *Microsoft Encarta Online Encyclopedia 2004*, <http://encarta.msn.com>.
50 Eriksson, Wallensteen and Sollenberg, 'Armed Conflict, 1989–2002', p. 594.
51 Gleditsch, 'The Future of Armed Conflict', p. 7.
52 Mary Kaldor and Robin Luckham, 'Global Transformations and New Conflicts', *IDS Bulletin – Institute of Development Studies* 32 (2) (April 2001), abstract.
53 Yahya Sadowski, 'Ethnic Conflict', *Foreign Policy* 111 (Summer 1998).
54 Smith, 'Interventionist Dilemmas and Justice', in Anthony McDermott (ed.) *Humanitarian Force* (Oslo: PRIO, 1997), PRIO-Report No. 4/97, p. 16.
55 Uwe Buse, 'Spiegel des 21. Jahrhunderts: die zukunft des krieges', *Der Spiegel* 26 October 1999, p. 2. Author's translation.
56 Martin Van Creveld, *The Transformation of War* (New York: The Free Press, 1991), pp. 192–223.
57 Kaldor and Luckham, 'Global Transformations and New Conflicts'.
58 William R. Ayres, 'A World Flying Apart? Violent Nationalist Conflict and the End of the Cold War', *Journal of Peace Research* 37 (1) (January 2000), pp. 105–17.
59 Kofi Annan, 'Two Concepts of Sovereignty', *The Economist* 10 September 1999.
60 Juan Enriquez, 'Too Many Flags', *Foreign Policy* 116 (fall 1999), p. 48.
61 Robert I. Rotberg, 'Failed States in a World of Terror', *Foreign Affairs* 81 (4) (July–August 2002), p. 131.
62 See Bundesverfassungsschutzgesetz, *Verfassungsschutzbericht 2002*, <http://www.bmi.bund.de/Annex/de_24336/Verfassungsschutzbericht_2002.pdf>. Accessed June 2004.
63 Stephen Castles and Mark J. Miller, *The Age of Migration: International Population Movements in the Modern World* (Houndmills: Macmillan, 1998), p. 276.
64 Stein Tønnesson, 'A "Global Civil War"?' *Security Dialogue* 33 (3) (September 2002), p. 389.
65 ibid.; Mackinlay, *Globalisation and Insurgency*; Martha Crenshaw, 'Why is America the Primary Target? Terrorism as Globalised Civil War', in Charles W. Kegley Jr. (ed.) *The New Global Terrorism: Characteristics, Causes, Controls* (Upper Saddle River, NJ: Prentice Hall, 2003), pp. 160–73; and MacGregor Knox, 'America is Fighting a Global Civil War', *Financial Times* 14 April 2003.
66 Ann Scott Tyson, 'Al Qaeda Broken, but Dangerous', *The Christian Science Monitor* 24 June 2002.
67 Daniel Benjamin and Steven Simon, 'Al-Qaeda's Dangerous Metamorphosis', *Los Angeles Times* 11 November 2002. See also Diana Muriel, 'Terror Moves to

the Virtual World', *CNN.com* 8 April 2004; and Jeremy Reynalds, 'Terror Group Finds New Home on Internet', *Talon News* 9 April 2004.

68 Reuven Paz, 'Virtual al-Qaïdah', Presentation at an international workshop on 'Modern Trends of Islamic Movements', in Oslo, Norway, February 2003.

69 Thomas Friedman, *Longitudes and Attitudes* (New York: Farrar, Strauss, Giroux, 2002), p. 6.

70 ibid.

71 For RAF, see Stefan Aust, *The Baader-Meinhof Group* (London: The Bodley Head, 1987).

72 Richard Clarke quoted in '60 minutes: Clarke's Take On Terror', *CBS News* 30 March 2004.

73 Robin Cook quoted in Nicholas Watt, 'Bin Laden wanted invasion', *The Guardian* 21 July 2004.

74 Cited in 'Full transcript of bin Ladin's speech', *al-Jazeera*, 30 October 2004, <http://   english.aljazeera.net/NR/exeres/79C6AF22–98FB–4A1C-B21F–2BC36E87F61F. htm>. Accessed November 2004.

75 For a similar argument, see Brigitte L. Nacos, 'The Terrorist Calculus behind 9–11: A Model for Future Terrorism?' *Studies in Conflict and Terrorism* 26 (1) (2003), pp. 1–16.

76 Paul Collier and Anke Hoeffler, 'Greed and Grievance in Civil Wars', World Bank Research Paper 21 October 2001, <http://www.worldbank.org/research/conflict/papers/greedgrievance_23oct.pdf>. Accessed April 2004; David Keen, *The Economic Functions of Violence in Civil Wars* (Oxford: Oxford University Press, 1998), Adelphi Paper No. 320; Mats Berdal and David Keen, 'Violence and Economic Agendas in Civil Wars: Some Policy Implications', *Millennium: Journal of International Studies* 26 (3) (1997), pp. 1–24; and Kaldor, *New and Old Wars*.

77 Cited in Mackinlay, *Globalisation and Insurgency*, p. 17.

78 Kaldor and Luckham, 'Global Transformations and New Conflicts'.

79 John Mueller, 'The Remnants of War: Thugs as Residual Combatants', Paper for the Conference on 'Identifying Wars', Uppsala University, 8–9 June 2001, <http://www.pcr.uu.se>. Accessed April 2004, paraphrased in Gleditsch, 'The Future of Armed Conflict', p. 13.

80 Mark Duffield cited in Jonathan Goodhand and David Hulme, 'From Wars to Complex Political Emergencies: Understanding Conflict and Peace-Building in The New World Disorder', *Third World Quarterly* 20 (1) (February 1999), p. 19. See also Berdal and Keen, 'Violence and Economic Agendas in Civil Wars', p. 2.

81 See, for example, Paul B. Rich, 'Warlords, State Fragmentation and the Dilemma of Humanitarian Intervention', *Small Wars and Insurgencies* 10 (1) (spring 1999), pp. 78–96; and Goodhand and Hulme, 'From Wars to Complex Political Emergencies', p. 19.

82 Mackinlay, *Globalisation and Insurgency*, pp. 17–20.

83 Mackinlay, *Globalisation and Insurgency*, p. 15.

84 Berdal and Keen, 'Violence and Economic Agendas in Civil Wars', pp. 2, 4, 22–3.

85 Ray Abrahams, *Vigilant Citizens: Vigilantism and the State* (Cambridge: Polity Press, 1998), p. 169. See also Berdal and Keen, 'Violence and Economic Agendas in Civil Wars', pp. 18–19; and Jean-Marie Guéhenno, 'The Impact of Globalisation on Strategy', *Survival* 40 (4) (1998–9), pp. 12–13.

86 For examples from Canada, see Margaret Purdy, 'Targeting Diasporas: The Canadian Counter-Terrorism Experience', University of British Columbia, Vancouver, Armed Groups Project, working paper, October 2003, <http://www.armedgroups.org/_media/Purdy_paper.pdf>. Accessed May 2004; and Stewart

Bell, *Cold Terror: How Canada Nurtures and Exports Terrorism Around the World* (Toronto: John Wiley & Sons, 2004).

87 CSIS Director quoted in 'Charities Could Be Funding Foreign Terrorists', *Globe and Mail* 18 November 1998.

88 A French intelligence officer noted about the *banlieue*: 'When the extremists take control, violence goes down. Islam brings discipline. But then we have to watch that neighborhood for a different reason. For the extremists, there are two kinds of territory: conquered territory and territory that remains to be conquered.' See Sebastian Rotella, 'Europe Holds Fertile Soil for Jihadis Terror: French Rampage Shows What can Happen When Alienation, Crime and Extremism Mix', *Los Angeles Times* 5 December 2001.

89 Gilles Kepel, *Jihad: The Trail of Political Islam* (Cambridge: Mass.: Harvard University Press, 2002), pp. 291–2.

3 INTERNATIONAL RELATIONS AND POLITICS

1 President George W. Bush Jr. quoted in The White House, *National Security Strategy of the United States*, September 2002, <http://www.whitehouse.gov/nsc/nssall.html>. Accessed April 2004.

2 I am indebted to Dr Annika S. Hansen for her contributions to an early draft of this chapter.

3 Richard Higgott, 'American Unilaterism, Foreign Economic Policy and the "Securitisation" of Globalisation', Singapore, Institute of Defence and Strategic Studies, October 2003, working paper No. 52, <http://www.ntu.edu.sg/idss/workingpapers/wp52.pdf>. Accessed April 2004.

4 John Ikenberry (ed.) *America Unrivalled*, p. 1, cited in Higgott, 'American Unilaterism, Foreign Economic Policy and the "Securitisation" of Globalisation', p. 1.

5 Zalmay Khalilzad and Ian Lesser (eds) *Sources of Conflict in the Twenty-First Century: Regional Futures and U.S. Strategy* (Santa Monica, Calif.: Rand, 1998), p. 10.

6 The above-mentioned Rand report is illustrative in this respect: it asserts that in the unlikely event of a US withdrawal from the world stage, the 'implications would be staggering', leading to widespread instability and conflict, endangering former friends and encouraging former adversaries. See Khalilzad and Lesser, *Sources of Conflict in the Twenty-First Century*, p. 11.

7 See for example, Immanuel Wallerstein, *The Decline of American Power: the U.S. in a Chaotic World* (New York and London: The New Press, 2003); Volker Bornschier and Christopher Chase-Dunn, *The Future of Global Conflict* (London: Sage, 1999); and OECD, *Globalisation and Linkages to 2020: Can Poor Countries and Poor People Prosper in the New Global Age?* (Paris: OECD, 1997), working papers 5–90. For US military overstretch, see Mark Mazzetti, 'Stretched Thin', *USNews.com* 2 February 2004; and 'Bush Ramps Up Military Spending in 2.4 Trillion Dollar Budget', *AFP* 2 February 2004.

8 Bornschier and Chase-Dunn, *The Future of Global Conflict*, p. 1.

9 See book review of Joseph S. Nye, Jr., *The Paradox of American Power*, in *Futurecasts* 4 (2) (February 2002), <http://www.futurecasts.com>. Accessed June 2004.

10 Robert Looney, 'From Petrodollars to Petroeuros: Are the Dollar's Days as an International Reserve Currency Drawing to an End?' <http://www.ccc.nps.navy.mil/si/novo3/middleeast.asp>. Accessed September 2004.

11 ibid.

12 OECD, *Globalisation and Linkages to 2020*, p. 21; and Khalilzad and Lesser, *Sources of Conflict in the Twenty-First Century*, p. 12.

13 OECD, *Globalisation and Linkages to 2020*, p. 21.
14 NIC, *Global Trends 2015*, p. 36.
15 James F. Hoge, 'A Global Power Shift in the Making', *Foreign Affairs* 83 (4) (July–August 2004), pp. 2–3.
16 June Teufel Dreyer, 'The Limits to China's Growth', *Orbis* 48 (2) (spring 2004), p. 246.
17 William C. Wohlforth, 'Transatlantic Relations in a Unipolar World', *Geneva Centre for Security Policy – Occasional Paper Series*, No. 41 (August 2002), p. 10.
18 Canadian Department of National Defence, *Strategic Assessment 2003* (Ottawa, September 2003, Project Report 2003/11), <http://www.forces.gc.ca/admpol/eng/doc/strat_2003/pdf/sa_2003_e.pdf>. Acessed May 2004, p. 145.
19 Canadian Department of National Defence, *Strategic Assessment 2003*, pp. 66, 145.
20 ibid., pp. 65–71, 145–6.
21 Samuel P. Huntington, 'The Lonely Superpower', *Foreign Affairs* 78 (2) (March–April 1999); and William C. Wohlforth, 'Transatlantic Relations in a Unipolar World', *Geneva Centre for Security Policy – Occasional Paper Series*, No. 41 (August 2002).
22 Huntington, 'The Lonely Superpower', p. 36.
23 ibid., p. 37.
24 The notion of soft power is taken from Joseph S. Nye, Jr., *The Paradox of American Power* (Oxford: Oxford University Press, 2002).
25 Hoffmann, 'Clash of Globalisations', p. 113.
26 See for example Christopher Marquis, 'U.S. Image Abroad Will Take Years to Repair, Official Testifies', *New York Times* 5 February 2004.
27 Huntington, 'The Lonely Superpower', p. 43.
28 Bornschier and Chase-Dunn, *The Future of Global Conflict*, pp. 1–5.
29 ibid., p. 9.
30 Thomas J. Volgy, Lawrence E. Imwalle and Jeff J. Corntassel, 'Structural Determinants of International Terrorism: The Effects of Hegemony and Polarity on Terrorist Activity', *International Interactions* 23 (2) (1997), pp. 207–31.
31 Richardson, 'Terrorists as Transnational Actors', p. 211.
32 NIC, *Global Trends 2015*, p. 50.
33 Bergesen and Lizardo, 'International Terrorism and the World System'.
34 John Soule noted in his study of the conflict in Northern Ireland that the terrorist attacks and the counter-terrorist responses assumed an almost 'ritualistic' character. Peter Waldman has noted how important vengeance has been in terrorism. See John Soule, *A Case Study of Terrorism: Northern Ireland 1970–1990* (New York: Carnegie, 2004), Case Study No. 5; and Peter Waldman, 'Revenge Without Rules: On the Renaissance of an Archaic Motif of Violence', *Studies in Conflict and Terrorism* 24 (6) (November 2001), pp. 435–50.
35 Carl Boggs, 'Militarism and Terrorism: The Deadly Cycle', *Democracy and Nature* 8 (2) (July 2002), pp. 241–59.
36 ibid.
37 See, for example, Peter F. Hirst, 'New and Old Technologies: Choice of Strategy and Targets', Gunnar Jervas (ed.), *FAO Report on Terrorism* (Stockholm: The Swedish Defence Research Establishment, 1998), pp. 111–28.
38 See for example James K. Campbell, 'Excerpts from Research Study "Weapons of Mass Destruction and Terrorism: Proliferation by Non-state Actors" ', *Terrorism and Political Violence* 9 (2) (summer 1997), pp. 24–56; Gavin Cameron, 'Multi-Track Microproliferation: Lessons from Aum Shinrikyo and Al-Qaida', *Studies in Conflict and Terrorism* 22 (4) (October–December 1999), pp. 277–309;

and 'The New Terrorism: Coming Soon to a City Near You', *The Economist* 15 August 1998.

39 Marilyn W. Thompson, 'The Pursuit of Steven Hatfill', *Washington Post* 14 September 2003, p. W06.

40 WMD is here taken to mean militarily effective nuclear, biological and, to a lesser extent, chemical weapons, with a lethality far exceeding that of conventional arms. For an assessment of Aum's biological-weapons programme, see William Rosenau, 'Aum Shinrikyo's Biological Weapons Program: Why Did it Fail?' *Studies in Conflict and Terrorism* 24 (4) (July 2001), pp. 289–301.

41 John Parachini, 'Putting WMD Terrorism into Perspective', *Washington Quarterly* 26 (4) (autumn 2003), pp. 37–50.

42 There is some disagreement about whether availability of sufficient material of weapons-grade HEU is the only technical barrier to terrorist use of a nuclear bomb.

43 'Country Profiles: Argentina & Brazil', *Global Security Institute*, San Francisco, <http:// www.gsinstitute.org/resources/countries/argentina_brazil.shtml>.

44 'Brazil, China Discuss Nuclear Production Agreement', *Agência Estado* 25 May 2004, <http:// www.aebrazil.com/highlights/2004/mai/25/40.htm>; 'Sources: Brazil Blocks Nuclear Inspectors', *CNN.com* 4 April 2004; and Carmen Gentile, 'Brazil: We're Not Hiding Nuclear Agenda', *UPI* 5 April 2004.

45 CIA, 'Unclassified Report to Congress on the Acquisition of Technology Relating to Weapons of Mass Destruction and Advanced Conventional Munitions, 1 January Through 30 June 2003'.

46 'IAEA Finds Traces of Highly Enriched Uranium in Iran: report', *AFP* 11 March 2004.

47 According to some analysts, an Israeli attack on Iranian nuclear plants is 'inevitable'. See 'Will Israel Strike Iran Facilities?', *Defense News* 4 October 2004, pp. 1, 6.

48 Nicolas D. Kristof, 'The Legacy of Dr. Khan', *International Herald Tribune* 27 August 2004.

49 Ian O. Lesser, 'Weapons of Mass Destruction in the Middle East: Proliferation Dynamics and Strategic Consequences', in Nora Bensahel and Daniel L. Byman (eds) *The Future Security Environment in the Middle East: Conflict, Stability, and Political Change* (Santa Monica, Calif.: Rand, 2004), pp. 253–98; and National Intelligence Council, 'Global Trends 2020 – east Asia', paper prepared for 'Commonwealth Conference', 8 December 2003, <http://www.cia.gov/nic/pdf_gif_2020_support/2003_12_08_papers/dec8_eastasia.pdf>. Accessed July 2004, p. 9.

50 Detailed accounts of al-Qaida's early efforts at acquiring radiological material comes from the court-room testimony of bin Laden aide Jamal Ahmad al-Fadl as well as from corroborated statements of Bulgarian businessman and former intelligence officer Ivan Ivanov, who have described meeting bin Laden in April 2001. See Ackerman and Bale, 'Al-Qaïda and Weapons of Mass Destruction'.

51 'UN Nuclear Watchdog Investigating Spread of Black Market', *AFP* 8 March 2004; 'Police Say Sri Lankan Implicated in Nuclear Ring Free To Leave Malaysia' *AFP* 22 February 2004; 'Malaysia Says Nuclear Middleman Reveals Iran, Libya Deals', *AFP* 20 February 2004; Joelle Stolz, 'The Libyan Inventory Recorded by the IAEA Reveals a Network Running from Malaysia to the Netherlands [in French]', *Le Monde* 13 February 2004; and Françoise Chipaux, 'Pakistan is at Heart of Global Nuclear Black Market [in French]', *Le Monde* 13 February 2004.

52 Stolz, 'The Libyan Inventory Recorded by the IAEA Reveals a Network Running

from Malaysia to the Netherlands [in French]'; and Chipaux, 'Pakistan is at Heart of Global Nuclear Black Market'.

53 Chipaux, 'Pakistan is at Heart of Global Nuclear Black Market'.

54 I am indebted to Dr Morten Bremer Mærli to this information. See his *Crude Nukes on the Loose: Preventing Nuclear Terrorism by Means of Optimum Nuclear Husbandry, Transparency, and Non-Intrusive Fissile Material Verification* (Oslo: University of Oslo, 2004), Ph.D. thesis.

55 I am indebted to Chief Scientist Steinar Høibråthen at the FFI for this information.

56 Charles D. Ferguson and William C. Potter, *The Four Faces of Nuclear Terrorism* (Monterey: Center for Non-Proliferation Studies, 2004).

57 Sharon K. Weiner, 'Preventing Nuclear Entrepeneurship in Russia's Nuclear Cities', *International Security* 27 (2) (fall 2002), pp. 126–58. See also Deborah Yarsike Ball, 'The Security of Russia's Nuclear Arsenal: The Human Factor', Lawrence Livermore National Laboratory, PONARS Policy Memo No. 91, October 1999, <http://www.csis.org/ruseura/ponars/policymemos/pm_0091.pdf>. Accessed May 2004.

58 According to a 2003 US General Accounting Office report, as many as 254 of 612 sources of radioactive materials which had been reported stolen worldwide in the past eight years had not been recovered. How many of these were HEU incidents is unknown. See 'NBC: Radioactive Materials Missing: Citing Threat of "dirty bombs," GAO report says U.S. fails to protect against theft', *MSNBC News* 13 June 2003.

59 Scott Parrish, 'Illicit Nuclear Trafficking in the NIS', issue brief, CNS NIS Nonproliferation Programme, March 2002, <http://www.nti.org/e_research/e3_8a.html>. Accessed October 2004.

60 Mark Franchetti, 'Inspector Claims Russia has Hushed Up Nuclear Thefts', *Sunday Times* 13 October 2002. For other examples, see Charles J. Hanley, 'Central Asia Emerges as Source of "Dirty Bomb" ', *AP* 15 June 2002; and Anna Badkhen, 'Raid in Georgia Triggers "Dirty bomb" Fears: Police Seize Radioactive Materials', *San Francisco Chronicle* 17 June 2003.

61 Mark Franchetti, 'Inspector Claims Russia has Hushed Up Nuclear Thefts', *Sunday Times* 13 October 2002.

62 These secret programmes 'involved building and testing a cluster munition, modeled on a Soviet bioweapon, to spread biological agents', 'the production of non-pathogenic bacterial spores that were then dried and weaponized', using only commercially available materials, the 'genetically engineer[ing of] *Bacillus anthracis* (the causative agent of anthrax) to recreate a Soviet strain thought to be resistant to the U.S. vaccine'. See Mark Wheelis and Malcolm Dando, 'Back to Bioweapons?' *Bulletin of the Atomic Scientists* 59 (1) (January–February 2003), pp. 40–6, <http://www.thebulletin.org/article.php?art-ofn=if03wheelis>. Accessed September 2004.

63 Thompson, 'The Pursuit of Steven Hatfill', p. W06.

64 Wheelis and Dando, 'Back to Bioweapons?'

65 Kenneth Alibek, 'Terrorist and Intelligence Operations: Potential Impact on the U.S. Economy', statement before the Joint Economic Committee, US Congress, 20 May 1998, <http://www.house.gov/jec/hearings/intell/alibek.htm>. Accessed May 2004.

66 ibid.

67 Daniel Feakes, 'Global Civil Society and Biological and Chemical Weapons', in Mary Kaldor, Helmut Anheier and Marlies Glasius (eds) *Global Civil Society Yearbook 2003* (London: LSE, 2003), Chapter 5.

68 NATO, 'Combating Terrorism at Sea', *NATO Briefing* April 2004, <http://www.nato.int/docu/briefing/terrorism_at_sea-e.pdf>. Accessed May 2004.

69 Ann Markusen, 'The Rise of World Weapons', *Foreign Policy* No. 114 (spring 1999), pp. 40–51. For a similar argument, see Martin C. Libicki, 'Rethinking War: The Mouse's New Roar?' *Foreign Policy* No. 117 (Winter 1999–2000), pp. 10–43.

70 For the crisis in Albania in January–February 1997 and the international peacekeeping intervention that followed, see Georgios Kostakos and Dimitris Bourantonis, 'Innovations in Peacekeeping: The Case of Albania', *Security Dialogue* 29 (1) (March 1998), pp. 49–58.

71 'Warheads with Mustard, Sarin Gas Found by Polish Troops in Iraq: Rumsfeld', *AFP* 1 July 2004; Liza Porteus, 'Tests Confirm Sarin in Iraqi Artillery Shell', *FoxNews.com* 19 May 2004; 'Official: Tests Confirm Sarin in Iraq Bomb', *Associated Press* 25 May 2004; and William Branigin and Joby Warrick, 'Deadly Nerve Agent Sarin Is Found in Roadside Bomb: Weapon Probably Not Part of a Stockpile, Experts Say', *Washington Post* 18 May 2004, p. A14.

72 Bob Drogin, 'The Other Weapons Threat in Iraq', *Los Angeles Times* 10 October 2004.

73 ibid.

74 National Intelligence Council, 'Global Trends 2020 – east Asia', p. 9.

75 See for example Owais Tohid, 'Pakistan and its Proliferator' *Christian Science Monitor* 6 February 2004; 'Al-Qaeda Trying to Acquire Small Nukes', *Times of India* 9 October 2002; and 'U.S. Says al Qaeda Exploring Russian Market for Weapons', *Washington Times* 8 October 2002.

76 Pål Aas, 'The Threat of Mid-Spectrum Chemical Warfare Agents', *Prehospital and Disaster Medicine* 18(4) (January 2003), pp. 306–12, <http://pdm.medicine.wisc.edu/184%20pdfs/aas.pdf>. Accessed April 2005.

77 Toxins are biological agents, which owe their pathogenicity to toxic substances that they themselves generate (WHO's definition).

78 Aas, 'The Threat of Mid-Spectrum Chemical Warfare Agents', p. 5. See also Rachel Nowak, 'Killer Virus', *New Scientist* 10 January 2001; 'US Develops Lethal New Viruses', *New Scientist* 29 October 2003; and 'Virus Synthesised in a Fortnight', *New Scientist* 14 November 2003.

79 Alibek, 'Terrorist and Intelligence Operations: Potential Impact on the U.S. Economy'.

80 See for example 'Technology and Terrorism', Draft Interim Report NATO Parliamentary Assembly, Sub-Committee on The Proliferation of Military Technology, April 2001, <http://www.nato-pa.int>. Accessed May 2004.

81 Aas, 'The Threat of Mid-Spectrum Chemical Warfare Agents', p. 6.

82 Monty G. Marshall, 'Regime Authority, Opportunity, and Outbreaks of State Failure Events', *Paper for Uppsala Conference on Conflict Data*, 8–9 June 2001.

83 Samuel Huntington, *The Third Wave* (Norman, Okla.: University of Oklahoma Press, 1991).

84 For studies on democratisation in the Middle East, see the classic study Ghassan Salamé (ed.) *Democracy Without Democrats? The Renewal of Politics in the Muslim World* (London: I. B. Tauris, 1994). See also Najib Ghadbian, *Democratisation and the Islamist Challenge in the Arab World* (Boulder, Col.: Westview Press, 1997).

85 Marshall, 'Regime Authority, Opportunity, and Outbreaks of State Failure Events', p. 123.

86 Their ability to mobilise world opinion and rally support for opposition groups was clearly demonstrated during the Zapatista uprising in Mexico. See David

Ronfeldt and Armando Martínez, 'A Comment on the Zapatista "Netwar", in John Arquilla et al. (eds) *Networks, Netwar, and Information-Age Terrorism* (Washington, DC: Rand, 1998), pp. 369–91. For a general study of transnational actors in global politics, see Peter Willetts, 'Transnational Actors and International Organizations in Global Politics', in John Baylis and Steve Smith (eds) *The Globalisation of World Politics: An Introduction to International Relations* (Oxford: Oxford University Press), pp. 287–310. For the role of NGOs in armed conflicts, see Farouk Mawlawi, 'New Conflicts, New Challenges: The Evolving Role for Non-Governmental Actors', *Journal of International Affairs* 46 (2) (winter 1993), pp. 391–413; and Brynjar Lia and Annika S. Hansen, 'Civil Military Co-Operation and Co-Ordination in Peace Support Operations [in Norwegian]', *FFI Research Report* No. 97/05161 (Kjeller: FFI, 1997).

87 Willetts, 'Transnational Actors and International Organizations in Global Politics', p. 301.

88 See discussion in Peter Ferdinand (ed.) *The Internet, Democracy, and Democratization* (London: Frank Cass, 2000), Special Issue on Democratisation. See also Chris Sprigman, 'Democratic Hacks', *Foreign Policy* No. 138 (September–October 2003), pp. 1, 90; and James McGirk, 'Smart Mob Rule', *Foreign Policy* No. 136 (May 2003), pp. 2, 92.

89 In fact, one recent study analysing data of 127 countries from 1970 to 1996 has found that economic globalisation measured in trade openness and portfolio (financial) investment flows tend to negatively affect democratic governance, while foreign direct investments have the opposite effect, although it weakens over time. See Quan Li and Rafael Reuveny, 'Economic Globalisation and Democracy: An Empirical Analysis', research paper, the Political Science Department at Penn State University, undated. <http://polisci.la.psu.edu/faculty/li/research-_papers/GLODEM39.pdf>. Accessed June 2004. See also David Cingranelli, and David L. Richards, 'Respect for Human Rights After the End of the Cold War', *Journal of Peace Research* 36 (5) (September 1999), p. 512.

90 Bellin follows the tradition in political science which views democracy as 'neither an evolutionary necessity nor a conjectural outcome; rather it is the product of *struggle* in which social forces play a central role. Interest, not enlightenment, drives regime change, and among the panoply of interest that animates people politically material change trump all others'. See Eva Bellin, 'Contingent Democrats: Industrialists, Labor and Democratisation in Late-Developing Countries', *World Politics* 52 (2) (January 2000), p. 177.

91 ibid., p. 205.

92 ibid.

93 Cingranelli and Richards, 'Respect for Human Rights after the End of the Cold War'.

94 ibid.

95 Fareed Zakariya, 'The Rise of Illiberal Democracy', *Foreign Affairs* 76 (6) (November–December 1997), pp. 22–43. For a counterargument, see A. Karatnycky, 'The 1998 Freedom House Survey: The Decline of Illiberal Democracy', *Journal of Democracy* 10 (1) (January 1999), pp. 112–25.

96 Anita Schjølset, 'Democratic Waves Revisited: Types of Democracy and Conflict across Time and Space', Paper for International Studies Association Conference, Los Angeles, 14–18 March 2000, p. 22.

97 ibid., p. 1.

98 Karatnycky, 'The 1998 Freedom House Survey: The Decline of Illiberal Democracy', p. 115.

99 Since 1995 the electoral democracies that have seen a deepening climate of

respect for political rights and civil liberties include the Dominican Republic, El Salvador, Honduras, India, Mali, Nicaragua, Papua New Guinea, the Philippines, Romania, Taiwan and Thailand. See Karatnycky, 'The 1998 Freedom House Survey: The Decline of Illiberal Democracy', pp. 115–16.

100 'World Conflict List 1999', National Defense Council Foundation <http://www.ndcf.org/conflict_list/world99.html>. Accessed June 2004.

101 Orlando J. Pérez, 'Democratic Legitimacy and Public Insecurity: Crime and Democracy in El Salvador and Guatemala', *Political Science Quarterly* 118 (4) (winter 2003/2004), pp. 627–45.

102 'Building an International Human Rights Agenda: Resisting Abuses in the Context of the "War on Terror" ', Amnesty International <http://web.amnesty.org/report2004/hragenda-1-eng>. Accessed May 2004.

103 Gleditsch, 'The Future of Armed Conflict', p. 27.

104 Karatnycky, 'The 1998 Freedom House Survey', p. 115.

105 Carothers, 'Democracy: Terrorism's Uncertain Antidote', p. 404.

106 Ben Aris, 'President Hailed as Prophet', *Daily Telegraph* 20 February 2003.

107 Pepe Escobar, 'Peaceful Jihad', *Asia Times Online* 25 November 2003.

108 'Kyrgyzstan: Radical Islamic Organization Faces Internal Split', *Peace and Justice Update* 7 (6) (24 October 2003), <http://peace.sandiego.edu/Fall03updates/10–24–03.pdf>. Accessed September 2004. The IHT nevertheless remains committed to its non-violent course, see for example, 'Hizb ut-Tahrir Members Rescue Uzbek and Kyrgyz Security Officers From Mob', *Radio Free Europe/Radio Liberty Newsline*, 25 May, 2004, <http://www.rferl.org/news line/2004/05/2-tca/tca-250504.asp>. Accessed September 2004.

109 The categorisation of Israel as a 'free' country is questionable, in light of its gross human-rights abuses in the Israeli-controlled West Bank and Gaza and its systematic use in these areas of an apartheid-like system of military laws applicable to Palestinians only.

110 The others are Myanmar, Cuba, North Korea, and Turkmenistan.

111 Karatnycky, 'The 1998 Freedom House Survey' and 'Freedom in The World 2004: Combined Average Ratings – Independent Countries', Freedom House, Washington, DC, <http://www.freedomhouse.org/research/freeworld/2004/combined2004.pdf>. Accessed July 2004.

112 For an account of Algeria's aborted democratisation process, see Luis Martinez, *The Algerian Civil War 1990–1998* (London: Hurst, 2000); Claire Spencer, 'Algeria in Crisis', *Survival* 36 (2) (summer 1994), pp. 149–63; Daniel Heradstveit, *Political Islam in Algeria* (Oslo: Norwegian Institute of International Affairs, 1997); and Shahin, *Political Ascent*.

113 Abdo Baaklini, Gilan Denoux and Robert Springborg, *Legislative Politics in the Arab World: The Resurgence of Democratic Institutions* (Boulder, Col.: Lynne Rienner, 1999).

114 Nora Bensahel, 'Political Reform In The Middle East', in Nora Bensahel and Daniel L. Byman (eds) *The Future Security Environment in the Middle East: Conflict, Stability, and Political Change* (Santa Monica, Calif.: Rand, 2004), pp. 15–55.

115 Carothers, 'Democracy: Terrorism's Uncertain Antidote', p. 404.

116 ibid., p. 405.

117 Ted Robert Gurr and Monty G. Marshall, *Peace and Conflict 2003: A Global Survey of Armed Conflicts, Self-Determination Movements, and Democracy* (College Park, Md.: University of Maryland Press, 2003), p. 20.

118 Pluchinsky, 'Terrorism in the Former Soviet Union', p. 119.

119 ibid. See also 'The Caucasus: Where Worlds Collide', *The Economist* 19 August 2000, pp. 17–19.

120 Ahmed Rashid, *Jihad: The Rise of Militant Islam in Central Asia* (New Haven, Conn.: Yale University Press, 2002).
121 Roy Licklider, 'The Consequences of Negotiated Settlements in Civil Wars, 1945–1993', *American Political Science Review* 89 (3) (September 1995), pp. 681–90.
122 Gurr, 'Terrorism in Democracies: Its Social and Political Bases'; and Engene, *Patterns of Terrorism in Western Europe, 1950–95*.
123 Two exceptions are the merger of Arab Republic of Yemen and People's Democratic Republic of Yemen in May 1990 (followed by a civil war) and the unification of Germany after the end of the Cold War.
124 These include Abkhazia, Aboriginals of Australia, Acheh, Ahwazi, Albanians in Macedonia, Assyria, Bashkortostan, Batwa, Bougainville, Buryatia, Cabinda, Chechen Republic of Ichkeria, Chin, Chittagong Hill Tracts, Chuvash, Circassia, Cordillera, Crimean Tatars, East Turkestan, Gagauzia, Greek minority in Albania, Hungarian minority in Romania, Ingushetia, Inkeri, Iraqi Turkoman, Ka Lahui Hawaiʻi, Karenni State, Khmer Krom, Komi, Kosova, Kumyk, Kurdistan, Lakota, Maohi, Mapuche, Mari, Mon, Montagnards, Nagalim, Nuxalk, Ogoni, Rusyn, Sanjak, Scania, Shan, Sindh, South Moluccas, Taiwan, Tatarstan, Tibet, Tuva, Udmurt, West Papua, Zanzibar. See their web site <http://www.unpo.org>.
125 'Self Determination and Conflict Transformation', UNPO, <http://www.unpo.org/news_detail.php?arg=01&par=87>.
126 ibid.
127 Writing on secessionist conflicts in the OSCE Europe, Pavel Baev observes that it is not only the sheer number of secessionist conflicts that is striking, but 'the capacity of the secessionist drive to achieve victory as well'. Pavel Baev, 'External Interventions in Secessionist Conflicts in Europe in the 1990s', *European Security* 8 (2) (1999), p. 27.
128 Tanisha M. Fazal, 'State Death in the International System', *International Organization* 58 (2) (spring 2004), pp. 311–44.
129 NIC, *Global Trends 2015*, pp. 46–7.
130 ibid., pp. 46–7.
131 Baev defines secessionist conflicts as 'violent confrontations between a state and an armed grouping seeking to take control over certain territory inside this state with the aim of establishing an independent state'. See Baev, 'External Interventions in Secessionist Conflicts in Europe in the 1990s', p. 23.
132 ibid., p. 31.
133 Rajan Menon and Graham Fuller, 'Russia's Ruinous Chechen War', *Foreign Affairs* 79 (2) (March–April 2000), pp. 32–44. This is not to say that the Russian federation will disintegrate, however. Instead, as Nunn and Stulberg observe, '[m]ore and more, Russia's restless regions are asserting themselves in domestic and international affairs, whether Moscow lets them or not'. They argue therefore that the West 'must learn to contend with a larger cast of actors who are both unfamiliar and unruly'. Sam Nunn and Adam N. Stulberg, 'The Many Faces of Modern Russia', *Foreign Affairs* 79 (2) (March–April 2000), pp. 54–62.
134 The Puerto Rican Fuerzas Armadas de Liberación Nacional (FALN) (Armed Forces of National Liberation) was believed to be behind nearly 130 bombings, mostly in New York and Chicago, in the 1970s and early 1980s. The Front de Libération du Québec (FLQ) perpetrated a series of bombings, bank hold-ups, and kidnappings, causing at least five deaths between 1963 and 1970. In October 1970, the FLQ kidnapped the British Trade Commissioner, the Quebec Vice-Premier and Minister of Labour, Pierre Laporte, whom they subsequently killed. See *Wikipedia – The Free Encyclopedia* at <http://en.wikipedia.org/wiki/FLQ>.

135 Eric Hobsbawm, 'Uncontrollable Capitalism: Golden Economic Era Ends Forever . . .', *CCPA Monitor* July–August 1995.
136 Rotberg, 'Failed States in a World of Terror', pp. 132–3. For a classical study of the concept of collapsed states, see I. William Zartman, (ed.) *Collapsed States: The Disintegration and Restoration of Legitimate Authority* (Boulder, Col.: Lynne Rienner, 1995).
137 James D. Fearon and David D. Laitin, 'Neotrusteeship and the Problem of Weak States', *International Security* 28 (4) (spring 2004), p. 41.
138 Rotberg, 'Failed States in a World of Terror', p. 130.
139 For a good account on the use of violence in the Algerian civil war, see Stathis Kalyvas, 'Wanton and Senseless? The Logic of Massacres in Algeria', *Rationality and Society* 11 (3) (August 1999), pp. 243–85. See also Martinez, *The Algerian Civil War 1990–1998*.
140 A Fatah-dominated militia Palestinian Armed Struggle Command (PASC), created back in 1969, is still the formal police, organising guards for schools and social institutions, regulating traffic and investigating petty crime. In the face of eighteen or so different armed groups active in the camp, all providing security for its own leaders and headquarters, the PASC's policing authority is still diluted, despite PLO efforts to make the PASC 'the only security reference point' in the camp. An agreement on co-ordination existed between the nationalist and Islamist forces in the camp, but had only limited effect in curbing inter-factional fighting. See 'Who Governs Whom in 'Ayn al-Hilwah [in Arabic]', *al-Wasat* (London) 514 (3 December 2001), pp. 30–1; and Lia, *A Police Force Without a State*, Chapter 2.
141 'Asbat al-Ansar (Band of Partisans)', Profile by the Terrorism Project, Center of Defense Information (CDI), 25 November 2002, <http://www.cdi.org/terrorism/asbat.cfm>. Accessed April 2004.
142 See 'From Afghan Arabs to Iraqi Arabs: The Wave of Violence is the Violence Coming from Iraq [in Arabic]', *Shuun Suudiyya* (Riyadh) 18 (July 2004).
143 There is a greater awareness of economic agendas in civil wars. See, for example, Berdal and Keen, 'Violence and Economic Agendas in Civil Wars'; and Mark Duffield, 'Globalisation and War Economies: Promoting Order to the Return of History?' *Fletcher Forum of World Affairs* 23 (2) (fall 1999), pp. 21–36.
144 Timoth W. Luke and Gerard Toal, 'The Fraying Modern Map: Failed States and Contraband Capitalism', *Geopolitics* 3 (3) (winter 1998), pp. 14–15.
145 Simon Montlake, 'Pirates ahead!' *Christian Science Monitor* 18 March 2004.
146 Jeremy McDermott, 'Colombian Rebels Beat Path to Peru', *BBC News* 6 February 2004.
147 Jeremy McDermott, 'Shining Path Back as FARC Exports Terror', *Telegraph* 13 September 2003.
148 For the triborder area, see 'The Lebanese Link in Suspected Latin American Militant Fundraisers', *Daily Star* 1 July 2003, <http://www.dailystar.com.lb/01_07_03/art21.asp>. Accessed July 2003.
149 McDermott, 'Shining Path Back as FARC Exports Terror'.
150 See case study in Martha K. Huggins (ed.), *Vigilantism and the State in Modern Latin-America: Essays on Extralegal Violence* (New York: Praeger, 1991). See also Tim Lester, 'Brazil: Favela Wars', *Foreign Correspondent* on *ABC News* 27 May 2003; Marcus Warren, 'Brazil's Next Leader Faces Gang Menace', *Telegraph* 26 October 2002; Gareth Chetwynd, 'Deadly Setback for a Model Favela', *Guardian* 17 April 2004; and 'Narkobander i full krig på Rios beste vestkant', *Aftenposten* (Oslo) 1 October 1004, p. 6.
151 Most countries in the Middle East and North Africa are not self-sufficient

in food production. Oil revenues often account for the majority of their foreign-currency earnings.

152 Bronson, 'Cycles of Conflict in the Middle East and North Africa'.

153 See, for example, Ian Lesser, 'Unresolved Issues: Assignments for the North and South', *Afers Internacionales* 38–9, <http://www.cidob.org/Ingles/Publicaciones/Afers/38–39.html>. Accessed June 2004.

154 Brynjar Lia, 'Security Challenges in Europe's Mediterranean Periphery: Perspectives and Policy Dilemmas', *European Security* 8(4) (winter 1999), pp. 46–7.

155 Åshild Kjøk et al., 'Restoring Peace or Provoking Terrorism? Exploring the Links Between Multilateral Military Interventions and International Terrorism', *FFI Research Report* No. 2003/01547 (Kjeller: FFI, 2004), <http://rapporter.ffi.no/rapporter/2003/01547.pdf>. Accessed August 2004.

156 Alex Morrison, Douglas A. Fraser, and James D. Kiras (eds) *Peacekeeping with Muscle: The Use of Force in International Conflict Resolution* (Clementsport: Canadian Peacekeeping Press, 1997); and Marrack Goulding, 'The Use of Force by the United Nations', *International Peacekeeping* 3 (1) (spring 1996), pp. 1–18.

157 Thomas G. Weiss, 'Contemporary Views on Humanitarian Intervention and China: "The Responsibility to Protect" ', Paper to the National Committee on United States–China Relations, January 2002, <http://www.ncuscr.org/article-sandspeeches/weiss%20final%203-11-pdf.pdf>, p. 3. Accessed August 2004.

158 ibid., p. 6. For a discussion of the evolution of humanitarian intervention concept, see John Tirman, 'The New Humanitarianism: How Military Intervention Became the Norm', *Boston Review* (December 2003/January 2004), <http://bostonreview.net/BR28.6/tirman.html> Accessed August 2004; and Kofi Annan, 'Walking the International Tightrope', *New York Times* 19 January 1999, p. A19.

159 According to Glennon, '[t]he new system acknowledges something else that the U.N. Charter overlooks: that the major threats to stability and well-being now come from internal violence more often than they do from cross-border fighting – and that to be effective, international law needs to stop the former as well as the latter'. See Michael J. Glennon, 'The New Interventionism. The Search for a Just International Law', *Foreign Affairs* 78 (3) (May–June 1999), pp. 2–7.

160 Fearon and Laitin, 'Neotrusteeship and the Problem of Weak States', p. 41.

161 Fernanda Faria, 'Crisis Management in sub-Saharan Africa: The Role of the European Union', *Occasional Paper* No. 51 (Paris: EU Institute for Security Studies, April 2004), <http://www.iss-eu.org/occasion/occ51.pdf> Accessed August 2004; and Jonathan Stevenson, 'Africa's Growing Strategic Resonance', *Survival* 45 (4) (winter 2003–4), pp. 153–72.

162 For a recent study of the co-operation between the UN and regional organisations in peace operations, see Michael Pugh and W. P. S. Sidhu (eds) *The United Nations and Regional Security: Europe and Beyond* (Boulder Col.: Lynne Rienner, 2003).

163 Thalif Deen, 'Annan Wants Regional Bodies to Share Peacekeeping', *IPS* 17 March 1999; and 'Major Military Exercise to Boost ECOWAS Forces', *IRIN News* at UN Office for the Coordination of Humanitarian Affairs, 28 May 2004, <http://www.irinnews.org/report.asp?reportid=41330&selectregion=west_africa & selectcountry=west_africa>. Accessed July 2004.

164 *The Report of the UN Panel on Peace Operations* (Brahimi Report), UN General Assembly document A/55/305-S/2000/809, 21 August 2000, <http://www.who.int/disasters/hbp/general/documents/brahimi_report.pdf>. Accessed May 2004.

165 Adianto P. Simamora, 'UN Welcomes ASEAN Peacekeeping Force, Promises Help', *Jakarta Post* 27 February 2004.

166 Faria, 'Crisis Management in sub-Saharan Africa', p. 55.
167 ibid.
168 ibid., pp. 34–8.
169 ibid.
170 At the G8 summit in 2004, the US stated that 'we acknowledge that expanding global capability for peace support operations is a critical element to a safer and more secure world'. See 'G-8 Action Plan: Expanding Global Capability For Peace Support Operations', Bush administration's statement at the G8 summit, <http://www.g8usa.gov/pdfs/0610ActionPlanPeaceOperations.pdf>, p. 4. Accessed September 2004.
171 Bradley Graham, 'Bush Plans Aid to Build Foreign Peace Forces', *Washington Post* 19 April 2004, p. A01.
172 'G-8 Action Plan: Expanding Global Capability For Peace Support Operations', p. 2.
173 ibid., p. 3.
174 Michael Yermolaev, 'Russia's International Peacekeeping and Conflict Management in the Post-Soviet Environment', in Mark Malan (ed.) *Boundaries of Peace Support Operations: The African Dimension* (ISS Monograph Series No. 44, February 2000, Pretoria: Institute for Security Studies).
175 'Indonesia Proposes ASEAN Peacekeeping Force: Official', *AFP* 21 February 2004; and Adianto P. Simamora, 'UN Welcomes ASEAN Peacekeeping Force, Promises Help', *Jakarta Post* 27 February 2004.
176 Adrian Kuah, 'The ASEAN Security Community: Struggling with the Details', *IDSS Commentary* No. 21/2004, 15 June 2004, <http://www.ntu.edu.sg/idss/Perspective/IDSS212004.pdf>. Accessed June 2004.
177 'Philippines Looking Forward to Talks on ASEAN Peacekeeping Force', *AFP* 26 February 2004.
178 International Peace Academy, *The UN, the EU, NATO and Other Regional Actors: Partners in Peace?* (New York: International Peace Academy, 11–12 October 2002), <http://www.iss-eu.org/activ/content/brochure.pdf>. Accessed July 2004, pp. 24, 32–3.
179 Virginia Page Fortna, 'Does Peacekeeping Keep Peace? International Intervention and the Duration of Peace After Civil War', *International Studies Quarterly* 48 (2) (June 2004), pp. 269–92.
180 Fen Osler Hampson, *Nurturing Peace: Why Settlements Succeed or Fail* (Washington, DC: United States Institute of Peace, 1996), p. 13.
181 Lake and Rothchild, 'Containing Fear', p. 72.
182 See, for example, William R. Ayres, 'A World Flying Apart?' p. 112.
183 ibid., p. 113.
184 See Stephen John Stedman, 'Spoiler Problems in Peace Processes', *International Security* 22 (2) (fall 1997), pp. 5–53; Pierre M. Atlas and Roy Licklider, 'Conflict Among Former Allies After Civil War Settlement: Sudan, Zimbawe, Chad and Lebanon', *Journal of Peace Research* 36 (1), pp. 35–54; Andrew Kydd and Barbara F. Walter, 'Sabotaging the Peace: The Politics of Extremist Violence', *International Organization* 56 (2) (April 2002), pp. 263–96; and R. Williams Ayres, 'Enemies of Peace: Spoilers in Ethnic Conflict Peace Processes', paper for International Studies Association Convention, Portland, Oregon, 26 February–2 March 2003.
185 Gleditsch, 'The Future of Armed Conflict', p. 28.
186 Graham, 'Bush Plans Aid to Build Foreign Peace Forces', p. A01.
187 Samuel Huntington, 'The Clash of Civilisations?' *Foreign Affairs* 72 (3) (summer 1993), pp. 22–8.

188 'Full text: "Bin Laden's message" ', *BBC News* 12 November 2002.

189 Thomas G. Weiss, 'Contemporary Views on Humanitarian Intervention and China: "The Responsibility to Protect" ', paper to the the National Committee on United States–China Relations, January 2002, <http://www.ncuscr.org/articlesandspeeches/weiss%20final%203-11-pdf.pdf>. Accessed May 2004, p. 6.

190 For example, the G4 group consisting of Brazil, Japan, Germany and India has been formed with a view to secure each of them a permanent seat in the UN Security Council.

191 'US Plans to Invade Sudan', press release, the Media Office of Hizb ut-Tahrir, Wilayah of Sudan 3 May 2004, <http://www.hizb-ut-tahrir.info/english/sudan/2004/may0304.htm>. Accessed May 2004.

192 The ICISS presented its report, *The Responsibility to Protect*, to UN Secretary-General Kofi A. Annan on December 18, 2001. See ICISS homepage at <http://www.dfait-maeci.gc.ca/iciss-ciise/report-en.asp>. Accessed May 2004.

193 Abrahm Chayes, 'The Use of Force in the Persian Gulf', in Lori Fisler Damrosch and David J. Scheffer (eds) *Law and Force in the New International Order* (Boulder, Col.: Westview, 1991), p. 7.

194 'All Well After 7-Hour Hijack Drama', *Aftenposten* (Oslo) 4 November 1994, <http://www.norwaves.com/norwaves/Volume2_1994/v2nw40.html>. Accessed June 2003.

195 See, for example, Jonathan Farley, 'The Mediterranean: Southern Threats to Northern Shores?' *The World Today* 50 (2) (February 1994), pp. 33–6.

196 Stephen John Stedman 'Spoiler Problems in Peace Processes'.

197 Tore Bjørgo, 'Terrortrusselen under Golfkrigen [The Terrorist Threat During the Gulf War]', *Internasjonal Politikk* 50 (3) (1992), pp. 245–57.

198 Kjøk et al., 'Restoring Peace or Provoking Terrorism?'

199 Robert O. Keohane, *International Institutions and State Power* (Boulder, Col.: Westview Press, 1989), p. 163.

200 Ernst B. Haas, *Beyond the Nation-State* (Stanford, Calif.: Stanford University Press, 1964).

201 The Arab Magreb Union (AMU) was forced to freeze its activities in 1995 due to a long-standing conflict between Morocco and Algeria over the West Saharan issue. See Brynjar Lia, 'The Quest for Regional Security in the Southern Mediterranean: The Role of European and Arab Security Organisations', *FFI Research Report* No. 99/02252 (Kjeller FFI, 1999), <http://www.mil.no/multimedia/archive/00005/Lia-R–99–02252_5567a.pdf>, pp. 92–5.

202 Alemayehu Geda and Haile Kibret, 'Regional Economic Integration in Africa: A Review of Problems and Prospects with a Case Study of COMESA', *Working Paper* No. 125, Department of Economics, School of Oriental and African Studies.

203 OECD, *Globalisation and Linkages to 2020*, p. 22.

204 For two different views, see Robert Looney, 'The Cancun Conundrum: What Future for the World Trade Organization?' *Strategic Insights* 2 (10) (October 2003), <http://www.ccc.nps.navy.mil/si/oct03/trade.pdf>. Accessed April 2004; and Mark Ritchie and Kristin Dawkins, 'A New Beginning for WTO After Cancun', *Foreign Policy In Focus (FPIF) Commentary*, 10 October 2003, <http://www.fpif.org/commentary/2003/0310fairtrade.html>. Accessed May 2004.

205 Gill Bates, 'China's New Security Multilateralism and its Implications for the Asia-Pacific Region', in SIPRI, *SIPRI Year Book 2004 – Press Release* (Stockholm: SIPRI, 9 June 2004), p. 13.

206 ibid.

207 See CTC web site at <http://www.un.org/Docs/sc/committees/1373/about.html>.

208 See, for example, 'SA wants SADEC to join forces to fight terrorism', *Channel Africa* 30 January 2004, via <http://www.africaonline.com/site/articles/1,3,55011.jsp>. Accessed May 2004.
209 Magnus Ranstorp with Jeffrey Cozzens, 'The European Terror Challenge', *BBC News* 24 March 2004.
210 CIA sources, cited by Rohan Gunaratna in his *Inside al-Qaida: Global Network of Terror* (New York: Columbia University Press, 2002), p. 6.
211 Lizardo, 'The Effect of Economic and Cultural Globalisation on Anti-U.S. Transnational Terrorism 1971–2000'.
212 See, for example, John Baylis and Steve Smith (eds) *The Globalisation of World Politics: An Introduction to International Relations* (Oxford: Oxford University Press, 1999).
213 Willetts, 'Transnational Actors and International Organizations in Global Politics', p. 289.
214 Mary B. Anderson, 'Humanitarian NGOs in Conflict Intervention', in Chester A. Crocker, Fen Osler Hampson, Pamela Aal (eds) *Managing Global Chaos: Sources and Responses to International Conflict* (Washington, DC: United States Institute of Peace Press, 1996), p. 344.
215 ibid., pp. 344, 346.
216 Lizardo. 'The Effect of Economic and Cultural Globalisation on Anti-U.S. Transnational Terrorism 1971–2000'.
217 UNDP, *Human Development Report 2002: Deepening Democracy in a Fragmented World* (New York and Oxford: Oxford University Press, 2002), p. 103. Another study from 1999 reports of *c.* 10,000 single-country NGOs that have significant international activities, and 4,700 INGOs. See Willetts, 'Transnational Actors and International Organizations in Global Politics', p. 290.
218 UNDP, *Human Development Report 2002*, p. 102.
219 Hoffmann, 'Clash of Globalisations', p. 109.
220 Samir Ragab, 'Mubarak Sets Record Straight for the Misinformed in Geneva', *The Egyptian Gazette* 10 December 2003.
221 Carrie A. Meyer, The Economics and Politics of NGOs in Latin America, (Westport, Conn.: Praeger, 1999), pp. 17–24.
222 Robert J. Milano, 'NGO–Government Relations: The Case of Mexico City', research paper, Milan Graduate School, New School University, May 2002, <http://www.newschool.edu/milano/urban/projects/mexicongo.pdf>. Accessed June 2004. See also 'Mexico's Fox Ends One-Party Rule', *BBC News* 1 December 2000.
223 Milano, 'NGO–Government Relations'.
224 Brynjar Lia and Annika S. Hansen, 'Civil Military Co-operation and Co-ordination in Peace Support Operations [in Norwegian]', *FFI Research Report* No. 97/05161 (Kjeller: FFI, 1997), p. 17.
225 Grey Frandsen, 'A Guide to NGOs: A Primer about Private, Voluntary, Non-Governmental Organizations that Operate in Humanitarian Emergencies Globally: Case Study: NGOs in Afghanistan', Center for Disaster and Humanitarian Assistance Medicine (CDHAM), August, 2003, <http://www.cdham.org/media/pdfs/Afghanistan.pdf>. Accessed May 2004, p. 11.
226 Feargal Cochrane, 'Beyond Political Elites: A Comparative Analysis of the Roles and Impacts of Community Based NGOs in Conflict Resolution Activity', *Civil Wars* 3 (2) (summer 2000), pp. 1–22.
227 Wrighte, 'The Real Mexican Terrorists', p. 215; and David F. Ronfeldt, John Arquilla, Graham E. Fuller, Melissa Fuller, *The Zapatista 'Social Netwar' in Mexico* (Washington, DC: Rand, 1998), Rand Report No. MR-994-A.

228 Lia, *A Police Force Without a State*, Chapter 4.
229 Don D'Cruz, 'Dangerous Liaisons', *IPA Review* 53/4 (September 2002), <http://www.ipa.org.au/units/ngowatch/articles/ddcindonesia1.html>. Accessed May 2004.
230 See, for example, Joseph Brewda, 'London's Terrorism Support Apparatus: Environmentalism, Indigenism, and NGOs', *Executive Intelligence Review* 10 November 1995, <http://www.larouchepub.com/other/1995/2245_terror_support.html>. Accessed May 2004. For NPA's co-operation with SPLA, see also Torill Nordeng, 'Norsk folkehjelp: Gir ikke opp Sør-Sudan', *Aftenposten* 21 October 1992; and 'Sudan-gerilja kritiserer norsk nødhjelp', *Aftenposten* 8 June 1998.
231 Moisés Naím, 'Al Qaeda, The NGO', *Foreign Policy* March/April 2002, pp. 99–100.
232 'Transnational Violence and Seams of Lawlessness in the Asia-Pacific: Linkages to Global Terrorism', executive summary, Conference at Asia-Pacific Center for Security Studies, 19–21 February 2002, <http://www.apcss.org/Conference/CR_ES/020219ES.htm>. Accessed May 2004.
233 Lizardo, 'The Effect of Economic and Cultural Globalisation on Anti-U.S. Transnational Terrorism 1971–2000', p. 22.
234 'The New Face of Insurgency', *RAND Research Brief* No. RB-7409-OTI (Washington, DC: Rand, 2001), <http://www.rand.org/publications/RB/RB7409/>. Accessed May 2004.

4 THE GLOBAL MARKET ECONOMY

1 Abu Ubayd al-Qirshi, 'The 9/11 Raid [in Arabic]', *Majallat al-Ansar* 1 (September 2002).
2 See, for example, 'The Bloodletting American Losses: Report on the US Economic, Social, Political, and Military Losses Following the Manhattan Raids Until the Recent Events in Iraq [in Arabic]', Markaz al-Buhuth wa'l-Dirasat al-Islamiyya web site, undated. Available on several Arabic-language jihadist web sites, including Muntadiyat Shabakat al-Hisbah, <http://www.alhesbah.org/v/showthread.php?t=531>. Accessed April 2005.
3 John J. Lumpkin, 'U.S. Worried Al-Qaida Targeting Oil', *Associated Press* 17 October 2002.
4 Jason Burke, 'Leader Tells How They Killed, then Ate, Slept and Prayed', *Observer* 6 June 2004.
5 'FBI: al-Qaida Operative Used Student Visa', *Associated Press* 14 October 2004.
6 See Robert MacCulloch, 'The Impact of Income on the Taste for Revolt', *American Journal of Political Science* 48 (4) (October 2004), pp. 830–48; Volker Bornschier and Christopher Chase-Dunn, *Transnational Corporations and Underdevelopment* (New York: Praeger, 1985); Edward Muller and Mitchell A. Seligson, 'Inequality and Insurgency', *American Political Science Review* 82 (2) (June 1987), pp. 425–51; Terry Boswell and William J. Dixon, 'Dependency and Rebellion: A Crossnational Analysis', *American Sociological Review* 55 (4) (1990), pp. 540–59; and Engene, *Patterns of Terrorism in Western Europe, 1950–95*, p. 194.
7 Raimo Väyrynen, 'Collective Violence in a Discontinuous World: Regional Realities and Global Fallacies', *International Social Science Journal* 38 (4) (1986), p. 515.
8 Gleditsch, 'The Future of Armed Conflict', p. 12. For a discussion of poverty and terrorism, see Lia, 'Causes of Terrorism'.
9 Pierre-Noël Giraud, 'Inequalities: Facts and Debates', English translation of

article published in *Sociétal* 35 (January 2002), <http://www.cerna.ensmp.fr/documents/png-societal-eng-02.pdf>. Accessed April 2004, p. 5.

10 UNDP, *Human Development Report 1999*, pp. 3, 11.

11 ibid.

12 François Bourguignon and Christian Morrison, 'Inequality Among World Citizens: 1820–1992', *American Economic Review*, 92 (4) (September 2002), pp. 727–44.

13 Albert J. Bergesen and Michelle Bata, 'Global and National Inequality: Are They Connected?' *Journal of World-Systems Research* 8 (1) (winter 2002), pp. 130–44.

14 Julio Carabaña, 'Unequal Inequalities: Growing and Fading, Good and Bad', paper for Symposium on 'Growing Inequalities', ESA Congress, Murcia, 23 September 2003, <http://www.ucm.es/info/socio6ed/profesorado/jcm/esa-murcia.pdf>. Accessed April 2004, p. 3. See also UNDP, *Human Development Report 2002*, p. 19.

15 Glenn Firebaugh, 'The Myth of Growing Global Income Inequality', paper for 'RC28 on Social Stratification and Mobility', Oxford, 10–12 April 2002, <http://www.nuff.ox.ac.uk/rc28/papers/firebaugh.pdf>. Accessed April 2004; and Glenn Firebaugh and Brian Goesling, 'Accounting for the Recent Decline in Global Income Inequality', *American Journal of Sociology* 110 (2) (September, 2004, pp. 283–312).

16 See, for example, Salvatore J. Babones, 'Population and Sample Selection Effects in Measuring International Income Inequality', *Journal of World-Systems Research* 8 (1) (winter 2002), pp. 8–28.

17 Carabaña, 'Unequal Inequalities'; and UNDP, *Human Development Report 2002*, p. 19

18 Peter Dicken, *Global Shift: Transforming the World Economy* (London: Paul Chapman, 1998), p. 68.

19 Manuel Castells, 'Information Technology, Globalisation and Social Development' *UNRISD Discussion Paper* (September 1999), p. 7.

20 Louisa Lim, 'China's Wealth Gap Widens to Gulf', *BBC News* 26 February 2004.

21 ibid.; Louisa Lim, 'China's Uighurs Lose out to Development', *BBC News* 19 December 2003; and Canadian Department of National Defence, *Strategic Assessment 2003*, pp. 65–6.

22 Hoffmann, 'Clash of Globalisations', p. 108.

23 Giraud, 'Inequalities: Facts and Debates', p. 10.

24 Nita Rudra, 'Globalisation and the Decline of the Welfare State in Less-Developed Countries', *International Organisation* 56 (2) (spring 2002), pp. 411–45.

25 Bruce Scott, 'The Great Divide in the Global Village', *Foreign Affairs* 80 (1) (January–February 2001), pp. 160–77.

26 Cingranelli and Richards, 'Respect for Human Rights After the End of the Cold War', pp. 511–34. Dicken describes this trend as 'interpenetration' between national economies. Dicken, *Global Shift*, p. 68.

27 Paul Hirst and Graham Thompson, *Globalisation in Question* (Cambridge: Polity Press, 1996), p. 51.

28 UNCTAD, *The Least Developed Countries Report 2004*, (New York: United Nations, 2004), <http://www.unctad.org/>. Accessed May 2004.

29 Geoffrey Jones, *The Evolution of International Business: An Introduction* (London: Routledge, 1996), p. 310.

30 Canadian Policy Research Initiative, *Canada 2005: Global Challenges and Opportunities* Vol. I (25 February 1997), <http://policyresearch.schoolnet.ca/keydocs/global/>. Accessed June 2000.

31 UNCTAD, *The Least Developed Countries Report 2004*, 'Highlights'.

32 Nancy Birdsall, 'Why Inequality Matters: The Developing and Transitional Economies', conference paper, 'The World Economy in the Twenty-First Century: Challenges and Opportunities', Mt. Holyoke College, South Hadley, Massachusetts, February 18–19, 2000, <http://www.mtholyoke.edu/acad/econ/bird5.pdf>. Accessed April 2004; and UNDP, *Human Development Report 1999*, pp. 3, 6.

33 Castells, *End of Millennium*, p. 164.

34 Birdsall, 'Why Inequality Matters'. See also Michelle Bata, and Albert J. Bergesen, 'Global Inequalities: An Introduction', *Journal of World-System Research* 7(1) (winter 2002), pp. 2–6.

35 Lindsay Lowell and Allan Findlay, 'Migration of Highly Skilled Persons from Developing Countries: Impact and Policy Responses: Synthesis Report', Geneva, December 2001, International Migration Papers No. 44, <http://www.ilo.org/public/english/protection/migrant/download/imp/imp44.pdf>. Accessed April 2004.

36 Hirst and Thompson, *Globalisation in Question*, pp. 117–18.

37 UNDP, *Human Development Report 1999*, p. 3.

38 Bernadette D. Proctor and Joseph Dalaker, 'Poverty in the United States: 2002', US Department of Commerce: US Census Bureau, September 2003, <http://www.census.gov/prod/2003pubs/p60–222.pdf>. Accessed May 2004.

39 Pablo Antolín, Thai-Thanh Dang and Howard Oxley, 'Poverty Dynamics in Four OECD Countries', OECD, Economics Department Working Papers No. 212, 30 April 1999, <http://www.oecd.org/dataoecd/57/21/1868105.pdf>, Accessed May 2004, p. 25.

40 See, for example, Taryn Ann Galloway and Rolf Aaberge, 'Assimilation Effects on Poverty Among Immigrants in Norway', Oslo: University of Oslo, Department of Economics, Memorandum No. 07/2003, <http://www.oekonomi.uio.no/memo/memopdf/memo0703.pdf>. Accessed May 2004, p. 24.

41 Predrag Bejakoviæ, 'Poverty, Inequality and Social Exclusion in The European Union and Croatia', in Rüdiger Pintar (ed.) *Croatian Accession to The European Union; Institutional Challenges*, Vol. II, (Zagreb: Institute of Public Finance and Friedrich Ebert Stiftung, December 2003), <http://ijf.hr/eng/EU2/Bejakovic.pdf>, Chapter 4. Accessed April 2004.

42 Hamish McRae, *The World in 2020. Power, Culture and Prosperity: A Vision of the Future* (London: HarperCollins, 1994), pp. 106–7.

43 Rudra, 'Globalisation and the Decline of the Welfare State in Less-Developed Countries', pp. 411–12.

44 'Land of the Free Agent', *The Economist* 18 May 2001.

45 Daniel H. Pink, *Free Agent Nation: How America's New Independent Workers Are Transforming the Way We Live* (New York: Warner Books, 2001)

46 McRae, *The World in 2020*, pp. 104–5.

47 For the situation in the UK, see Steve Schifferes, 'The Trade Unions' Long Decline', *BBC News* 8 March 2004.

48 Mazur argues for a recovery of labour unions and an adjustment to the progressing internationalisation. He suggests that the recent protests in Seattle were a reflection of the loss of voice. Jay Mazur, 'Labor's New Internationalism', *Foreign Affairs* 79 (1) (January–February 2000), pp. 80–1.

49 For the concept of horizontal inequality, see Black, 'The Geometry of Terrorism'.

50 Alan B. Krueger and Jitka Maleckova, 'Education, Poverty, and Terrorism: Is There a Causal Connection?' paper for the World Bank's Annual Bank Conference on Development Economics, April 2002, <http://http://econ.worldbank.org/files/14988_Alan_Krueger.pdf>. Accessed April 2004.

51 Gleditsch, 'The Future of Armed Conflict'.
52 Engene, *Patterns of Terrorism in Western Europe, 1950–95.*
53 Kurt Finsterbusch, 'The Social Impacts of Scarcity and Likely Political Responses to Scarcity in Institutionally Developed Societies', in Michael N. Dobkowski and Isidor Wallimann (eds) *The Coming Age of Scarcity: Preventing Mass Death and Genocide in The Twenty-First Century* (Syracuse, NY: Syracuse University Press, 1998), p. 162.
54 Engene, *Patterns of Terrorism in Western Europe, 1950–95.*
55 Ronaldo Munck, *Globalisation and Labour: The New 'Great Transformation'* (London and New York: Zed Books, 2002), p. 163.
56 ibid.
57 RAND-MIPT database on <http://www.mipt.org/>.
58 'The New Red Brigades/Communist Combatant Party', Center for Defense Information web site, 30 January 2004, <http://www.cdi.org/friendlyversion/printversion.cfm?documentid=2019>. Accessed May 2004. See also Gaspare Barbiellini Amidei, 'Red Brigades: Few but Dangerous', *Corriere della Sera* 19 July 2004.
59 For al-Qaida in Europe, see Petter Nesser, 'Jihad in Europe: A Survey of the Motivations for Sunni Islamist Terrorism in Post-Millennium Europe', *FFI Research Report* No. 2004/01146 (Kjeller: FFI, 2004), <http://http:// rapporter.ffi.no/rapporter/2004/01146.pdf>. Accessed June 2004.
60 Interviews with British Scotland Yard officials; and 'Insight: British Raids', *CNN.com* 30 March 2004.
61 I debunk the common thesis that poverty is irrelevant in explaining terrorism in Lia, 'Causes of Terrorism', Chapter 3. See also Li and Schaub, 'Economic globalisation and transnational terrorism'; and Christina Paxson, 'Comment on Alan Krueger and Jitka Maleckova, "Education, Poverty, and Terrorism: Is There a Causal Connection?" ', Princeton University, 8 May 2002, <http://www.w-ws.princeton.edu/~rpds/downloads/paxson_krueger_comment.pdf>. Accessed May 2004.
62 Manuel Castells, *The Power of Identity: The Information Age: Economy, Society and Culture* (Oxford: Blackwell, 1997), p. 303.
63 McRae, *The World in 2020*, pp. 142, 144.
64 'Report of the Working Group on Transnational Corporations', in *For the Record 2002* (Ottawa: Human Rights Internet Online, March 2003), <http://www.hri.ca/fortherecord2003/vol1/globalisationpp.htm#workinggroup>. Accessed May 2004.
65 Mark Herkenrath and Volker Bornschier, 'Transnational Corporations in World Development: Still the Same Harmful Effects in an Increasingly Globalised World Economy?' *Journal of World-System Research* 9 (1) (winter 2003), p. 105.
66 Kriengsak Chareonwongsak, *The Future Society of Asia* (Munich and Thailand: Institute of Future Studies for Development, August 2001), <http://www.cap.uni-muenchen.de/fgz/downloads/asia.pdf>, p.17. Accessed July 2004.
67 Willetts, 'Transnational Actors and International organizations in Global Politics', p. 296.
68 Chareonwongsak, *The Future Society of Asia*, p. 17.
69 Paul De Grauwe and Filip Camerman, 'Are Multinationals Really Bigger than Nations?' *World Economics Magazine* 2 (4) (April–June 2003), pp. 23–37; and Martin Wolf, 'Countries Still Rule the World', *Financial Times* 6 February 2002.
70 In recent studies, the economic size of TNCs has been calculated based on value-added data, not sales figures, as was done previously, making the comparison with the GDP of states more sound. The UNCTAD study cited below estimated

value added for TNCs as 'the sum of salaries and benefits, depreciation and amortization, and pre-tax income'. See 'Are Transnationals Bigger than Countries?' *UNCTAD* Press Release 12 August 2002.

71 ibid.

72 ibid.

73 Paul De Grauwe and Filip Camerman, 'Are Multinationals Really Bigger than Nations?' *World Economics Magazine* 2 (4) (April–June 2003), pp. 23–37.

74 See Peter H. Merkl (ed.) *Political Violence and Terror: Motifs and Motivations* (Berkeley, Calif.: University of California Press, 1986), pp. 342–3.

75 See statistics in US Department of State's annual reports *Patterns of Global Terrorism*. According to former FBI bomb expert Robert Quigley, businesses had also been the target of 52 per cent of the 3,163 bombing attacks that took place in 1994, while 34 per cent were aimed at civilian government facilities, and 12 per cent at police and military facilities. See Jack Kelly, 'Safety at a Price: Security is a Booming, Sophisticated, Global Business', *Post-Gazette* 13 February 2000, <http://www.post-gazette.com/headlines/20000213security1.asp>.

76 Dan Murphy, 'US Multinational Companies Wary of Backlash', *Christian Science Monitor* 21 April 2003.

77 Mark Herkenrath and Volker Bornschier, 'Transnational Corporations in World Development: Still the Same Harmful Effects in an Increasingly Globalised World Economy?' *Journal of World-System Research* 9 (1) (winter 2003), p. 105.

78 Willetts, 'Transnational Actors and International Organizations in Global Politics'; and Hirst and Thompson, *Globalisation in Question*, p. 98.

79 See for example the US-based NGO *CorpWatch; Holding Corporations Responsible* at <http://corpwatch.radicaldesigns.org/index.php>. Accessed May 2004.

80 Andreas Wegner and Daniel Möckli, *Conflict Prevention: The Untapped Potential of the Business Sector* (Boulder, Col.: Lynne Rienner, 2002); and Mark Tran, 'UK: New Taskforce to Tackle "Attacks" on Corporate Business', *Guardian* 6 July 2004.

81 'Report of the Working Group on Transnational Corporations', in *For the Record 2002* (Ottawa: Human Rights Internet Online, March, 2003), <http://www.hri.ca/fortherecord2003/vol1/globalisationspp.htm#WorkingGroup>. Accessed May 2004. See also 'The UN and Business', Global Policy web site, <http://www.globalpolicy.org/reform/indxbiz.htm>. Accessed May 2004.

82 Juliette Bennett, 'Multinational Corporations, Social Responsibility and Conflict', *Journal of International Affairs* 55 (2) (spring 2002), pp. 393–410.

83 Stephen R. Miller, 'Corporations Fight to Avoid Accountability', CorpWatch web site, 7 July 2004, <http://corpwatch.radicaldesigns.org/article.php?id=11427>. Accessed July 2004.

84 Pratap Chatterjee, 'New Halliburton Whistleblowers Say Millions Wasted in Iraq', *CorpWatch* 16 June 2004, <http://www.corpwatch.org/article.php?id=11373>. Accessed July 2004.

85 Praful Bidwai, 'Enron Teaches Tough Lessons for Developing World', *Inter Press Service* 7 February 2002.

86 For example, the UN Center on Transnational Corporations advised Third World governments on how to negotiate with multinationals, and it also oversaw negotiations of a Code of Conduct for TNCs.

87 UN Committee on Trade and Development, 'Multinational Corporations (MNCs) in Least Developed Countries (LDCs)', Global Policy web site, <http://www.globalpolicy.org/reform/2002/modelun.pdf>. Accessed July 2004.

88 Dicken, *Global Shift*, p. 276.

89 Jones, *The Evolution of International Business*, p. 304. One benefit is that TNCs function as vehicles for the transfer of information and technology, which

promotes trade flows and disseminates organisational and managerial skills, ibid., p. 314. See also Rajneesh Narula and John H. Dunning, 'Developing Countries Versus Multinational Enterprises in a Globalising World: The Dangers of Falling Behind', *Forum for Development Studies* 2 (1999), pp. 262, 268, 275.

90 Paul Hirst and Graham Thompson, *Globalisation in Question* (Cambridge: Polity Press, 1996), p. 98; and Willetts, 'Transnational Actors and International Organizations in Global Politics'. See also *Human Development Report 1999*, p. 8–10, 12.

91 Martin Wolf, 'Will the Nation-State Survive Globalisation?' *Foreign Affairs* 80 (1) (January–February 2001), pp. 178–90.

92 Paul N. Doremus, William W. Keller, Louis W. Pauly and Simon Reich, *The Myth of the Global Corporation* (Princeton, NJ: Princeton University Press, 1998).

93 Jones, *The Evolution of International Business*, p. 309.

94 Dicken argues that although boundaries become more permeable, and TNCs can pressure governments for preferential treatment, national governments nevertheless continue to exercise control over their economy by providing specific cultural, political, social and economic conditions for the economic activity within their borders and by setting concrete rules for economic activity in three major policy areas: trade, Foreign Direct Investment (FDI) and industry. See Dicken, *Global Shift*, pp. 112–13.

95 Kelly, 'Safety at a Price'.

96 For a press account from the UK, see 'The Police Have Failed us – So We've Hired a 6ft 6in Security Guard', *Daily Telegraph* 5 April 2004. For advocates of a further privatisation of policing in the USA, see 'Privatising the Long Arm of the Law', *Michigan Privatisation Report* 1998 No.4, Mackinac Center for Public Policy; and 'Prison Privatisation: A Growing National Trend', *Michigan Privatisation Report* 2004 No.1, Mackinac Center for Public Policy, <http://www.mackinac.org>. Accessed May 2004.

97 Gary T. Marx, 'Police and Democracy', in M. Amir and S. Einstein (eds) *Policing, Security and Democracy: Theory and Practice*, Vol. II (Huntsville, Ala.: Office of International Criminal Justice, 2001), <http://web.mit.edu/gtmarx/www/dempol.html>. Accessed May 2004.

98 The Polish Rutkowski Patrol was recently involved in an assault on three alleged Polish racketeers in Sweden. See 'Polish Private Eye Nabs Blackmailers in Sweden', *Reuters* 15 July 2004.

99 David Sklansky, 'The Private Police', *UCLA Law Review* 46 (4) (April 1999), pp. 1165–287.

100 Sarah Blandy and Diane Lister, 'Gated Communities: A Systematic Review of the Research Evidence', ESRC Centre for Neighbourhood Research, April 2003, CNR Paper No.12, <http://www.bristol.ac.uk/sps/cnrpapersword/cnr12sum.doc>. Accessed July 2004.

101 Haya El Nasser, 'Gated Communities More Popular, and Not Just for the Rich', *USA Today* 15 December 2002.

102 Manuel B. Aalbers, 'The Double Function of the Gate: Social Inclusion and Exclusion in Gated Communities and Security Zones', paper presented at the conference 'Gated Communities: Building Social Division or Safer Communities?' 18–19 September 2003, University of Glasgow, <http://www.bristol.ac.uk/sps/cnrpapersword/gated/aalbers.doc>. Accessed July 2004.

103 Louise Shelley, 'Transnational Organised Crime: The New Authoritarianism', in H. Richard Friman and Peter Andreas (eds) *The Illicit Global Economy and State Power* (Lanham, Md.: Rowman & Littlefield, 1999), pp. 44–5.

104 Mark Galeotti, *The Kremlin's Agenda* (Coulsdon: JANE's Information Group, 1995), pp. 108–9.

105 ibid.; and Louise Shelley, 'Transnational Organised Crime: The New Authoritarianism', p. 45, citing interview with Victor Illiukhin, Head of the Russian State Duma Committee on Security.
106 Lubov Savchenko, 'Moscow Security Services', US and Foreign Commercial Service, Business Information Service for the Newly Independent States, December 1999, <http://www.bisnis.doc.gov/bisnis>. Accessed June 2004.
107 Catherine Auer, 'In it For the Money', *Bulletin of the Atomic Scientists* 60 (2) (March–April 2004), pp. 42–3.
108 Kelly, 'Safety at a Price'.
109 Kevin O'Brien, 'Military-Advisory Groups and African Security: Privatised Peacekeeping?' *International Peacekeeping* 5 (3) (Autumn 1998), pp. 91, 97.
110 Peter W. Singer, 'Corporate Warriors: The Rise of the Privatised Military Industry and its Ramifications for International Security', *International Security* 26 (3) (winter 2001/2002), pp. 186–220.
111 Christian Jennings, 'Private US firm training both sides in Balkans', *Scotsman* 3 March 2001.
112 Brynjar Lia, *Building Arafat's Police: The Politics of International Police Assistance in the Palestinian Territories after the Oslo Agreement* (Reading: Ithaca, 2005), Chapter 9.
113 Singer, 'Corporate Warriors', p. 188.
114 'Gurkha Security Guards, Ltd.', Center for Public Integrity web site, searchable database on PMCs, <http://www.bop2004.org/bow/search. aspx?section= database&selection=company&id=11>. Accessed July 2004. See also Auer, 'In It For the Money', and O'Brien, 'Military-Advisory Groups and African Security'.
115 'Agreement for the Provision of Military Assistance dated this 31 Day of January 1997 between the Independent State of Papua New Guinea and Sandline International', The Worldwide Web Virtual Library: Papua New Guinea, <http:// coombs.anu.edu.au/specialproj/png/topics/hiredbackos2.htm>. Accessed July 2004.
116 'Conflict, Inc.: Selling the Art of War', *Center for Defense Information/America Defense Monitor* 7 December 1997, <http://www.cdi.org/adm/1113/transcript. html>. Accessed July 2004.
117 Ian Traynor, 'The Privatisation of War; $30 Billion Goes to Private Military; Fears Over "Hired Guns" Policy', *Guardian* 10 December 2003.
118 'Sandline Mercenaries Operating In Iraq', *Pacific Media Watch* 17 June 2004; David Leigh, 'Who Commands the Private Soldiers?' *Guardian* 17 May 2004; Jamie Wilson, 'Private Security Firms Call for more Firepower in Combat Zone', *Guardian* 17 April 2004; and Robert Fisk and Patrick Cockburn, 'Deaths of Scores of Mercenaries Hidden from View', *Star* 13 April 2004.
119 Jonathan Franklin, 'US Contractor Recruits Guards for Iraq in Chile', *Guardian* 5 March 2004.
120 Estimates from Singer, 'Corporate Warriors', p. 199; and Barry Yeoman, 'Soldiers of Good Fortune', *Independent Weekly* 3 July 2003, <http://www.indyweek.com/ durham/2003-07-23/cover.html>. Accessed July 2004.
121 Auer, 'In It For the Money'.
122 Singer, 'Corporate Warriors', p. 187.
123 David Leigh, 'Who Commands the Private Soldiers?'
124 Ian Traynor, 'The Privatisation of War: $30 Billion Goes to Private Military; Fears Over "Hired Guns" Policy'.
125 According to one source, the US military already relies on private contractors to maintain some 28 per cent of all weapons systems. See Yeoman, 'Soldiers of Good Fortune'.

126 Robert Fisk and Patrick Cockburn, 'Deaths of Scores of Mercenaries Hidden from View'.
127 Yeoman, 'Soldiers of Good Fortune'.
128 ibid.
129 O'Brien, 'Military-Advisory Groups and African Security: Privatised Peace-keeping?' p. 80.
130 Singer, 'Corporate Warriors', p. 187.
131 ibid., p. 186.
132 Jennings, 'Private US Firm Training Both Sides in Balkans'.
133 Singer, 'Corporate Warriors', p. 213.
134 In Sierra Leone he was arrested and served a prison term, but Israeli authorities intervened behind the scenes to get Klein released, as they also did on previous occasions, probably due to close links with prominent Israeli politicians and his distinguished military career before he turned mercenary. In 1991, he was only convicted of illegal export of military arms and information to a Colombian group, and received a fine of 13,400 US dollars. For his reported links with the deceased Revaham Ze'evi, see Scott Thompson, 'Gen. Ze'evi Lived and Died by the Sword', *Executive Intelligence Review*, 26 October 2001, <http://www.larouchepub.com/other/2001/2841gen_zeevi.html>. Accessed July 2004. See also 'Who is Israel's Yair Klein and What was he Doing in Colombia and Sierra Leone?' DemocracyNow web site 1 June 2000, <http://www. democracynow.org/article.pl?sid=03/04/07/0232255>. Accessed July 2004; 'Private Israeli Firms Sell Security', *Associated Press* 8 July 1998; and 'Press Briefing by Enrique Ballesteros, Special Raporteur on Question of Mercenaries', *UN Press Release* 25 March 1999, <http://www.unhchr.ch/huricane/huricane.nsf/0/97d57726fd8999c08025673f0062f6aa?opendocument>. Accessed July 2004.
135 Douglas Farah, 'Al Qaeda Cash Tied to Diamond Trade: Sale of Gems From Sierra Leone Rebels Raised Millions, Sources Say', *Washington Post* 2 November 2001, p. A01.
136 Rindle had maintained contacts with UNITA since he served as a South African army liaison officer to the UNITA during the Apartheid era.
137 ' "Mercenaries" Back in Prison Court', *BBC News* 22 July 2004.
138 'Policeman Killed in Robbery', *Aftenposten* (Oslo) 5 April 2004.
139 David Montero, 'Guns "R" U.S.', *The Nation* 14 November 2002, <http://www.thenation.com/doc.mhtml?i=20021202&s=montero>. Accessed July 2004.
140 Chris Kahn, 'Virginia Trailer Park a Terrorist Haven?' *Associated Press* 26 December 2001.
141 Between 1980 and 1990, al-Fuqra members have been either convicted or suspected in twelve assassinations and seventeen fire-bombings, according to one source. See 'Sniper Link to al-Fuqra Probed: Investigators Suspect Connection with Radical Islamist organisation', *WorldNetDaily* 11 November 2002, <http://www.worldnetdaily.com/news/article.asp?article_id=29608>. Accessed July 2004; John J. Miller, 'A Junior al Qaeda ... Right here at home: Meet al Fuqra', *National Review Online* 31 January 2001, <http://www.nationalreview.com/flash-back/flashback-miller013102.shtml>. Accessed July 2004; 'Jamaat ul-Fuqra', South Asia Terrorism Portal, <http://www.satp.org/satporgtp/countries/pakistan/terroristoutfits/jamaat-ul-fuqra.htm>. Accessed July 2004; and 'Al-Fuqra Holy Warriors of Terrorism', *Anti-Defamation League Report* 1993, <http://www.adl.org/extremism/moa/al-fuqra.pdf>. Accessed July 2004.
142 ' "Holy Wars" web site is shut down', *The Times* (London) 4 October 2001. A part of the text of the now-defunct Sakina Security Services web site was available in July 2004 at œhttp://seclists.org/lists/politech/2001/Oct/0024.html>. A

spokesman interviewed by the British newspaper *The Independent* denied any terrorist links: 'We're running a security company and nowhere on the web site does it say we train terrorist fighters for jihad'. The course title was 'just a name, my friend, the same as Jewish kids going to Israel'. Cited in 'MP investigates fundamentalist', *The Independent* 26 September 2001.

143 Zain-ul Ibidin said his web site was part of a 'bona-fide commercial venture in the training of people who wanted to be involved in the completely lawful security business, such as bodyguards.' See ' "Holy Wars" ' web site is shut down', *The Times* (London) 4 October 2001; and 'Sakina Security Services, Ltd'., Center for Public Integrity web site, searchable database on PMCs, <http://www.bop2004.org/bow/search.aspx?act=advanced>. Accessed July 2004.

144 'Communiqué from The Islamic Army of Iraq General Command', albasrah.net web site, translated by Jihad Unspun web site 15 July 2004, <http://www.jihadunspun.net/index-side_internal.php?article=10466&list=/home.php&>. Accessed 20 July 2004.

145 Susan Strange, *The Retreat of the State: The Diffusion of Power in the World Economy* (Cambridge: Cambridge University Press, 1996), p. 121.

146 Mayra Buvinić and Andrew R Morrison, 'Living in a More Violent World', *Foreign Policy* 118 (spring 2000), p. 66; and Kal Raustaliala, 'Law, Liberalization and International Narcotics Trafficking', *New York University Journal of International Law and Politics* 32 (1) (1999), pp. 89–145, citing UNODC reports from 1997.

147 Robert K. Schaeffer, *Understanding Globalisation: The Social Consequences of Political, Economic and Environmental Change* (Lanham, Md.: Rowman & Littlefield, 1997), pp. 329–31.

148 Thomas M. Sanderson, 'Transnational Terror and Organised Crime: Blurring the Lines', *SAIS Review* 24 (1) (winter/spring 2004), <http://www.saisreview.org/PDF/24.1sanderson.pdf>, p. 52.

149 According to the UN's Global Report on Crime and Justice, cited in Buvinić and Morrison, 'Living in a More Violent World', p. 66.

150 Schaeffer, *Understanding Globalisation*, pp. 329–34.

151 US Drug Enforcement Administration, 'Drug Intelligence Brief: Burma Country Brief', May 2002, <http://www.usdoj.gov/dea/pubs/intel/02021/02021.html>. Accessed October 2004; and 'Transnational Violence and Seams of Lawlessness in the Asia-Pacific: Linkages to Global Terrorism', Executive Summary, Conference at Asia-Pacific Center for Security Studies, 19–21 February 2002, <http://www.apcss.org/Conference/CR_ES/020219ES.htm>. Accessed July 2004.

152 According to the director of the UN Office on Drugs and Crime (UNODC), heroin sells in Kabul at 1 US dollar per gram, and retails in Europe at 100 US dollars. See 'Entire Societies Need to Get Involved in Countering Drug Abuse, UN Commission on Narcotic Drugs Told, as it Begins 47th session', *UN Press Release* 13 March 2004, <http://www.un.org/News/Press/docs/2004/socnar894.doc.htm>. Accessed July 2004.

153 ibid., citing a report by UNODC on Global Survey on Ecstasy and Amphetamine-Type Stimulants (ATS).

154 Kal Raustaliala, 'Law, Liberalization and International Narcotics Trafficking', *New York University Journal of International Law and Politics* 32 (1) (1999), p. 102.

155 ibid., p. 92. For a similar argument, see also Peter Andreas, 'When Policies Collide: Market Reform, Market Prohibition, and the Narcotization of the Mexican Economy', in H. Richard Friman and Peter Andreas (eds) *The Illicit Global Economy and State Power* (Lanham, Md. Rowman & Littlefield, 1999), pp. 125–41.

156 For definitions, see 'Children and Human-Trafficking', Interpol web site, <http://www.interpol.int/public/thb/default.asp>. Accessed July 2004; or United Nations Office on Drugs and Crime (UNODC), 'Fact Sheet on Human-Trafficking', <http://www.unodc.org/unodc/en/trafficking_victim_consents.html#facts>. Accessed July 2004.

157 Yves Engler, 'Bush's Mexican Gambit: The Fallout from NAFTA', *Counter-Punch* 8 January 2004, <http://www.counterpunch.org/engler01082004.html>. Accessed July 2004.

158 Louise Shelley, 'Identifying, Counting and Categorising Transnational Criminal Organisations', *Transnational Organised Crime* (5) 1 (spring 1999), pp. 1–18.

159 Thomas Homan, 'Statement for Bureau of Immigration and Customs Enforcement, The Department of Homeland Security Regarding a Hearing on "Alien Smuggling" before House Subcommittee on Immigration, Border Security, and Claims Committee on the Judiciary', 24 June 2003, <http://usinfo.state.gov/regional/ea/chinaaliens/homan.htm>. Accessed July 2004.

160 US Department of State, 'Trafficking in Persons Report', 14 June 2004, <http://www.state.gov/g/tip/rls/tiprpt/2004/>. Accessed July 2004.

161 ibid., introduction.

162 'UN-Appointed Expert on Human-Trafficking to Protect Rights of Victims', *EuropaWorld* 23 April 2004, <http://www.europaworld.org/week174/unappointed23404.htm>. Accessed July 2004; and 'People Smuggling', Interpol web site, <http://www.interpol.int/public/thb/peoplesmuggling/default.asp>. Accessed July 2004.

163 'Roundtable Discussion on the Trafficking of Women', Guest lecture by Dr Aurora de Dios, 19 April 2003, the Asia Foundation, <http://asiafoundation.or.kr/board/download.html?bbs_id=program4&type=1&doc_num=2>. Accessed July 2004.

164 Nicholas Marsh and Aaron Karp, 'Global Small Arms Transfers: Insights and Mysteries', *Small Arms Survey 2003: Development Denied*, summary, p. 3, <http://www.smallarmssurvey.org/yearbook%202003/yb2003_en_presskit_ch3.pdf>. Accessed October 2004. See also Buvinić and Morrison, 'Living in a More Violent World', pp. 66–7; and Peter Lewis Young, 'Clandestine Trade in Arms: A Matter of Ways and Means', *Jane's Intelligence Review* (May 2000), pp. 48–51.

165 For example, in Ecuador some 872 persons were arrested for possessing and trafficking in weapons in 2002 and while only seven were arrested for possessing and trafficking in explosives. 'Evaluation of Progress in Drug Control 2001–2002: Ecuador', Inter-American Drug Abuse Control Commission, <http://www.cicad.oas.org/mem/eng/reports/progress_2001–2002/ecuador%20-%20eng.pdf>. Accessed July 2004.

166 'Vietnamese Court Hands Down Stiff Jail Terms in Explosives Case', *Agence France Presse* 23 February 2001; and '47 Dead in Explosion in Northern China', *Agence France-Presse* 17 July 2001.

167 'Bomber has Confessed, China Says', *CNN.com* 27 March 2001; and 'China Arrests Suspected Bomb Supplier', *CNN.com* 27 March 2001.

168 Estonia, for example, reported c.280 incidents according to the study, which was similar to per capita level in Peru and Lebanon.

169 United Nations, 'Results of the Study on the Illicit Manufacturing of and Trafficking in Explosives by Criminals and their Use for Criminal Purposes', Report of the Secretary-General, United Nations Economic and Social Council, 23 January 2002, <http://www.unodc.org/pdf/crime/commissions/11comm/9add1e.pdf>. Accessed July 2004, p. 12.

170 ibid., p. 13.

171 'Press review by Daniela Lazarova', *Radio Praha* 15 March 2004, <http://www.radio.cz/en/article/51700>. Accessed July 2004.

172 Although Norwegian black-market explosives are mostly used on private building lots, the reported theft of nearly 600 kilograms of explosives and 5,000 detonators from commercial stockpiles shortly after the Madrid bombings caused much concern. For recent reports of explosive thefts in Norway, see 'Vil ha sprengstoff-amnesti', *Aftenposten* 20 April 2004; 'Bedre sikring: For lett å stjele sprengstoff', *Nettavisen* 5 April 2004; 'Tilstod tyveri av 50 kilo dynamitt', *Nettavisen* 26 March 2003; 'Dynamitt stjålet i Bergen', *Nettavisen* 10 March 2003; 'Frykter dynamitt-ulykke i Ålesund', *Nettavisen* 26 July 2002; 'Stjal 100 kilo dynamitt: eksplosivt tyveri i Østfold', *Nettavisen* 22 March 2000; '300 kilo dynamitt på avveie', *Nettavisen* 3 January 2000; '660 kilo dynamitt stjålet på Gol', *Nettavisen* 2 April 2004; 'Stjal 660 kg dynamitt', *Nettavisen* 9 June 2004; and 'Ikke farlig: stjålet dynamitt går til private', *Nettavisen* 7 April 2004.

173 'Greece Seizes Ship Loaded with Explosives', *Voice of America News* 23 June 2003.

174 United Nations Office on Drugs and Crime (UNODC), 'Fact Sheet on Human-Trafficking', <http://www.unodc.org/unodc/en/trafficking_victim_consents.html#facts>. Accessed July 2004.

175 James O. Finckenauer and Jennifer Schrock, 'Human-Trafficking: A Growing Criminal Market in the U.S.', Washington DC: US Department of Justice, National Institute of Justice, 2000, <http://www.ojp.usdoj.gov/nij/international/ht.html>. Accessed July 2004; 'UN-Appointed Expert On Human-Trafficking To Protect Rights of Victims', *EuropaWorld* 23 April 2004, <http://www.europaworld.org/week174/unappointed23404.htm>. Accessed July 2004; and Margaret E. Beare, 'Illegal Migration: Personal Tragedies, Social Problems, or National Security Threats?' in Phil Williams (ed.) *Illegal Immigration and Commercial Sex: The New Slave Trade* (London: Frank Cass, 1999), Special issue of Transnational Organised Crime, p. 38.

176 Angelique Chrisafis, 'Fears of Triad Link to Body Found in Car', *Guardian* 5 June 2004. For recent examples of triad activities in South Africa, Ireland and the United Kingdon, see also 'Mafia, Triads Bring Sex Workers into SA', *iAfrica.com* 24 March 2003. For a survey of Chinese organised crime in Europe, see Emil W. Plywaczewski, 'Chinese Organised Crime in Western and Eastern Europe', US Department of State, International Information Programmes, <http://http://usinfo.state.gov/regional/ea/chinaaliens/polishprof.htm#ewp3>. Accessed July 2004.

177 H. Richard Friman and Peter Andreas, 'Introduction: International Relations and the Illicit Global Economy', in H. Richard Friman and Peter Andreas (eds) *The Illicit Global Economy and State Power* (Lanham, Md.: Rowman & Littlefield, 1999), p. 12.

178 Carlos Resa-Nestares, 'Transnational Organised Crime in Spain: Structural Factors Explaining its Penetration', in Emilio C. Viano (ed.) *Global Organised Crime and International Security* (Aldershot: Ashgate, 1999), pp. 47–62.

179 Dina Siegel, 'The Transnational Russian Mafia', in Dina Siegel, Henk van de Bunt and Damian Zaitch (eds) *Global Organised Crime: Trends and Developments* (Dordrecht: Kluwer Academic, 2003), pp. 51–62.

180 Gerben Bruinsma and Wim Bernasco, 'Criminal Groups and Transnational Illegal Markets', *Crime, Law and Social Change* 41 (1) (February 2004), pp. 79–94.

181 Klaus von Lampe, 'Assessing Organised Crime: The Case of Germany', *ECPR Standing Group eNewsletter Organised Crime* 3 (September 2002), <http://http://people.freenet.de/kvlampe/kvlecprnl0309.pdf>. Accessed July 2004, pp. 8–11.

182 Castells, *End of Millennium*, p. 180.

183 Willetts, 'Transnational Actors and International Organisations in Global Politics', p. 298.
184 Duffield, 'Globalisation and War Economies: Promoting Order to the Return of History?' See also Goodhand and Hulme, 'From Wars to Complex Political Emergencies'.
185 Conversation with security officials from the former Soviet republic of Georgia. September 1999.
186 Russia's Ministry of Interior, *Sostoyanie pravoparyadka v Rossiskoi Federatsii i osnovnye rezul'taty deyatel'nosti organov vnutrennikh del i vnutrennikh voisk v 1999 godu* (Moscow: Russia's Ministry of Interior, 1999); and Russia's Ministry of Interior and UN Office for Drug Control and Crime Prevention, *The Drug Situation in the Russian Federation* (Moscow, 1999).
187 Rolf-Inge Vogt Andrésen 'Report from a Fact-Finding Mission to Moscow 10–13 April 2000 [in Norwegian]', *FFI-Reiserapport* No. 2000/02343 (Kjeller: FFI, 2000), p. 8.
188 'Serbia's Uncertain Future', *Radio Free Europe/Radio Liberty* 9 January 2004.
189 See for example 'Albanian Government Adopts Anti-Mafia Law', *Radio Free Europe/Radio Liberty* 17 July 2004.
190 Randy Willoughby, 'Crouching Fox, Hidden Eagle: Drug Trafficking and Transnational security: A Perspective from the Tijuana–San Diego Border', *Crime, Law and Social Change* 40 (1) (July 2003), pp. 113–42. The DEA is more diplomatic in its reports, but concedes that the drug cartels 'remain powerful'; they possess 'abundant financial resources' and are 'adept at corrupting or intimidating public officials'. See 'Mexico: Country Profile 2003', US Drug Enforcement Administration, November 2003, <http:// www.usdoj.gov/dea/pubs/intel/03047/03047.pdf>. Accessed July 2004, p. iii.
191 Marcos Pablo Moloeznik, 'The Military Dimension of the War on Drugs in Mexico and Colombia', *Crime, Law and Social Change* 40 (1) (July 2003), pp. 107–12; and Marcos Pablo Moloeznik, 'The Challenges to Mexico in Times of Political Change', *Crime, Law and Social Change* 40 (1) (July 2003), pp. 7–20.
192 'Islamic Movement of Uzbekistan Controls Drug Traffic to Central Asia, Special Services Say', *Pravda* 30 May 2001, citing an interview with Bolot Dzhanuzakov, head of the National Security Service of Kirghizia; 'The Islamic Movement of Uzbekistan (IMU)', Center for Defense Information (CDI) web site 25 March 2002; and Justin L. Miller, 'The Narco-Insurgent Nexus in Central Asia and Afghanistan', *The National Interest* 7 May 2003.
193 Nelson Forte Flores. 'US Report Cites Reasons RP Can't Curb Illegal Drugs', *Manila Time* 21 June 2004, citing a report by the US Department of State's International Narcotics Control Strategy Report (INCSR).
194 'Drugs And Terrorism: A New Perspective', Drug Intelligence Brief, US Drug Enforcement Administration (DEA), September 2002, <http:// www.usdoj.gov/dea/pubs/intel/02039/02039.html>. Accessed July 2004. For PKK's drug-related network in Norway, see Oslo Police District/Intelligence Department, 'Crime in Oslo and the Financing of International Terrorism [in Norwegian]', unclassified report, No. 2004/1, pp. 18–20.
195 Of these, hashish- and ecstasy-trafficking were the most important sources of income. Interview with Spanish counter-terrorism official, September 2004; 'Spanish Judge: Morocco Flush with al-Qaida: Europe must Shield itself from Militants across Strait, Garzon says', *Associated Press* 16 July 2004; and Steven Brooke, 'Outside View: Financing al-Qaida 2.0', *United Press International* 29 June 2004.
196 Thomas M. Sanderson, 'Transnational Terror and Organised Crime: Blurring the

Lines', *SAIS Review* 24 (1) (winter/spring 2004), <http://www.saisreview.org/pdf/24.1sanderson.pdf>. Accessed July 2004, p. 50.

197 Sari Horwitz, 'Cigarette Smuggling Linked to Terrorism', *Washington Post* 8 June 2004, p. A01.

198 The CIA's Global Trends 2015 project predicted that '[o]ver the next 15 years transnational criminal organizations will become increasingly adept at exploiting the global diffusion of sophisticated information, financial, and transportation networks'. See NIC, *Global Trends 2015*, p. 41.

199 See, for example, Kjøk et al., 'Restoring Peace or Provoking Terrorism?'.

200 See, for example, the first paragraphs in al-Qaida's 'Declaration from the World Islamic Front for Jihad against the Jews and the Crusaders [in Arabic]', first published in the London-based pan-Arab newspaper *al-Quds al-Arabi* on 23 February 1998, p. 3, where the economic plunder is one key theme: 'First, for over seven years the United States has been occupying the lands of Islam in the holiest of places, the Arabian Peninsula, *plundering its riches*, dictating to its rulers, humiliating its people, terrorizing its neighbours, and turning its bases in the Peninsula into a spearhead through which to fight the neighbouring Muslim peoples' [my emphasis].

201 Brynjar Lia and Åshild Kjøk, 'Energy Supply as Terrorist Targets? Patterns of "Petroleum Terrorism" 1968–99', in Daniel Heradstveit and Helge Hveem (eds) *Oil in the Gulf: Obstacles to Democracy and Development* (Aldershot: Ashgate, 2004), pp. 100–24.

202 'Saudis Search for Clues after Militant Attack; 22 people Killed in Khobar; Britain Warns More Strikes Likely', *Associated Press* 31 May 2004; John J. Lumpkin, 'U.S. Worried Al-Qaida Targeting Oil', *Associated Press* 17 October 2002; Jeff Gerth, 'Pro-Qaeda Oil Workers a Sabotage Risk for Saudis', *New York Times* 3 February 2003; and Vince Cannistraro and Risa Molitz, 'Al Qaeda Oil Plot Could Cripple U.S. Economy', *ABCNews.com* 13 February 2003.

203 Al-Qaida audio tape quoted in John J. Lumpkin, 'U.S. Worried Al-Qaida Targeting Oil'.

204 See, for example, Michael L. Ross, 'What Do We Know about Natural Resources and Civil War?' *Journal of Peace Research* 41 (3) (May 2004), pp. 337–56; Michael L. Ross, 'Does Oil Hinder Democracy?' *World Politics* 53 (April 2001), pp. 325–61; Giacomo Luciani, 'The Oil Rent, the Fiscal Crisis of the State and Democratisation', in Ghassan Salamé (ed.) *Democracy Without Democrats? The Renewal of Politics in the Muslim World* (London: I. B. Tauris, 1994), pp. 130–55; and Robert Looney, 'Iraqi Oil: A Gift from God or the Devil's Excrement?' *Strategic Insights* 2 (7) (July 2003), <http://www.ccc.nps.navy.mil/si/july03/middleeast2.asp>. Accessed April 2004.

205 Countries with a recent history of civil war are more likely to experience political violence again. See Gleditsch, 'The Future of Armed Conflict', p. 17.

206 These countries included Bahrain, Kuwait, Oman, Qatar, Saudi Arabia, United Arab Emirates, Algeria, Egypt, Iran, Libya and Yemen. See statistics in Bright E. Okogu, 'The Middle East and North Africa in a Changing Oil Market', research paper, International Monetary Fund, 5 September 2003, <http://www.imf.org/external/pubs/ft/med/2003/eng/okogu/okogu.htm>. Accessed July 2004.

207 Luciani, 'The Oil Rent, the Fiscal Crisis of the State and Democratisation', p. 152.

208 Lia and Kjøk, 'Energy Supply As Terrorist Targets?', p. 105.

209 Paul Blustein, 'Oil Prices Reach New Peak as Terrorism Anxieties Jump: Some Worry Saudi Attack Exposes Global Weaknesses', *Washington Post* 2 June 2004, p. A10.

210 Herman Franssen, 'Oil: Market Fundamentals versus Geopolitical Realities',

Middle East Institute Policy brief, 5 February 2004, <http://www.mideasti.org/articles/doc196.html>; 'The Future of Energy: The End of the Oil Age', *The Economist* 23 October 2003; and 'OPEC: Still Holding Customers over a Barrel', *The Economist* 23 October 2003.

211 IEA, 'Executive Summary', *World Energy Outlook 2002*, (Paris: IEA, 2002), <http://library.iea.org/textbase/weo/pubs/weo2002/weo2002_1sum.pdf>. Accessed July 2004, pp. 26–7.

212 IEA, 'Executive Summary', *World Energy Outlook 2002*, (Paris: IEA, 2002), <http://library.iea.org/textbase/weo/pubs/weo2002/weo2002_1sum.pdf>. Accessed July 2004, p. 29. See also NIC, *Global Trends 2015*, pp. 8–9, 30.

213 'The Future of Energy: The end of the Oil Age', *The Economist* 23 October 2003. See also Conrad de Aenlle, 'Alternative Energy still Awaits its Day', *International Herald Tribune* 24 August 2004.

214 IEA, 'World Energy Investment Outlook: Asia-Pacific Energy Investment Challenges: 2003 Insights', presentation by Claude Mandil, Japan Press Center, 17 November 2003, <http://library.iea.org/dbtw-wpd/textbase/speech/2003/mandil/jpc.pdf>. Accessed July 2004.

215 NIC, *Global Trends 2015*, p. 28.

216 IEA, 'World Energy Investment Outlook: North American Energy Investment Challenges', presentation by Mr Claude Mandil at CSIS Seminar, November 2003, <http://library.iea.org/dbtw-wpd/textbase/speech/2003/mandil/csis.pdf>. Accessed July 2004, p. 8.

217 Lia, 'The Quest for Regional Security in the Southern Mediterranean'.

218 John Calabrese, 'Beyond Barcelona: The Politics of the Euro-Mediterranean Partnership', *European Security* 6 (4) (winter 1997), p. 91.

219 Information from 'Algeria: Sector Analysis', *ArabDatanet* June 2003, <http://www.arabdatanet.com/country/profiles/profile.asp?ctryname=algeria&ctryabrv=al&navtitle=sector%20analysis>. Accessed July 2004; and 'Libya Country Analysis Brief', *Energy Information Administration* January 2004, <http://www.eia.doe.gov/emeu/cabs/libya.html>. Accessed July 2004.

220 Calabrese, 'Beyond Barcelona', p. 91; Ahmad Aghrout and Martin S. Alexander, 'The Euro-Mediterranean New Strategy and the Maghreb Countries', *European Foreign Affairs Review* 2 (3) (fall 1997), p. 312; and IEA, *North Africa Oil and Gas* (Paris: OECD, 1996), pp. 81–5, 158.

221 IEA, 'Outlook for Gas Demand and Supply to 2020', presentation by Dr Fatih Birol at conference on Natural Gas Transit and Storage in South-east Europe, 31 May–1 June 2002, <http://www.worldenergyoutlook.org/papers/nmcfat.pdf>. Accessed July 2004, pp. 2–3, 5, 9.

222 IEA, 'Executive Summary', *World Energy Outlook 2002*, (Paris: IEA, 2002), <http://library.iea.org/textbase/weo/pubs/weo2002/weo2002_1sum.pdf>. Accessed July 2004, p. 30.

223 ibid.

224 IEA, 'World Energy Investment Outlook: North American Energy Investment Challenges', p. 8.

225 IEA, 'The IEA in 2003 and Long-Term Energy Security', presentation, Energy Seminar at the Paul H. Nitze School of Advanced International Studies (SAIS), Johns Hopkins University, November 2003, <http://library.iea.org/dbtw-wpd/textbase/speech/2003/mandil/sais.pdf>. Accessed July 2004.

226 Both 'put options' and 'short-selling' allow the purchaser to make a profit when the stock price falls. See more on the suspicios trading prior to 9/11 in Marilynn M. Rosenthal, 'Markets Hold 9–11 Clues: Activity Before Attacks Indicates People had Prior Knowledge', *Ann Arbor News* 13 June 2004, at <http://www.

mlive.com/columns/aanews/index.ssf?/base/news-0/108712190945891.xml>.
Accessed July 2004.

227 Lia and Kjøk, 'Energy Supply As Terrorist Targets?'

228 Paul Kemezis, 'Algeria Blast Has Officials Rethinking LNG Safety', *Engineering News-Record* 30 January 2004, <http://www.enr.com/news/powerIndus/archives/040202.asp>. Accessed July 2004.

229 ibid.

230 Oppenheimer, 'Terrorism Threats to Infrastructure Security', *Jane's Terrorism and Security Monitor* 1 January 2003.

231 Jerry Havens, 'Terrorism: Ready to Blow?' *Bulletin of the Atomic Scientists* 59 (4) (July/August 2003), pp. 16–18, <http://www.thebulletin.org/issues/2003/ja03/ja03havens.html>. Accessed July 2004.

232 ITERATE database.

233 Charlie Savage, 'Ex-Official Links LNG Tankers, Al Qaeda: Clarke Aide says Hub was Entryway', *Boston Globe* 30 March 2004.

234 Rohan Gunaratna, 'Al-Qaeda Adapts to Disruption', *Jane's Intelligence Review* 1 February 2004.

235 'U.S.: Padilla Planned to Blow up Apartments', *Associated Press* 1 June 2004.

236 Mark Hosenball and Evan Thomas, 'The Biggest Catch Yet: Khalid Shaikh Mohammed, a.k.a. "The Brain", was Planning Horrific New Attacks on the United States', *Newsweek* 10 March 2003.

237 The potential danger of this can be gleaned from the scope of accidents involving natural gas, such as the recent tragedy in Belgium in July 2004 where fifteen people where killed and more than 100 injured at the industrial area of Ghislenghien, about 20 miles south-east of Brussels, due to an explosion in a high pressure pipeline transporting natural gas from the Belgian port of Zeebrugge to northern France. It was described as 'the country's worst industrial gas disaster for more than 35 years'. See Margaret Neighbour, 'Belgian pipeline blast kills 15', *Scotsman* 31 July 2004.

238 International Energy Agency, *North Africa Oil and Gas*, p. 89.

239 The Barcelona Declaration signed in November 1995 establishes a broad co-operative framework between the EU and the other states bordering on the Mediterranean, including a plan for establishing a Mediterranean free-trade area by the year 2010.

240 I have expanded more upon this in Lia, 'Security Challenges in Europe's Mediterranean Periphery'.

5 THE DEMOGRAPHIC FACTOR

1 Cited in Robert D. Kaplan, 'The Coming Anarchy', *Athlantic Monthly* 273 (2) (February 1994), p. 46.

2 See for example Jack A. Goldstone, 'Demography, Environment, and Security', in Paul F. Diehl and Nils Petter Gleditsch (eds) *Environmental Conflict* (Boulder, Col.: Westview, 2001), pp. 84–108; and Henrik Urdal, 'The Devil in the Demographics: How Youth Bulges Influence the Risk of Domestic Armed Conflict, 1950–2000', paper presented to the International Studies Association 43rd Annual Convention New Orleans, La., 24–27 March 2002, <http://www.isanet.org/noarchive/urdal.html>. Accessed December 2004.

3 Valerie M. Hudson and Andrea Den Boer, 'A Surplus of Men, a Deficit of Peace: Security and Sex Ratios in Asia's Largest States', *International Security* 26 (4) (spring 2002), pp. 5–38.

4 Schaeffer, *Understanding Globalisation*, p. 217.

5 Roger Smith, 'Scarcity and Genocide', in Michael N. Dobkowski and Isidor Wallimann (eds) *The Coming Age of Scarcity* (Syracuse, NY: Syracuse University Press, 1998), pp. 199–219.

6 Cited in Schaeffer, *Understanding Globalisation*, p. 218.

7 ibid.

8 ibid.

9 Schaeffer refers to what he terms the 'Sexual Revolution, which altered the relations between the sexes in the first world and in many Third World countries, and thereby reduced birth rates considerably. The second revolution was the "Green Revolution", which greatly increased food production through technological innovations. See ibid., pp. 222–30.

10 In the 1960s, for example, the United Nations estimated the world's population to exceed 7.5 billion at the end of the century i.e. 1.5 billion too many.

11 NIC, *Global Trends 2015*, p. 19; and 'World Demographic Trends', report of the Secretary-General, United Nations Department of Economic and Social Information and Policy Analysis, Population Division, No. E/CN.9/1997/9, Table 2.

12 For example, a UN study recorded a 38 per cent reduction in prices on 'basic foods' during the 1980s. Schaeffer, *Understanding Globalisation*, pp. 222–5.

13 Smith, 'Scarcity and Genocide', p. 217.

14 Buvinić and Morrison, 'Living in a More Violent World', p. 62; and NIC, *Global Trends 2015*, p. 19.

15 See for example Eugene Linden, 'The Exploding Cities of the Developing World', *Foreign Affairs* 75 (1) (January/February 1996), pp. 52–65.

16 N'Dow quoted by Williams, 'Terrorism and Organised Crime: Convergence, Nexus, or Transformation?', p. 81.

17 See, for example, 'Parallel Power Flexes Muscle in Brazil', *Drug War Chronicle* 28 February 2003, <http://www.stopthedrugwar.org>. Accessed September 2004; and Michael Day, 'Crime Groups Turn to Terrorism in Rio de Janeiro', *Jane's Intelligence Review* 1 August 2003.

18 Buvinić and Morrison, 'Living in a More Violent World', p. 62.

19 See NIC, *Global Trends 2015*, p. 25.

20 Buvinić and Morrison, 'Living in a More Violent World', pp. 58ff.; and McRae, *The World in 2020*, pp. 109–10.

21 Buvinić and Morrison, 'Living in a More Violent World', p. 61.

22 See, for example, NIC, *Global Trends 2015*, pp. 8, 20.

23 For example, South Africa's population is projected to be only 38.7 million in 2015, down from 43.4 million in 2000. See NIC, *Global Trends 2015*, p. 19.

24 According to Buvinić and Morrison, 'a key feature of aggressive behaviour: once it occurs, it tends to reoccur.' They term this phenomenon 'criminal inertia'. They also believe that 'globalisation breeds violence', because 'globalisation has aggravated income inequalities throughout the world, spread a culture of violence through increased communication and media, and expanded trade in death industries such as firearms and drugs'. ibid., pp. 61, 63.

25 NIC, *Global Trends 2015*, p. 25.

26 Lia, 'Security Challenges in Europe's Mediterranean Periphery', pp. 45–6.

27 Remy Leveau, 'Youth Culture and Islamism in the Middle East', in Laura Guazzone (ed.) *The Islamist Dilemma: The Political Role of Islamist Movements in the Contemporary Arab World* (Reading: Ithaca Press, 1995), p. 266.

28 ibid., p. 265.

29 Hudson and Den Boer, 'A Surplus of Men, a Deficit of Peace'.

30 Buvinić and Morrison, 'Living in a More Violent World', p. 61.

31 See for example 'Russia's Dwindling Population', *Stratford Intelligence Update* 9

May 2000; Mark Lawrence Schrad, 'Abnormal Demographics', *Foreign Affairs* 83 (4) (July/August 2004), pp. 150–1; NIC, *Global Trends 2015*, p. 25; and Rodger Doyle, 'Assembling the Future: How International Migrants are Shaping the Twenty-First Century', *Scientific American* 286 (2) (February 2002), p. 30.

32 The term 'more developed nations' includes Europe, northern America, Australia, New Zealand and Japan. Figures are taken from 'World Demographic Trends', report of the Secretary-General, United Nations Department of Economic and Social Information and Policy Analysis, Population Division, No. E/CN.9/1997/9, Table 2.

33 McRae, *The World in 2020*, pp. 109–10, 112, 199–203.

34 See for example J. M. Taw and Bruce Hoffman, *The Urbanization of Insurgency: The Potential Challenge to US Army Operations* (Washington, DC: Rand, 1994); and Brian Nichiporuk, *The Security Dimension of Demographic Factors* (Santa Monica, Calif.: Rand, 2000), p. xx.

35 See for example Daniel L. Byman et al., *Trends in Outside Support for Insurgent Movements* (Washington, DC: RAND, 2001); Purdy, 'Targeting Diasporas'; and Lia and Kjøk, 'Islamist Insurgencies, Diasporic Support Networks, and Their Host States'.

36 Beare, 'Illegal Migration', p. 20.

37 *World Refugee Survey 2003*, Table 3 <http://www.refugees.org/wrs2003.cfm.htm>, and *World Refugee Survey 2004*, Table 1, <http://www.refugees.org/data/wrs/04/pdf/key-statistics.pdf>. Accessed October 2004.

38 See 'Trends in International Migration Reflect Increasing Labour-Related Immigration and Persistent Integration Problems' 21 January 2004, <http://www.oecd.org/document/50/0,2340,en_2649_33931_24968882_1_1_1_1,00.html>. Accessed October 2004.

39 NIC, *Global Trends 2015*, p. 23.

40 'World Demographic Trends', report of the Secretary-General, United Nations Department of Economic and Social Information and Policy Analysis, Population Division, No. E/CN.9/1997/9, p. 2, <http://www.itcilo.it/actrav/actrav-english/telearn/global/ilo/seura/migworld.htm>. Accessed May 2000.

41 McRae, *The World in 2020*, pp. 117–18.

42 George Joffé, 'The Economic Factor in Mediterranean Security', *International Spectator* 31 (4) (October–December 1996), p. 67.

43 Rodger Doyle, 'Assembling the Future: How International Migrants Are Shaping the Twenty-First Century', p. 30.

44 ibid.

45 Riva Kastoryano, 'Transnational Participation and Citizenship: Immigrants in the European Union', University of Oxford, Transnational Communities Programme working paper No. 20, <http://www.transcomm.ox.ac.uk/working%20papers/riva.pdf>. Accessed October 2004.

46 Williams, *Illegal Immigration and Commercial Sex*, p. 2.

47 Beare, 'Illegal Migration', p. 21.

48 Alejandro Porte, *The Economic Sociology of Immigration* (New York: Russel Sage Foundation, 1995), cited in Beare, 'Illegal Migration', p. 16.

49 Beare, 'Illegal Migration', p. 16.

50 ibid., p. 37.

51 ibid., p. 20.

52 NIC, *Global Trends 2015*, p. 23.

53 ibid., p. 42.

54 Phil Magers, 'Analysis: Texas Has New Majority', *United Press International* 27

August 2004, citing Steve Murdock, the Texas state demographer at the University of Texas at San Antonio.

55 See Yeh Ling-Ling, 'The Immigration Time Bomb: Declare a Moratorium', *Las Vegas Review-Journal* 23 July 2001, <http://www.diversityalliance.org/docs/time-bomb-lvrj.html>. Accessed October 2004. See also Phil Magers, 'Analysis: Texas has New Majority'; Daphne Spain, 'The Debate in the United States over Immigration', <http://usinfo.state.gov/journals/itsv/0699/ijse/spain.htm>; and Frank Zoretich, 'N.M. Will Secede to New Nation, Prof. Says', *Albuquerque Tribune* 17 February 2000, <http://209.157.64.200/focus/f-news/1100577/posts>. Accessed October 2004.

56 Stephan Thernstrom, 'The Myth of the Minority Majority', *Hoover Digest* 1 (winter 2002), <http://www.hooverdigest.org/021/thernstrom.html>. Accessed October 2004.

57 Castles and Miller, *The Age of Migration*, p. 279.

58 Nichiporuk, *The Security Dimension of Demographic Factors*, p. xiv.

59 NIC, *Global Trends 2015*, p. 42.

60 Gleditsch, 'The Future of Armed Conflict', p. 28.

61 See, for example, 'Nørrebrox i flammer', *Aftenposten* (Oslo) 17 August 1997.

62 ' "White Wolves" linked to Soho bomb', *BBC News* 30 April 1999; Tom Buerkle, 'London Bombing Suspect Is Charged: 22-Year-Old Man Held for 3 Murders as Officials Hope Terror is Ended', *International Herald Tribune* 3 May 1999; and 'Press Release: Soho Bomb', *Outage!* 30 April 1999, <http://outage.nabumedia.com>. Accessed October 2004.

63 Castles and Miller, *The Age of Migration*, p. 279.

64 Writing about globalisation and its impact on ethnic diasporas, Robin Cohen argues that five interlinked processes are at work: 'a world economy with quicker, denser transactions; altered flows in international migration (more contractual relationships, family visits, sojourning, as opposed to permanent settlement); the development of "global cities" that reside more in global than national roles; the creation of cosmopolitan and local cultures; and deterritorialisation of social identity, challenging the hegemonising nation state's claim to make an exclusive citizenship, and an increase in multiple forms of identification.' See Robin Cohen, *Global Diasporas: An Introduction* (London: UCL Press, 1997), cited in Vincent Miller, 'Mobile Chinatowns: the Future of Community in a Global Space of Flows', *Social Issues* 2 (1) (January 2004), <http://www.whb.co.uk/socialissues/vol2vm.htm>. Accessed October 2004.

65 NIC, *Global Trends 2015*, p. 47.

66 ibid., pp. 24, 41.

67 Nichiporuk, *The Security Dimension of Demographic Factors*, p. xv.

68 CSIS report cited in 'Terrorism Update: Canada and Terrorism', Anti-Defamation League, posted January 2004, <http://www.adl.org/terror/tu/tu_0401_canada.asp>. Accessed July 2004.

69 Singer and Wildavsky, *The Real World Order*.

70 See his article in Roberto Aliboni, George Joffé, and Tim Niblock (eds) *Security Challenges in the Mediterranean* (London: Frank Cass, 1996).

71 CSIS report cited in 'Terrorism Update: Canada and Terrorism', Anti-Defamation League posted January 2004, <http://www.adl.org/terror/tu/tu_0401_canada.asp>. Accessed July 2004.

72 Interview with Scotland Yard official, June 2004.

73 Rosie Cowan and Richard Norton-Taylor, 'MI5 Agents Foil Bomb Plot', *Guardian* 31 March 2004.

74 Beare, 'Illegal Migration', p. 20.

75 Jennifer Loven, 'Bush's Immigrant-Legalizing Plan Could Draw Hispanics to GOP', *Associated Press* 7 January 2004; and Yves Engler, 'Bush's Mexican Gambit: The Fallout from NAFTA', *CounterPunch* 8 January 2004, <http://www.counterpunch.org/engler01082004.html>. Accessed July 2004, citing the *New York Times* 27 December 2003 and the *Globe and Mail* 3 January 2004.
76 Ben Hall, 'Immigration in the European Union: Problem or Solution?' *OECD Observer* October 2000, <http://www.oecdobserver.org/news/fullstory.php/aid/337>. Accessed October 2004.
77 Jolyon Howorth, 'France and the Mediterranean in 1995: From Tactical Ambiguity to Inchoate Strategy?' *Mediterranean Politics* 1 (2) (autumn 1996), pp. 157–75.
78 Personal conversation with NATO officers involved in the operation, Jåttå headquarters, Norway, May 2004.
79 Beare, 'Illegal Migration'.
80 Aghrout and Alexander, 'The Euro-Mediterranean New Strategy and the Maghreb Countries', p. 313.
81 The latter figure is an estimate by Spain's counter-terrorism judge Baltasar Garzon's in July 2004. See Daniel Woolls, 'Spain Judge: 1,000 in Morocco Pose Threat', *Associated Press* 15 July 2004. See also 'Terrorism Update: Canada and Terrorism', Anti-Defamation League posted January 2004, <http://www.adl.org/terror/tu/tu_0401_canada.asp>. Accessed July 2004; and Roman Kupchinsky and Tereza Nemcova, 'The Changing Face of Human-Trafficking', *RFE/RL Organised Crime and Terrorism Watch* 4 (13) 24 May 2004.
82 Italian police report cited in Kupchinsky and Nemcova, 'The Changing Face of Human-Trafficking'.

6 IDEOLOGICAL SHIFTS

1 Cited in 'Voice seems to be al Qaeda leader calling for uprising', *CNN.com* 1 October 2004, via <http://www.cnn.com/2004/world/meast/10/01/zawahiri.transcript/index.html>.
2 Lia, 'Causes of Terrorism', Chapter 2.
3 Francis Fukuyama, *The End of History and the Last Man* (London: Hamish Hamilton, 1992).
4 Samuel Huntington, 'The Clashes of Civilisation?' *Foreign Affairs* 72 (3) (summer 1993), pp. 22–8.
5 Robert Kaplan, 'The Coming Anarchy', *Atlantic Monthly* 273 (2) (February 1994), pp. 44–76.
6 For a discussion of cores and counter-cores in the international system, see Bornschier and Chase-Dunn, *The Future of Global Conflict*.
7 'The New Red Brigades/Communist Combatant Party', Center for Defense Information 30 January 2004, <http://www.cdi.org/friendlyversion/printversion.cfm?documentid=2019>. Accessed May 2004. See also Gaspare Barbiellini Amidei, 'Red Brigades: Few but Dangerous', *Corriere della Sera* 19 July 2004.
8 Philip Willan, 'Italy Downplays Red Brigades File Find', *Independent* 21 October 2004.
9 A proponent of this view is John Gray. See his 'Geopolitics and the Limits of Growth', *Globalist* 17 March 2004.
10 See for example Graham Fuller and Ian Lesser, *A Sense of Siege: The Geopolitics of Islam and the West* (Boulder, Col.: Westview Press, 1995); and François Burgat and William Dowell, *The Islamic Movement in North Africa* (Austin, Tex.: University of Austin Press, 1993).
11 For the Sunni-Shiite convergence in political Islam, see, for example, Hamid Enayat, *Modern Political Islamic Thought* (London: Macmillan, 1982).

12 For two recent studies of the Muslim Brothers and Islamism in Egypt, which both emphasise the modernising features of these movements, see Bjørn Olav Utvik, 'The Modernising Force of Islamism', in John L. Esposito and François Burgat (eds) *Modernizing Islam: Religion in the Public Sphere in Europe and the Middle East* (London: Hurst Publishing, 2003); and Lia, *The Society of the Muslim Brothers in Egypt 1928–1942*, pp. 279–87.

13 The term 'salafi' or 'salafist', (or in Arabic *al-salafi* pl. *al-salafiyyun*), requires an explanation. It literally means 'those who look to our forefathers.' The salafists seek to reform Islam by purging it of syncretism and what they perceive as illegal innovation, which entered Islam during the long decline since the era of the Prophet and the four Rightly Guided Caliphs, who led the Muslim community after the Prophet's death. The salafists believe that only by ridding Islam of these superstitions, and by returning to the pristine Islam of these forefathers (in Arabic, *salaf*, *aslaf*), can Islam rise up from centuries of colonial humiliation and regain its strength and hegemonic position in the world. Mainstream salafism originally was and to some extent still is apolitical and non-violent in many countries. It has often concerned itself with outward forms of religious practice such as dress codes, beards for men etc. Although salafis often reject the label wahhabism, they are very influenced by Saudi wahhabist theology and often benefit from Saudi financial support. In Saudi Arabia, there are salafi activists among both pro-regime and dissident clerics. For a discussion of Islamism in Saudi Arabia, see Mansur al-Nuqaydan, 'The Islamist Map in Saudi Arabia and the Question of Repudiation [in Arabic]', *Al-Wasat*, 28 February 2003; and 'Saudi Arabia Background: Who are the Islamists?' (Amman, Riyadh, Brussels: International Crisis Group, Middle East Report No. 31, 21 September 2004), <http://www.icg.org// library/documents/middle_east_north_africa/iraq_iran_gulf/31_saudi_arabia_ backgrounder.pdf>. Accessed October 2004.

14 In Saudi Arabia, clerics like Shaykh Nasir bin Hamad al-Fahd, Shaykh Ali bin Khudayr al-Khudayr, and the deceased Shaykh Hamud al-Uqla, are thought to be amongst the leading figures of the new salafi-jihadi trend. For al-Qaida, the deceased Abdallah Azzam and the imprisoned Abu Qatadah al-Filastini, are also important.

15 Cited in 'Why Salafi-Jihadism? [in Arabic]', Global Islamic Media Centre, 5 September 2003, <http://groups.yahoo.com/group/globalislamicmedia>. Accessed October 2003.

16 A Saudi Islamic researcher goes so far as to state that '[t]hey [the extremist groups] were all born out of the womb of Salafi thought.' See al-Nuqaydan, 'The Islamist Map in Saudi Arabia and the Question of Repudiation [in Arabic]'.

17 The slogan is taken from the literature of Shaykh Abdallah Azzam, Osama bin Laden's ideological mentor and a founder of the Maktab al-Khidmat, an organ-isation that facilitated the influx of fighter-volunteers during the Afghan liber-ation war in the 1980s. For a collection of biographies on Abdallah Azzam, see <http://www.geocities.com/pwhce/wotbio.html>. Accessed November 2003.

18 See, for example, the declaration of support by the Algerian GSPC to al-Qaida in 'Algerian rebels offer support to al Qaeda', *Reuters* 22 October 2003.

19 National Intelligence Council, 'Social Identity and the Roots of Future Conflict', paper by Stuart J. Kaufman for the Global Trends 2020 project, <http:// www.cia.gov/nic/pdf_gif_2020_support/2003_11_06_papers/kaufman_panel-2_nov6.pdf>. Accessed July 2004.

20 Peter Beyer, *Religion and Globalisation* (London: Sage Publications, 1997), p. 226.

21 See Brynjar Lia et al., 'Nuclear Material, Gas and Microbes as Terrorist Weapons? An Analysis of Terrorist Groups' Interest in, and Use of, Non-Conventional

Weapons [in Norwegian]', *FFI Research Report* No. 2001/02930 (Kjeller,: FFI, 2002), <http://www.mil.no/multimedia/archive/00004/Lia-R-2001-02930_4569a. pdf>; and James K. Campbell, 'Chemical and Biological Weapons Threats to America: Are We Prepared?' testimony before the US Senate Judiciary Subcommittee on Technology, Terrorism and Government Information and the Senate Select Committee on Intelligence, 22 April 1998, <http://judiciary.senate.gov/old-site/campbell.htm>. Accessed October 2004. For a database on doomsday cults, see Rick A. Ross Institute for the Study of Destructive Cults, Controversial Groups and Movements,

22 Michael Barkun, 'Millenarians and Violence: The Case of the Christian Identity Movement', in Thomas Robbins and Susan J. Palmer (eds) *Millenium, Messiahs, and Mayhem: Contemporary Apocalyptic Movements* (London and New York: Routledge, 1997), p. 247. See also Dennis Camire and John Hanchette, 'Extremist Sects Spreading and Sharpening', *Salt Lake Tribune* 30 March 1997, p. 12.

23 Bradley C. Whitsel, 'Catastrophic New Age Groups and Public Order', *Studies in Conflict and Terrorism* 23 (1) (January–March 2000), pp. 21–36.

24 Jahn R. Hall and Philip Schuyler, 'The Mystical Apocalypse of the Solar Temple', in Thomas Robbins and Susan J. Palmer (eds) *Millenium, Messiahs, and Mayhem: Contemporary Apocalyptic Movements* (New York: Routledge, 1997), pp. 285–311.

25 Beyer, *Religion and Globalisation*, p. 225.

26 ibid.

27 ibid., p. 226

28 Felipe Fernández-Armesto, 'Religion', in John Gribbin et al. *The Future is Now: Predicting the twenty-first Century* (London: Weidenfeld & Nicolson, 1998), p. 58.

29 ibid., p. 59.

30 ibid.

31 NIC, *Global Trends 2015*, p. 42.

32 Daniel A. Metraux, 'Religious Terrorism in Japan: The Fatal Appeal of Aum Shinrikyo', *Asian Survey* 35 (12) (December 1999), p. 1141.

33 ibid., pp. 1148–50.

34 Ulrich Beck, *Die Feindlose Demokratie, Ausgewählte Aufsätze* (Stuttgart: Philipp Reclam Jr., 1995).

35 John Arquilla, David Ronfeldt and Michele Zanini, 'Networks, Netwar, and Information-Age Terrorism', in Ian O. Lesser, Bruce Hoffman, John Arquilla, David F. Ronfeldt, Michele Zanini, and Brian Michael Jenkins (eds) *Countering the New Terrorism* (Washington, DC: Rand, 1999), p. 48.

36 ibid.

37 ibid.

38 A 'counterculture' can be defined as a cluster of ideological or religious movements, organisations and interest groups loosely organised around a set of basic tenets and slogans in opposition to the established order.

39 Castells, 'Information Technology, Globalisation and Social Development', p. 7.

40 Beyer, *Religion and Globalisation*, p. 2.

41 Kegley, *International Terrorism: Characteristics, Causes, Controls*, p. 104. Paul Wilkinson is a typical proponent of this school.

42 See for example threats from Hamas to launch attacks on Israeli and Jewish targets abroad in Ewen MacAskill, 'Israel Steps Up Security Abroad, Fearing Reprisals', *Guardian* 24 March 2004; Arieh O'Sullivan, 'A Strike Outside the Ballpark', *Jerusalem Post* 27 September 2004; and Bertus Hendriks, 'Syria under Pressure after Damascus Attack', *Radio Netherlands* 27 September 2004, <http://www.rnw.nl/hotspots/html/syr040927.html>. Accessed October 2004. Several prominent Iraqi insurgent groups, including the Islamic Army in Iraq and the

Qaidat al-Jihad Organisation in the Land of the Two Rivers have vowed to carry out attacks abroad, including in the United States. See, for example, 'Letter to the American People', [in Arabic], Yahoo Group iaiiraq, 2 January 2005, <http://groups.yahoo.com/group/iaiiraq/menage/339>. Accessed January 2005.

43 I am indebted to Prof., Tore Bjørgo for information on right wing contacts with animal-rights activism. For examples of co-operation between Islamic militants and neo-Nazi groups, see Peter Finn, 'Germany Bans Islamic Group: Recruitment of Youths Worried Officials', *Washington Post* 16 January 2003, p. A14.

44 Hoffman, *Inside Terrorism*; and Campbell, 'Chemical and Biological Weapons Threats to America: Are We Prepared?'

7 OUR TECHNOLOGICAL FUTURE

1 Black, 'The Geometry of Terrorism', p. 24.

2 Jasper McKee, 'The Technology of Terrorism' Canadian Association of Physicists (CAP) <http://www.cap.ca/pic/archives/58.1(2002)/editorial.html>. Accessed October 2004. See also Wilkinson, *Technology and Terrorism*, p. 6.

3 National Research Council, Committee on Science and Technology for Countering Terrorism, *Making the Nation Safer: The Role of Science and Technology in Countering Terrorism*, (Washington, DC: National Academies Press, 2002), <http://www.nap.edu/pdf/web_ready/0309084814.pdf>. Accessed October 2004.

4 Jackson, 'Technology Acquisition by Terrorist Groups', p. 203.

5 Hirst, 'New and Old Technologies: Choice of Strategy and Targets', p. 111.

6 Castells, *The Rise of Network Society*; and Dorothy Denning, *Information Warfare and Security* (Reading, Mass.: ACM Press Books, 1999).

7 NIC, *Global Trends 2015*, p. 28.

8 See for example Heikki Seppä, 'Future Technologies: From Bloototh to RFID', VTT Technical Research Centre of Finland, 11 February 2004, <http://www.tekes.fi/eng/events/m2m/machineseminar.pdf>. October 2004.

9 For a recent and widely acknowledged study of vulnerabilities and security risks in the Norwegian telecommunication network, see Janne M. Hagen and Kjell Olav Nystuen, 'Protection of Society with a Focus on Public Telecommunication [in Norwegian]', *FFI Research Report* No. 99/00240 (Kjeller: FFI, 1999).

10 Sharon Gaudin, '2003 "Worst Year Ever" for Viruses, Worms', *Internetnews* 23 December 2003, <http://www.internetnews.com/dev-news/article.php/3292461>. Accessed October 2004.

11 Subimal Bhattacharjee, 'Q1 2004 Tops In Cyber Attacks', *Financial Express* 3 May 2004.

12 See, for example, Center for Strategic and International Studies (CSIS), *Cybercrime . . . Cyberterrorism . . . Cyberwarfare . . . Averting an Electronic Waterloo* (Washington, DC: CSIS, 1998), pp. 51–5; and Kenneth C. Watson, 'Creating the Department of Homeland Security: Consideration of the Administration's Proposal', prepared witness testimony to the House Committee on Energy and Commerce, July 9, 2002, <http://energycommerce.house.gov/107/hearings/07092002hearing629/watson1072.htm#_ftn2>. Accessed October 2004.

13 Joshua Green, 'The Myth of Cyberterrorism', *Washington Monthly* November 2002, <http://www.washingtonmonthly.com/features/2001/0211.green.html>. Accessed October 2004.

14 GAO, 'Computer Security: Progress Made, but Critical Federal Operations and Assets Remain at Risk', testimony by United States GAO, House of Representatives, 19 November 2002, <http://www.gao.gov/new.items/d03303t.pdf>. Accessed October 2004.

15 Dorothy Denning, 'Activism, Hactivism and Cyberterrorism: The Internet as a Tool for Influencing Foreign Policy', Georgetown University, <http://www. terrorism.com/documents/denning-infoterrorism.htm>. Accessed March 2000, p. 19. See also Denning's statement in 2004 in Erwin Lemuel G. Oliva, 'US Expert Says No Such Thing as Cyberterrorism Yet', *INQ7.net* 15 June 2004, <http:// www. crime-research.org/news/06.15.2004/428>. Accessed October 2004. A definition used by the FBI is the following: 'cyberterrorism is the premeditated, politically motivated attack against information, computer systems, computer programs, and data which results in violence against noncombatant targets by subnational groups or clandestine agents'. See Denning *Information Warfare and Security*, p. 69.

16 'First Cyberterrorist Attack Reported', *Reuters* 5 May 1998.

17 'Islamic Hackers Step Up Attacks', *BBC News* 29 October 2002.

18 For example on Muntadayat *al-mâsada al-Jihadiyya*, <http://www.alm2sda.net/vb/ index.php>. Accessed October 2004.

19 Hirst, 'New and Old Technologies: Choice of Strategy and Targets', p. 125.

20 Transnational terrorist attacks affecting civilian infrastructure have mostly been targeted at people, not the infrastructure itself. In civil wars, however, insurgents and guerrilla movements have often targeted domestic civilian infrastructure to weaken the government's ability to fight. See Brynjar Lia, 'Is Civilian Infrastructure Likely Target for Terrorist Groups in Peace-time?' [in Norwegian]' *FFI Research Report* No. 2000/01703 (Kjeller: FFI, 2001), <http://www.mil.no/ multimedia/archive/00004/Lia-R-2000-01703_4935a.pdf>, pp. 17ff.

21 Denning, 'Activism, Hactivism and Cyberterrorism'.

22 See Uri Fisher, 'Information Age State Security: New Threats to Old Boundaries', *Journal of Homeland Security* November 2001, <http://www. homelandsecurity.org/journal/articles/fisher.htm>. Accessed October 2004. See also Elizabeth Becker, 'Pentagon Sets Up New Center for Waging Cyberwarfare', *New York Times* 8 October 1999.

23 See, for example, Michael Whine, 'Islamist Organisations on the Internet', *Terrorism and Political Violence* 11(1) (spring 1999), pp. 123–32; and Kelly R. Damphouse and Brent L. Smith, 'The Internet: A Terrorist Medium for the Twenty-First Century'; Harvey W Kushner (ed.) *The Future of Terrorism: Violence in the New Millenium* (London: Sage, 1998), pp. 208–24.

24 Investigators have reportedly found bomb-making manuals such as *Big Book on Explosives*, *The Anarchist's Cookbook*, *The Homemade C4*, etc., in the possession of terrorists. See Hirst, 'New and Old Technologies: Choice of Strategy and Targets', p. 116.

25 In mid-October 2004 the *Encyclopedia for Preparation for Jihad* (*Mawsûat al-Îdad*) was available on these web sites: <http://www.geocities.com/m_e3dad4/>, <http://www.geocities.com/m_ali3dad4>, <http://www.geocities.com/m_u3dad4>, <http://www.geocities.com/m_alu3dad4>, <http://www.geocities.com/i3dad_ jihad4>, <http://www.geocities.com/i3dad_jehad4>, <http://www.geocities.com/ m_ale3dad4>.

26 Gary R. Bunt, *Islam in the Digital Age: E-jihad, On-line Fatwas, and Cyber Islamic Environments* (London: Pluto Press, 2003).

27 Barnaby Page, 'U.S.–Israeli Site Hacked, Mideast Link Uncertain', *TechWeb* 3 November 2000.

28 Steve Wright, *An Appraisal of the Technology of Political Control* (Luxembourg: European Parliament, Directorate General for Research, Scientific and Technological Options Assessment (STOA) Programme, 1998), p. 4, <http://cryptome. org/stoa-atpc.htm>. Accessed May 2000.

29 Translated text as appeared on web site, <http://www.spyshop.no>. Accessed June

2004. The company was investigated by the police after equipment from the store was used in a high-profile robbery.

30 Anonymous (Michael Scheuer), *Imperial Hubris: Why the West is Loosing the War on Terror* (Washington, DC: Brassey's, 2004), p. 83.

31 Moisé Naím, 'The Fourth Annual Grotius Lecture: Five Wars of Globalisation', *American University International Law Review* 18 (1) (2002), p. 14.

32 'Technology and Terrorism', Draft Interim Report, NATO Parliamentary Assembly, Sub-Committee on The Proliferation of Military Technology, April 2001, <http://www.nato-pa.int.> Accessed May 2004.

33 I am indebted to Dr Åke Sellström, Director of Swedish Defence Research Institute's NBC Defence Department in Umeå, Sweden for this information.

34 See Michael Gips, 'A Remote Threat', *Security Management Online* October 2002, <http://www.securitymanagement.com/library/001324.html>. Accessed July 2004; Dennis M. Gormley, 'UAVs and Cruise Missiles as Possible Terrorist Weapons', in James Clay Moltz (ed.) *New Challenges in Missile Proliferation, Missile Defense, and Space Security* (Monterey: Center for Nonproliferation Studies, August 2003), occasional papers No. 12, pp. 3–10, <http://cns.miis.edu/pubs/opapers/op12/op12.pdf>. Accessed July 2004; and Eugene Miasnikov, 'Threat of Terrorist Unmanned Aerial Vehicles: Technical Aspects [in Russian]', Center for Arms Control, Energy and Environmental Studies at Moscow Institute of Physics and Technology, Dolgoprudny, June 2004, <http://www.armscontrol.ru/UAV/rus/UAV%20report.pdf>. Accessed June 2004.

35 According to data collected by Louis R. Mizell, a private-security expert and ex-U.S. intelligence officer, cited in Gips, 'A Remote Threat'.

36 Roger Davies, 'Improvised Mortar Systems: An Evolving Political Weapon', *Jane's Intelligence Review* May 2001, pp. 12–15.

37 US Department of State, *Patterns of Global Terrorism 2001* (Washington, DC: Office of the Coordinator for Counter-terrorism, 21 May 2002), Appendix B; and 'Mujahedeen-e-Khalq: Iranian rebels', Council of Foreign Affairs <http://www.terrorismanswers.com/groups/mujahedeen.html>. Accessed October 2004.

38 *Encyclopedia of Preparation for Jihad* (*Mawsúat al-i'dad*), <http://www.geocities.com/m_e3dad4/>. Accessed October 2004.

39 Information from presentations at a conference on international terrorism and intelligence in the UK, summer 2004.

40 Bruce Simpson, 'The Low Cost Cruise Missile: A Looming Threat?' 20 May 2002, <http://aardvark.co.nz/pjet/cruise.shtml>. Accessed October 2004.

41 Hirst, 'New and Old Technologies: Choice of Strategy and Targets', p. 117. The Algerian GIA reportedly planned to down a hijacked airplane over Paris in December 1994.

42 A study on recent advances in nanotechnolocy predicts that electronically erasable and rewritable paper for books, magazines and newspapers, will be available within five to ten years. Clifton Coles, 'Nanotech Advances in Next 15 years', *The Futurist* 37 (4) (July–August 2003), pp. 8–9, citing William Illsey Atkinson, *Nanocosm: Nanotechnological and the Big Changes Coming from the Inconceivably Small* (New York: American Management Association, 2003).

43 For the effect of the new electronic media around 1970, see Hoffman, *Inside Terrorism*, pp. 136–7. For other studies of media and terrorism, see for example Brigitte L. Nacos, *Mass-Mediated Terrorism: The Central Role of the Media in Terrorism and Counter-Terrorism* (Lanham, Md.: Rowman & Littlefield, 2002); and Michel Wieviorka, *The Making of Terrorism* (Chicago, Ill. and London: Chicago University Press, 1993), pp. 42–51. For a counterargument to Wievorka,

see Paul Wilkinson, 'The Media and Terrorism: A Reasessment', *Terrorism and Political Violence* 9 (2) (summer 1997), pp. 51–64.

44 Wright, 'Executive Summary', p. 1.

45 ibid., p. 3.

46 Richard Clutterbuck, 'Keeping Track of Terrorists after 1992', in Alex P. Schmid and Donald D. Crelinsten (eds) *Western Responses to Terrorism* (London: Frank Cass, 1998), p. 306.

47 Duncan Campbell, *Interception Capabilities 2000* (Luxembourg: European Parliament, Directorate General for Research, Scientific and Technological, Options Assessment (STOA) Programme, 1999), p. 18, <http://www.iptvreports.mcmail.com/ic2report.htm>. Accessed June 1999.

48 ibid., pp. 22–3.

49 Ralph Vartabedian, 'U.S. Funnels Billions to Science to Defend Against Terrorism', *Los Angeles Times* 7 March 2004.

50 Spencer S. Hsu and Sari Horwitz, 'Impervious Shield Elusive against Drive-By Terrorists', *Washington Post* 8 August 2004, p. A01.

51 ibid.

8 CONCLUSION

1 For the concept of social distance, see Black, 'The Geometry of Terrorism'.

SELECT BIBLIOGRAPHY

Abdallah, Abdel Mahdi, 'Causes of Anti-Americanism in the Arab World: A Socio-Political Perspective', *Middle East Review of International Affairs* 7 (4) (December 2003), pp. 62–73.

Adams, Thomas K., 'The New Mercenaries and the Privatization of Conflict', *Parameters: US Army War College Quarterly* 29 (2) (Summer 1999), pp. 103–16.

Andrésen, Rolf-Inge Vogt, 'Terrorism and Organised Crime in Post-Soviet Russia', *FFI Research Report* No. 2001/03417 (Kjeller: FFI, 2001).

Anonymous (Michael Scheuer), *Through Our Enemies' Eyes: Osama bin Laden, Radical Islam, and the Future of America* (Washington, DC: Brassey's, 2002).

—— *Imperial Hubris: Why the West is Losing the War on Terror* (Washington, DC: Brassey's, 2004).

Arquilla, John, David Ronfeldt and Michele Zanini, 'Networks, Netwar, and Information-Age Terrorism', in Ian O. Lesser, Bruce Hoffman, John Arquilla, David F. Ronfeldt, Michele Zanini and Brian Michael Jenkins (eds) *Countering the New Terrorism* (Washington, DC: Rand, 1999), pp. 39–84.

Barber, Benjamin R., *Jihad vs. McWorld: How Globalism and Tribalism are Reshaping the World* (New York: Ballantine, 1996).

—— *Jihad vs. McWorld: Terrorism's Challenge to Democracy* (London: Corgi, 2003).

Barkun, Michael, 'Millenarians and Violence: The Case of the Christian Identity Movement', in Thomas Robbins and Susan J. Palmer (eds) *Millenium, Messiahs, and Mayhem: Contemporary Apocalyptic Movements* (London and New York: Routledge, 1997), pp. 247–60.

Baylis, John and Steve Smith (eds) *The Globalization of World Politics: An Introduction to International Relations* (Oxford: Oxford University Press, 1999).

Berdal, Mats and David Keen, 'Violence and Economic Agendas in Civil Wars: Some Policy Implications', *Millennium: Journal of International Studies* 26 (3) (1997), pp. 795–818.

Bergesen, Albert J. and Omar Lizardo, 'International Terrorism and the World System', *Sociological Theory* 22 (1) (March 2004), pp. 38–52.

Beyer, Peter, *Religion and Globalization* (London: Sage, 1997).

Bjørgo, Tore (ed.) *Root Causes of Terrorism* (London and New York: Routledge, 2005).

Black, Donald, 'The Geometry of Terrorism', *Sociological Theory* 22 (1) (March 2004), pp. 14–25.

Buvinić, Mayra and Andrew R. Morrison, 'Living in a More Violent World', *Foreign Policy* 118 (spring 2000), pp. 58–72.

Byman, Daniel L., Peter Chalk, Bruce Hoffman, William Rosenau and David Brannan, *Trends in Outside Support for Insurgent Movements* (Washington, DC: Rand, 2001).

Castells, Manuel, *The Rise of Network Society: The Information Age: Economy, Society and Culture* (Oxford: Blackwell, 1996).

—— *The Power of Identity: The Information Age: Economy, Society and Culture* (Oxford: Blackwell, 1997).

—— *End of Millennium: The Information Age: Economy, Society and Culture* (Oxford: Blackwell, 1998).

Central Intelligence Agency, *Terrorist CBRN: Materials and Effects*, CTC-2003-40058, June 2003, <http://www.cia.gov/cia/reports/terrorist_cbrn/CBRN_threat.pdf>. Accessed April 2004.

Cha, Victor D., 'Globalization and the Study of International Security', *Journal of Peace Research* 37 (3) (May 2000), pp. 391–403.

Chua, Amy, *World on Fire: How Exporting Free Market Democracy Breeds Ethnic Hatred and Global Instability* (New York: Anchor, 2003).

Cohen, Eliot A., 'History and the Hyperpower: Empire's New Clothes', *Foreign Affairs* 83 (4) (July/August 2004), pp. 49–64.

Collier, Paul and Anke Hoeffler, 'Greed and Grievance in Civil Wars', World Bank Research Paper, 21 October 2001.

Crenshaw, Martha, 'Why America? The Globalization of Civil War', *Current History* 100 (650) (December 2001), pp. 425–32.

Cronin, Audrey Kurth, 'Behind the Curve: Globalization and International Terrorism', *International Security* 27 (3) (winter 2002–3), pp. 30–58.

Denning, Dorothy, *Information Warfare and Security* (Reading, Mass.: Addison-Wesley, 1999).

Doran, Michael, 'Somebody Else's Civil War', *Foreign Affairs* 81 (1) (January/February 2002), pp. 22–42.

Duffield, Mark, 'Globalisation and War Economies: Promoting Order to the Return of History?' *Fletcher Forum of World Affairs* 23 (2) (fall 1999), pp. 21–36.

Engene, Jan Oskar, *Patterns of Terrorism in Western Europe, 1950–95* (Bergen: University of Bergen, 1998), Ph.D. thesis.

Enriquez, Juan, 'Too Many Flags', *Foreign Policy* 116 (fall 1999), pp. 1–49.

Feldmann, Andreas and Maiju Perälä, 'Nongovernmental Terrorism in Latin America: Re-Examining Old Assumptions', Working Paper No. 286, The Kellogg Institute, Notre Dame, Indiana, July 2001, <http://www.nd.edu/~kellogg/WPS/286.pdf>. Accessed April 2004.

Giddens, Anthony, *The Consequences of Modernity* (Cambridge: Polity Press, 1990).

Gleditsch, Nils Petter, 'The Future of Armed Conflict', The Madame Madeleine Feher European Scholar-in-Residence Lecture, Bar-Ilan University, Israel, December 2002, <http://www.biu.ac.il/SOC/besa/feher6.pdf>. Accessed April 2004.

Guéhenno, Jean-Marie, 'The Impact of Globalisation on Strategy', *Survival* 40 (4) (winter 1998–9), pp. 5–19.

Guelke, Adrian, *The Age of Terrorism and the International Political System* (London: I. B. Tauris, 1997).

Gunaratna, Rohan, *Inside Al Qaeda: Global Network of Terror* (New York: Columbia University Press, 2002).

Gurr, Ted Robert, 'Terrorism in Democracies: When It Occurs, Why It Fails', in

Charles W. Kegley Jr., *The New Global Terrorism: Characteristics, Causes, Controls* (Upper Saddle River, NJ: Prentice Hall, 2003) pp. 202–15.

Hegre, Håvard, Rannveig Gissinger, Nils Petter Gleditsch, 'Globalization and Internal Conflict', in Gerald Schneider, Kathrine Barbieri and Nils Petter Gleditsch (eds) *Globalization and Armed Conflict* (Lanham, Md. and Oxford: Rowman & Littlefield, 2003), pp. 251–75.

Herkenrath, Mark and Volker Bornschier, 'Transnational Corporations in World Development: Still the Same Harmful Effects in an Increasingly Globalized World Economy?' *Journal of World-System Research* 9 (1) (winter 2003), pp. 105–39.

Hirst, Peter, 'New and Old Technologies: Choice of Strategy and Targets', in Gunnar Jervas (ed.) *FOA Report on Terrorism* (Stockholm: Swedish Defence Research Establishment, 1998), pp. 111–28.

Hoffman, Bruce, *Inside Terrorism* (New York: Columbia University Press, 1998).

Hoffmann, Stanley, 'Clash of Globalizations', *Foreign Affairs* 81 (4) (July/August 2002), pp. 104–15.

Homer-Dixon, Thomas, 'The Rise of Complex Terrorism', *Foreign Policy* 128 (January/February 2002), pp. 52–62.

Huntington, Samuel, 'The Lonely Superpower', *Foreign Affairs* 78 (2) (March/April 1999), pp. 35–49.

Inglehart, Ronald and Wayne E. Baker, 'Modernization's Challenge to Traditional Values: Who's Afraid of Ronald McDonald?' *The Futurist* 35 (2) (March/April 2001), pp. 16–21.

International Energy Agency, *World Energy Outlook 2002* (Paris: IEA, 2002).

International Institute of Strategic Studies, *Strategic Survey 2003/4* (Oxford: Oxford University Press, 2004).

Kaldor, Mary, *New and Old Wars: Organised Violence in a Global Era* (Stanford, Calif.: Stanford University Press, 1999).

Kepel, Gilles, *Jihad: The Trail of Political Islam*, trans. Anthony F. Roberts, (Cambridge, Mass.: Harvard University Press, 2002)

Khalilzad, Zalmay and Ian Lesser (eds) *Sources of Conflict in the 21st Century: Regional Futures and U.S. Strategy* (Santa Monica, Calif.: Rand, 1998).

Khashan, Hilal, 'Collective Palestinian Frustration and Suicide Bombings', *Third World Quarterly* 24 (6) (December 2003), pp. 1049–67.

Kimmel, Michael S., 'Globalization and its Mal(e)contents: The Gendered Moral and Political Economy of Terrorism', *International Sociology* 18 (3) (September 2003), pp. 603–20.

Kjøk, Åshild, Thomas Hegghammer, Annika S. Hansen and Jørgen Kjetil Knudsen, 'Restoring Peace or Provoking Terrorism? Exploring the Links between Multi-lateral Military Interventions and International Terrorism', *FFI Research Report* No. 2003/01547 (Kjeller: FFI, 2004). <http://www.rapporter.ffi.no/rapporter/2003/01547.pdf>. Accessed April 2005.

Kushner, Harvey W. (ed.) *The Future of Terrorism: Violence in the New Millenium* (London: Sage, 1998).

Laqueur, Walter, *The New Terrorism* (Oxford: Oxford University Press, 1999).

Le Billon, Philippe, 'Buying Peace or Fuelling War? The Role of Corruption in Armed Conflict', *Journal of International Development* 15 (4) (2003), pp. 413–26.

Li, Quan and Drew Schaub, 'Economic Globalization and Transnational Terrorism:

A Pooled Time-Series Analysis', *Journal of Conflict Resolution* 48 (2) (April 2004), pp. 230–58.

Lia, Brynjar, *A Police Force Without a State: A History of the Palestinian Security Forces in the West Bank and Gaza* (Reading: Ithaca Press, 2005).

—— *Building Arafat's Police: The Politics of International Police Assistance in the Palestinian Territories after the Oslo Agreement* (Reading: Ithaca Press, 2005).

—— 'Causes of Terrorism: An Updated and Expanded Review of the Literature', *FFI Research Report* No. 2005/04307 (Kjeller: FFI, 2005).

—— 'Security Challenges in Europe's Mediterranean Periphery: Perspectives and Policy Dilemmas', *European Security* 8(4) (winter 1999), pp. 27–56.

—— *The Society of the Muslim Brothers in Egypt 1928–1942: The Rise of an Islamic Mass Movement* (Reading: Ithaca Press, 1998).

Lia, Brynjar and Thomas Hegghammer, 'Jihadi Strategic Studies: The Alleged al-Qaida Policy Study Preceding the Madrid Bombings', *Studies in Conflict and Terrorism* 27 (5) (September–October 2004), pp. 355–375.

—— 'Islamist Insurgencies, Diasporic Support Networks, and Their Host States: The Case of the Algerian GIA in Europe 1993–2000', *FFI Research Report* No. 2001/03789 (Kjeller: FFI, 2001).

Lia, Brynjar and Åshild Kjøk, 'Energy Supply As Terrorist Targets? Patterns of "Petroleum Terrorism" 1968–99', in Daniel Heradstveit and Helge Hveem (eds) *Oil in the Gulf: Obstacles to Democracy and Development* (Aldershot: Ashgate, 2004), pp. 100–24.

Lia, Brynjar and Katja H.-W. Skjølberg, 'Warum es zu Terrorismus kommt: Ein Überblick über Theorien und Hypothese zu den Ursacken des Terrorismus', *Journal für Konflikt und Gewaltforschung* 6 (1) (spring 2004), pp. 121–63.

Libicki, Martin C., 'Rethinking War: The Mouse's New Roar?' *Foreign Policy* 117 (winter 1999–2000), pp. 10–43.

Linden, Eugene, 'The Exploding Cities of the Developing World', *Foreign Affairs* 75 (1) (January–February 1996), pp. 52–65.

Lizardo, Omar A., 'The Effect of Economic and Cultural Globalization on Anti-U.S. Transnational Terrorism 1971–2000', research paper, Univeristy of Arizona, 16 June 2004, <http://www.members.cox.net/~olizardo/terror_glob.pdf>. Accessed June 2004.

Luke, Timoth W. and Gerard Toal, 'The Fraying Modern Map: Failed States and Contraband Capitalism', *Geopolitics* 3 (3) (winter 1998), pp. 14–33.

MacCulloch, Robert, 'The Impact of Income on the Taste for Revolt', *American Journal of Political Science* 48 (4) (October 2004), pp. 830–48.

Mackinlay, John, *Globalisation and Insurgency* (Oxford: Oxford University Press, 2002), Adelphi paper No. 352.

Maskaliunaite, Asta, 'Terrorism and Globalization: Recent Debates', *Rubikon E-journal* October 2002, <http://venus.ci.uw.edu.pl/~rubikon/forum/terrorism.htm>. Accessed May 2004.

Matthews, Jessica, 'Power Shift', *Foreign Affairs* 76 (1) (January–February 1997), pp. 50–66.

Mousseau, Michael, 'Market Civilization and its Clash with Terror', *International Security* 27 (3) (winter 2002–3), pp. 5–29.

Naím, Moisé, 'The Fourth Annual Grotius Lecture: Five Wars of Globalization', *American University International Law Review* 18 (1) (2002), pp. 1–18.

National Intelligence Council, *Global Trends 2015: A Dialogue about the Future with Nongovernment Experts*, NIC 2000–02, December 2000.

—— 'Global Trends 2020: East Asia', paper for the Global Trends 2020 Project, 8 December 2003.

—— 'The Middle East to 2020', paper for the Global Trends 2020 project, 8 December 2003.

Nesser, Petter, 'Jihad in Europe: A Survey of the Motivations for Sunni Islamist Terrorism in Post-Millennium Europe', *FFI Research Report* No. 2004/01146 (Kjeller: FFI, 2004).

Nichiporuk, Brian, *The Security Dimension of Demographic Factors* (Santa Monica, Calif.: Rand, 2000).

al-Qirshi, Abu Ubayd, 'The September 11th Raid [in Arabic]', *Majallat al-Ansar* 1 (September 2002).

Rapoport, David C., 'The Four Waves of Rebel Terror and September 11', *Anthropoetics* 8 (1) (spring–summer 2002), <http://www.anthropoetics.ucla.edu/ap0801/terror.htm#b1>. Accessed April 2004.

Rashid, Ahmed, *Jihad: The Rise of Militant Islam in Central Asia* (New Haven, Conn.: Yale University Press, 2002).

Raustaliala, Kal, 'Law, Liberalization and International Narcotics Trafficking', *New York University Journal of International Law and Politics* 32 (1) (1999), pp. 89–145.

Resa-Nestares, Carlos, 'Transnational Organized Crime in Spain: Structural Factors Explaining its Penetration', in Emilio C. Viano (ed.) *Global Organized Crime and International Security* (Aldershot: Ashgate, 1999), pp. 47–62.

Rosenau, William, 'Aum Shinrikyo's Biological Weapons Program: Why Did it Fail?' *Studies in Conflict and Terrorism* 24 (4) (July 2001), pp. 289–301.

Rudra, Nita, 'Globalization and the Decline of the Welfare State in Less-Developed Countries', *International Organization* 56 (2) (spring 2002), pp. 411–45.

Ronfeldt, David F., John Arquilla, Graham E. Fuller and Melissa Fuller, *The Zapatista 'Social Netwar' in Mexico* (Washington, DC: Rand, 1998), Rand Report No. MR-994-A.

Ross, Jeffrey Ian and Ted Robert Gurr, 'Why Terrorism Subsides: A Comparative Study of Canada and the United States', *Comparative Politics* 21 (4) (July 1989), pp. 405–26.

Ross, Michael L., 'What Do We Know about Natural Resources and Civil War?' *Journal of Peace Research* 41 (3) (May 2004), pp. 337–56.

Schaeffer, Robert K., *Understanding Globalization: The Social Consequences of Political, Economic and Environmental Change* (Lanham, Md.: Rowman & Littlefield, 1997).

Schmid, Alex and Janny de Graaf, *Violence as Communication: Insurgent Terrorism and the Western News Media* (Beverly Hills, Calif.: Sage, 1982).

Schmid, Alex P. and Albert J. Jongman, *Political Terrorism: A New Guide to Actors, Authors, Concepts, Data Bases, Theories and Literature* (Amsterdam: SWIDOC, 1988).

Schmid, Alex P. and Donald D. Crelinsten (eds) *Western Responses to Terrorism* (London: Frank Cass, 1998).

Senechal de la Roche, Roberta, 'Collective Violence as Social Control', *Sociological Forum* 11 (1) (March 1996), pp. 97–128.

Shearer, David, *Private Armies and Military Intervention* (Oxford: IISS/Oxford University Press, 1998), Adelphi Paper No. 316.

Shelley, Louise, 'Transnational Organized Crime: The New Authoritarianism', in H. Richard Friman and Peter Andreas (eds) *The Illicit Global Economy and State Power* (Lanham, Md.: Rowman & Littlefield, 1999), pp. 25–51.

Siegel, Dina, Henk van de Bunt and Damian Zaitch (eds) *Global Organized Crime: Trends and Developments* (Dordrecht: Kluwer Academic, 2003).

Silke, Andrew, 'Lords of Discipline: The Methods and Motives of Paramilitary Vigilantism in Northern Ireland', *Low Intensity Conflict and Law Enforcement* 7 (2) (autumn 1998), pp. 121–56.

Singer, Max, and Aaron B. Wildavsky, *The Real World Order: Zones of Peace, Zones of Turmoil* (London: Chatham House Publishers, 1993).

Singer, Peter W., 'Corporate Warriors: The Rise of the Privatized Military Industry and Its Ramifications for International Security', *International Security* 26 (3) (winter 2001/2), pp. 186–220.

Sprinzak, Ehud, 'Right-Wing Terrorism in a Comparative Perspective: The Case of Split Delegitimization', in Tore Bjørgo (ed.) *Terror From the Extreme Right* (London: Frank Cass, 1995), pp. 17–43.

Sprinzak, Ehud and Idith Zertal, 'Avenging Israel's Blood (1946)', in Jonathan B. Tucker (ed.) *Toxic Terror: Assessing Terrorist Use of Chemical and Biological Weapons* (Cambridge, Mass.: MIT Press, 2000), pp. 17–41.

Stern, Jessica, *Terror in the Name of God: Why Religious Militants Kill* (New York: HarperCollins, 2003).

Strange, Susan, *The Retreat of the State: The Diffusion of Power in the World Economy* (Cambridge: Cambridge University Press, 1996).

Takeyh, Ray and Nikolas Gvosdev, 'Do Terrorist Networks Need a Home?' *The Washington Quarterly* 25 (3) (summer 2002), pp. 97–108.

Taylor, Bron, 'Religion, Violence and Radical Environmentalism: From Earth First! to the Unabomber to the Earth Liberation Front', *Political Violence and Terrorism* 10 (4) (winter 1998), pp. 1–42.

The 9/11 Commission Report: Final Report of the National Commission on Terrorist Attacks Upon the United States (New York: Norton & Co, 2004).

Tønnesson, Stein, 'A "Global Civil War"?' *Security Dialogue* 33 (3) (September 2002), pp. 389–91.

Volgy, Thomas J., Lawrence E. Imwalle and Jeff J. Corntassel, 'Structural Determinants of International Terrorism: The Effects of Hegemony and Polarity on Terrorist Activity', *International Interactions* 23 (2) (1997), pp. 207–31.

Wieviorka, Michel, *The Making of Terrorism* (Chicago, Ill.: Chicago University Press, 1993).

Wilhelmsen, Julie, 'When Separatists Become Islamists: The Case of Chechnya', *FFI Research Report* No. 2004/00445 (Kjeller: FFI, 2004).

Wilkinson, Paul, 'The Media and Terrorism: A Reassessment', *Terrorism and Political Violence* 9 (2) (summer 1997), pp. 51–64.

Willetts, Peter, 'Transnational Actors and International Organizations in Global Politics', in John Baylis and Steve Smith (eds) *The Globalization of World Politics: An Introduction to International Relations* (Oxford: Oxford University Press, 1999), pp. 287–310.

Windsor, Jennifer L., 'Promoting Democratization Can Combat Terrorism', *The Washington Quarterly* 26 (3) (summer 2003), pp. 43–58.

Wrighte, Mark R, 'The Real Mexican Terrorists: A Group Profile of the Popular Revolutionary Army (EPR)', *Studies in Conflict and Terrorism* 25 (4) (July 2002), pp. 207–25.

Zakariya, Fareed, 'The Rise of Illiberal Democracy', *Foreign Affairs* 76 (6) (November–December 1997), pp. 22–43.

INDEX

human-trafficking 123, 127, 157
humanitarian interventions 74, 81–2
Huntington, Samuel 42–3, 60, 81, 160

IAEA *see* International Atomic Energy
  Agency
ICBL *see* International Campaign to
  Ban Landmines
ICC (International Criminal Court) 89
ICISS (International Commission on
  Intervention and State Sovereignty) 83
identity 19, 24, 83, 95, 154
ideologies 8*f*, 159–69, 194–5;
  implications for terrorism 160, 168–9;
  Islamism 162–5; postulate 159–60;
  religious extremism 165–6; resurgent
  left? 161–2, 161*f*, 169; trends 160–8,
  161*f*
IEA *see* International Energy Agency
IEMF (Interim Emergency
  Multinational Force) 75
'illiberal democracies' 61–2
improvised explosive devices (IEDs)
  179–80
IMU (Islamic Movement of Uzbekistan)
  129
Independent, The 227 n142
India 41, 42, 49, 54, 82, 88, 98, 136, 146,
  162
individualisation 101, 102, 167
Indonesia 65, 68, 69, 77, 82, 87, 94
information technologies 20, 171, 172–6;
  in conventional terrorism 175–6;
  cyberterrorism 173–5, 182;
  globalisation 60–1; implications for
  terrorism 171, 173–6, 178; network
  complexity 172–3; postulate 171;
  trends 144, 172–8
informational capitalism 21, 100,
  168
INGOs (international non-governmental
  organisations) 16, 91–5, 190; definition
  92; funding 93; implications for
  terrorism 91, 94–5; postulate 91;
  proliferation 91–3
institutions 19, 89–90
insurgencies 12, 15, 33–4, 35–6, 156,
  161–2
Inter-American Democratic Charter 77
interdependence 20
Interim Emergency Multinational Force
  (IEMF) 75

International Atomic Energy Agency
  (IAEA) 50, 52, 52*f*, 53*f*
International Campaign to Ban
  Landmines (ICBL) 19–20, 92
international co-operation 198 n5
International Commission on
  Intervention and State Sovereignty
  (ICISS) 83
International Criminal Court (ICC) 89
International Energy Agency (IEA) 135,
  136, 137–8
International Islamic Relief
  Organisation (IIRO) 95
international relations *see*
  democratisation; INGOs; military
  interventions; multilateralism;
  peacekeeping; state formation and
  failure; weapons of mass destruction;
  world order
international terrorism 11, 39
internationalised internal conflicts 27–8
IRA (Irish Republican Army) 117, 139;
  see also PIRA
Iran: economy 41; opium production
  122; political Islam 163, 164; regime
  63, 72, 82; Revolutionary Guard Corps
  (IRGC) 81; terrorism 179; WMD 50,
  51, 54, 55*t*, 57, 59
Iran–Iraq war 27, 29
Iraq: Islamism 163, 169, 175; Operation
  'Iraqi Freedom' 25, 31, 42, 72, 79, 81,
  84–5, 86, 89; private military
  companies 114, 115; resistance 29, 30,
  64, 70; WMD 54, 55–6, 55*t*, 57, 59
Irish Republican Army *see* IRA
Islamic Army of Iraq 119, 175
Islamic Movement of Uzbekistan (IMU)
  129
Islamism 10, 29, 37, 81–4, 107–8, 156–7,
  162–5, 178
Israel 23, 26, 50, 55*t*, 63, 71–2, 81, 82,
  145*t*, 156, 174
Italy 104, 107, 126, 136, 137, 147, 157–8,
  162

Jamaat al-Fuqra (JF) 117–18, 226 n141
Japan 54, 88, 123, 136, 147, 165, 166
Jenkins, Brian 14
jihadism 104, 160, 163–4, 176, 176*f*, 178,
  187, 189; *see also* salafi-jihadism
Jonestown/People's Temple cult 165
Jordan 63, 71, 93, 145*t*

Uppsala University Conflict Data
  Project 25, 30
urbanisation 141, 142, 143–4, 145–6,
  147
Uzbekistan 63, 66, 90

Venezuela 71, 77
Vietnam 27, 88, 124
vigilantism 13, 14, 35, 36
violence 12, 13, 14, 144, 154

Wackenhut Corporation 111
wahhabism 163, 238 n13
war *see* armed conflicts
weapons 34, 123–5, 178–80
weapons of mass destruction (WMD)
  45–59, 188–9; Al-Qaida 46–9, 51,
  57; CBW proliferation 45–6, 47,
  53–9, 55*t*, 165, 178–9, 183;
  implications for terrorism 45;
  and non-state actors 20;
  nuclear proliferation 45, 49–53,

52*f*, 53*f*, 55*t*, 128; postulate 45–6;
  terrorism 3
Weather Underground 96
West Bank 30, 82, 145*t*
White Wolves 153
Woolsey, R. James 14
World Bank 41, 103
world order 16, 39–45, 188; economy
  41–2; implications for terrorism 30,
  44–5; military power 42; postulate
  39–44; regional powers 42–3;
  uni-multipolar system 42–3;
  US hegemony 40–1, 42–3
World Trade Organisation (WTO) 88–9
WorldCom 109

Yemen 63, 81, 145, 156
Yugoslavia 26, 54

Zain-ul Ibidin, Sulayman Bilal 118, 227
  n143
Al-Zawahiri, Ayman 159